Cambridge Studies in Early Modern British History

Series editors

ANTHONY FLETCHER
Emeritus Professor of English Social History, University of London

JOHN GUY
Visiting Fellow, Clare College, Cambridge

JOHN MORRILL
*Professor of British and Irish History, University of Cambridge, and
Vice-Master of Selwyn College*

This is a series of monographs and studies covering many aspects of the history of the British Isles between the late fifteenth century and the early eighteenth century. It includes the work of established scholars and pioneer work by a new generation of scholars. It includes both reviews and revisions of major topics and books, which open up new historical terrain or which reveal startling new perspectives on familiar subjects. All the volumes set out detailed research into our broader perspectives and the books are intended for the use of students as well as of their teachers.

For a list of titles in the series, see end of book.

Print Culture and the Early Quakers

The early Quaker movement was remarkable for its prolific use of the printing press. Carefully orchestrated by a handful of men and women who were the movement's leaders, printed tracts were an integral feature of the rapid spread of Quaker ideas in the 1650s. Drawing on very rich documentary evidence, this book examines how and why Quakers were able to make such effective use of print. As a crucial element in an extensive proselytising campaign which also used public preaching, confrontation, silence and symbolic performance, printed tracts enabled the emergence of the Quaker movement as a uniform, national phenomenon. The book explores the impressive organisation underpinning Quaker pamphleteering and argues that the early movement should not be dismissed as a disillusioned spiritual remnant of the English revolution, but was rather a purposeful campaign which sought, and achieved, effective dialogue with both the body politic and society at large. The Quakers' vibrant use of the press sheds light not only on the significance of print in early modern society, but also on our understanding of political and religious participation in the 1650s.

KATE PETERS is Lecturer in Archives and Records Management, University College London.

PRINT CULTURE AND THE EARLY QUAKERS

KATE PETERS

CAMBRIDGE
UNIVERSITY PRESS

CAMBRIDGE UNIVERSITY PRESS
Cambridge, New York, Melbourne, Madrid, Cape Town, Singapore, São Paulo

Cambridge University Press
The Edinburgh Building, Cambridge CB2 2RU, UK

Published in the United States of America by Cambridge University Press, New York

www.cambridge.org
Information on this title: www.cambridge.org/9780521770903

First published 2005

Printed in the United Kingdom at the University Press, Cambridge

A catalogue record for this book is available from the British Library

Library of Congress Cataloguing in Publication data
Peters, Kate.
Print culture and the early Quakers / Kate Peters.
p.   cm. – (Cambridge studies in early modern British history)
Includes bibliographical references (p.) and index.
ISBN 0 521 77090 4
1. English prose literature – Quaker authors – History and criticism.   2. English prose
literature – Early modern, 1500–1700 – History and criticism.   3. Christian literature –
Publishing – England – History – 17th century.   4. Christianity and literature – England –
History – 17th century.   5. Pamphlets – Publishing – England – History – 17th century.
6. Tracts – Publishing – England – History – 17th century.   7. Christian literature,
English – History and criticism.   8. Printing – England – History – 17th century.
9. Quakers – England – History – 17th century.   10. Quakers in literature.
I. Title.   II. Series.
PR120.O34P48   2004
289.6′41′09032 – dc22   2003064043

ISBN-13 978-0-521-77090-3 hardback
ISBN-10 0-521-77090-4 hardback

CONTENTS

ILLUSTRATIONS

ACKNOWLEDGEMENTS

The initial research for this book was undertaken while I was a graduate student, and was funded by a postgraduate award from the British Academy, and by studentships from Corpus Christi College, Cambridge, and the Prince Consort and Thirlwell Fund of the Faculty of History at Cambridge. I am grateful to all of these bodies, and mindful that postgraduate studies were more easily undertaken a decade ago than they are today.

Most of the research was carried out in the extremely peaceful setting of the Friends' House Library, London, where I was always made very welcome. I am grateful to Malcolm Thomas and all the librarians for their help and enthusiasm. It was a pleasure to work there. I am grateful to the following publishers who have kindly allowed me to re-work material which has appeared in print elsewhere: to the editors of *Prose Studies*, for allowing me to re-work material in Chapter 1; to David Chadd of the Centre of East Anglian Studies, for permission to re-use the material in Chapter 3; to Ashgate publishing for permission to re-work material appearing in Chapter 4; and to the editors of *Studies in Church History* for material which appears in Chapter 5. The illustrations are reproduced from the Thomason Tract Collection by permission of the British Library, which I gratefully acknowledge.

This book is largely, and belatedly, the product of my doctoral thesis, and I would like to thank a number of scholars who have helped over the years. I owe the largest debt of gratitude to two inspiring historians: my doctoral supervisor at Cambridge, Patrick Collinson, whose perceptive questions helped me to think in new ways about my work and were fundamental in shaping my arguments; and my undergraduate tutor, Ann Hughes, who encouraged me to undertake the research in the first place, and has remained an enthusiastic and attentive reader of my work ever since. I am very grateful to both of them. Colleagues in the History Department at Birmingham University also provided a supportive and pleasant environment in which to work, and I am particularly grateful to Professor Eric Ives and Richard Cust for their help. The thesis examiners, William Lamont and John Morrill, made many helpful suggestions on the revision of the text; John Morrill in particular encouraged me to publish, and made useful comments on the draft of Chapter 8. Anthony Fletcher has remained warmly encouraging and patient beyond merit. I am also grateful to a number of other historians and friends who have shown an interest in my work, and have offered helpful comments at various stages: Lynn Botelho, Mario Caricchio (for sharing his knowledge of Giles Calvert), Patricia Crawford, Colin Davis, Mark Goldie, Arnold Hunt, Caroline Litzenberger, Frank McGregor, Rosemary Moore, Nigel Smith, Margaret Spufford, Alex Walsham, Helen Weinstein and Andy Wood.

The preparation of this book for publication was delayed in part by a lengthy itinerancy in search of gainful employment. The final chapter of the book was written during a period of research leave from the School of Library, Archive and Information Studies at UCL. I am very grateful to the Head of School, Susan Hockey, for granting me this leave, and for her strong encouragement of my research, as well as to colleagues in the School who covered for me in my absence. The book has been delayed further by the imperatives of nature: the birth of my children, Tom, Alice and Edward Frearson, has inevitably, if happily, interrupted my work. I am grateful to Valerie Smith and Vicky Silvester for ably providing the childcare without which I could not have completed this project. My parents have assisted willingly in this as in so many ways, and I thank them for their support throughout.

I am, finally, grateful to my husband, and erstwhile fellow historian, Michael Frearson, who from the beginning has encouraged, discussed and proofread my work, and more recently also looked after the children and cooked the dinners. This book is dedicated to him.

ABBREVIATIONS

A. R. Barclay Mss	Abram Rawlinson Barclay Manuscripts, Friends' House Library, London
Audland's Journal	'The Journal of John Audland, 1654', in 'Letters of John Audland, 1653', Ms Box P2/15, Friends' House Library, London
BDBR	*Biographical Dictionary of British Radicals in the Seventeenth Century,* ed. Richard Greaves and Robert Zaller, 3 vols., Brighton, 1982–1984
BL	British Library, London
CSPD	*Calendar of State Papers Domestic*
CUL	University Library of Cambridge
DNB	*Dictionary of National Biography*
DQB	Dictionary of Quaker Biography, typescript collection of biographical details of Quakers, Friends' House Library, London
FHL	Friends' House Library, London
JFHS	*Journal of the Friends' Historical Society*
Nuttall, EQL	Geoffrey Nuttall, 'Early Quaker letters from the Swarthmoor Mss to 1660', typescript calendar and index with annotations, London 1952, Friends' House Library, London.
Portfolio	Portfolio Manuscript Collections, Friends' House Library, London.
PRO	Public Record Office, London (since 2003 the National Archives).
STC	Donald Wing, *Short-title Catalogue of Books Printed in England, Scotland, Ireland Wales and British North America, 1641–1700,* 2nd edn, 3 vols., New York, 1972–1988

Sw Mss	Swarthmoor Manuscripts, Friends' House Library, London
Sw Trs	Transcriptions of the Swarthmoor Manuscripts, Friends' House Library, London

CONVENTIONS USED IN THE TEXT

The Quakers were highly articulate, but they were not literary. Their spelling and their syntax are unusually erratic, even for the seventeenth century. In quotations I have kept to the original spelling. However, I have, where necessary, inserted words in square brackets in order to clarify the meaning, and have occasionally inserted punctuation for the same reason. Most abbreviations and contractions have been expanded, and upper-case 'F' substituted for 'ff'.

References to printed tracts include the *STC* reference number as well as the author and title, for ease of identification. Where page numbers in the printed tracts are missing or incorrect, the signature number is given.

Where dates of mss are uncertain they are placed in square brackets. Unless otherwise stated, all manuscripts referred to are from collections at Friends' House Library, London.

Introduction

The early Quaker movement is remarkable for its prolific use of the printing press. Quaker leaders began to publish their ideas in tracts and broadsides in late 1652; by the end of 1656, nearly three hundred titles had been printed, an average of more than one new Quaker book each week. Their zealous use of the press challenges established opinions about the significance of the Quakers, and about the role of print in the English revolution. Quakers in the 1650s are widely seen as a group of religious dissidents who were disillusioned with English political society, and who were historically significant as a thorn in the side of Commonwealth and Protectorate governments rather than for any more positive contribution. This book, based on a systematic and chronological reading of the tracts published between 1652 and 1656, and of the many letters produced by the movement's leaders, argues on the contrary that Quakers were highly engaged with contemporary political and religious affairs, and were committed in very practical ways to the establishment of Christ's kingdom on earth. Their printed tracts were used very explicitly to involve everyone in this process, urging all people to heed the light of Christ within them, and to uphold the law of God in all aspects of religious and political life. The pamphleteering activities of the early Quaker movement demonstrate that print enabled a form of political participation in the society of the 1650s: through it, Quakers expected to achieve substantial political and religious change.

Histories of the early Quaker movement invariably describe a group of religious radicals, first apparent in the north of England in 1652, which became a national phenomenon over the summer of 1654, when Quaker preachers conducted a campaign across the whole country.[1] The genesis of

---

[1] The story of the emergence of the Quaker movement has been amply told by William C. Braithwaite, *The beginnings of Quakerism* (London, 1912: 2nd edn, Cambridge, 1955), Braithwaite, *The second period of Quakerism* (London, 1919: 2nd edn, Cambridge, 1961). Two other monographs offer important interpretations: Hugh Barbour, *The Quakers in puritan England* (New Haven, 1964), and Barry Reay, *The Quakers and the English revolution* (London, 1985).

1

the Quaker movement consisted in the linking up of puritan sects and Seeker congregations across Yorkshire, Lancashire and Westmorland, through the rousing preaching, initially of the Leicestershire-born lay preacher George Fox, and later of other key preachers like James Nayler, Edward Burrough and Francis Howgill, all of whom were experienced lay preachers to gathered churches or Seeker congregations.[2]

The Quakers' religious beliefs were central to the emergence of a movement which was highly participatory, both in the demands it placed on its followers, and in the expectation to change the outside world. Quakers rejected the central predestinarian tenets of Calvinist puritanism: they believed that the light of Christ was present within each individual and that this could lead to salvation and to perfection.[3] This entailed an aggressive proselytising campaign in which Quakers sought to awaken literally every one to Christ's inner light. The individual religious participation of those 'convinced' was also central. Quakers emphasised the guidance of the spirit above the scriptures or other formal doctrinal expressions, and indeed juxtaposed the spirit to all things 'carnal' or outward.[4] This led them to abandon formal structures of religious worship, and to argue against any church which emphasised formal worship and professional ministry, especially one financed through a compulsory tithe system. It also underpinned the Quakers' social egalitarianism. The belief that everyone was spiritually equal fostered the practice of abandoning honorific titles, of using the egalitarian 'thee' rather than the respectful 'you'; and refusing to doff hats or swear oaths which stressed human hierarchies above God. It was also used to justify the fact that women preached and participated fully in religious leadership.[5] Quakers had also been very recent participants within the radical politics of the 1640s: Quaker leaders

[2] The most recent narrative of Fox's early preaching which linked these communities is in H. L. Ingle, *First among friends: George Fox and the creation of Quakerism* (Oxford, 1994). See also William G. Bittle, *James Nayler: the Quaker indicted by Parliament* (York, 1986); and for wider accounts of the early work of Quaker ministers, see the accounts in Norman Penney (ed.), *First Publishers of Truth* (London, 1907). W. C. Braithwaite has shown us that there were links between some of these communities prior to the preaching of Fox: W. C. Braithwaite, 'The Westmorland and Swaledale Seekers in 1651', *JFHS* 5: 1 (1908), 3–10.

[3] For studies which place Quakers within the context of puritanism, see Geoffrey Nuttall, *The holy spirit in puritan faith and experience* (Oxford, 1946); Nuttall, *Studies in Christian enthusiasm* (Wallingford, Penn., 1948); Hugh Barbour, *Quakers in puritan England*; Braithwaite, *Beginnings of Quakerism*, pp. 1–26; R. W. Acheson, *Radical puritans in England 1550–1660* (London, 1990).

[4] Maurice Creasey, '"Inward" and "outward": a study in early Quaker language', *JFHS* supplement 30 (1962).

[5] Christopher Hill, *The world turned upside down: Radical Ideas during the English Revolution* (Harmondsworth, 1987); Barry Reay, 'Quakerism and society' in J. F. McGregor and B. Reay (eds.), *Radical religion in the English revolution* (Oxford, 1986), pp. 141–64; Kenneth Carroll, 'Quaker attitudes towards signs and wonders', *JFHS* 54: 2 (1977), 70–84; Carroll, 'Sackcloth and ashes, and other signs and wonders', *JFHS* 53: 4 (1975), 314–25. For attitudes to sexual equality in the early Quaker movement, see Keith Thomas, 'Women and the civil war

were drawn from the army and the Levellers.[6] More broadly, membership was drawn from the middling, mainly rural sections of society, excluding the very poor and the very rich: 'most belonged to the relatively comfortable middle section of the community and were slightly wealthier than the population at large'.[7]

Historians are loath to attribute too much significance to the proliferation of radical religious sects of the 1650s, arguing that their importance has been exaggerated. Nevertheless, Quakers are still considered important to the history of the Commonwealth and Protectorate. Numerically they certainly appear more significant than other religious groupings. At the Restoration, Quakers comprised nearly 1 per cent of the entire population, while in their stronghold of Westmorland, 3.3 per cent of the population were Quakers.[8] John Morrill, in an article which warned against being 'dazzled by the emergence of the radical sects', conceded that the Quakers probably changed the numerical significance of the sectaries' challenge to puritanism.[9]

The significance of the Quakers to the history of the 1650s is largely negative. In *The world turned upside down*, Christopher Hill described the Quakers as political radicals drawing on long-standing traditions of social protest and anticlericalism. Their appearance was, for Hill, a consequence of the failed revolution of 1647 to 1649: the emergence of the Quakers, he argued, 'witnessed *both* to the defeat of the political Levellers *and* to the continued existence of radical ideas'.[10] Hill's argument was shaped in part by the research of Alan Cole, whose work was seminal in countering the largely

---

sects', *Past and Present* 13 (1958), 42–62, Phyllis Mack, *Visionary women: ecstatic prophecy in seventeenth-century England* (Berkeley, 1992), Patricia Crawford, *Women and religion in England 1500–1720* (London, 1993); Christine Trevett, *Women and Quakerism in the seventeenth century* (York, 1991).

[6] M. E. Hirst, *The Quakers in peace and war* (London, 1923) was the first to identify the links between Quakers, the army and the navy. Her work has been consolidated by Alan Cole, 'The Quakers and politics, 1652–1660', unpublished Ph.D thesis, University of Cambridge, 1955; and by Barry Reay, 'Early Quaker activity and reactions to it, 1652–1664', unpublished D Phil. thesis, University of Oxford, 1979.

[7] Reay, *Quakers and the English revolution*, p. 21. See also Ernest E. Taylor, 'The first Publishers of Truth: a study', *JFHS* 19 (1922), 66–81; Alan Cole, 'The social origins of the early Friends', *JFHS* 48 (1957), 99–118; Barry Reay, 'The social origins of early Quakerism', *Journal of Interdisciplinary History* 11: 1 (Summer 1980), 55–72; Richard Vann, *The social development of English Quakerism, 1655–1755* (Cambridge, Mass., 1969); Vann, 'Quakerism and the social structure in the interregnum', *Past and Present* 43 (1969), 71–91.

[8] Reay, *Quakers and the English revolution*, p. 29. In comparison, it has been estimated that the entire Baptist population comprised no more than one quarter of a percentage of the national population. Cited in Ronald Hutton, *The British republic, 1649–1660* (London, 1990), pp. 30–31.

[9] John Morrill, 'The church in England 1642–9', in John Morrill (ed.), *Reactions to the English Civil War, 1642–1649* (London, 1982), p. 90, n. 4.

[10] Christopher Hill, *The world turned upside down*, p. 240; Hill, *The experience of defeat* (Harmondsworth, 1985).

denominational view that early Quakers were pacifist and aloof from political life, and who established the Quakers' political links with the New Model Army, Levellers and governments of the 1650s.[11] Yet Cole refused to allow the Quakers' much significance as active political participants in the early 1650s. Cole argued that the spiritualism of the early Quakers precluded them from any positive political action. The Quakers, he argued, were disillusioned by the political and religious reforms of the Commonwealth which betrayed the principles on which the civil wars had been fought. As a result, Quakers increasingly distanced themselves from 'carnal' governments which compromised religious conviction, and emphasised instead adherence to religious ideals and practice determined by the light of Christ within each individual. The form of political activity in which Quakers participated, Cole argued, was their prophetic mission to judge and witness against the political and religious corruption around them, denouncing clergy, magistrates, landowners and Cromwell himself. The Quakers' refusal to compromise with their former comrades excluded them from the political mainstream: they were politically significant to the 1650s as a marginal group of committed but unrealistic radicals, witnesses rather than actors, and sufferers rather than agents.[12]

Barry Reay's later study of the Quakers and the English revolution consolidated Cole's argument that the Quakers played little active part in the history of the 1650s.[13] Reay pointed out the strong denominational influence in Quaker history, which, by emphasising the longevity of the movement, and the long-term success of figures like George Fox, has obscured the movement's origins, and removed it from the immediate political context of the Interregnum. Reay's work sought to reintegrate the Quakers into the history of the 1650s, arguing that the early Quaker movement was an important means of understanding the social and political context of the English revolution. In a self-conscious attempt to eschew the weight of retrospective Quaker records, Barry Reay based much of his research on non-Quaker records: court records of Quaker prosecutions, government papers and anti-Quaker pamphlets, and in consequence discovered very widespread hostility to the Quakers. The nature of Reay's research therefore led him to consider the Quakers as troublemaking outsiders, and his thesis, that hostility to the Quakers was significant to the collapse of the republic in 1659–60, has contributed to the notion that Quakers had little that was positive to contribute to the history of the 1650s; and that they were significant

---

[11] Cole, 'Quakers and politics', esp. pp. 1–36. See also Cole, 'The Quakers and the English revolution', *Past and Present* 10 (1956), 39–54.

[12] Cole, 'Quakers and politics', pp. 22–36; 37–77.

[13] Barry Reay, 'Early Quaker activity'; Reay, *The Quakers and the English revolution*.

primarily for the conservative reactions they provoked at all levels of society.[14]

Within the context of the 1650s the Quakers are thus seen as the radical remnant of a failed revolution, having lost faith in the republican regimes, and, driven by a rather inward mysticism, with little positive to offer in the way of political solutions. This view has been assimilated into broader accounts of the 1650s. John Morrill wrote that all the religious sects were politically anarchistic; none 'had ambitions to set up particular constitutional forms'; and their criticism of the regimes was half-hearted: they were 'under no illusion that a Stuart Restoration would be much worse for them'.[15] Derek Hirst reiterated Barry Reay's argument that fear of the Quakers was their most important feature. In an article arguing that 'too much has been made of the sects' by historians, he went on to emphasise that it was the Quaker threat to ministers and magistrates which, 'though familiar, is too little heeded'.[16]

In the past fifteen years, there has been a sustained assault on the significance of radicalism in the 1640s and 1650s, as part of the broader revision of the English civil war and revolution.[17] It is no longer possible, as did both Alan Cole and Barry Reay, to describe the Quakers as a popular radical movement (although Barry Reay also showed that the Quakers provoked enormous popular hostility).[18] More recent work on popular culture has suggested that truly 'popular' religion centred on traditional religious worship; that Anglican ceremony remained central to the religious inclinations of most people; and that it was successfully maintained throughout the 1650s. Research for this and earlier periods has increasingly focused on how 'ordinary' people experienced their religion in the aftermath of the reformation, rather than on unusual and rather esoteric religious separatists, who have enjoyed disproportionate attention.[19]

---

[14] Barry Reay, 'Popular hostility towards Quakers in mid-seventeenth-century England', *Social History* 5: 3 (1980), 387–407; Reay, 'The Quakers, 1659, and the restoration of the monarchy', *History* 63 (1978), 193–213; Reay, 'Quakerism and society', pp. 21, 164.

[15] John Morrill, *The nature of the English revolution* (London, 1993), pp. 26–27.

[16] Derek Hirst, 'The failure of godly rule in the English republic', *Past and Present* 132 (1991), 33, 36.

[17] J. C. Davis, 'Radicalism in a traditional society: the evaluation of radical thought in the English Commonwealth, 1649–60', *History of Political Thought* 3: 2 (1982), 193–213; a useful account of the impact of revisionism is the editors' introduction in Richard Cust and Ann Hughes (eds.), *Conflict in early Stuart England* (London, 1989), pp. 1–46.

[18] Cole, 'The Quakers and the English revolution', 39–40; Reay, *Quakers and the English revolution*, p. 1; Reay, 'Popular hostility towards Quakers', 387–407.

[19] John Morrill, 'The church in England, 1642–49', pp. 89–114; John Spurr, *The restoration Church of England, 1646–1689* (London and New Haven, 1991), pp. 1–20; Eamon Duffy, 'The Godly and the multitude in Stuart England', *Seventeenth Century Journal* 1: 1 (1986), 31–55; Patrick Collinson, *The religion of protestants: the church in English society,*

Criticism of historians' overemphasis on radical religion reached its apotheosis in the work of Colin Davis, who in 1986 published a short monograph arguing that the most flamboyant of the radical sects of the 1650s, the Ranters, did not exist 'either as a small group of like-minded individuals, as a sect, or as a large-scale, middle-scale or small movement'.[20] Davis's argument was raised in criticism at the over-reliance by historians on a handful of printed tracts, some of which were by 'Ranter' authors, and others were lewd gutter-press denunciations of the Ranters, presenting them as the worst sign yet of divine wrath. The Ranter tracts themselves, Davis maintained, held little common 'doctrine' and there was scant evidence that the authors even knew each other; the hostile gutter-press attacks on the Ranters were more revealing about contemporary fears than about the nature of radical religion in the Commonwealth. 'There was no Ranter movement, no Ranter sect, no Ranter theology.'[21]

Davis's work gained notoriety for its attack on Christopher Hill and the Communist Party Group historians, whom he accused of exploiting the seventeenth-century Ranter 'myth' to further their own interpretation of the English revolution.[22] Beyond the vituperative exchanges, though, Davis did highlight methodological problems which remain unanswered either by him or his critics. In the final round of the debate, the question revolved around whether the Ranters constituted 'a number of groups, some loosely linked, with related and alarming ideas on the nature of God and on sin'; or whether we should talk of a Ranter 'milieu', or 'moment'.[23] For Davis, the key issue is to identify a socially cohesive group of people with a 'shared ideology reflected behaviourally' of practical antinomianism.[24] The role of print in all this remains unexplored but is implicitly central. Davis implied, though he has not pursued the argument, that a coherent religious movement (or at least one which may be traced by historians) is constituted by the relationship between authors of tracts, the tracts themselves, and responses of their audiences.

1559–1625 (Oxford, 1982); Tessa Watt, *Cheap print and popular piety, 1550–1640* (Cambridge, 1991); Margaret Spufford, 'The importance of religion in the sixteenth and seventeenth centuries' in Margaret Spufford (ed.), *The world of rural dissenters, 1520–1725* (Cambridge, 1995); Anthony Fletcher, 'The godly divided: the end of religious unity in protestant England', *Seventeenth Century 5*: 2 (1990), 185–94.

[20] J. C. Davis, *Fear, myth and history: the Ranters and the historians* (Cambridge, 1986), p. 75.

[21] *Ibid.*, p. 124.

[22] For the responses and subsequent debate, see G. E. Aylmer, 'Did the Ranters exist?', *Past and Present* 117 (1987), 208–19; Christopher Hill, 'The lost Ranters? A critique of J. C. Davis', *History Workshop Journal* 24 (1987), 134–40; E. P. Thompson, 'On the Rant', in G. Eley and W. Hunt (eds.), *Reviving the English revolution* (London, 1988); J. C. Davis, 'Fear, myth and furore: reappraising the "Ranters"', *Past and Present* 129 (1990), 79–103; Bernard Capp, 'Fear, myth and furore: reappraising the Ranters. Comment 2', *Past and Present* 140 (August 1993), 164–271.

[23] Capp, 'Fear, myth and furore', 171.   [24] *Ibid.*, 207.

The misuse of, and over-reliance upon, printed sources is a theme common to much of the recent revisionism of the English civil war.[25] The collapse of censorship in 1641 unleashed a flood of pamphleteering, as a result of which domestic news and a wide spectrum of political and religious ideas were published on an unprecedented scale. Much of this material was systematically collected by a London stationer, George Thomason, resulting in his own financial ruin, but rendering much of the pamphlet literature accessible to subsequent historians.[26]

Christopher Hill argued that the sudden expansion in publishing had a revolutionary impact. Previously suppressed ideas were expressed; styles of writing changed; authors became journalistic and wrote with a purpose, developing methods which aimed to persuade wider audiences.[27] The assumptions behind Hill's arguments are familiar to literary scholars, and particularly new historicists, who are keen to locate literary texts within a social or political context, and thus to make explicit links between language and action and to explore 'the kinds of public intervention that speech and writing can make'.[28] They are more inclined to argue, without the reserve of political historians towards the period, that 1640–1660 was a time of literary and linguistic innovation. Nigel Smith has shown how the political upheavals at the centre of society were reflected in a crisis over the meanings of words and the significance of literary styles and genres.[29] Sharon Achinstein has argued that the diversity of opinions published were symptomatic of the wider conflict in the public sphere. The debates over language itself, and over the possibility of a universal language, were highly significant: 'because public expression was becoming the means by which political and social differences were made known'.[30] In an article published in 1996, David Zaret argued that the emergence of printed petitions in the 1640s transformed petitioning from an essentially secret, deferential and apolitical means of addressing Parliament into a dialogic and highly public form of political lobbying. The

---

[25] Editors' introduction in Kevin Sharpe and Peter Lake (eds.), *Culture and politics in early Stuart England* (London, 1994), pp. 1–20, esp. p. 2.

[26] Lois Spencer, 'The professional and literary connexions of George Thomason', *The Library* (5th ser.) 13 (1958), 102–18; Spencer, 'The politics of George Thomason', *The Library* (5th ser.) 14 (1959), 11–27.

[27] Christopher Hill, 'Radical prose in seventeenth-century England: from Marprelate to the Levellers', *Essays in Criticism* 32: 2 (April 1982), 95–118; cf. Hill, 'Censorship and English literature', in *The collected essays of Christopher Hill* (3 vols., Brighton, 1985–86), vol. I, *Writing and revolution in seventeenth-century England* (Brighton, 1985), pp. 32–62.

[28] David Norbrook, *Writing the English republic: poetry, rhetoric and politics, 1627–1660* (Cambridge, 1999), p. 10.

[29] Nigel Smith, *Literature and revolution in England, 1640–1660* (London and New Haven, 1994); Smith, *Perfection proclaimed: language and literature in English radical religion, 1640–1660* (Oxford, 1989).

[30] Sharon Achinstein, 'The politics of Babel in the English revolution' in James Holstun (ed.), *Pamphlet wars: prose in the English revolution* (London, 1992), p. 17.

circulation of printed petitions, Zaret argued, led in very practical ways to the invention of public opinion: petitions invoked the authority of the public opinion they represented, and petitioners began publicly to demand action from Parliament, including constitutional reform, based on their petitions.[31]

There is a wide gap between the attitude of essentially literary scholars, and that of historians, to the proliferation of print in the 1640s and 1650s. Historians more concerned with the political significance of the decades are very wary of print as an accurate historical source. The fact that print is assumed to be propagandistic is taken as proof that it is a poor reflection either of what happened, or of how people experienced events. John Morrill queried Hill's heavy reliance on printed material: 'unless one has dirtied one's hands with the grime of the Commonwealth Exchequer Papers, and unless one has ploughed through a cross-section of the surviving Assize Files and county committee papers, the nature of the revolutionary experience will remain elusive'.[32] William Lamont has argued that the sheer quantity and literary range of material in the Thomason collection effectively prevents any accurate assessment of its content; and maintained that the only way to judge it is in the context of extraneous manuscript material.[33] Printed sources are often assumed to be misleading. Morrill and Walter argued that perceptions of disorder in the English revolution were inflated by printed reports of riot: the 'reality', they claimed, was far more peaceable.[34] Beyond the reliability of the content, there are also serious, and important, reservations about the accessibility of printed tracts. Although expanding, literacy levels were low; and although print was easier to read than handwriting, most people could not read. The abundance of printed information does not automatically equate with a universally or uniformly informed populace.[35] This, indeed, is a point insufficiently addressed by some literary

---

[31] David Zaret, 'Petitions and the "invention" of public opinion in the English revolution', *American Journal of Sociology* 101: 6 (May 1996), 1497–1555, esp. 1499. I am grateful to Ann Hughes for drawing my attention to this article. See also the work of Dagmar Freist, *Governed by opinion: politics, religion and the dynamics of communication in Stuart London, 1637–1645* (London, 1997).

[32] John Morrill, 'Review article: Christopher Hill's revolution', *History* 27: 241 (1989), 249.

[33] William Lamont, 'Pamphleteering, the Protestant consensus and the English revolution', in R. C. Richardson and G. M. Ridden (eds.), *Freedom and the English revolution: essays in history and literature* (Manchester, 1986), pp. 72–89, esp. p. 73. He draws his argument from Conrad Russell, 'Losers', *London Review of Books* 6: 18 (1984), 20–22.

[34] John Morrill and John Walter, 'Order and disorder in the English revolution', reprinted in J. S. Morrill, *The nature of the English revolution*, pp. 359–61, 373.

[35] David Cressy, *Literacy and the social order: reading and writing in Tudor England* (Cambridge, 1980); Margaret Spufford, 'First steps in literacy: the reading and writing experiences of the humblest seventeenth-century autobiographers', *Social History* 4: 3 (1979), 407–35; Keith Thomas, 'The meaning of literacy in early modern England' in G. Bauman (ed.), *The written word: literacy in transition* (Oxford, 1986); Adam Fox, 'Ballads, libels and popular ridicule in Jacobean England', *Past and Present* 145 (1994), 47–83.

scholars, whose work often focuses on the cultural experiences of a literary minority.[36]

The work of Davis in particular, and the hesitancy of other historians in general, calls for a sustained and detailed study of how contemporaries made use of print. The Quakers lend themselves to such an investigation. Not only did they produce, and preserve, a significant number of tracts; they also wrote and preserved thousands of letters in the course of their extensive campaigning, which describe their pamphleteering activities. Furthermore, we can be sure from a number of other sources that the Quakers 'existed': they were not a figment of their own or others' propaganda. A primary concern of this book is to show how and why Quakers published tracts as part of their successful missionary campaign; to examine how a group of people in the mid-seventeenth century were able to make use of print to spread their ideas; and to identify the impact of print on the growth of a successful, national movement.

A second concern is to argue that if we examine pamphleteering as an activity in its own right, it becomes necessary to reassess the early Quaker movement and the nature of its political participation. Recent non-denominational historiography has presented the early Quakers in a negative light, as eccentric troublemakers who merely hastened the popular, conservative reaction which brought down the republic. While this is true in some respects, the Quakers' own zealous and sustained use of the press describes a very purposeful and organised movement which requires explanation.

It is in this context that the denominational tradition of Quaker historiography needs to be discussed. The history of the early Quaker movement is dominated by its denominational tradition: indeed, its unassailability as a movement of importance in the 1650s owes a great deal to the fact that Quakers survived into the Restoration and beyond, and that Quaker leaders were very meticulous in the preservation and cataloguing of their records. During the decades following the Restoration, the Quaker movement consolidated into a formally organised church. Part of this involved the establishment of particular, monthly and quarterly meetings in each county, and of a series of central, London-based meetings: the Yearly meeting, the Morning meeting and the Meeting for Sufferings. The local meetings kept regular records of membership, as well as of births, marriages and deaths, and these form a crucial aspect of subsequent estimates of the size and make-up of the early Quaker movement. The central meetings played an important role in

---

[36] See Thomas Corns's stimulating account of the prose styles of Lilburne and Milton: Thomas N. Corns, 'The freedom of reader-response: Milton's *Of Reformation* and Lilburne's *The Christian Mans Triall*' in R. C. Richardson and G. M. Riddens (eds.), *Freedom and the English revolution*, 93–110.

shaping the collections of Quaker records: the Second Day Morning Meeting regulated all Quaker publications from 1673 onwards, monitoring the content of new books, and ensuring that copies of each one were retained. The Second Day Morning Meeting and the Meeting for Sufferings also initiated the collection and cataloguing of all Quaker books 'From the Beginning or First Appearance of the said People', which originated the Friends' reference library which is still extant today.[37] The Second Day Morning Meeting instigated too the posthumous publication of Fox's papers and his *Journal* after his death in 1691; its first Recording Clerk, Ellis Hookes, was responsible in the 1670s for publishing the edited works of some of the most prolific authors of the 1650s: James Parnell, Edward Burrough, Francis Howgill and William Smith, all of whom were dead.[38] In the 1660s, Ellis Hookes also compiled two substantial manuscript volumes of Sufferings; and as part of this catalogued some of the vast collections of letters at Swarthmoor Hall which dated from the 1650s.[39]

Much of our knowledge of Quakers in the 1650s is thus directly attributable to the efforts of a later generation of Quakers, intent on preserving the memory of early Quaker ministers who had died prematurely, and also on preventing the publication of enthusiastic or politically dangerous works which would have compromised the Quaker movement of the Restoration period. The implications of the Quakers' self-censorship have long been known: the omission of references in his published *Journal* to Fox's frequent meetings with Cromwell and the projection of the 1661 Peace Testimony back into the 1650s are two notorious instances in which the political origins of the Quakers were to some extent obscured by subsequent denominational writing.[40]

A rather less sinister implication of such a strong denominational tradition has been the obfuscation of the actual origins of the Quaker movement. As Christopher Hill wrote of reading Fox's *Journal*: 'one at once becomes aware of a gap between the events described and the apparent reasons for

[37] Thomas O'Malley, '"Defying the powers and tempering the spirit": a review of Quaker control over their publications 1672–1689', *Journal of Ecclesiastical History* 33: 1 (1982), 72–88; Anna Littleboy, 'Devonshire House Reference Library, with notes on early printers and printing in the Society of Friends', *JFHS* 18: 1 (1921), 1–16; John Whiting, *A catalogue of Friends Books* (London, 1708), cited in Anna Littleboy, 'Devonshire House Reference Library' *JFHS* 18: 3 (1921), 66–69.

[38] T. Edmund Harvey, 'Introduction' in George Fox, *The Journal of George Fox*, ed. Norman Penney (2 vols., Cambridge, 1911), vol. I, pp. ix–xxviii; Norman Penney, 'Our recording clerks: Ellis Hookes', *JFHS* 1: 1 (1903), 18.

[39] Norman Penney, 'Ellis Hookes', 15.

[40] T. Edmund Harvey, 'Introduction' in *The Journal of George Fox*, ed. Penney, vol. I, pp. ix–xxviii; Alan Cole, 'The Quakers and politics', pp. 16–36; Christopher Hill, *The world turned upside down*, pp. 241–48.

them'.[41] Historians tend to take for granted both the appearance and the survival of Quakers, over decades when other radical religious sects were rapidly disappearing.[42] Yet our understanding of how the Quaker movement did grow and thrive is very important, especially in light of Davis's critique of the Ranters which has forced historians to think more precisely about how radical movements should be defined. By focusing explicitly on Quaker sources contemporaneous to the 1650s, this book examines sources generated in the course of the early Quaker campaign, which by definition describe the organisation and establishment of a national 'Quaker' movement. The Quakers' pamphleteering activities, recorded in letters and by the tracts themselves, provide very clear evidence of precisely how a national network of contacts was established; and how a coherent set of ideas was disseminated nationally.

The book is divided into three sections. The first section deals with the organisation of Quaker pamphleteering in the early 1650s, describing the close links between the movement's leadership and the production of Quaker tracts, examining the broad scope of potential audiences, and showing how the concerted use of printed tracts aided the establishment of a nationally based movement by 1654 (see Chapters 1, 2 and 3). The second section examines the role of print in the emergence of a recognisable Quaker identity and the development of a nascent Quaker discipline in two case-studies, showing how printed tracts contributed textually to the establishment of a discernible, coherent and national movement. Chapter 4 discusses the exploitation of the term 'Quaker' in the tracts, which in a variety of ways was used to signify a cohesive and elect group of people. Chapter 5 explores how the presentation of one doctrinal issue associated with the Quaker movement – that of women's public preaching – was presented in print, and contextualised by the rather different picture presented by the manuscript correspondence. The Quakers used their tracts self-consciously, it will be argued, to suggest a national, disciplined and godly movement. The final section of the book argues that the Quakers' use of print indicates that the movement emerged as a national campaign which very specifically aimed to achieve further religious reform and the immediate establishment of a godly commonwealth (see Chapters 6, 7 and 8). That this was done through widespread and meticulous pamphleteering reveals much about the role of print and political participation in the mid-seventeenth century. Quakers did not offer wholesale constitutional solutions, but demanded instead specific changes; they

---

[41] Hill, *World turned upside down*, p. 232.
[42] Muggletonians are an exception. William Lamont, 'The Muggletonians 1652–1979: a "vertical approach"', *Past and Present* 99 (1983), 22–40; Barry Reay, 'The Muggletonians: a study in seventeenth-century English sectarianism', *Journal of Religious History* 9: 1 (1976), 32–49; C. Hill, B. Reay and W. Lamont, *The world of the Muggletonians* (London, 1983).

did not deliver abstract political commentary, but demanded their audiences participate directly in religious reformation. By understanding Quaker pamphleteering, it is possible to describe how Quakers actually participated in the political life of the interregnum, and to argue that, however threatening, marginal and eccentric their ideas, Quakers engaged seriously with contemporary issues, and were able in consequence to build a national, successful movement and maintain a coherent and effective dialogue with the body politic.

Part I

Authorship, production and readership

1

Writing and authority in the early Quaker movement[1]

The practical importance of writing in the formation of the early Quaker movement is rarely acknowledged by its historians. Those who do, concentrate rather on the importance of written Quaker records in the establishment of a mature denominational tradition. The survival of 'Quakerism' has entailed the cataloguing and retention of early written records, the structuring of Quaker writing into first and second 'generations,' and the compilation of posthumous testimonies and collected editions of the works of individuals deemed noteworthy to the early movement.[2] The process of codifying doctrines, and of recording 'canonical' or 'dogmatic' writings, is an important feature in establishing any new denominational tradition.[3] Its process within the context of the Quaker movement has been well studied already.[4] Indeed, the fact that scholars refer to 'Quaker' writing in some way as stylistically unified and denoting distinctive characteristics underlines the success of the denominational cataloguing of Quaker records. Collections of Quaker works have been studied in order to identify from them aspects

---

[1] An earlier version of this chapter appeared in Thomas N. Corns and David Loewenstein (eds.), *The emergence of Quaker writing: dissenting literature in seventeenth-century England* (London, 1995), pp. 6–24.

[2] For specific accounts of the post-Restoration shaping of Quaker records, see Anna Littleboy, 'Devonshire House Reference Library', *JFHS* 18: 1 (1921), 1–16; Norman Penney, 'Our recording clerks: Ellis Hookes', *JFHS* 1: 1 (1903), 12–22; Thomas O'Malley, ' "Defying the powers and tempering the spirit": a review of Quaker control over their publications 1672–89', *Journal of Ecclesiastical History* 33 (1982), 72–88; Arnold Lloyd, *Quaker social history, 1669–1738* (London, 1950), pp. 147–56.

[3] Max Weber, *The sociology of religion*, trans. Ephraim Fischoff (Boston, 1963), p. 64.

[4] Bryan Wilson, 'An analysis of sect development', in Bryan Wilson (ed.), *Patterns of sectarianism: organisation and ideology in social and religious movements* (London, 1967), pp. 22–45, and Wilson, *Religion in sociological perspective* (Oxford, 1982), pp. 89–120. For attempts to describe the Quaker movement in this way, see Elizabeth Isichei, 'From sect to denomination among English Quakers', in Wilson (ed.), *Patterns of sectarianism*, pp. 161–81; Richard Vann, *The social development of English Quakerism, 1655–1755* (Cambridge, Mass., 1969), pp. 197–208. Perhaps the most crucial work in this context is Arnold Lloyd, *Quaker social history*.

of doctrine or style which can be understood as characteristic of the Quaker movement.[5]

The careful analysis of writing within the development of the Quaker denominational tradition, however, has obscured the significance of contemporary writing to the growth of the Quaker movement in the first half of the 1650s. The authors of Quaker tracts were also the movement's leadership, and their function as authors was central to their authority as leaders. This chapter will emphasise the immediate practicalities involved in Quaker pamphleteering, and argue that Quaker writing was produced primarily as an intrinsic part of the organisation of the movement.

It is often held that writing, and the performance of formal written sermons, were anathema to early Quakers. Early Quaker worship was predominantly silent; worshippers spoke only when 'moved' to do so by divine inspiration, and the very process of writing down these utterances undermined their divine spontaneity. Richard Bauman, who carried out an ethnographic study of Quaker language, stated that 'Quaker religious speaking was all spontaneous'; and that there were 'principled reasons for not taking down these utterances in writing'.[6] The abundance of written documentary evidence produced by Quakers themselves is thus removed from the context of the 1650s and seen instead as part of the subsequent Quaker impulse to record their own denominational history. Bauman went on to base a study of Quaker speaking on the 'doctrinal, polemical and personal documents' which he claimed were a tribute to the 'remarkable Quaker penchant for documenting their activities for posterity'.[7]

---

[5] The literature about 'Quaker' writing and language is vast. Initially it stemmed from the Quakers' own denominational writings. See, for example, Luella M. Wright, 'Literature and education in early Quakerism', *University of Iowa Humanistic Studies* 5: 2 (1933), 5–60; Wright, *The literary life of early Friends* (New York, 1932), Maurice Creasey, '"Inward" and "outward": a study in early Quaker language', *JFHS* supp. 30 (1962); Howard H. Brinton, *Quaker journals: varieties of religious experience among Friends* (Wallingford, Penn, 1972); Hugh Barbour and Arthur Roberts (eds.), *Early Quaker writings, 1650–1700* (Michigan, 1973). The accessibility of the Quaker records, however, has meant that literary and linguistic scholars have also studied them as a literary entity. The first important work in this context was Jackson I. Cope, 'Seventeenth-century Quaker style', *Publications of the Modern Languages Association*, 71: 2 (1956), 725–54. See also Hugh Ormsby-Lennon, 'From Shibboleth to apocalypse: Quaker speechways during the puritan revolution', in P. Burke and R. Porter (eds.), *Language, self and society: a social history of language* (Cambridge, 1991); Nigel Smith, 'Hidden things brought to light: enthusiasm and Quaker discourse', in Corns and Loewenstein (eds.), *The emergence of early Quaker writing*. Finally, a very important area of study has been by an ethnographer of speaking, Richard Bauman, who has explicitly studied 'Quaker' speech within an ethnographic framework. Richard Bauman, 'Aspects of seventeenth-century Quaker rhetoric', *The Quarterly Journal of Speech* 56 (1970), 67–74; Bauman, *Let your words be few: symbolism of speaking and silence among seventeenth-century Quakers* (Cambridge, 1983).

[6] Bauman, *Let your words be few*, p. 11.   [7] *Ibid.*, p. 12.

Similarly, the process of conversion and formal admission, often recorded in written form in other separatist churches, was not documented in the Quaker movement; 'conversion' was deemed to be an ongoing process which could not be articulated by a single statement or certificate.[8] Instead, some Quakers wrote narratives of their spiritual experiences, mainly for evangelistic purposes after the formal establishment of local meetings in the 1660s and 1670s.[9] Richard Vann identified a 'paradox' in the very study of Quaker history, arguing that although Quaker insistence on the immediacy of the inner light for their religious experience was 'almost uniquely hostile to history', the same emphasis caused the abundance of written spiritual autobiography on which early Quaker history is based.[10] In Vann's analysis, early autobiographical writing formed part of the establishment of denominational tradition.

The quest for an authoritative account of early 'Quaker' doctrine has also led scholars to examine Quaker writing teleologically, within the context of its denominational history. Robert Barclay's *Apology for the true Christian divinity*, published first in Latin in 1676, was the first major statement of Quaker doctrine.[11] Hugh Barbour, in his attempt to describe the importance of 'early Quaker writing', argued that it was highly individualistic: there existed no theological 'canon' of Quaker literature before 1700; and Quakers wrote 'as each felt led'.[12] All early Quaker writing, Barbour argued rather extravagantly, 'reflected personal involvement in a cosmic struggle'.[13]

More recently, scholars have stressed the importance of inner experience in early Quaker writing, and have examined Quaker literature chiefly for examples of a seventeenth-century sense of self.[14] Within the context of radical writing in the English revolution, Nigel Smith considered Quaker writing as a peculiar expression of 'self', arguing that Quakers exhibited an extreme degree of self-denial.[15] In very similar vein, Phyllis Mack and Elaine Hobby have studied the published works of Quaker women as early explorations of a female sense of self, arguing that their works depended often on a negation

---

[8] See Vann, *The social development of English Quakerism*, pp. 1–46; Patricia Caldwell, *The puritan conversion narrative: the beginnings of American expression* (Cambridge, 1983); Nigel Smith, *Perfection proclaimed: language and literature in English radical religion 1640–1660* (Oxford, 1989), pp. 23–25.

[9] Owen Watkins, *The puritan experience* (London, 1972), pp. 161, 182; chapters 10 and 11 of Watkin's work provide a broad and very important study of Quaker testimonial writing within the context of puritan autobiography. See also Nigel Smith, *Perfection proclaimed*, pp. 53–54.

[10] Vann, *The social development of English Quakerism*, pp. 1–2.

[11] W. C. Braithwaite, *The second period of Quakerism* (Cambridge, 1961), pp. 385–98; Rufus M. Jones, *Spiritual reformers in the sixteenth and seventeenth centuries* (London, 1914), pp. 343–49; Cope, 'Seventeenth-century Quaker style', 752–53.

[12] Barbour and Roberts (eds.), *Early Quaker writings*, p. 14.　　[13] *Ibid.*

[14] Brinton, *Quaker journals*.　　[15] Nigel Smith, *Perfection proclaimed*, pp. 66–72.

of their gender and the subjugation of their female identities beneath their relationship with the divine and their role as prophets.[16]

The assumption is thus that the primary purpose of early Quaker writing was to record immediate and highly individualistic religious experience and hence to define the mystical relationship between the author and the divine; and that this was appropriated into denominational writing in the 'second generation' of the Quaker movement. To a certain extent, this argument is not incorrect. Early Quaker tracts were heavily steeped in the immediate religious experience of the authors; and, as will be seen, such experience was crucial to the authority of Quaker authors. Yet the emphasis on the personal or mystical element of Quaker writing alone should not be allowed to negate or obscure its practical function of proselytisation and the publishing of Quaker beliefs.

By no means all Quakers felt obliged to write down the story of their own spiritual conversion; and Quaker publications were not all concerned primarily with spiritual autobiography. Richard Vann thought that the 'seventy' Quakers who had published 'some account of the Lord's dealings with them' in the first two generations of the movement is an impressive figure, compared with other sectarians' autobiographies.[17] Barry Reay's estimate that there could have been as many as 60,000 Quakers in England by 1660 puts this figure into perspective.[18] By no means all Quakers were moved to leave a written record of their religious awakening or relationship with the divine. Writing was not an inherent part of being a Quaker.

The practical importance of writing and authorship, and their significance to the establishment of the Quaker movement, is demonstrated in two separate works written by Edward Burrough, a prominent Quaker leader and spokesman originally from Underbarrow in Westmorland.[19] Both of

---

[16] Elaine Hobby, *Virtue of necessity: English women's writing, 1649–1688* (London, 1988), pp. 36–37, 40–49; Phyllis Mack, *Visionary women: ecstatic prophecy in seventeenth-century England* (Berkeley, 1992); Elaine Hobby, '"Oh Oxford thou art full of filth": The prophetical writings of Hester Biddle, 1629[?]–1696', in Susan Sellers (ed.), *Feminist criticism: theory and practice* (London, 1991), pp. 157–69. See also Mack, 'The prophet and her audience: gender and knowledge in the world turned upside down', in G. Eley and W. Hunt (eds.), *Reviving the English revolution* (London, 1988). A recent 'literary' approach to Quaker writing, which includes feminist literary scholarship, is Corns and Loewenstein (eds.), *The emergence of Quaker writing.*

[17] Vann, *The social development of English Quakerism*, p. 20.

[18] Barry Reay, *The Quakers and the English revolution* (London, 1985), p. 11.

[19] Edward Burrough was born in 1634 (or 1632) and was thus about eighteen years old when he first encountered George Fox in 1652. As a Quaker preacher he travelled to London, Bristol and Ireland, as well as much of England, often in the company of his companion Francis Howgill. He died in Newgate prison in February 1663, one of the many Quaker victims of Restoration religious persecution. Little is known of his social origins, although an early biographer clearly implies that he was of wealthy, Anglican parents and had been educated at grammar school; his association with the Quakers led effectively to his being

Burrough's works, written respectively in 1659 and 1662, attempted to record the brief history of the movement. In 1659, at the age of twenty-six, Edward Burrough exercised sufficient authority in the movement to publish with George Fox, 'a true account, of our first beginning and coming forth in the world', in which he described the humble origins of a few 'followers of the Lamb', 'in scorn called Quakers'.[20] In this first historical account, published as the preface to George Fox's *Great mistery of the great whore unfolded*, Edward Burrough described how the Quakers had, seven years earlier, 'first Journied out of Westmerland, through Cumberland, Northumberland, and into some parts of Scotland, and Durham, York-shire, Lancashire, Cheshire etc.', until they arrived, in 1654, in London.[21]

The purpose of Burrough's historical account was undoubtedly linked to the immediate political context in which it was written. *The great mistery of the great whore unfolded* was a calendar of all the printed debates between Quakers and their adversaries over the past seven years, published under the authoritative and unifying name of George Fox. In the preface, Burrough emphasised the consistency of the Quakers' opposition throughout the 1650s, to 'Anabaptists, Independents, Presbyters, Ranters and many others' alike, 'shewing that the controversie on our part is just, and equal, against them all'.[22] He also argued that the integrity of the Quakers' religious campaign lay behind their objection to the political regimes of the interregnum:

then we saw not only the performance and practice in Church state, and in Religious orders were corrupted, but also Government, and Magistracy, and all things in civil state were not aright in the sight of the Lord.[23]

The work appeared at the point in English history when Quakers were at the height of their political influence, publicly welcoming the reinstatement of the Rump Parliament, and playing an active role in national politics. Lists of Quakers eligible to serve as justices were submitted to Parliament; others regained their commissions in the army.[24] As such, the issue of a folio volume outlining the consistency of Quaker belief in liberty of conscience, and the relevance of their beliefs to the proper government of the nation, was an

---

thrown out of the family home. *DNB*; Ernest Taylor, 'The first Publishers of Truth: a study', *JFHS* 19 (1922), 67; Elizabeth Brockbank, *Edward Burrough: a wrestler for truth 1634–1662* (London, 1949), esp. pp. 14, 16–17; W. C. Braithwaite, *The beginnings of Quakerism* (Cambridge, 1955), p. 90.

[20] Edward Burrough, 'Epistle to the Reader', in George Fox, *The great mistery of the great whore unfolded* (London, 1659), STC F1832, sigs. a2r and b2r. The date printed on the title page of the work is 1659; Burrough's *Epistle* is dated November 1658 (sig. d2v).

[21] *The great mistery of the great whore*, sigs. b4v, cr.   [22] *Ibid.*, sig. a2r.   [23] *Ibid.*, sig. b3r.

[24] Barry Reay, 'The Quakers, 1659 and the restoration of the monarchy', *History* 63 (1978), 195, 200–01.

act of considerable political acumen.[25] The Quakers, Burrough argued, had consistently opposed all that was wrong in England in the turbulent 1650s, and they had suffered for it; they were now in a position of moral superiority and could, with the considerable credibility of 'having received power from on high',[26] comment and advise upon the frightening political vacuum which the nation now faced.

In the rather sober circumstances of 1662, Edward Burrough wrote a shorter history of the 'Beginning of the worke of the Lord and the first Publication of Truth', this time with specific reference to the movement's history in the city of London.[27] Burrough's manuscript testimony of 1662 was written more modestly, 'to be presented to the Meeting of Men [in London] to be read amongst them'. Although it told the same story of the first movings of the Lord in his few chosen 'Instruments', who 'began to publish and declare the things of the kingdom of God', the purpose of this later history was to consolidate, by describing their establishment and maintenance, regular meetings of 'Men Freinds' in the city of London.[28]

Both of Burrough's early commentaries on the origins of the Quaker movement place considerable significance on the printed tracts which appeared in the 1650s. *The great mistery of the great whore* was, after all, a calendar of the Quakers' printed disputations. In his preface to them, Burrough was not only justifying their validity; he also invited, should the reissue of these previous publications fail to convince, the ultimate national debate: 'if any, especially of the heads and Rulers have doubts or jealousies raised in them, concerning us', Burrough wrote, they should call for a dispute between 'four, ten, twenty, thirty, more or fewer of us' with 'as many of the wisest and ablest of the Priests and Professors . . . at any place in England, at what place, time, and for what continuance, as they shall ascribe and consent unto'.[29] The appearance of such a call at such a moment underlines that the Quakers expected their writings to challenge and persuade a wide audience. Its publication demonstrates that Quaker tracts in the 1650s served an immediate interactive function with the political nation at large.

---

[25] The Quakers' political participation in supporting the recall of the Rump Parliament in 1659 is discussed by Alan Cole, 'The Quakers and politics, 1652–1660', unpublished Ph. D thesis, University of Cambridge, 1955, esp. pp. 78–103; and more recently by Barry Reay, 'The Quakers, 1659, and the restoration of the monarchy'. See also Austin Woolrych, 'The Good Old Cause and the fall of the Protectorate', *Cambridge Historical Journal* 13: 2 (1957), 133–61.

[26] *The great mistery of the great whore*, sig. b3r.

[27] Edward Burrough, 'A testimony concerning the beginning of the worke of the Lord . . . in this cittie of London' (1662), in 'Mary Pennington her Book, being copies of severall papers of friends, which she transcribed for her dear father', FHL Temp. Mss 752 [fols. 6–15].

[28] Burrough, 'A testimony' [fols. 6r–v].

[29] *The great mistery of the great whore*, sig. c3r. See Barry Reay, 'The Quakers, 1659, and the restoration of the monarchy', for an account of the hostility of many puritan ministers towards Quakers during the months of upheaval in 1659.

The latter work, unprinted and addressed to private meetings of Quakers in the rather solemn context of 1662, allows a more refined view of the Quakers' use of print. In describing the establishment of Quaker meetings in London, Edward Burrough listed the affairs which had been managed by those local meetings, 'for the prosperous carrying on the good work of the Lord so hapily begun in the Citty':

(to whitt) concerning providing convenient meeting places for the publishing of truth; and how the poor people that believed should be honestly taken care for, that no want should be amongst them; and that the sick, and weak, and impotent should be visited and provided for; and that such Servants as were put away out of their services for receiving the truth, should be looked after, and placed in some honest imployments.[30]

Burrough emphasised very strongly that these tasks of social organisation belonged to the 'friends of the City', and 'were not proper for us of the Ministry'. Warming to his theme of the distinction between the social role of local meetings and the loftier pursuits of Quaker 'ministers', Burrough expanded:

neither had we the opportunities of such exercises, being wholly devoted to the worke of the Ministry, to which we were ordained of God, and were continually exercised in preaching the Gospell, in answering Books and Manuscripts put forth against us, and in Disputes and Conventions with such as opposed the truth.[31]

Burrough's two historical accounts underline that writing was intended to be proactive in publicising and furthering the Quaker movement. As Burrough described it, answering books was the work of a Quaker 'ministry', 'ordained of God', with very distinct responsibilities from other members of the Quaker movement. It is the role of Quaker leaders as the movement's principal authors which will now be considered.

Nearly one hundred named Quaker authors had had their writings published by 1656, contributing to a total of nearly three hundred (291) publications.[32] The most prolific authors emanated from the original communities in Yorkshire and Westmorland visited by George Fox in 1652: eight men (James Nayler, George Fox, Richard Farnworth, James Parnell,

[30] Burrough, 'A testimony' [fol. 8r]. His reference to 'publishing of truth' refers to Quakers speaking or preaching at their meetings; Burrough was writing specifically about the meeting established at the Bull and Mouth, Aldersgate, which was also the site of the Quaker Thomas Simmonds's printing house. Chapter 2 will discuss in more detail the organisation behind early Quaker printing.

[31] Burrough, 'A testimony' [fol. 8v].

[32] Based on a study of Joseph Smith's *Descriptive catalogue of Friends' books* (2 vols., London, 1867), and followed up in Donald Wing, *Short-title catalogue of books printed in England, Scotland, Ireland, Wales and British North America, 1641–1700*, 2nd edn (3 vols., New York, 1972–88), and G. K. Fortescue (ed.), *Catalogue of the pamphlets, books, newspapers and manuscripts relating to the Civil War, the Commonwealth, and Restoration, collected by George Thomason, 1640–1661* (2 vols., London, 1908).

Edward Burrough, Francis Howgill, William Dewsbery and Richard Hubberthorne) individually wrote more than half of all Quaker publications in this period. Yet their influence was still greater than this. A significant number of the early tracts were composite, either containing a variety of sections written by different people, or listing a number of people as joint authors of a whole tract. These composite works were often inspired or directed by the original core of Quaker authors, who organised the contributions of the less prolific Quaker authors. Thus James Nayler actually contributed to almost one in five of all Quaker publications between 1652 and 56; at the other end of the spectrum, thirty-three authors contributed to the joint authorship of only one tract each, and nearly half of all named authors appeared as contributors to tracts rather than as individual authors.[33]

The select group of individuals responsible for the publication of Quaker books between 1652 and 1656 lends credence to the notion of a Quaker ministry responsible for writing, described by Edward Burrough in 1662. The notion of a Quaker ministry, however, runs contrary to many basic conceptions surrounding the early Quaker movement.[34] The Quakers were and are famous for their denunciation of the trained ministers of the Church of England, deriding them as 'hireling priests' who made a 'trade in other men's words' and relied on their worldly learning to command religious authority. Yet despite this, there was within the early Quaker movement a body of men and women acting as an effective leadership. Known within the denominational tradition as the First Publishers of Truth, these 'ministers' were itinerant preachers, numbering between 60 and 240, who travelled the country and were initially responsible for the spread of Quaker ideas.[35] It is precisely these leaders who are best known within the early history of the Quaker movement: figures like George Fox, James Nayler, Edward Burrough and William Dewsbery. It is also these individuals who wrote the majority of Quaker tracts.

In 1974 the ethnographer Richard Bauman identified the Quaker minister as enjoying a 'particular communicative role', and suggested that the act of speaking itself defined the early Quaker ministry.[36] Since no formal structures existed for electing ministers, Bauman argued, it was the process of public

[33] For further analysis see M. K. Peters, 'Quaker pamphleteering and the development of the Quaker movement, 1652–1656', unpublished Ph.D thesis, University of Cambridge, 1996, pp. 26–29.

[34] H. H. Gerth and C. Wright Mills (eds.) *From Max Weber: essays in sociology* (1948; reprinted London, 1993), p. 317.

[35] Norman Penney (ed.), *The First Publishers of Truth*, JFHS Supps. 1–5 (London, 1907); Ernest Taylor, 'The first publishers of truth: a study', *JFHS* 19 (1922), 66–81.

[36] Richard Bauman, 'Speaking in the light: the role of the Quaker minister' in Richard Bauman and Joel Sherzer (eds.), *Explorations in the ethnography of speaking* (Cambridge, 1974), p. 144.

speech at a meeting which signalled that the speaker was divinely inspired. Although as an ethnographer of speaking Bauman was concerned with the spoken authority of Quaker ministers, his argument can be extended to manuscript papers and printed tracts. Quaker leaders themselves elided the differences, so often highlighted by historians, between their spoken, written or printed declarations: 'The Lord speaks to thee by the mouth of his Servants in word and writing', Edward Burrough had 'warned' the nation in a tract published in 1654, and continued, 'I write not as from man . . . but as from the eternal and spiritual light':

for who Speaks, Writes, or Declares, from the light of God . . . Speaks, Writes, and Declares not as from man . . . but as from God, whose light is spiritual . . . and from this light did the Prophets and Ministers of God . . . Speak, Write, and Declare . . . and from this light . . . did all the holy men of God Write, and Declare.[37]

The process of writing played an important practical role in the establishment and maintenance of the Quaker ministry. There are very few written records relating to the process of how one became a Quaker minister, and Bauman's argument, that it was determined by speaking from the word of God, is very convincing. The letters and manuscripts circulated by Quaker leaders, however, reveal a good deal about how their authority was exercised, and demonstrates that their ministerial status was consolidated, often very pragmatically, by the written word.

Basic structures for internal discipline were laid down and enforced through papers written and distributed by the itinerant Quaker leaders. In a paper to 'Frends', later dated by George Fox 'abought 1653', the Yorkshire-born Quaker William Dewsbery addressed 'the word of the living God to his Church he hath Called and Chosen out of the world'.[38] In it, Dewsbery advised that 'in every perticuler meetting of Frinds Sarvants and Children of the most high God,' 'their be chosen from amongst you one or two who are the most growne in the power and life' who should take 'Charg and Care over the flocke of god in that place'.[39] Those chosen, Dewsbery continued, should not 'Rulle as lords over gods heritag', nor 'by Constrant', nor 'for Filthy lucker', but 'in all pueritty to be examples to the flocke'. They should keep order by appointing regular meetings – one a week as well as on First Days, or Sundays. There should be general meetings with other local groups

---

[37] Edward Burrough, *A warning from the Lord to the inhabitants of Underbarrow, and so to all the Inhabitants in England* (London, 1654), STC b6057, pp. 25, 37, 36.

[38] William Dewsbery, born in 1621, was actually one of the oldest of the original Quaker ministers and was therefore perhaps well placed to advise on the setting up of churches. He had served in the army; and had been connected to the Balby group where he encountered Fox in 1651: *BDBR*.

[39] William Dewsbery [1653], Sw Mss 3: 19.

every two or three weeks; and in remote areas where members were scattered over great distances, meetings should last for three or four hours, 'as the lord orders'. If any should 'walk disorderly', Dewsbery advised those acting as the elders of the meeting 'to deal planly with them in Reproveing them and ministering to the puer in the Conscienc', at first privately, then if necessary before the whole meeting, with the support of 'two or three more that are the most grown in the truth', and finally with the support of members of other meetings. If the back sliders were still unreformed, Dewsbery counselled: 'Charg them to depart from amongst you, (so Cast them out).'[40]

This document has been seen as important in laying down a basic structure for church discipline which would be widely applied in later years.[41] It is also highly revealing about the roots of the Quaker movement, and the role of the itinerant preachers and their writings in its growth. Copies of letters like Dewsbery's would be carried by itinerant preachers, and used by them when they visited and revisited the localities where they preached their message. In so doing, a homogeneous and networked series of meetings could be established. Thus two years later, in March 1655, and from the other end of England, Henry Fell reported a 'very Serviceable' meeting at Gravesend in Kent, to George Fox, and asserted, 'it is likely Some thinge may be brought forth here if a meetinge be but kept up on the first dayes, and some friends in the ministry to come amongst them'.[42]

Quaker ministers did not only oversee the appointment of local meetings, and the choosing of local 'elders'. At a national level, they also informed one another about the success or otherwise of their preaching. Thus Henry Fell wrote to Fox of the Gravesend meeting: 'I thought good to lay this before thee, that thou might be mindfull of it': effectively, Henry Fell was advising Fox to organise the supply of more ministers.[43] Many other letters similarly informed of the need for more ministers in particular areas, or simply recorded the setting up of local meetings.

The ministers also exercised a degree of authority over one another, again enforced through written letters which were copied and circulated among them. Letters of recommendation could be sent: from Ireland, Edward

---

[40] Dewsbery, Sw Mss 3: 19. There were a number of similar documents circulating in the Quaker movement in the 1650s: see Arnold Lloyd, *Quaker social history*, pp. 1–16.

[41] Braithwaite, *Beginnings of Quakerism*, p. 140.

[42] Henry Fell to George Fox, Gravesend, 27 March 1655, Sw Mss 4: 167.

[43] The effectiveness of such requests is illustrated by the fact that within three weeks, a letter written by George Taylor, the chief co-ordinator of ministerial correspondence based at Kendal in Westmorland, reported that two named ministers, John Storey and John Wilkinson, were on their way to Kent; and by the end of April seven unnamed 'friends' from the north were operating in Kent and Surrey. George Taylor, 14 April 1655, Sw Mss 1: 219; Francis Howgill and Edward Burrough, 30 April 1655, Caton Mss 3: 150.

Burrough wrote to colleagues in London about 'one Jo: Parrat [Perrot]', who 'hath bene with me about a weeke', and who had helped Burrough to write the papers and notes necessary for his proselytising. Perrot was, Burrough wrote, 'a pretty Man, and servicable as to me for writeing'.[44] From London a year later, Edward Burrough sent a letter to 'the churches of Christ in Ireland', recommending to them 'my deare Brother and faithfull Companion in the kingdom of Jesus, called Humphrey Norton', whom Burrough sent to Ireland 'as a faithfull labourer, to be be received by you in the name of him that sends him'. Burrough emphasised Humphrey Norton's strengths:

I doubt not, but that the flocke will receive refreshment; the weake will be strengthned, and weary and heavy laden will be comforted; and the body will be Edefied, and for this cause hath the Lord chosen him, into thy service, to manifest further unto you the power of the gospell of god by his ministry.[45]

Just as ministers could be commended by one another, so they could also be denounced. Edward Burrough's suggestion in 1662 that local meetings should ensure 'that such Servants as were put away out of their services for receiving the truth, should be looked after, and placed in some honest imployments' demonstrates the ephemerality of the Quaker ministry.[46] Again, the written record of ejection was important. In 1655 the Quaker minister and author Christopher Atkinson, guilty of fornication with one of his Quaker colleagues, was cast out of the movement in a document formally witnessed by fellow ministers, which was then read out loud at a meeting of local Quakers. The ministers who oversaw his ejection originated mostly from the north of England. At the time, they were all preaching in East Anglia, and met together in Norwich specifically in order to deal with the Atkinson crisis. Although the statement of Atkinson's ejection was formally read to the meeting in Norwich, news of the trouble was conscientiously sent back to the Quaker ministers' communication headquarters at Swarthmoor Hall in Lancashire.[47]

---

[44] Edward Burrough to Robert Dring and Gerrard Roberts, Waterford, 21 January 1656, Markey Mss. p. 103. John Perrot, who came from near Waterford, was later the subject of considerable ministerial scandal and division when he argued that the inner leadings of the spirit should override practical considerations of organisation, including the holding of prearranged meetings and the Quakers' refusal to remove their hats during worship. Braithwaite, *Second period of Quakerism*, pp. 228–50.

[45] Edward Burrough, 9 June 1656, Sw Mss 6: 34. Humphrey Norton originally came from Durham, and in London acted as a correspondent with Quakers in Kendal, organising the funding of the movement. Like John Perrot, Humphrey Norton subsequently fell out with Fox and other Quaker leaders. See Braithwaite, *Beginnings of Quakerism*, pp. 235–37, George Fox, *The journal of George Fox*, ed. Norman Penney (2 vols., Cambridge, 1911), vol. I, p. 441; vol. II, p. 314. For the importance of the Kendal fund, see below, Chapter 2.

[46] Burrough, 'A testimony' [fol. 8r].

[47] Richard Clayton to Margaret Fell, 12 July 1655, Sw Trs 1: 564–65. The witnesses were John Stubbs, William Caton and Thomas Symonds; other ministers present were Richard

In 1656, Robert Collinson of Kendal, previously responsible for distributing books in the area, was formally cast out by letter for 'breach of the unity by false Imitated power from whence proceeded false Judgement'.[48] Collinson's 'false judgement', according to those who wrote the statement denouncing him, had been against 'the ministry of Christ, unto which we are called'. Collinson had specifically attacked the ministers' authority to preach, and had 'denied all that which was spoaken by all of us . . . and said that all which was spoaken here was only a forme of words, without the life and power and bad us stay at home and be silent, and goe not Idleing up and downe'.[49]

As with Christopher Atkinson, the account of Collinson's rebellion and excommunication was written down and 'given forth to go abroad amonge freinds for the Cleareing of the lords truth'.[50] The status of the ministers' utterances was central to their ministry. Those who were deemed to speak with the word of God were accorded due authority. Those who operated without the 'life and power', or, as in Collinson's case, failed to recognise the authority of God's word, were formally cast out. The process of 'casting out' itself required a formal, written statement, ratified by the authority of Quaker ministers.

Written records, in the form of manuscript letters, were thus generated by the Quaker ministers as part of the organisation of the early movement. It was essential that the central core of itinerant preachers informed each other of satisfactory or unsatisfactory preaching, and of the need for ministers in particular localities. Although the individual spirituality of each author was emphasised in order to establish the authenticity of their awakening, a major purpose of the letters was to establish a coherent movement.

Quaker leaders also used their writing as an instrument to convince potential followers. The early correspondence between Quaker ministers demonstrates that they placed enormous value on papers and printed tracts as a means of awakening people to the 'light within'. A key figure in the development of publishing was the Yorkshire Quaker Thomas Aldam, a leading member of the gathered church in Balby, South Yorkshire, where George

---

Hubberthorne, George Whitehead and Richard Clayton. Apart from Thomas Symonds, all of these were men from the northwest of England. See Chapter 3. This was the culmination of a long dispute between Atkinson and his fellow ministers in East Anglia which had been running since December 1654, apparently occasioned by Atkinson's unseemly relations with a woman. See Sw Mss 1: 239; Sw Trs 2: 569, 2: 589; and also Vann, *The social development of English Quakerism*, p. 18.

[48] For Collinson as the distributor of books around Kendal, see Richard Farnworth, 7 January 1653, Sw Mss 4: 83.

[49] 'Excommunication of Robert Collinson', signed by Francis Howgill, John Audland and Edward Burrough, 17 March 1656, Sw Trs 2: 485; Braithwaite, *Beginnings of Quakerism*, pp. 344–45.

[50] 'Excommunication of Robert Collinson', Sw Trs 2: 485.

Fox travelled in 1651.[51] Aldam was imprisoned in York Castle for disturb-ing a puritan minister in May 1652 and remained in gaol for two-and-a-half years. While in prison Aldam collaborated with a handful of his fellow prisoners in organising the publication of some of the earliest pamphlets.[52] Aldam's kinsman Richard Farnworth of nearby Tickhill was, for the first year of Quaker publishing, the most prolific Quaker author, and Aldam co-authored a number of tracts with him.[53] The partnership of Aldam and Farnworth in producing printed tracts was central to the development of the Quaker campaign; Aldam's contribution was organisational, and probably also financial.[54] It was from prison in York that he sent manuscripts down to London for printing, and organised the distribution of printed tracts across the north of England. Aldam was in little doubt as to the efficacy of using printed books, and was keen to impress this upon fellow Quaker minis-ters. In 1652 he wrote to George Fox and urged him to take up the printed books, 'which will be verye servisable for weake frends, and Convinceing the world'.[55] Aldam also informed Margaret Fell at Swarthmoor Hall that writing was effective. At his trial at the York Assizes in March 1653, he explained to her: 'I was made to write very much, and to cleambe it upon the walles as they went in and out . . . and many people were made to owne the truth and were silent.'[56] Elizabeth Hooton, Thomas Aldam's fellow pris-oner at York, was similarly enthusiastic. While Aldam's concern was with proselytisation, however, Hooton's motivation was slightly different. She explained in a letter to Fox: 'I am much kept to writinge, and my eys are tender, that I cannot abide to write for verye much.' Despite this ailment,

---

[51] Thomas Aldam (d. 1660) remains biographically rather obscure. He lived in Warmsworth, South Yorkshire, and was a wealthy yeoman. In 1651 he was an established leader of the gathered church at Balby; and it was to this community that Fox travelled in 1651 after his release from Derby gaol. Geoffrey Nuttall, *Studies in Christian enthusiasm* (Wallingford, Penn., 1948), pp. 25–38; *DNB*; *BDBR*.

[52] Thomas Aldam, S. Buttivant, J. Harwood, T. Lawson, J. Nayler and B. Nicholson, *A brief discovery of the threefold estate of Antichrist* (London, 1653), *STC* A894B; Thomas Aldam, M. Fisher, J. Holmes, E. Hooton, B. Nicholson and W. Pears, *False prophets and false teachers described* [1652], *STC* A894BA.

[53] Richard Farnworth (c.1630–66) was connected to Thomas Aldam through Aldam's uncle, Thomas Lord, with whom Farnworth lived before being thrown out for his increasingly radical views. Aldam and Farnworth were later connected by marriage with the Stacey family. See Geoffrey Nuttall, 'Notes on Richard Farnworth', *JFHS* 48 (1956), 79–84; and P. Holzenberg and R. Greaves, *BDBR*. Farnworth's publications with Thomas Aldam were: Richard Farnworth and Thomas Aldam, *A discovery of truth and falsehood* (London, 1653) *STC* F479A; Aldam, *An Easter-Reckoning, or, A Free-will Offering* (London, 1653), *STC* F480; Aldam, *The generall-good to all people* (London, 1653) *STC* F483; Aldam, *Gods covenanting with his people*, (London, 1653); Aldam, *The priests ignorance and contrary walkings* (London, 1655); *STC* F492; (2nd edn. 1656), *STC* F492A.

[54] See below, Chapter 2.

[55] Thomas Aldam to George Fox, 1652, A. R. Barclay Mss 1: 71, fols. 206–07.

[56] Thomas Aldam to Margaret Fell, 1653, Sw Mss 3: 43.

she stated that she kept 'single Coppies of what I have send [*sic*] forth'; and copies of anything her fellow prisoners were 'moved to write'.[57] Writing in this case was not a spontaneous outburst, but was valued highly enough for duplicates to be kept for use on later occasions. The proselytising value of tracts and handwritten papers was constantly emphasised. Margaret Fell was sure that manuscripts she was sending to press 'will worke for the glory of my father'.[58] Richard Farnworth, travelling through his native county of Yorkshire in April 1653, was even more optimistic about the worth of his books, claiming: 'the truth doth spread much abroad by the Bookes that is in Printe, and now there is as many written as is Sufficient for the Downefall of Antichrists Kingdome'.[59]

Printed tracts and manuscript papers were produced as an intrinsic part of the ministers' proselytising. Edward Burrough's recommendation of the ministerial capabilities of John Perrot in Ireland, cited above, stemmed from his need for books to 'doe their service'.[60] The failure of a consignment of books to Ireland, where Burrough worked an extensive preaching campaign between 1655–56, led him to complain to his book suppliers in London, 'we have great want of bookes, which is the sanse of our much writing, abundance have I written. Scarce a day these severall weekes hath passed over, wherein I have not written one thing or other, many times I have had want of a good writer with me.'[61]

---

[57] Thomas Aldam and Elizabeth Hooton to George Fox, Autumn 1652, A. R. Barclay Mss 1: 16, fol. 54. This statement is extremely significant to our understanding of the Quaker movement. There are a handful of letters remaining from the summer of 1652, the time of Elizabeth Hooton's arrest. It is Hooton's impulse to keep copies of letters which may lie behind our understanding that the Quaker movement 'began' in the summer of 1652.

[58] Margaret Fell to Thomas Fell, February 1653, Abraham Mss [1].

[59] Richard Farnworth to Thomas Aldam [April 1653], Portfolio 36: 151. The date of Farnworth's letter may be significant. There were growing tensions between the Army and the Rump Parliament at the beginning of 1653 before the Rump's final dissolution by Cromwell and his troops in April 1653: tensions about which, as Chapter 7 will show, the Quakers were well aware. The dissolution of the Rump Parliament may well have been seen by Farnworth as part of the 'Downefall of Antichrists Kingdome' which he thought his books would produce. The classic account of the dissolution of the Rump Parliament is still Blair Worden, *The Rump Parliament 1648–1653* (Cambridge, 1974); and Worden, 'The Bill for a new representative?', *English Historical Review* 86 (1971); see also Austin Woolrych, *Commonwealth to Protectorate* (Oxford, 1986).

[60] Edward Burrough to Robert Dring, Dublin, 22 August, 1655, Markey Mss, p. 13. He wrote again on 22 November asking for some manuscripts which he had sent to the press in London to be sent back to him, 'if yu have not wholly forgotten us'; and guaranteed that they would be 'serviceable for the world': Edward Burrough to Robert Dring and Gerrard Roberts, Waterford, 22 November 1655, Markey Mss, p. 98. In May 1656, John Audland wrote to Edward Burrough, who by now had returned to London, informing him that the consignment of books bound for Ireland had been lost with the boat transporting them. Audland to Burrough, 12 May 1656, A. R. Barclay Mss 1: 110, fols. 317–18.

[61] Edward Burrough to Robert Dring and Gerrard Roberts, Waterford, 21 January 1656, Markey Mss, p. 103.

The practical value of writing was that papers, letters, or printed tracts could be more widely dispersed than oral preaching. There was, however, no straightforward or progressive transition from an oral to a written culture within the Quaker movement. Written addresses were integrated in very complex ways into an itinerant preaching campaign.

Quaker authors argued strongly for the equation of publishing and preaching. 'We would have all to call upon the Lord, while he is near, and to seek him while he may be found,' wrote the Quaker minister Thomas Atkinson, as part of a printed dispute with a puritan minister, 'and that is the intent of all our writing and printing, or coming to your Steeple-houses, or coming abroad for your souls good.'[62] Another author went to considerable and unusual etymological trouble to argue that preaching and publishing were synonymous:

Preaching is publishing, or declaring abroad, or telling to one another openly, whether by conference or any other way. Thus they preached or published, or told abroad what Christ had done to one that was deafe, and had an impediment in his speech *Mark* 7.36. *Ephphatha* they preached it, which word you know is used where preaching is expressed, and yet it signifies no more here but telling abroad; or publishing as it is rendered in the English.[63]

The equation of written and spoken declarations was important to the status of Quaker authors as leaders of the movement. There are many ways in which a printed tract, privately read, could be interpreted beyond the original intentions of the author. Once a book had passed through the hands of printers, proof-readers, booksellers and finally inquisitive and disillusioned religious radicals, the author could lose a good deal of control over interpretation, while public preaching allowed speakers to respond to questions and audience reaction.[64] As will be seen in Chapter 2, considerable efforts were made by the Quaker pamphleteers to control the ways in which their tracts were produced and read. In their own writing, authors tried to maintain their own personal status as preachers and prophets, and argued that their books should be regarded in the same light as their preaching: 'this was I moved of the Lord to write forth, to be set on the Crosses in *Westmerland*, and elsewhere', wrote John Camm in a tract published in 1654.[65] Richard Farnworth's enthusiasm for his written papers as a form of his own ministry led to some striking metaphors: 'truth doth spread very much abroad,' he

---

[62] Thomas Atkinson, in George Fox and Richard Hubberthorne, *Truths defence against the refined subtilty of the serpent* (n.p., 1653), STC F1970, p. 17.

[63] William Tomlinson, *A Word of Reproof to the Priests or Ministers* (London, 1653), STC T1855, p. 17.

[64] Roger Chartier, 'Texts, printings, readings' in Lynn Hunt (ed.), *The new cultural history* (London, 1989), pp. 154–75.

[65] J[ohn] C[amm], *A true discovery of the ignorance* (London, 1654), STC C393, p. 19.

reported in a letter to Fox, 'I have even beene nailed to the crosse in these parts.'[66] Farnworth also believed that his experience of the ministry, through writing, could be shared by his co-religionists; he wrote publicly to fellow Quakers: 'you may manifestly declare your selves to be the Epistles of Christ, to be seen and read of all men, you that are in union and fellowship with him, who are dispersed and scattered abroad'.[67] More privately he wrote to Margaret Fell: 'I am as a white paper book without any line or sentence but as it is revealed and written by the spirit.'[68]

The relationship for Quakers between the 'word' of God and the holy spirit diverged radically from earlier puritan positions, which argued that the spirit spoke only through, or in, the 'word'; and that the scriptures were the word of God. The idea that the holy spirit could manifest itself in other ways than the scriptures was more widely voiced by the 1640s and 1650s: but the Quaker argument, that the scriptures were only the 'letter', given forth by the apostles, was significantly different. Quakers argued that the holy spirit which had moved men to write the scriptures was also present in them; and that consequently their utterances – spoken or written – were as valid as those of the apostles. Thus the holy spirit, which was the original word of God, was distinguished from the 'letter', which was the Bible.[69] This had important ramifications for the status of the Quakers' own utterances, minimising the distinction between a written, printed or spoken form; but maximising the importance of the speaker or author. In April 1653, Richard Farnworth sent three manuscripts to Thomas Aldam for publication, and requested that he 'Read them over, and see that there be noe mistake in any.' Farnworth was particularly keen for Aldam to look over one work, *God's covenanting with his people*, and check his scriptural references in the concordance: 'thou meist sett a few [words] to it with the great Concordance but see that they be according to the Condition of that which they are set in to: or else let it bee'.[70] Effectively, Farnworth's written utterance, and Aldam's own understanding of it, were to take precedence over the Bible.

Such authority enabled written papers to be sent, on occasion, in place of the ministers themselves. Thus in November 1653 the Quaker Gervase Benson, a Yorkshire justice of the peace and former mayor of Kendal, travelled from the north of England to London, where members of the Barebones Parliament were discussing the possible abolition of tithes for lay

---

[66] Richard Farnworth to George Fox [November 1653], Sw Mss 3: 52.

[67] Richard Farnworth, *Light risen out of darkness* (London, 1654) *STC* F490, pp. 3–4.

[68] Richard Farnworth to Margaret Fell, Sw Mss 3: 51, as cited in Phyllis Mack, *Visionary women*, p. 173.

[69] Geoffrey Nuttall, *The holy spirit in puritan faith and experience* (Oxford, 1946), pp. 21–33, esp. p. 27. Nuttall does not emphasise so much the distinction made by the Quakers between the 'Word' and the 'Letter', although it is clearly present in the Quakers' early writings.

[70] Farnworth to Aldam [April 1653], Portfolio 36: 151.

impropriators. Benson's intentions were clearly political: he met with sympathetic MPs and addressed papers to them.[71] Benson had carried with him a manuscript of a tract written by James Nayler and George Fox, which he had printed, but too late to be distributed among the MPs before the Barebones Parliament resigned its power to Cromwell. The resultant tract stated rather forlornly: 'These Papers were prepared and intended to have been delivered to every member of Parliament, but before they could be got out the Parliament dissolved.'[72] The tract was published nevertheless. Its authors had written it hundreds of miles away from London, and had entrusted its publication and dissemination to Gervase Benson. Fox and Nayler were far more prolific authors, and thus better known, than Benson.[73] Their address to Parliament was expected to stand regardless of whether they would themselves deliver it: and was deemed more authoritative than Benson's spontaneous address, which remained unpublished.

That Quaker authors did not expect to accompany their writings, and indeed expected them to function in lieu of their preaching, is also clear from the distribution of unprinted papers. James Nayler, temporarily imprisoned in Appleby gaol in November 1652, sent a paper to George Fox to be 'coppied out' and sent 'into Furness'.[74] A paper written by Margaret Fell had a wider distribution: 'wee have Coppied one for the Bottom of Westmerland, and another for Cumberland and sent them away this day, we shall send another for Bishoprick [Durham] as speedily as may be', wrote the chief Quaker scribe George Taylor in 1654, suggesting an almost routine distribution of her papers.[75] Margaret Fell, whose last child was born in 1653, does not seem ever in the 1650s to have travelled very far from her home in Lancashire; like the incarcerated Nayler, she wrote papers to be sent further afield than she could travel. One of her papers was read aloud to a meeting in Sunderland one Sunday in August 1655, and carried the authority of her own spoken utterance: 'truly my hart was much broken to hear thy voyce, it was so pure and pleasant to my eares', wrote William Caton, a former member of the Fell household who had been present at the meeting.[76] Writing did not always

---

[71] For Benson's account of his visit to London, and attempt to meet the members of the Barebones Parliament, see Gervase Benson, 29 November 1653, Sw Mss 4: 32. For the wider political lobbying of Parliament by the Quakers, see below, Chapter 7.

[72] James Nayler *et al.*, *A lamentacion (by one of England's prophets)* (n.p., 1653), STC N292, p. 20.

[73] Nayler had had nine tracts published by the end of 1653; and Fox at least seven.

[74] James Nayler to George Fox [November 1652], Sw Mss 3: 69.

[75] George Taylor to Margaret Fell, October 1654, Sw Mss 1: 211.

[76] William Caton to Margaret Fell, 28 August 1655, Sw Mss 1: 375. William Caton had been the companion and schoolmate of George Fell, the son of Margaret and Thomas, and later had served as Margaret Fell's secretary. Born in 1636, and so aged about nineteen, he was, like many of his fellow ministers, very young. *Journal of George Fox*, ed. Penney, vol. I, p. 421; *DNB*.

suggest an immobilised author. Another paper 'given forth' by a very mobile James Nayler at Strickland Head, on his way into the Yorkshire dales, was intended by its Kendal scribes to 'goe through all as fast as might bee'.[77]

Writing was also used to emphasise and consolidate oral addresses. When foiled by his meeting with an apparently intransigent Oliver Cromwell in March 1654, Francis Howgill rehearsed their interview in print:

> when I had delivered what I was commanded, thou questioned it, whether it was the word of the Lord or not, and soughtest by thy reason to put it off; and we have waited some dayes since, but cannot speak to thee, therefore I was moved to write to thee, and clear my conscience, and to leave thee.[78]

After reiterating the warning that Cromwell was rebuilding in England everything that God had but recently destroyed, Howgill's tract issued another on the Lord's behalf: 'Wherefore thus saith the Lord, wilt thou limit me, and set bounds to me, when, and where, and how, and by whom I shall declare myself, and publish my name?'[79]

Quaker authors, then, produced papers and tracts to spread the word of God, which they claimed was within them: their writing was deemed to carry the authority of the spirit within them. In the same vein, their written tracts and papers were valued as specific instruments of 'convincement'. The process of reading was equated with that of conversion. Early Quaker tracts, especially the prefatory addresses to the reader, abound with metaphors which linked reading to the first awakenings in the reader of the sense of their 'inner light'. It is worth citing a long passage from a tract by Richard Farnworth to see how he described the process. This was an address written to 'the valiant Souldiery of the Army of the Lamb', in a tract published in 1653:

> Thou mayest see in this ensuing Treatise that the battle is begun, and the Beast is raging mad; but fear not, come into the battle, and bring with thee the girdle of truth, for the cause is Gods, and he will assist thee: do but read this little Paper put into thy hand, and it will beget desires in thee; If simplicity do but lead thee in the reading, and encourage thee to press on into the warfare; it may be thou wilt finde something in it that is hard to thee; but read on, and in the end thou wilt see the large love of God to us which is hated, and reviled, and shamefully intreated, which will let thee see, that it is the Lord that doth assist us by his power, and keepeth us both day and Eke each hour; leave not till thou hast read it over, and it will to thee the Enemies subtilties discover; then come away, and do not stay to hover. Deny thy self and follow the Lamb.[80]

---

[77] George Taylor to Margaret Fell, April 1655, Sw Mss 1: 220.

[78] Francis Howgill, in John Camm and Francis Howgill, *This was the word of the Lord* (London, 1654), STC C392, sig. A4r.

[79] *Ibid.*, sigs. A4r, A4v.

[80] Richard Farnworth, *An Easter-reckoning* (London, 1653), STC F480, sig. A3v.

Farnworth did not expect his readers to take their task lightly. In a similar preface he had warned the reader, 'this ensuing Treatise was not written for swine to snuffle upon'.[81] Nor was the process of their reading a simple revelation of the inner light; a first reading was expected to 'get desires' in the readers; they were expected to encounter something 'hard' in it; they were urged to 'read on' and 'press on into the warfare'; and again to 'leave not till thou hast read it over'. In similar passages in other tracts, Farnworth paid more attention to the difficulties to be encountered by his readers: 'take heed how thou dost pass thy Judgment; . . . it may be that thou mayst find something in it hard to be digested by thy carnal wisdom; take heed of calling truth railing, for all deceit must be cursed, burned, and cut down by the sword of the Spirit'.[82] Yet the process was not necessarily difficult: 'the cause is Gods, and he will assist thee'. Moreover, the reading could well be an aural process. The last few lines of Farnworth's prefatory address were written in rhyme; and his admission that his words could be taken as 'railing' suggest a primarily oral transmission.[83]

Reading was to be done with simplicity, 'a single eye',[84] or with 'Christian attention'.[85] And the rewards were high: 'it will shew thee the way that leadeth to salvation, and the true guide which it is written from, that thou mayest have union with him in the life and substance of it, without all question or doubt, to live in the life and power of the truth it self'.[86] As they urged their readers to read with simplicity and understanding, Quaker authors also implicitly and explicitly attacked other writing and preaching: the 'great swelling words of mans wisdome' by which the nation had been deceived. Farnworth assured his reader that his tract would contain none of the 'gilded expressions . . . that doth arise from the wisdom of the flesh, for they do but feed the fleshly minde, which must be destroyed with a sore destruction'.[87] '[M]inde not the multitude of words, least thou be deceived; Truth needs no covers', warned another.[88] High-flown language was rejected as the product of learned men who had gone to Oxford and Cambridge and indulged themselves 'with carnal words and weapons about carnal things'.[89] Quaker authors differentiated between their own tracts, written most often for 'the sake of the simple ones'; and all the others, written, the Quakers

---

[81] Richard Farnworth, *A discovery of faith* (London, 1653), STC F479, p. 3.

[82] Farnworth, *Light risen out of darkness*, p. 6.

[83] The combining of literary and oral techniques in the dissemination of libels or public ridicule is also discussed by Adam Fox, 'Ballads, libels and popular ridicule in Jacobean England', *Past and Present* 145 (1994), 63–65.

[84] Farnworth, *A discovery of faith*, p. 4.   [85] Farnworth, *Light risen out of darkness*, p. 6.

[86] Farnworth, *A discovery of faith*, p. 4.   [87] *Ibid.*

[88] A. P., Preface, in James Nayler, *An answer to the booke called the perfect pharise* [1654], STC N261, sig Av.

[89] James Nayler, *The power and glory of the Lord* (London, 1653), STC N302, p. 9.

argued, specifically to deceive. George Fox differentiated between 'the corrupt communication' and the 'pure communication'[90]; James Nayler was more prosaic:

Now though I abhorre striving for Master-hood in words or writing; yet for the sake of the simple ones, who not yet having the true judgement and salt in themselves to discerne of spirits, are subject to take great swelling words of mans wisdome, for the power of God unto salvation I am therefore moved to lay open some of the deceits in this Paper, that where truth and simplicity is in the heart, it may more cleerly judge of truth from deceit.[91]

The process of reading Quaker tracts was therefore expected by their authors to be altogether different from other forms of reading. Reading and writing came to nothing if they were not born of the holy spirit. Quaker tracts were intended to convince by exercising the reader in discovering the holy spirit or light within. There are strong parallels in this with what Nigel Smith identified as the Ranters' concern with 'language in its capacity as a bearer of divine truths, and its ability to communicate Ranter ideas to the illuminated and to other people'.[92]

The contention over the true nature of reading and writing also extended to the reading of the scriptures. For the Bible too, Quaker authors argued there was an 'inner' and an 'outer' reading. They argued that the scriptures had been written from the same holy spirit which now was moving Quaker authors to write their tracts and papers; but that the subsequent translations and interventions in the text itself were carnal perversions: 'the Scripture was not put in Chapter and Verse by the spirit,' wrote James Nayler, 'but the hireling Priests have done it to trade withall'.[93] Furthermore, Quaker authors argued that the scriptures were, like their own tracts, an instrument to aid Christ and his Disciples, themselves messengers of the same holy spirit, in their own preaching. The Bible did not lead of itself to the revelation of the light within: 'the Scriptures was used by Christ and his Apostles, to convince gaine-sayers, though they needed not them in regard of themselves, but had the same spirit that gave them forth, and was taught by it and not by the letter'.[94]

Another author, in the course of a printed disputation, argued similarly that knowledge of the Bible or other godly texts could never equate with personal knowledge of the inner light of Christ:

---

[90] George Fox, *The vials of the wrath of God* (London, 1654), STC F1975, p. 14.
[91] James Nayler, *A few words occasioned by a paper lately printed* [1654], STC N279, p. 3. Jackson Cope argued that the Quakers' style contributed to the growth of 'plain' prose more usually related to developments in science and philosophy than theology: see 'Seventeenth-century Quaker style', 725.
[92] Nigel Smith, *A collection of Ranter writings in the seventeenth century* (London, 1983), p. 30.
[93] Nayler, *An answer to the booke called the perfect pharise*, p. 15.   [94] *Ibid.*

What if a man could repeat all the Bible, thats larger, and better then thy Book, yet if the Unction within, the spirit of Christ live not in him, all will avail him nothing. If that seed remain not in him, how can he be guided into all truth. how can he keep himself, and not sin? Pen and Inck shall never make a sinner become a Saint.[95]

The scriptures, then, could be and had been abused by the ministry, 'wresting them for their own ends, adding and diminishing them to their own destruction'; and it was from such carnal readings that arose 'all these sects and opinions in the world'.[96] Quakers were adamant that reading was of no purpose if the light within was excluded by the reader. Yet they were equally adamant that the light of Christ was within every one. It was through the process of reading their own tracts, they suggested, untainted by centuries of interventions by the priesthood, that the first glimmerings of this light might be detected. Thereafter, Nayler argued, the true spirit of the scriptures would become clear; and the inner light 'will open all Parables and read all Scriptures within you in your measure, and so you will come to the Unitie with all Saints in measure, and so come to Christ the first born, even to the innumerable company of Angels, to the spirits of just men made perfect'.[97]

Quaker authors therefore claimed considerable authority for their own writings, and exercised authority through them. They wrote the Word of God, and as such enjoyed the same status as the Apostles. A proper reading of their own tracts, carefully directed by the ministers themselves, would enable the reader to recognise the true light of Christ within themselves. Such lofty purposes behind Quaker writing were recognised by their opponents in the puritan ministry, and were received at worst as blasphemy. Quaker books, it was pointed out at a very early date, were valued by the Quakers above the scriptures:

that they intend to magnify their writings and Epistles above or into an equality unto the holy Scriptures seems very probable, in that they put their papers very diligently into one another hands, but not so the Scriptures, and do some of them say, That it is alike for to take a sentence out of their letters and preach from it, as to take a sentence out of *Pauls* Epistles.[98]

The Essex minister John Stalham also condemned the Quakers' elevation of their pamphlets above those of anyone else:

They clamour, That the Gospel We preach, is from man, and by man: from the Printers and Stationers, but theirs is immediate altogether, for they are taught of God, and the

---

[95] Martin Mason, *The proud pharisee reproved* (London, 1655), STC m933, p. 10.

[96] James Parnell, *A shield of the truth* (London, 1655), STC p533, p. 9.

[97] James Nayler, *A discovery of the first wisdom from beneath* (London, 1653), STC n272, p. 4.

[98] Joseph Kellet, John Pomroy and Paul Glissen, *A faithful discovery of a treacherous design* (London, 1653), STC f568, p. 35.

Teaching of God is immediate in the least degree: And yet they deliver out all their revelations (as they call them) by writing; and they print at one time, more then they speak at a time; and it comes to our hands by the Printers and Stationers. Here they allow in themselves that which they condemne in others.[99]

Thus far, this chapter has argued that the process of writing, and the fact of authorship, was of great importance in the early Quaker movement. Those individuals who wrote the vast majority of Quaker tracts and papers were the effective leaders of the movement. They generated written records in the course of co-ordinating the movement; they wrote specifically as messengers of the holy spirit, and the act of writing physically dispersed their message, and implicitly their authority, faster and further than oral preaching. The final section of this chapter examines in more detail the ways in which Quaker writing emerged as a tool of the leadership, and concentrates specifically on the period 1652–1653, when Quaker leaders established their authority over a growing movement.

The catalyst to much early Quaker writing was the absence of preaching ministers from their local meetings. Many early Quaker printed tracts originated as manuscript letters written by itinerant ministers to their own meetings, or to meetings they had recently visited. Letters and tracts aimed to achieve a form of group cohesion and discipline which was necessitated by the absence of these key preaching figures.

In early 1652, George Fox travelled and preached among groups of Seekers in Yorkshire.[100] Here he revisited contacts he had made at least two years earlier, from Derby gaol, in particular groups centred around Balby and Tickhill in south Yorkshire, and Leeds and Wakefield to the north.[101] From these communities were garnered formidable Quaker ministers: Thomas Aldam, Richard Farnworth and Margaret Killam from around Balby; James Nayler and William Dewsbery from around Wakefield. In May 1652, Fox left the Yorkshire communities and travelled west towards Lancashire and Westmorland, where he met up with similar groups in Preston Patrick, and centred around Swarthmoor Hall in north Lancashire, home of the gentlewoman Margaret Fell.[102] Fox had spent six or seven months in Yorkshire; by the time he left he had made a sufficiently significant impression on them for

---

[99] John Stalham, *Contradictions of the Quakers* (Edinburgh, 1655), STC s5184, p. 25.

[100] A narrative of this early period is provided in Braithwaite, *Beginnings of Quakerism*, pp. 58–110. For a more recent account, see Larry H. Ingle, *First among friends: George Fox and the creation of Quakerism* (Oxford, 1994), chs 6–7.

[101] For evidence of Fox's contact with Richard Farnworth during Fox's imprisonment in Derby gaol in 1650–51, see Richard Farnworth to Fox, 1652, Sw Mss 3: 53; *Journal of George Fox*, ed. Penney, vol. I., pp. 16–37.

[102] It has also been established that formal links existed between the members of the Preston Patrick Westmorland meeting, and groups of Seekers in Swaledale, Yorkshire, before Fox's arrival in the area. W. C. Braithwaite, 'The Westmorland and Swaledale Seekers in 1651', *JFHS* 5: 1 (1908), 3–10.

enthusiasts to continue a written dialogue. In May 1652, Thomas Aldam was imprisoned at York Castle for interrupting the sermon of his parish minister. He was joined by Fox's former travelling companion from the Midlands, Elizabeth Hooton, in June, and Mary Fisher and Jane Holmes in August.[103] By November 1652, James Nayler, who had also been travelling around Lancashire, was imprisoned at Appleby, Westmorland. His fellow prisoner was Francis Howgill, who came from near Grayrigge, Westmorland, and was formerly an established preacher to the Preston Patrick Seekers.[104]

By the end of 1652, therefore, there was a growing need for regular and sustained communication between Quakers from Yorkshire and Lancashire. Moreover, as Richard Bauman argued that the authority of the Quaker ministers rested on their spoken word, the need for communication between preachers and local meetings would increase as their leaders undertook extended itinerant preaching. The new 'Quaker' communities were increasingly disrupted as their preachers travelled further afield, and underwent sometimes lengthy periods of imprisonment. Letters, the key means for leaders to maintain contact with the members of their local meetings, were carried by other Quakers, who visited and acquainted themselves with local groups, and thus further established themselves as figures of authority. Francis Howgill was greatly perturbed when unable to send letters from Appleby gaol in late 1652: 'we canot write but what we write privatly now no friend is to come at us no Leter to goe from us'.[105] Thomas Killam, Mary Aldam, Hannah Castley, Ann Dewsbery, Christopher Roods and Thomas Goodwin – members of the Balby and Wakefield meetings – all sent their greetings to James Nayler as he travelled with Fox in Westmorland and Lancashire, via a letter written by Richard Farnworth.[106] The prisoners at York sent their greetings to George Fox; the 'Balby friends' sent theirs to the prisoners at York; and asked also to be 'remembered' to Margaret Fell and George Fox.[107] The letters entailed the leaders' mutual recognition of their authority: greetings were exchanged between Thomas Aldam in York, and Margaret Fell in Swarthmoor, who had never met: 'my love doth breath out in the power of my fathers love made manifest in thee' wrote Aldam, 'thoughe I never sawe thy face, yet hereing the language of my father proceedinge from thee, and throughe thee . . .'[108]

---

[103] Braithwaite, *Beginnings*, p. 68; *Journal of George Fox*, vol. I., p. 37. See Anthony Pearson, *To the parliament of the common-wealth of England* (London, 1653), STC P992, for a comprehensive list of the prisoners at York, with the dates and causes of their imprisonment.

[104] Braithwaite, *Beginnings* pp. 111–12. For letters relating to their imprisonment, see A. R. Barclay Mss 1: 18, fols. 59–60; 1: 29, fol. 86, 1: 74, fols. 217–20; Sw Mss 3: 66.

[105] Francis Howgill to George Fox, Appleby [Nov/Dec] 1652, A. R. Barclay Mss 1: 18, fol. 60.

[106] Richard Farnworth to James Nayler and George Fox, September 1652, Sw Mss 4: 229.

[107] Thomas Aldam to George Fox, York, July 1652, A. R. Barclay Mss 1: 16, fol. 53.

[108] Thomas Aldam to Margaret Fell, York, 3 April 1653, Sw Mss 3: 43.

In their letters, the itinerant Quaker ministers asserted their authority over their own meetings, or over meetings which they had visited. 'Thomas Goodale [Goodaire], I charge thee by the lord that thou minde thy growth in him, and be faithful to what is comitted to thee', wrote Richard Farnworth in a letter to James Nayler's local Wakefield meeting, thirty miles north of Farnworth's home town of Tickhill. In the same letter he exhorted 'James' to 'watch over the weake ones, and improve thie talent to thie maisters use in faithfullnes', and 'frends' in general to 'meete often togather, and stir up that wich is puer [*sic*] in one another'.[109]

Richard Farnworth travelled and preached very extensively in his native Yorkshire, and in adjoining counties to the south, during the last half of 1652 and much of 1653.[110] Many of his letters were addressed to congregations, or individuals, whom he had met earlier on his travels. Letters sent to Margaret Fell at Swarthmoor Hall, Lancashire, included instructions to circulate copies of them 'to frends abrord . . . to be red at theire meetings'.[111] Newly gathered groups of Quakers in Westmorland were contacted by Margaret Fell on Farnworth's behalf, while Farnworth himself was gathering meetings of Quakers across Yorkshire. In November 1652, Farnworth visited the home of Gervase Benson, near Sedburgh, in the far northwest of Yorkshire, not ten miles from Kendal, and within easy reach of many former Preston Patrick Seekers.[112] Early in the following month, back on his home ground in Balby, Yorkshire, Richard Farnworth received one of the first consignments of printed books from London, and sent a few copies to Margaret Fell with instructions to send them 'Amonge them Frends there'; especially Underbarrow, Grayrigge, and one to Major Bousfield 'that Collo: Benson may see it'.[113] Farnworth also sent a covering letter, to be coppied out by Fell's scribes, and sent to all recipients of the books. The letter included exhortations to local groups to meet together often; and a warning to 'live not in words but minde the power of words'. Farnworth was scrupulously aware of his intended audiences. The letter to be circulated among friends was to 'Aquaint them with our affaires'; the private one for Margaret Fell she was to keep herself; another 'halfe sheet' was included especially for Major

---

[109] Richard Farnworth to James Nayler, Balby, 6 July 1652, Sw Trs 2: 11.
[110] By November 1652 he had visited Lincolnshire, Nottinghamshire and Derbyshire. Richard Farnworth to James Nayler and George Fox, Borrett, Sedburgh, November 1652, Sw Mss 3: 58.
[111] Richard Farnworth to Margaret Fell, Balby, 8 June 1653, Sw Mss 3: 46.
[112] Gervase Benson was a justice of the peace, former county commissioner for Westmorland, an alderman and former mayor of Kendal, public notary, and a colonel. I am grateful to Dr Colin Phillips of Manchester University for this information.
[113] Richard Farnworth to Margaret Fell, Balby, 2 December 1652, Sw Mss 3: 45. The book was probably Thomas Aldam *et al.*, *False prophets and false teachers described* [1652].

Bousfield and his wife, and by extension for Colonel Benson.[114] Different letters were sent between Quaker ministers, and between ministers and their congregations. Letters to individuals had a different function again. Shortly after his conversion in May 1653, Anthony Pearson requested that George Fox and James Nayler, who 'both know my condicon better then my selfe', should be moved 'if nether of them bee drawne this way, to helpe mee with their councell by letter'.[115] Some letters, therefore, could consist of individual counselling of those unsure in their faith; others were sent to sustain newly formed communities by providing them with news, religious invective and repeated instructions to hold regular meetings. Letters were sent where itinerant ministers previously had been in person, and were expected to play an important part in meetings for worship; James Nayler sent a paper to Margaret Fell with specific instructions which indicate the authority of both Nayler and Fell: 'that which I have receved of my father, for you and the rest that aways, I have here inclosed, let it be communicated to them, when you meete to breake the bread of life'.[116]

The earliest of Quaker tracts often included printed copies of letters between itinerant ministers. One of the first extant tracts to appear was entitled *A brief discovery of a threefold estate of Antichrist*. This included at its end an open letter sent from James Nayler in October 1652, from Kellett, Lancashire, to 'friends'. The main subject of the letter was a victorious description of a confrontation between Fox and Nayler, and magistrates at Lancaster. The letter included the by now familiar instruction to friends to 'meet often together'; as well as the stirring news that Justice Gervase Benson, Judge Thomas Fell and Colonel William West, all notable figures in the north-west with considerable legal powers, were 'much convinced of the truth'.[117]

The value of such printed newsletters was swiftly noted by Thomas Aldam, who had organised the printing of *A brief discovery* in time for distribution at his trial at the York assizes in March 1653: 'many Bookes wee sent Abroade in to the Contry, haveing them reddie and printed Letters', he explained to Margaret Fell.[118] Thereafter, printed letters containing news became commonplace: Thomas Aldam's account of his trial at York, in a letter to his wife

---

[114] Richard Farnworth to Margaret Fell, Balby, 2 December 1652, Sw Mss 3: 45. The half sheet for Gervase Benson has unfortunately not survived.

[115] Anthony Pearson to a 'Frende' [Margaret Fell?], Rampshaw, West Aukland, Co. Durham, 9 May 1653, Sw Mss 1: 87.

[116] James Nayler to Margaret Fell, 4 March 1654, Sw Mss 3: 4.

[117] Thomas Aldam, Samuel Buttivant, Benjamin Nicholson, John Harwood and James Nayler, *A brief discovery of a threefold estate of Antichrist* (London, 1653), STC A894B, pp. 11–13.

[118] Thomas Aldam to Margaret Fell, York, 3 April 1653, Sw Mss 3: 43. And compare this with the fact that this letter itself got reprinted in Richard Farnworth, *Gods covenanting with his people* (London, 1653), BL E703(6*).

Mary; James Nayler's letter to 'severall Friends about Wakefield', styling himself 'A prisoner at Appleby in Westmorland for the Truths sake', and warning his home congregation: 'O take heed of looking back, lest you be taken captive, and led back again, and so you come short of redemption'.[119]

Such 'news' letters were associated with absent ministers. The pattern of writing back to one's own meeting was repeated in a collection of letters written by itinerant ministers travelling along the Yorkshire coast in the winter of 1653, published as *Severall letters written to the saints most high*, in March 1654. One of the letters written by the Yorkshire minister, William Dewsbery, sternly reminded his readers, 'I am with you, though absent in body'; and he went on to warn them:

you have not been faithful many of you, in walking with the Lord, since you heard the Gospel of your Salvation; I charge you in the presence of the Lord God Almighty, and by his Power, every one of you examine your Consciences, which will witness with me.[120]

James Nayler, in a letter printed in the same collection, addressed 'To all dear Brethren and Friends in Holderness, and in the East parts of Yorkshire', was equally authoritative: 'dear friends, watch over one another, exhort, reprove, admonish in pure love and meekness of spirit, least you also be tempted . . . I shall be glad to see your faces in the flesh'.[121] Yet Nayler was also keen to emphasise the great worth of the mission which kept him away from his 'brethren': 'The Work of the Lord is great in those parts, and he carries it on with a high hand, he hath got himself the Victory.'[122] Nayler's travelling companion, John Whitehead, published a letter from Scarborough with the specific request: 'Let this be read when you are met together.'[123]

The first published Quaker tracts emerged out of the itinerant ministry of their authors, and were intended to consolidate Quaker meetings. The very existence of these tracts, and their close affinities with manuscript letters, underlines the intrinsic relationship between leaders, discipline and authors in the growing Quaker movement. The comparatively small number of authors of such tracts in 1652 and the early part of 1653 suggests a highly visible group of leading ministers who were able to dominate, or minister to, geographically dispersed groups of Quakers. The use of print suggests a large-scale movement at a very early date, where key figures were important enough to justify the widespread circulation of their letters and speeches.

Imprisonment, like itinerant preaching, also afforded the opportunity and occasion for writing tracts, and publicising Quaker ideas. The first Quaker

---

[119] Thomas Aldam, in Farnworth, *Gods covenanting with his people*, pp. 48–50; James Nayler, in Farnworth, *A discovery of faith*, pp. 14–16.
[120] William Dewsbery, James Nayler, John Whitehead and George Fox, *Several letters written to the saints most high*, London, 1654, STC D1272, p. 3.
[121] *Ibid.*, p. 9.   [122] *Ibid.*, p. 10.   [123] *Ibid.*, p. 12.

ministers were imprisoned at York for interrupting church sermons in May 1652; George Fox was arrested at Lancaster in October 1652 under the terms of the Blasphemy Act; Francis Howgill and James Nayler were imprisoned for the same reason at Appleby in November 1652. Like itinerant preaching, imprisonment meant the removal of Quaker leaders from their meetings, and the need for communication between them, as has been shown from the letters cited above.

Imprisonment led to more focused public campaigning. Once they were imprisoned, the presence of Quakers in a city or town gaol led very often to the sustained attention of Quakers from outside, as they protested against religious persecution, and publicised the causes of their co-religionists.[124] The imprisonment at York of Thomas Aldam, Mary Fisher, Jane Holmes, John Harwood and Benjamin Nicholson was the focus of such early itinerant activity, and subsequent publications. Farnworth and his followers from Balby went to visit them on different occasions; and in July 1652, the young daughters of Margaret Fell – seventeen and nineteen years old respectively – travelled unaccompanied from Swarthmoor to visit the York prisoners and to bring them letters from George Fox. This latter visit aroused the disapprobation of Thomas Aldam, who felt that York was too profane a place for such young women, and he sent them back again.[125]

Thomas Aldam recorded much activity in York initiated by the prisoners themselves in protest at their arrest, and reported in a letter to George Fox in July 1652: 'my sister Hooton is carried much forth to speaking . . . the Citie is in a greate rage, for truth strikeing at the head of the deceite, it causes the beastly part to fall into rage and madnesse'.[126] Elizabeth Hooton was also 'moved to write', to the same end. She wrote first to the 'Sheriffes and Justices', of whom 'there was many mett this last weeke together at Yorke'. Then she wrote 'two letters to the lawyers that was at a Court, in the Castle garth, and another to a Preist which she was moved to goe to speak to'.[127]

Thus writing was described as a self-conscious activity for the Quaker prisoners, closely linked to physical confrontation with their opponents, and carefully directed to those immediately concerned with the imprisonment of

---

[124] See Chapter 7 below for a discussion of the representations of imprisonments and trials.
[125] For Farnworth's description of a visit to York with a number of followers from Balby, see Richard Farnworth to James Nayler and George Fox, September 1652, Sw Mss 4: 229. For the visit of Margaret Fell's young daughters, see Thomas Aldam and Elizabeth Hooton to George Fox, York, [July] 1652, A. R. Barclay Mss 1: 16, fol. 52. For his disapproval, see Thomas Aldam to George Fox and others, York, [July] 1652, Sw Trs 1: 13. Margaret Fell's two elder daughters, Margaret and Bridget, were probably aged about nineteen and seventeen respectively at the time; Bonnelyn Young Kunze, *Margaret Fell and the rise of Quakerism* (London, 1994), p. x.
[126] Thomas Aldam and Elizabeth Hooton to George Fox, York, [July] 1652, A. R. Barclay Mss 1: 16, fols. 52–53.
[127] *Ibid.*, fol. 53.

people on the grounds of their religious beliefs. In the same month, Thomas Aldam described to George Fox a prototype for Quaker writing. They wrote much, he explained, to their 'gainsayers', 'who doe all that lies in to rend us odious to the world'; but the York prisoners did not stop there: 'what we doe write to them we doe write to the people to let them see that their folly might be discovered'. The gainsayers, he explained, 'conceale the letters, and will not let them be seene', whereas 'declaring and makeing knowne the same to the people causes many to come to us and many own the truth spoken'.[128]

The York prisoners wrote to their gainsayers and to 'the people' alike, hoping to shame the former and enlighten the latter. Thomas Aldam had defined a major purpose in Quaker writing: of publicising their cause to the 'people' or the outside world. In York this was facilitated by their highly publicised physical presence, augmented by the visits of other leading Quaker preachers. The high-profile preaching of Aldam and Hooton, and their lobbying of the religious and civil authorities in York, was augmented by writing and printed tracts. Writing was an intrinsic part of their public campaign for religious liberty.

When Thomas Aldam suggested to Fox that printed tracts were 'verye servisable' for 'weake frends' and 'Convinceing the world' alike, he highlighted the purposeful nature of Quaker writing.[129] 'Weak friends', in local meetings deserted by their habitual speakers, were sustained by letters and tracts sent back to them by their leaders. At the same time, 'the World' outside was subjected to a barrage of Quaker tracts and papers which publicised the Quaker campaign, under the names of a few choice leaders. Quaker writing was self-consciously all-embracing in the audiences it addressed. Sophisticated strategies were employed; distinctions were made between 'gainsayers' and 'the people'; the illiteracy or ignorance of audiences was taken into account. The Quaker belief that the light of God was within all men and women was crucial to their attitude towards written invective: the 'people' in its entirety had to be reached. Quaker authors thus made use of the written word in the fullest possible sense, in order that their message would reach the widest possible audience. The following chapter discusses how, practically, Quaker authors organised the printing, distribution and readership of their tracts in order to facilitate the dissemination of their beliefs.

[128] Thomas Aldam to George Fox and others, York, [July] 1652, Sw Trs 1: 13.
[129] Thomas Aldam to George Fox, 1652, A. R. Barclay Mss 1: 71, fols. 206–07.

2

The production and readership of Quaker pamphlets

Just as writing tracts and papers was the responsibility of a limited number of ministers in the early Quaker movement, so the more practical tasks of publishing, distributing, and overseeing the readership of the tracts were the preserve of the Quaker ministry. The tight control exercised by leaders over the tracts is the salient feature of their production, underlining that pamphlets were an integral part of the Quaker ministers' proselytising campaign. The elaborate organisation necessary for the production of the tracts developed in conjunction with the movement itself. A study of the production and distribution of the tracts therefore allows a wider insight into the organisation of a growing, national movement, and reinforces the argument that it was established by a strong leadership. This chapter will argue that printed tracts were produced as a very precise tool by Quaker leaders, who addressed specific audiences with particular tracts.

THE EXPANSION OF QUAKER PUBLISHING

As Chapter 1 has shown, the appearance of printed tracts in 1652 developed out of the exchange of manuscript papers between itinerant or incarcerated Quaker leaders and their local congregations. The adoption of printing is in itself evidence that the scope of the Quaker preachers' missionary work was increasing. Although Quaker ministers continued to use handwritten papers as an intrinsic part of their ministry, pinning them up on church doors, in market places, or handing them out at trials, it was increasingly obvious that printed tracts were an efficacious means of spreading ideas.[1] Edward Burrough was deeply troubled that his 'great want of bookes' in Ireland was slowing him down, complaining to his book-suppliers in London: 'Scarce a day these severall weekes hath passed over, wherein I have not written one thing or another.'[2] Printing also enabled the juxtaposition of local

---

[1] For examples of the circulation of manuscript papers, see Richard Farnworth, Sw Mss 3: 46–47; George Taylor, Sw Mss, 1: 212; Edward Burrough, Sw Trs 3: 491.
[2] Edward Burrough to Robert Dring, 22 August 1655, Markey Mss, p. 13.

experiences, and thus helped in the establishment of an apparently homogeneous movement. George Taylor of Kendal sent a manuscript to Margaret Fell and later to George Fox, suggesting that the account of his confrontation with a Kendal justice of the peace, John Archer, be published: 'I had thoughts onse to have this letter of his blasphemies printed that all might have seen him.'[3] Taylor's dispute with Archer was a local issue: John Archer had briefly imprisoned Taylor following a public confrontation. The manner of its publication underlines how print enabled a broader airing of Quaker grievances. George Taylor, an ironmonger from Kendal (of whom more later), was not encouraged to publish the account of his confrontation under his name alone, and it appeared instead as part of a larger and more authoritative publication by Gervase Benson, a justice of the peace and Kendal's former mayor, and a prolific Quaker author and spokesman.[4] Print, controlled by a handful of authors, facilitated the appearance of a uniform and extensive movement.

Alarmed contemporaries were also convinced that printing was an efficient tool of the Quaker leaders, and references to Quaker books became an integral part of published attacks on them, suggesting that puritan ministers' first encounter of the Quakers was through their books; and that as a result their perception was of Quakerism as a national phenomenon. The minister of Kirkby Stephen in Westmorland, Francis Higginson, complained that the 'Leaders of your Sect have taken a sinful liberty to themselves in their printed bookes', and remarked that their 'printed Libels' 'flye as thick as Moths up and down the Country'.[5] John Stalham, minister of Terling, Essex, encountered Quakers for the first time on a visit to Edinburgh in the spring of 1655. Curious, he made further enquiries, and was disconcerted to be presented very promptly with a ready-bound volume of more than thirty Quaker books. He incorporated their use of books into his attack on them, complaining: 'they print at one time, more then they speak at a time', and demonstrating the Quakers' dangerous views from a mixture of evidence from their books and their meetings. William Thomas, a puritan minister from Somerset, described Quaker books as 'Satans Library', 'purposely made little, that they may be made nimble, and passe with more speed, and at an easy rate, to infect the Nation'.[6] Quaker publications also attracted the unfavourable attention of the presbyterian booksellers Luke Fawne and his colleagues in

[3] George Taylor to Margaret Fell, 25 December 1654, Sw Mss 1: 211; Taylor to George Fox, 6 January 1655, Sw Mss 1: 212.
[4] George Taylor's accusations against John Archer appeared in Gervase Benson, *An answer to John Gilpin's book* (London, 1655), STC B1899, pp. 4–5.
[5] Francis Higginson, *A brief relation of the irreligion of the northern Quakers* (London, 1653), STC H1953, sig. a2.
[6] John Stalham, *Contradictions of the Quakers* (Edinburgh, 1655), STC S5184, p. 25; William Thomas, *Rayling Rebuked* (London, 1656), STC T989, sig. B4r.

1654. In 1652 the booksellers, concerned about the status of the Stationers' Company and the laxity of publishing law, had published *A beacon fired*, which complained about the ease with which Catholic books were imported and sold in England.[7] In 1654, the same publishers broadened their attack to include the unlicensed publications of Quakers and Socinians, and published *A second beacon fired*, calling for the suppression of their books. The very quantity of Quaker books, they warned, 'argues that there are many buyers, and the many buyers argue a great infection by them, which like a Gangrene spreads more and more.'[8]

The rate of Quaker publications increased with the geographical scope of the ministry. During 1652 and 1653, Quaker ministers operated primarily in the north of England, expanding the movement to the north towards Newcastle, Durham, Carlisle and the surrounding areas. By the end of 1653, more adventurous journeys were undertaken: to North Wales and Chester, to London, and to Cambridge.[9] In the summer of 1654, as elections for the first Protectorate Parliament were held, a concerted, national preaching campaign was undertaken by the Quaker ministers. This took them through many of the counties of England, as pairs of ministers followed different routes until they converged, in August, on London. John Audland and Thomas Ayrey spent two months travelling from Lancashire to Chester, down through the borders of England and Wales to Bristol, and as far west as Plymouth before journeying to London through Somerset, Wiltshire, Hampshire and Surrey, stopping as they travelled in major cities, market towns and villages.[10] Richard Hubberthorne, Elizabeth Williams and Elizabeth Fletcher travelled from Lancashire via Oxford, probably following the highway from Chester, through Staffordshire and Warwickshire. Other ministers, travelling from Yorkshire, took routes further to the east ignoring the capital: Ann Blaykling and James Parnell probably went directly from Yorkshire to Cambridge; George Fox, Richard Farnworth and Thomas Goodaire travelled around Leicestershire and Staffordshire in August and September 1654.[11] William Dewsbery, released from York prison on 27 July 1654, travelled

---

[7] Luke Fawne, Samuel Gellibrand, Joshua Kirton, John Rothwell, Thomas Underhill and Nathaniel Webb, *A beacon set on fire* (London, 1652), STC F564. William Clyde, *The struggle for the freedom of the press from Caxton to Cromwell* (London, 1934), pp. 225–33; 256–60.

[8] Luke Fawne et al., *A second beacon fired* (London, 1654), STC F565, p. 10. Francis Howgill and Edward Burrough issued their own reply: *The fiery darts of the divel quenched* (London, 1654). A copy of this was dated by George Thomason on 24 November 1654.

[9] William Braithwaite, *The beginnings of Quakerism* (London, 1955), chs 6–7.

[10] 'The Journal of John Audland, 1654', in 'Letters of John Audland, 1653', pp. 23–35. Hereinafter this document will be referred to as Audland's Journal.

[11] For Parnell and Blaykling see below, Chapter 3. For Farnworth and Goodaire, Richard Farnworth to 'Friends', Samuel Watson Collection, p. 44, as cited in Braithwaite, *Beginnings of Quakerism*, p. 176.

through Beverley and Hull to the 'great' towns of Lincoln, Nottingham, Newark, Oakham, Leicester and Wellingborough, before his arrest in Derby on 24 August.[12] By August, Francis Howgill, Edward Burrough, Richard Hubberthorne, John Camm, Thomas Ayrey and John Audland were engaged in constant preaching and meetings in London: in September they were joined by Christopher Atkinson, Miles Halhead, James Lancaster and Elizabeth Coward; Anthony Pearson was there in July and again in October.[13] Thus from the summer of 1654, Quaker preachers undertook far wider itineraries than hitherto: by the end of the year, Quakers from the north had reached Kent and Sussex, East Anglia, Scotland and France, and had established permanent bases in London and Bristol.[14]

The concerted expansion of the movement over the summer of 1654 is quite possibly connected to the holding of the first Protectorate elections in July. A large meeting of Quaker leaders, including Christopher Atkinson, Edward Burrough, John Audland and Francis Howgill, held at the home of Anthony Pearson in February 1654 may have been a planning meeting.[15] Shortly afterwards, two relatively senior Quakers, Francis Howgill and John Camm (aged about thirty-six and fifty respectively), travelled to London in March 1654, where they established contacts with religious sectaries, and held a meeting with Oliver Cromwell, subsequently publishing an account of their interview with him.[16] While in the capital they also concerned themselves with a number of publications, reporting to George Fox, 'thy former Answer to Eaton was in the press already we came there . . . but a sheet or two was but printed so we took it out and that we carried we have put in the press and that paper conserning London is in print'.[17] They also established important contacts in the brothers Robert Dring, linen draper, and Simon Dring, who lived respectively in Moorfields and Watling Street,

---

[12] William Dewsbery to Margaret Fell [August 1654], Sw Mss 4: 133. Geoffrey Nuttall dates this letter between Dewsbery's two imprisonments, Nuttall, *EQL*, p. 76.

[13] Audland's Journal, pp. 29–32; Francis Howgill to Robert Widder, 23 September 1654, Sw Trs 2: 485; Braithwaite, *Beginnings of Quakerism*, p. 161; Thomas Willan to Margaret Fell, October 1654, Sw Mss 1: 222.

[14] Braithwaite, *Beginnings of Quakerism*, chs 9–10. A very early foreign mission to France by Christopher Atkinson and two female travelling companions was mentioned in a letter by Francis Howgill to Robert Widder, 23 September 1654, Sw Trs 2: 485; and by Richard Hubberthorne to Margaret Fell, 17 January 1655, Sw Trs 2: 577.

[15] Edward Burrough to George Fox, 7 February 1654, Sw Mss 3: 14.

[16] I have taken their ages from the respective entries in the *DNB*. John Camm, born at Camsgill near Kendal, was a man of 'considerable property', who had already renounced the national church and formed his own congregation before forming links with Fox and the Quakers in 1652. For their publications about the meeting with Cromwell, see John Camm and Francis Howgill, *This was the word of the Lord which John Camm and Francis Howgill was moved to declare to Oliver Cromwell* (London, 1654), STC c392; John Camm, *Some particulars concerning the law, sent to Oliver Cromwell* (London, 1654), STC c391.

[17] Francis Howgill and John Camm to George Fox, 27 March 1654, A. R. Barclay Mss, 2: 127.

who already hosted religious meetings at their homes and were soon helping with the circulation of Quaker books; and with the Muggletonian Alexander Delamain, who undertook to distribute Quaker books in the capital.[18]

In July 1654, Anthony Pearson went to London for a meeting with Cromwell, and published a key political tract, *A few words to all judges, justices and ministers of the law in England*.[19] Pearson's political contacts were impressive, and important within the Quaker movement. Although still in his twenties, Pearson served as a justice of the peace in Durham, Westmorland and Cumberland, reputedly first encountering Quaker ideas when he sat on the bench at the trial of James Nayler at Appleby in January 1653. From 1648, Pearson had served as clerk to the radical MP Sir Arthur Haselrig in Newcastle, and acted as clerk and registrar for the Committee for Compounding. In 1652 he was appointed Sequestration Commissioner for Durham. His political colleagues included the robust republican opponents of the Protectorate, Arthur Haselrig and Sir Henry Vane. Pearson was a key political contact in the development of the early movement: as will be seen, Pearson was an important political pamphleteer for the Quakers.[20]

Beyond the role of Pearson in the movement's expansion over the summer of 1654, it is clear that Quakers more generally played a part in electioneering. Gervase Benson and Thomas Aldam urged that eligible Quakers use their vote in the second Protectorate elections of 1656; and Derek Hirst has shown how association with Quakers affected the political prospects of parliamentary candidates in Leeds in the same year.[21] It was reported in 1654 that Baptists stood in most places, and held meetings of two or three hundred in market towns as part of the election; and it is impossible to imagine that Quakers would remain aloof from these.[22] Quaker pamphlets aimed

---

[18] For the brothers Dring, see Braithwaite, *Beginnings of Quakerism*, pp. 157, 159, 376. Braithwaite asserts that Robert lived in Moorfields and Simon in Watling Street, although acknowledges some confusion. I have found two Watling Street addresses for Robert Dring: at the sign of the White Horse, and later at the sign of the Arrow; A. R. Barclay Mss 2: 177; Sw Mss 1: 66. For Alexander Delamain's letters to Quakers in Kendal, see Alexander Delamain to Thomas Willan, 27 June 1654, Sw Mss 3: 93.

[19] Anthony Pearson, *A few words to all judges, justices and ministers of the law in England* (London, 1654), STC P988 (copy dated by Thomason on 16 July 1654); Braithwaite, *Beginnings of Quakerism*, p. 161. See also Plate 13, p. 224.

[20] Anthony Pearson to Edward Burrough, 21 February 1654, Sw Mss 3: 35. His political instincts outlived his affiliation with the Quaker movement: he renounced them after the Restoration, and acted as under-sheriff for the country of Durham. See Amy Wallis, 'Anthony Pearson (1626–1666),' *JFHS* 51: 2 (1966), 77–95; *DNB; BDBR;* Pearson's political writings are also discussed more fully in Chapter 7 below.

[21] W. Alan Cole, 'The Quakers and politics, 1652–1660', unpublished Ph.D thesis, University of Cambridge, 1955, p. 40; Derek Hirst, 'The fracturing of the Cromwellian alliance: Leeds and Adam Baynes', *English Historical Review* 429 (October, 1993), 877, 889, 893–94.

[22] S. R. Gardiner, *The history of the Commonwealth and Protectorate, 1649–1656* (4 vols., London, 1894–1903), vol. III, p. 177; Fox, Nayler and Farnworth co-authored a tract, *To you that are called by the name of Baptists* [n.p., 1654], STC T1753, copy dated by Thomason 18 August 1654.

specifically at Cromwell and members of Parliament appeared over the summer of 1654.[23] It is clear from their journeys that the Quaker ministers had political contacts, and that they were in touch with political developments in the capital. John Audland and Thomas Ayrey stayed with Captain John Hering, former Barebones MP for Hereford on their journey down to London; on their return to Bristol in September 1654, they had made permanent links with notable Bristol figures: Denis Hollister, a former Barebones MP, and George Bishop, a Bristol merchant who was himself an unsuccessful candidate in the first Protectorate elections, and had been a senior civil servant under the Commonwealth.[24] The sudden concentration of Quaker ministers in London in August 1654, as newly elected MPs gathered there, must be understood in its political context.

In accordance with increased ministerial activity, the number of Quaker publications rose. From a total of twenty-eight Quaker publications in 1653, output rose to over sixty in 1654, and over one hundred publications appeared in 1655, an average of almost two new publications each week.[25] As the bookseller Luke Fawne perceived, this was indicative of a wider potential audience, of more 'buyers' for Quaker ideas as the geographical scope of the movement increased. Publication rates fell back to around 80 new publications in 1657 and 70 in 1658, reflecting perhaps a new cautiousness in the aftermath of the James Nayler affair in 1656, but rose sharply to over 150 in 1659, as the movement mobilised around the Good Old Cause and the recall of the Rump Parliament.[26]

As with the earliest Quaker publications, discussed in Chapter 1, ministers wrote tracts which were pertinent to the areas they visited. John Camm and Francis Howgill organised a number of publications directly relevant to the capital while they were there in March 1654, not only George Fox's broadside, *A warning to all in this proud city called London*, but also their

---

[23] George Fox, *A message from the Lord to the parliament of England* (London, 1654), *STC* F1863 (copy dated by Thomason 15 September 1654); *Something in answer to a petition to Oliver Cromwell* (London, 1654), *STC* s4659 (copy dated by Thomason 21 September 1654).

[24] 'Audland's journal', p. 25; Barry Reay, 'Early Quaker activity and reactions to it, 1652–1664' unpublished D Phil. thesis, University of Oxford, 1979, p. 66. For George Bishop see J. W. Martin, 'The pre-Quaker writings of George Bishop', *Quaker History* 74: 2 (1985), and below, Chapters 6 and 7.

[25] See M. K. Peters, 'Quaker pamphleteering and the development of the Quaker movement, 1652–1656', Cambridge University Ph.D thesis, 1996, p. 68.

[26] These figures are calculated from Wing's *STC* and do not include second or further editions of Quaker works. See also David Runyon's rather different figures, based on Joseph Smith's *Descriptive catalogue*, in Hugh Barbour and Arthur Roberts (eds.), *Early Quaker writings, 1650–1700* (Michigan, 1973), pp. 568–75. Runyon's figures are at variance with mine as he counted each individual contribution to a Quaker publication as a work in its own right. Nevertheless, Runyon's calculations do show the same pattern in the rates of publication by year.

own accounts of their meetings with Cromwell.[27] Through the contacts made by Howgill and Camm, another tract by George Fox, *To all that would know the way to the kingdom*, was published in June, a classic introduction to the Quakers' anti-Calvinist doctrine of inner light within all men, ideal for dissemination in London just as Quaker ministers themselves were to arrive there.[28] Other ministers published tracts relevant to the areas through which they travelled. Richard Farnworth, who travelled around Leicestershire and Staffordshire in the summer and autumn of 1654, published accounts of a series of debates he held with puritan ministers in the region; John Audland, who visited Bristol frequently from the summer of 1654 onwards, published replies to his critics around Bristol; Richard Hubberthorne, publishing as he travelled, first of all wrote a warning to the university of Oxford; and later described his imprisonments in Cambridge and Norwich.[29]

The same body of authors also continued to dominate publications. In 1653, Richard Farnworth, James Nayler and George Fox had written half of all the Quakers' publications. During the period 1654–1656, Farnworth, Nayler, Fox, Richard Hubberthorne, William Dewsbery, James Parnell and Francis Howgill single-handed wrote nearly half of all publications, and contributed to many more.[30] Most other authors contributing to Quaker tracts were primarily ministers from the north of England, figures like Gervase Benson, George Whitehead, Margaret Fell and Christopher Atkinson. Other authors were local men and women who had become involved in the Quaker ministers' preaching and imprisonments, and were clearly influenced by the writings of the national ministers. These newly recruited authors included, for example, Francis Ellington of Wellingborough, imprisoned with Dewsbery at Northampton in October 1654, and who wrote an account of his sufferings remarkably similar to those published earlier by

---

[27] George Fox, *A warning to all in this proud city called London* [n.p., 1654], *STC* F1982, which was dated by George Thomason on 30 March 1654; see Francis Howgill to George Fox, 27 March 1654, A. R. Barclay Mss 2: 127, fol. 4.

[28] George Fox, *To all that would know the way to the kingdom* ([London] 1654), *STC* F1942A. The first edition of this (*STC* F1942) was dated by Thomason on 12 March 1654; the second edition (F1942A) was dated by him 27 June 1654; for the organisation involved in distributing this in the capital before the arrival of Quaker missionaries from the north, see Sw Mss 3: 93.

[29] Richard Farnworth, *Truth cleared of scandals* (London, 1654), *STC* F512; Farnworthe, *A character whereby false christs may be known* (London, 1654), *STC* F475; John Audland, *The innocent delivered out of the snare* (London, 1655), *STC* A4196; Audland, *The schoolmaster disciplined* (London, 1655), *STC* A4197; Richard Hubberthorne, *A true testimony of the zeal of Oxford professors* (London, 1654), *STC* H3240; Hubberthorne, *The immediate call to the ministry of the gospel* (London, 1654), *STC* H3225; Hubberthorne, *The testimony of the everlasting gospel witnessed through sufferings* [Norwich, 1654], *STC* H3237. For a case-study of this kind of local pamphleteering, based on Hubberthorne's ministry in East Anglia, see below, Chapter 3.

[30] See Peters, 'Quaker pamphleteering', p. 27.

Dewsbery.[31] Thomas Symonds of Norwich, a weaver, was imprisoned with Richard Hubberthorne, Christopher Atkinson and George Whitehead in Norwich gaol, publishing an account of his sufferings under the auspices of those core Quaker authors in 1655, before publishing his own tract the following year.[32] Humphrey Smith, a native of Stoke Bliss in Herefordshire, had encountered Richard Farnworth early in 1655 and served a literary apprenticeship with him, appearing as the co-author of *Antichrist's man of war* in April 1655.[33] By August, Humphrey Smith travelled to Evesham as a Quaker minister in his own right, stirring up considerable local unrest, and wrote a number of tracts denouncing the local magistrates.[34] Thus, even as the movement expanded and the number of Quaker authors increased, the core of itinerant preachers from the original communities in Yorkshire, Lancashire and Westmorland continued to influence the output of Quaker publications.

THE ORGANISATION OF QUAKER PUBLISHING

The domination of Quaker publishing by a relatively small core of its leaders is even clearer when we turn to the organisation of the actual production and distribution of the tracts, which was controlled by a small handful of men and women. Of these, the most zealous was Thomas Aldam, a wealthy yeoman from Warmsworth in Yorkshire, who was imprisoned in May 1652 in York Castle, and who spent his two-year imprisonment organising the printing and distribution of books. As Chapter 1 has shown, Thomas Aldam

---

[31] Francis Ellington, *A true discovery of the ground of the imprisonment of Francis Ellington, Thomas Cocket and Edward Ferman* (London, 1655), *STC* T2683; compare with William Dewsbery *et al.*, *A true testimony of what was done* (London, 1655), *STC* T3123, Dewsbery, *A discovery of the grounds from whence the persecution did arise in Northamptonshire* (London, 1655), *STC* D1266.

[32] Simmonds contributed with George Whitehead and James Lancaster to Christopher Atkinson's tract, *Ishmael and his mother cast out into the wilderness* (London, 1655), *STC* A4127 (copy dated by Thomason 12 March 1655) before publishing alone: Thomas Simmonds, *The voyce of the just uttered* (London, 1656), *STC* S3804.

[33] Richard Farnworth and Humphrey Smith, *Antichrist's man of war apprehended* (London, 1655), *STC* F470. This was internally dated as April 1655; George Thomason dated his copy 20 June 1655. Richard Farnworth had been preaching in Worcestershire since February 1655: Braithwaite, *Beginnings of Quakerism*, p. 194. For the extent of his preaching and networking in Herefordshire in April, see Richard Farnworth to Fox, 26 April 1655, Sw Mss 3: 55.

[34] Stephen Roberts, 'The Quakers in Evesham, 1655–1660: a study in religion, politics and culture', *Midland History* 16 (1991), 63–85. Humphrey Smith published *The cruelty of the magistrates of Evesham in Worcestershire* (London, 1655), *STC* S4055; and *Something further laid open of the cruel persecution* (London, 1656), *STC* S4072. He was also a signatory to the more inflammatory *Representation of the government of the borough of Evesham* (London, 1655), *STC* R1104, presented to the Lord Protector in protest at the harsh treatment at the hands of the Evesham authorities.

was emphatic in his recommendations of the advantages of printing from the outset of the movement, urging George Fox to 'write as often as thou canst to mee for what Bookes frends would have,' and outlining to him the two central functions of Quaker publishing: 'they are Bookes which will be verye servisable for weake frends, and Convinceing the world'.[35] Thomas Aldam was also instrumental in suggesting to Margaret Fell that she play a prominent role in organising and overseeing publications on a regular basis. In a letter to Fell, unfortunately undated but certainly written before mid-1654, Aldam described his imprisonment at York as a literally god-given opportunity to organise printing; and urged that his work should be carried on by others too:

> There is one thinge whiche I have Beene moved much in, that there might bee meanes Amongst you used to send forth 2 or 3 whoe are made free to followe such a Callinge as to keepe the markets in your County with Bookes. It Comes to mee often there shall bee A great Service to Confound those great Babilonish prefaces. . . . As the Lord hath sett mee here in the place where hee hath appointed mee to be faithfull to gett these printed soe it is required of you in your place to Carrye this the Testimonie of the Trueth abroad. Make some Contribution Amongst you and let some goe in.[36]

Aldam's suggestion, to 'keepe the markets in your County with Bookes', and to fund the printing on the basis of local contributions, exactly describes early Quaker publishing. Prior to a permanent Quaker presence in London, Aldam in Yorkshire and Fell in Lancashire between them co-ordinated most publications: as the movement expanded nationally, other regional contacts were found to help the distribution and financing of publications. The development of regular Quaker publishing was symptomatic of a nationally coherent movement, and indeed contributed to its establishment. In this respect, Margaret Fell's position at Swarthmoor Hall was crucial as she was to co-ordinate not only Quaker publishing, but much of the national organisation and campaigning.

   In order to organise printing, Aldam and Fell needed contacts with London, where most Quaker books were published, initially by Giles Calvert, nationally renowned as a radical publisher, and increasingly after 1656 by Thomas Simmonds, a publisher who was also a Quaker and who worked from the main Quaker meeting house in London, the Bull and Mouth.[37] Thomas Aldam's contacts with Giles Calvert and the London press were through the army.[38] His earliest extant letter specifically concerned with

[35] Thomas Aldam to George Fox, 1652, A. R. Barclay Mss 1: 71, fols. 206–07.
[36] [Thomas Aldam] to Margaret Fell, A. R. Barclay Mss 2: 159, fols. 99–100.
[37] Thomas O'Malley, 'The press and Quakerism, 1653–59', *JFHS* 54: 4 (1979), 169–84; Altha Terry, 'Giles Calvert's publishing career', *JFHS* 25 (1938), 45–49; Russell Mortimer, 'The first century of Quaker printers', *JFHS* 40 (1948), 37–49; Maureen Bell, 'Elizabeth Calvert and the "Confederates"', *Publishing History* 32 (1992), 5–49.
[38] For a broader discussion of these army links, see below, Chapter 7.

printing was dated 19 February 1653, when Thomas Aldam wrote to a 'deare Frend', Captain Amor Stoddard in London, asking him to send the two or three hundred copies of 'the discoverie of the false Temple and the true Temple if it be printed, with the other of the Priests of the world'.[39] The books, published in London by Giles Calvert, were to be carried up by carrier to York, and Aldam requested Stoddard to 'send mee word in thy Letter what thou didst pay for the printinge of them, and I shall use some meanes to send the money . . . by the Carrier which brings the bookes'.[40] The relationship between Aldam, Captain Stoddard and the London press continued for the next two years, until Aldam's release from prison.[41]

Amor Stoddard remains a relatively obscure figure in the early Quaker movement. He appears as a close companion to George Fox in Fox's *Journal;* and is deemed to have met Fox in Nottinghamshire as early as 1647.[42] By 1653 at the latest he had a London address, in Long Alley, Moorfields, and was supplying northern Quakers with publications from the Council of Officers in London.[43] Stoddard may have been the Captain Stoddard in John Lambert's northern regiment of horse, which could easily have made him an acquaintance of James Nayler, Lambert's former quartermaster, and of other Yorkshire Quakers, and thus explain his links with Aldam.[44]

While Aldam's contacts with Giles Calvert were through Stoddard, Margaret Fell had a different channel of communication, through her husband Thomas. Thomas Fell was a relatively wealthy member of the Lancastrian gentry, a former MP in the Long Parliament, and an assize judge on

---

[39] Thomas Aldam to Captain Stoddard, 19 February 1653, A. R. Barclay Mss 1: 15, fol. 51. He was referring to one of his own works, published by Giles Calvert, *A brief discovery of a threefold estate of Antichrist* (London, 1653), STC A894B, which included a section entitled 'A description of the true and false temple' (pp. 1–7). 'The priests of the world' could refer to another section of this same tract, entitled 'A description of the false ministry', but beginning with the phrase 'The Priests of the world' (p. 7).

[40] Thomas Aldam to Captain Stoddard, 19 February 1653, A. R. Barclay Mss 1: 15, fols. 51–52. The manuscript had been carried down to London by Samuel Buttivant, who also wrote the preface to the tract. Buttivant had informed the York prisoners by letter that the books were expected to be printed on 3 February.

[41] See Thomas Aldam to Amor Stoddard, 21 June 1653, A. R. Barclay Mss 1: 17, fol. 58; Thomas Aldam to Oliver Cromwell, 29 August 1654, Portfolio 1: 5; Richard Farnworth to Fox, Sw Mss 3: 52.

[42] *The Journal of George Fox* Norman Penney, ed. (2 vols., Cambridge, 1911), vol. i, pp. 185, 187, 189–90, 198, 261, 431. Penney did not elucidate on the military career of Stoddard, indicating only that he was 'styled' a captain by Friends.

[43] For his London address, see Thomas Aldam to Captain Stoddard, 21 June 1653, A. R. Barclay Mss 1: 17, fol. 58; for his role in forwarding the declaration of the Officers of the Army in January 1653, see Thomas Aldam to Captain Stoddard, 19 February 1653, A. R. Barclay Mss 1: 15, fol. 50, and below, Chapter 7.

[44] For Captain Stoddard, see Charles Firth and Godfrey Davies, *The regimental history of Cromwell's army* (2 vols., Oxford, 1940), vol. i, p. 257. Stoddard is also identified as a soldier by M. E. Hirst, *The Quakers in peace and war* (London, 1923), p. 529. For Nayler, see William Bittle, *James Nayler 1618–1660* (York, 1986), pp. 3–8.

the North Wales and Cheshire Circuit. He was a member of the county elite: vice-chancellor of the duchy of Lancaster and justice of the peace; he had also profited from sales of land during the civil war.[45] Allied to Fell was Colonel William West, like Fell a Lancashire JP, and profiteer from the civil war, but politically active as a member of the Nominated 'Barebones' Parliament of 1653.[46] West and Fell were both in London for political and professional reasons; both were instrumental in organising publications before the establishment of a permanent Quaker presence in mid-1654. In a letter dated 18 February 1653 (the day before that sent by Aldam to Stoddard), Margaret Fell sent a number of manuscripts from Swarthmoor to her husband in London, requesting him to get them printed, and stressing the importance of the task: 'I pray thee doe not neglect, for I am sure if they be published, they will worke for the glory of my father.'[47]

At least two of the manuscripts she enclosed were published by Giles Calvert.[48] Like Stoddard and Aldam, the Fells therefore had established contact with Calvert by February 1653. The frequent presence of Thomas Fell and William West in London continued to play an important role in Quaker publishing. As a Barebones MP, West himself distributed Quaker books in London.[49] In November 1653, on one of the earliest missions out of the native Quaker counties to Wales, Richard Hubberthorne and his travelling companion John Lawson were imprisoned in Chester gaol. From there, they wrote to Margaret Fell at Swarthmoor Hall, requesting first that 'any bokes or printed papers' should be sent to a Wrexham shopkeeper called Edward More; and secondly that she inform them of the London addresses of Thomas Fell and William West, so that 'if I have anythinge from the Lord to write to them I may know where they are'.[50] Lawson and Hubberthorne were also

---

[45] Bonnelyn Young Kunze, *Margaret Fell and the rise of Quakerism* (London, 1994), pp. 29–30; *DNB*.

[46] Young Kunze, *Margaret Fell*, pp. 35, 79. Woolrych identified West as a Radical (Independent): Austin Woolrych, *Commonwealth to Protectorate* (Oxford, 1982, reprinted 1986), p. 430.

[47] Margaret Fell to Thomas Fell, 1653, Abraham Mss [1].

[48] George Fox *et al.*, *Sauls errand to Damascus* (London, 1653), STC F1894; James Nayler, *Several petitions answered* (London, 1653), STC N316A.

[49] A copy of James Nayler's tract entitled *The power and glory of the Lord shining out of the North* (London, 1653), STC N302, held by Cambridge University Library, states that it was 'rec'd from Col. Wm. West 20 August 1653' (CUL Syn. 7. 65. 57, p. 26); George Thomason dated his copy 17 August.

[50] Richard Hubberthorne to Margaret Fell, [November] 1653, Sw Mss 4: 66. During this period, Hubberthorne published a disputation with Vavasour Powell's gathered church in Wrexham, *Truth cleared and the deceit made manifest* [n.p.], (1654), STC H3241, which unfortunately recorded neither its place of publication nor the name of its publisher. That Hubberthorne was in contact with other Quaker publishing ventures at this time is indicated by another contemporary publication. Hubberthorne's *Truths defence against the refined subtilty of the serpent* (London, 1653), STC F1970, co-authored with George Fox, was published for the York bookseller Thomas Wayte and a copy dated by George Thomason on 19 December

concerned about the impact of a derisive work by John Gilpin, *The Quakers shaken*, which they had encountered on their travels: 'Let ther be some of gilpines booke answered,' they urged Fell, 'for it is scattered all over these parts.'[51] Thus, through Margaret Fell and her husband, itinerant preachers maintained communication channels which facilitated the writing, publishing and distribution of Quaker books on a national scale.

The vast majority of Quaker tracts stated that they were printed in the capital.[52] Tracts which were apparently not printed in London tended to be those published while their authors were travelling abroad, or were isolated publications by authors who do not figure centrally in the organisation of Quaker ministers. Others were broadsides. The few publications by the main Quaker authors which were not printed in London were primarily early ones, dating from 1653. It would be wrong to attribute too much to the bibliographic information provided in the tracts, which were unlicensed, and until 1656 were published in the main by Giles Calvert with little competition from other publishers. There is nothing in the correspondence to suggest that Quakers used any presses outside London. Most itinerant Quaker authors, therefore, probably through Fell or Aldam, found the means to sustain regular contact with the London presses.

We know relatively little about ease of access to the press in the 1650s.[53] The government gained some measure of control over the press after the regulatory chaos of the 1640s, and in its legislation, control of the press passed from the Stationers' Company to Parliament and the government. The Printing Act of September 1649 limited printing to London, and to York and Finsbury for Bible production; required printers to enter into a £300 bond with the government; and stipulated that all books and pamphlets were to be licensed. Beyond the bond to the government, most regulation lay, as it had under previous legislation, with the Stationers' Company. The Printing Act of January 1653 restated much of the earlier legislation, although focusing

1653. At about the same time, Thomas Wayte published Nayler and Fox's *Lamentacion (by one of Englands Prophets) over the ruines of this oppressed nacion* ([n.p.], 1654), *STC* N292: Thomason dated his copy 29 January 1654. Clearly, Hubberthorne was in contact with other Quaker publishing ventures during his missionary work in Cheshire and Wales.

[51] John Lawson to Margaret Fell [November, 1653], Sw Mss 4: 69.
[52] Peters, 'Quaker pamphleteering', p. 76.
[53] The most recent studies of the use of the press in this focus either on the 1640s, or on the Restoration period: see Anthony Cotton, 'The London Newsbooks in the Civil War: their political attitudes and sources of information', unpublished D Phil. thesis, University of Oxford, 1971; Dagmar Freist, 'The formation of opinion and the communication network in London 1637–c.1645', unpublished Ph.D thesis, University of Cambridge, 1992; John Hetet, 'A literary underground in restoration England: printers and dissenters in the context of constraint, 1660–89', unpublished Ph.D thesis, University of Cambridge, 1987. The exception is Maureen Bell, 'Women publishers of puritan literature in the mid-seventeenth century: three case studies', unpublished Ph.D. thesis, University of Loughborough, 1987, which very usefully focuses on the work of Elizabeth Calvert, wife of Giles.

the powers of regulation with the Council of State.[54] The 1653 Act was operative until 28 August 1655; thereafter, under the Protectorate, the press was regulated by direct orders of Cromwell and through three appointed commissioners.[55] It is after 1655 that censorship is deemed to have been harshest and most effective.

The attitude both of Quakers and of their opponents suggests that access to printing presses was straightforward and relatively easy. Quaker authors complained bitterly at suggestions that their publishing should be stopped, but not at the fact that it was. James Nayler drew very clear parallels between restraints on religious freedom and regulation of the press, and denounced leaders of northern gathered churches who had petitioned the government to take control of the press in order to curb the Quakers. Press censorship was, according to Nayler: 'a way by which your Forefathers the bishops did long uphold their beastly Kingdom, and the Papist before them; for, if none might Print or speak against it, then all your deceit might goe for Truth undiscovered, as it has done many years', and Nayler went on to chide his opponents: 'you have not that Truth that is able to defend it self against all Errors, printed and preached whatsoever, which did never seek to the powers of men to protect it'.[56]

Opponents of the Quakers who petitioned the government for legislation against them suggested that their publications be curbed. In his first printed exchange with the Quakers, Richard Baxter reproached them for complaining about the lack of religious freedom: 'Never age in the world, I think, under a Christian Magistrate, had less cause to complain of want of liberty for preaching; what Liberty would you have? Nay, you have the Libertie of Printing, which is more than Preaching.'[57] Baxter (at the same time providing useful insight into the aural nature of print) was emphatic that the power of the Quakers lay with their unbridled use of the press:

Is it not a case to be lamented by every true Christian that in *England* such language as is contained in this Pamphlet, should be suffered to be spoken in the ears of the Nation by the Press? Should not those faithful Ministers that are near our Rulers,

---

[54] Frederick Siebert, *Freedom of the press in England 1476–1776. The rise and decline of government controls* (Urbana, Ill., 1952), 222–29; Clyde, *Struggle for the freedom of the press*. A more recent study of government control of the press is Michael Seymour, 'Pro-government propaganda in interregnum England, 1649–1660', unpublished Ph.D thesis, University of Cambridge, 1986.

[55] Siebert, *Freedom of the press*, pp. 229–31.

[56] James Nayler, *Churches gathered against Christ and his kingdom* (London, 1654), STC N267, pp. 11–12.

[57] Richard Baxter, *The Worcester-shire petition . . . defended* (London, 1653), STC B1455, p. 23. This was a response to Thomas Aldam *et al.*, *A brief discovery of a threefold estate of Antichrist* (London, 1653), STC A894B, which in turn had been written in reply to *The humble petition of many thousands . . . of the county of Worcester* (London, 1652), STC B1285.

remember them of the sin and danger of this? . . . Oh ye Honorable Rulers of this Commonwealth; . . . Doth it not concern you what language the Subjects hear or speak? Language as well as other objects doth make an Impression on the mind: Should your Subjects receive such impressions as this doth tend to? If it be tender consciences that you indulge, I beseech you consider whether those be the words of a tender conscience? and whether Powder Plotting Papists, may not on the same grounds expect Liberty?[58]

Baxter's attack on the wanton printing of dangerous ideas also attacked their main agent in the printing industry. Baxter emphasised that Giles Calvert in particular enjoyed far too much freedom and must be held responsible for the spread of dangerous doctrines, reproving the government:

I do not speak only of your bearing with the Writers, but that one *Giles Calvert*, shall be suffered for so many years to publish such a multitude of these Reproaches to the world, and openly to own it with his name subscribed! . . . I abhor as much as most do, too rigorous restrictions, and not bearing with each other in tolerable differences: But that a Pulpit should be Satans Oracle, or a place to make Christianity contemned, is very sad. Let all the Apothecaries in *London* have liberty to keep open shop: But O do not under that pretence, let a man keep an open shop of poysons, for all that will to destroy themselvs freely; as *Giles Calvert* doth for soul-poysons. No, nor suffer any to be an Apothecary, that knows not poyson from Physick.[59]

Despite the fact that opponents of the Quakers expressed concern at the apparent laxity of press censorship, and that Quakers denounced calls for regulation of the press as part of their oppression, such polarised positions were rhetorical, and both were based on the premise that Quaker publishing was, for the time being, unhampered. Furthermore, the equation of radical religion with a demand for freedom of expression is not straightforward. The Quakers themselves called on the government for some forms of printing to be regulated, and attacked ballad and newsmongers. 'It is very hard', wrote Margaret Fell to her husband shortly after the passage of the 1653 Printing Act, 'that the press should bee open for all pamfletes and ballats and must be shut against the Truth.'[60] In a pamphlet distributed in London in December 1653, just after the inauguration of the Protectorate, George Fox demanded proper regulation of the printing press by the government: 'I charge you by the Lord, that no ballads nor jesting books be suffered to be printed, for they stir up lightness and wantonness, and gather the people together to exercise their minds in that which drawes from God.'[61]

It is clear from their output alone that Quakers enjoyed relatively easy access to the press. Over half of all Quaker publications between 1653 and

---

[58] *Ibid.*, pp. 33–34.   [59] *Ibid.*, pp. 35, 39.
[60] Margaret Fell to Thomas Fell, 1653, Abraham Mss [1].
[61] George Fox, *Newes coming up out of the north sounding towards the south* (London, 1654), *STC* F1867, p. 23. George Thomason dated his copy 21 December 1653.

1656 were printed for Giles Calvert, many of which were to be sold at his shop, the Black Spread Eagle, on Ludgate Hill near St Paul's Cathedral.[62] Calvert's domination of Quaker publishing diminished after 1656 and his role was filled increasingly by the publisher Thomas Simmonds, who, like Calvert, was notorious as a 'radical' publisher, but unlike him was probably actually a Quaker. Thomas Simmonds was married to Giles Calvert's sister, Martha Simmonds, herself an outspoken Quaker leader who played a prominent part in the internal upheavals caused by James Nayler at the end of 1656, and Calvert's demise as the Quakers' main publisher after 1656 has been linked to the ructions caused by the Simmonds–Nayler scandal. What is significant for the purposes of this study is that, at the outset of the movement, northern Quaker authors turned readily to Calvert as a well-known radical publisher; and that he contributed not only by publishing their books, but assisted more generally in the early organization of the movement.

Giles Calvert had published works by Winstanley, William Walwyn, Jacob Boehme and Henry Niclaes.[63] As has been seen, he attracted the ire of Richard Baxter, and earlier of the heresiographer Thomas Edwards.[64] Baxter's frustration lay in the fact that Calvert operated as a radical publisher without any constraints, 'openly', 'with his name subscribed'. Shortly after he first made contact with the Quakers, Calvert was appointed for a brief time as one of the publishers to the Council of State.[65] Although the Quaker historian Altha Terry believed that this position enabled him to publish the Quakers' books with relative freedom, he did not hold the position beyond the calling of the 'Barcbones' Nominated Assembly, and it was probably limited to the period of the interregnum Council between the expulsion of the Rump Parliament in April and the calling of Barebones in July 1653.[66]

[62] Peters, 'Quaker pamphleteering', p. 81.
[63] Calvert had published works by John Saltmarsh, William Dell, the regicides Hugh Peter and John Cook, the Leveller William Walwyn, and the *Agreement of the People*, about half the works written by Winstanley, as well as works by Jacob Boehme and Henry Niclaes. H. R. Plomer, *Dictionary of booksellers and printers . . . 1641–1667* (Oxford, 1907). See also Altha Terry, 'Giles Calvert's publishing career', 45–49; J. S. T. Hetet, 'A literary underground in restoration England: printers and dissenters in the context of constraint, 1660–89', unpublished Ph.D thesis, University of Cambridge, pp. 124–32; Maureen Bell, 'Women publishers', pp. 127–30; Nigel Smith, *Perfection proclaimed: language and literature in English radical religion* (Oxford, 1989), pp. 148, 188.
[64] Thomas Edwards, *Gangraena* (3 vols., London, 1646), vol. ii, p. 9, vol. iii, p. 62.
[65] Calvert, along with Henry Hills, Robert Ibbotson and Thomas Brewster, was being considered for the job by John Thurloe on 11 May 1653, *CSPD* 1,652–53, p. 320. He appeared as printer to the Council of State on 10 and 11 June in the registers of the Stationers' Company, but not thereafter. G. E. B. Eyre (ed.), *A transcript of the registers of the Company of Stationers 1640–1708* (3 vols., London, 1913, reprinted Gloucester, Mass., 1967), vol. i, pp. 419, 420.
[66] Altha Terry, 'Giles Calvert's publishing career', p. 45. The old Council of State was dissolved with the Rump Parliament; a new one was established on 29 April 1653. Gardiner, *Commonwealth and Protectorate*, vol. ii, pp. 264–65; 273.

His role as publisher of Quaker books both preceded and postdated this position.

The legal status of Calvert's Quaker publications is difficult to gauge. None was formally licensed; and only a handful – apparently arbitrarily – were entered in the registers of the Stationers' Company.[67] Calvert's pamphlets rarely included the identity of his printers. Given the family ties with Martha Simmonds, it seems unlikely that Calvert would have regarded Thomas Simmonds as professional competition and therefore he would have had little commercial need to register their work or protect his printers. Perhaps reflecting growing governmental concern over the Quakers, and the increased desire under the Protectorate to control the press, Calvert was under government surveillance in 1655 and 1656. Intelligence reports in January 1655 of a major Quaker meeting at Swannington, Leicestershire noted, 'they have a printer with them, and sixe are constantly writing'. Calvert was later identified as the printer, and in February his shop was reportedly ransacked by the authorities of the Protector. In May 1656 he was formally questioned before the Council of State.[68] Yet even these tighter restrictions were hardly paralysing. During February 1655, in the aftermath of the Swannington meeting, the bookseller George Thomason obtained no Quaker pamphlets: in March, he obtained fourteen of them, ten of them published in Calvert's name. Calvert and the Quakers maintained the ability to produce printed tracts, with relatively little difficulty or even subterfuge.

In addition to providing a relatively secure publishing service, Giles Calvert was an important contact among radical communities in London. As Quaker preachers travelled, Calvert's shop was the first destination for them. When John Audland called John Wilkinson and John Storey to London for their first visit in April 1655, he advised them to 'Enquire at London to Gilles Callvert shop at the black spred Eagle', where Calvert would direct them to the Quaker Robert Dring's house. This underlines that Calvert's shop would be easy to find for newcomers to London, while Calvert himself would

[67] These were John Stubbs and William Caton, *A true declaration of the bloody proceedings of the men in Maidstone* (London, 1655), STC S6072, entered by Calvert in the Stationers' Company register on 20 June 1655; James Nayler, *Love to the lost* (London, 1656), entered 9 February 1656; Martin Mason, *The boasting Baptist dismounted* (London, 1656), entered 23 April 1656; Miles Halhead and Thomas Salthouse, *The wounds of an enemie in the house of a friend* (London, 1656), entered 21 March 1656; Richard Farnworth, *The priests ignorance* (London, 1656), entered 1 April 1656; Henry Clark, *A cloud of witnesses* (London, 1656), entered 29 March 1656; Edward Burrough, *A trumpet of the Lord* (London, 1656); Eyre, *A transcript of the registers*, vol. I, p. 486; vol. II, pp. 36, 50, 41, 44, 36, 38. I am grateful to Mario Caricchio for sharing these references with me, and for his discussions of Calvert's publishing role.

[68] Thomas Birch (ed.), *A collection of the State Papers of John Thurloe* (7 vols., London, 1742), vol. III, pp. 94, 116; Hetet, 'A literary underground in restoration England', p. 130; George Taylor to Margaret Fell, 26 February 1655, Sw Mss 1: 214; *CSPD* (1656), p. 308.

initiate people into the London Quaker community.[69] Christopher Atkinson, Miles Halhead and James Lancaster all visited Calvert's shop in the summer and autumn of 1654, immediately following their arrival in London from the north of England.[70] Calvert was also used as a forwarding address for letters, both before and after the major influx of Quaker ministers to London in the summer of 1654: 'Loving Frend Giles Calvert', went one such, 'get these lynes to our deer frend and brother G[eorge] F[ox] I desire. And if he be gone out of the City, some of our northerne frends likely may be there to carry it.'[71]

Giles Calvert also played a more formal role within the organisation of the early Quaker movement, lending sometimes large amounts of money to Quakers in the capital. It remains unclear whether the money he lent was actually in the form of books, for which he expected to be reimbursed later, or in the form of more direct loans of money. Calvert 'lent' £3 10s. to Christopher Atkinson when he arrived in London in October 1654, and twenty shillings to Miles Halhead and James Lancaster in September 1654; but in both cases there is evidence that the Quaker ministers had obtained books from Calvert at the same time.[72] By the following year, a more formal relationship had been established which suggests that Calvert acted as supplier to regional book distributors. In July 1655, John Audland asked Francis Howgill and Edward Burrough to pay Giles Calvert £20 'upon Jordans account' for books, and noted that if they could not pay, they should at least note down the expense on the account 'leaste it be forgoten', and Audland would try to raise the money himself from friends around Bristol.[73] In March 1656, Robert Dring, who had responsibility for organising

[69] John Audland to John Wilkinson and John Storey, 1 April 1655, A. R. Barclay Mss 1: 28, fol. 82. Wilkinson and Storey were both itinerant ministers originally from Westmorland.

[70] George Taylor and Thomas Willan to Margaret Fell, annual accounts 1654, Sw Mss 1: 208; Taylor and Willan to Fell, 14 October 1654, 1: 209; Thomas Willan to Margaret Fell, 26 November 1654, Spence Mss 3: 7.

[71] Thomas Taylor to George Fox, Lichfield, 16 March 1655, Sw Mss 3: 30. For further examples of correspondence directed to Calvert, see: Alexander Delamain and John Bridges to Thomas Willan, 27 June 1654, Sw Trs 4: 99; John Audland to Francis Howgill and Edward Burrough, 13 September 1654, A. R. Barclay Mss 2: 157, fol. 88; Edward Burrough to Robert Dring, 22 October 1655, Markey Mss, p. 13.

[72] Taylor and Willan to Fell, 14 October 1654, Sw Mss 1: 209; Taylor and Willan to Fell, annual accounts 1654, Sw Mss 1: 208; Willan to Fell, 26 November 1654, Spence Mss 3: 7; Francis Howgill to Robert Widder, 23 September 1654, Sw Trs 2: 485.

[73] John Audland to Edward Burrough and Francis Howgill, 14 July 1655 (or 56?), A. R. Barclay Mss 2: 177, fol. 151. 'Jordan' was possibly Thomas Jordan, a grocer of Maryport Parish, Bristol, who died in 1688, and who, with his wife Lydia, née Hollister, was signatory to the marriage of George Fox and Margaret Fell in Bristol in 1669. He does not appear among the wealthier Bristol Merchant Venturers of the order of George Bishop, William Rogers, Thomas Speed and William Yeamans, and wealthy traders like Dennis Hollister, Thomas Goldney and Edward Pyott: see R. S. Mortimer, 'Bristol Quaker merchants', *JFHS* 45: 1 (1953), 81–91; DQB.

Burrough's publications from Ireland, and who was also an acquaintance of Amor Stoddard, noted that he had received £5 10s. from Calvert, 'whereof 50 s[hillings] is monyes G[eorge] Scafe had on my account'.[74] Thus different individuals, often local retailers, had separate accounts with Calvert, for supplying books to different regions. A letter to Margaret Fell in August 1655 from George Taylor, another regional supplier of books in Kendal, informed her that he had received a variety of tracts to the value of eleven shillings, which he would not touch 'till I hear from thee or Gyles Calvert'.[75] Whether as a supplier of books or credit, Giles Calvert played an important, and active, part in the organisational development of the Quaker movement.

The early contact established with Giles Calvert through Thomas and Margaret Fell, and Thomas Aldam and the army, was of considerable practical importance. Regular access to Giles Calvert's shop in order for books to be published necessitated an organisational structure to supply, distribute and finance a substantial number of books. Calvert himself clearly helped in these tasks. Publishing thus was an intrinsic part of the escalation of the Quaker movement, not only in the intellectual spreading of ideas, but in the arrangements necessary for the practical dissemination of the books and manuscripts themselves.

In order for the manuscripts to reach London safely for printing, and for the published tracts to be distributed back to local meetings of Quakers, it was necessary to establish a reliable and widespread network of safe addresses and trustworthy contacts. The close correlation between the expansion of itinerant preaching, the establishment of a communications network, and the national distribution of books, is an important feature in the growth of the early movement, which underlines the close relationship between printed books and oral preaching, and throws light on radical networks generally. From the movement's beginnings, a very major concern voiced by itinerant ministers in their correspondence was the establishment of safe addresses and new contacts. In this context, Margaret Fell at Swarthmoor Hall was the central figure in the establishment of the movement: after she was 'convinced of the truth' by George Fox's preaching in May 1652, her home became an organisational headquarters, and a vast number of letters were sent to her, informing her of the itineraries of each minister.

The establishment of an address within this network was important. Following his first meeting with George Fox, Anthony Pearson wrote a letter in May 1653 which described ecstatically his convincement, and then more practically mentioned that a Kendal carrier came every fortnight 'within a mile of my house', and requested that letters for him should be left with one

---

[74] Robert Dring to George Taylor, 28 March 1656, Sw Mss 1: 285. For Dring's work in distributing books and papers to Burrough in Ireland, see Markey Mss., pp. 13, 98, 103. For his association with Amor Stoddard, see A. R. Barclay Mss 2: 157; Sw Trs 2: 549.

[75] George Taylor to Margaret Fell, 25 August 1655, Sw Mss 1: 294.

Peter Huggens.[76] Other contacts were more ephemeral, as itinerant ministers travelled longer distances. In November 1652, Richard Farnworth was sent a letter from Swarthmoor Hall which went first to his address in Balby, Yorkshire, and was then sent on to Derbyshire, where Farnworth was preaching among the congregation of a gathered church.[77] By January 1653, Farnworth informed Margaret Fell of another forwarding address, instructing her to send any letters 'by Kendall caryers to Ardsley near Wakefield', and to arrange for them to be left at 'A Smiths shopp for either Thomas Goodaire or William Nayler'.[78] In this way, Farnworth maintained steady contact with Fell.

The main focus for the establishment of such a network of addresses and contacts was the co-ordination of national preaching, of which the distribution of books was seen as an integral part. Here again, there was fairly tight control, within the constraint that ministers preached as they were 'moved' by God. The main co-ordinator of Quaker preaching around Bristol, John Audland was unimpressed to discover that John Wilkinson and John Storey, whom he had expected in Bristol, had gone instead to Cumberland, and wrote to Margaret Fell in complaint: 'we would say nothing contrary to the freedome of any but the worke is great as ever was, more then wee can supply'.[79] Occasionally pleas were made for the supply of more preachers: 'the care and burdin of freinds is so great on every hand, that we can hardly gitt any settlement among them', was the complaint of Howgill and Burrough to George Fox; 'deare heart lett Alex [Alexander Parker] come a season, to help us least our nett breake and we sufer loose [loss]'.[80] The network of 'national' preachers and local meetings also enabled suitable itineraries to be set up within specific localities. John Audland called for two women preachers to be sent to him at Olverstone in Gloucestershire, stating that 'heare are friends enough to recave them for presente: and when they are heare, it will be seene what places they are fitt for'.[81]

The establishment of a co-ordinated national network of preachers and meetings effectively aided the distribution of books and letters, underlining the importance of books as a tool of the itinerant preachers and thus the interdependence of the spoken and written word. Describing their preaching to Baptists, Independents and soldiers in Dover, John Stubbs and William Caton emphasised their success with the postmaster, 'a temperate spirit and very hopefull', and with a shoemaker, Luke Howard, who had been a Baptist for ten or eleven years, but was now 'Clearly Convinced'. It was to Luke

---

[76] Anthony Pearson [to Margaret Fell?], 9 May 1653, Sw Mss 1: 87.
[77] Richard Farnworth to Margaret Fell, 2 December 1652, Sw Mss 3: 45.
[78] Richard Farnworth to Margaret Fell, 7 January 1653, Sw Mss 4: 83.
[79] John Audland to Margaret Fell [1655], Caton Mss 3, p. 419.
[80] Francis Howgill to George Fox, 21 March 1657, A. R. Barclay Mss 1: 34, fol. 97.
[81] John Audland to Edward Burrough, 26 April 1656, A. R. Barclay Mss 1: 116, fol. 331.

Howard's shop, they suggested, that 'a dozen of some sorts of bookes which you thinke would bee serviceable' should be sent.[82] Although it was common for local shopkeepers to act as recipients of books and letters, it was primarily important that the itinerant Quaker ministers were sure of their convincement, before forwarding their names and addresses to Margaret Fell in Swarthmoor, or to London contacts.[83]

Quaker ministers invested similar trust and scrutiny in the transport of their books and letters. Manuscripts and letters were often carried by itinerant ministers themselves, or by trusted and known friends. In 1652, Richard Farnworth sent some letters on to George Fox, and urged him to speak to the messenger:

I sent them by John Snodin, as thou canst, send me word if thou have Received them, I was moved to chardge him to deliver them to thie owne hand that thou mightest speake to him, for I saw his condition and had spoken to him before.[84]

George Taylor in Kendal similarly advised Margaret Fell to use the services of one James Moore, 'for hee is deare and pretiouse to mee, and serviseable in the truth in his place'.[85]

Common carriers were also used, especially with the carriage of large consignments of books from London to the north of England.[86] Carriers were certainly preferable to the postal system as far as security was concerned. Another Kendal Quaker saw fit to warn Margaret Fell:

I received a letter for thee by the post and send it to thee by Thomas Pearson, it came singell by itt self and I know nott who sent it for their came 6 or 7 in the parcell and none of them did menshen it but George Taylor thinks it came from Richard Hubberthorne, thou may send me word by this bearer if it did soe, I did threaten the post man and saide I thought it had bene inclosed in some, but he denied and said it was as it came to him.[87]

---

[82] John Stubbs and William Caton to Francis Howgill and Edward Burrough, Dover, 19 March 1655, Sw Mss 3: 151.

[83] For shopkeepers as recipients for books and letters, see Portfolio 36: 103; Sw Trs 1: 359; Sw Trs 2: 569, 571, 575, 599; Sw Mss 1: 121; Sw Mss 4: 66, 257; A. R. Barclay Mss 1: 28, fol. 82; 2: 170, fol. 139; 2: 177, fol. 152. On one occasion the gaoler at Launceston prison was trusted to receive letters; Sw Trs 1: 628.

[84] Richard Farnworth to George Fox, 1652, Sw Mss 3: 53.

[85] George Taylor to Margaret Fell, 1654, Sw Mss 1: 211. For other examples of Quakers or named and trusted friends carrying letters, see Sw Mss 1: 9, 12, 42, 222, 235, 236, 237, 238, 249, 286, 288, 387; Sw Mss 3: 53; Sw Mss 4: 83; Sw Mss 6: 34; Sw Trs 3: 547, Caton Mss 3: 420. John Lilburne acted as messenger for Quaker ministers in Dover; A. R. Barclay Mss 1: 170, fol. 139. On another occasion, letters were brought from Ireland by a 'filthy deceitful wench' who was being sent home after an unsuccessful stint as a minister; Sw Trs 1: 568. For soldiers who were used as messengers, see Sw Mss 3: 55.

[86] For examples of the use of common carriers, see Portfolio 32: 56; Sw Mss 1: 87, 206, 214, 372; Sw Trs 2: 564.

[87] Thomas Willan to Margaret Fell [1654] Sw Mss 1: 222. For other examples of the troubled use of the postal service, see Sw Mss 1: 209, Spence Mss 3: 7.

The distribution of books and letters, therefore, was controlled by the ministers themselves, who decided whom to trust as messengers and recipients, and informed their colleagues about them. This was a wider part of the national ministerial campaign, and part of a developing network of contacts and local meetings.

The financing of Quaker publishing was also an integral part of the Quaker leaders' organisation. Thomas Aldam was confident of 'finding the means' to pay for one of the first sets of books printed for Giles Calvert in 1653. Other ministers similarly indicated that they would send money for books they used on their journeys. John Stubbs and William Caton, sending to London for a dozen books for Dover, promised 'wee shall endeavour to get money for them'.[88] Edward Burrough ordered books by price, asking for twenty shillings' worth to be sent to Ireland.[89] Larger consignments were sent at the request of ministers promising to pay later: Richard Farnworth asked Francis Howgill to get 100 copies of one of his books published, and arranged for a local man to send the wholesale price back via the carrier, with money from the sales of the books to be collected later.[90] Quaker books, especially those recounting events which had taken place in the locality, were thus sometimes sold by the ministers themselves or by their chosen distributors.

As the scale of the movement grew, it becomes more apparent that money for books (and the organisation of preachers generally) was raised by local groups, again at the behest of the itinerant ministers: in 1655 William Caton wrote of a 'General Meeting' in Sunderland, where 'friends is to bring their mony' for the 'Collection'.[91] The impulse for such organisation came from the itinerant ministers. From Crayke in North Yorkshire, William Dewsbery wrote to Thomas Aldam in York, requesting '3 or 4 dusan of books of such sorts as thou finds moved to send', including any currently at the printer's, which would assist him in his ministry there and in the market towns of Bedale and Northallerton. The local people 'would have sent some mony but they have not much in the outward', Dewsbery explained, 'I have sent thee ashiling towards the paying for them.' He suggested to Aldam that, although the local people were not sufficiently 'rased up' to buy books, they would 'look of books if they might have them lent'; and were certainly fired up enough to 'desparc them abrod'.[92] Dewsbery had thus assessed the needs of a specific locality, which involved the establishment of some kind of lending library of Quaker books, as well as the possibility of local Quakers,

[88] William Caton and John Stubbs to Edward Burrough and Francis Howgill, 19 March 1655, Sw Mss 3: 151.
[89] Edward Burrough to Robert Dring, 22 November 1655, Markey Mss, p. 98.
[90] Richard Farnworth to Francis Howgill and Edward Burrough [?1654], Portfolio 32: 56.
[91] William Caton to Margaret Fell, 28 August 1655, Sw Mss 1: 375.
[92] William Dewsbery to Thomas Aldam, August 1654, Portfolio 36: 103.

undertaking the selling or wider dissemination of books. All of this suggests strongly that the responsibility for book distribution was a central strand of preaching activity among all of the main Quaker leaders.

THE KENDAL FUND AND BOOK PRODUCTION

Book distribution was recorded most systematically at Kendal, by an iron-monger called George Taylor. From 1654, Taylor's shop was used as a for-warding address for nearby Swarthmoor Hall, for, as has been suggested in the chapter so far, George Taylor sent weekly letters to Margaret Fell enclos-ing letters and books which had arrived for her at his house. In addition to his function in copying and forwarding letters, George Taylor was also made responsible for organising the financing of the movement, collecting money from local meetings in Westmorland, Cumberland and Lancashire, and dis-bursing it among itinerant ministers. Taylor worked with another Quaker, Thomas Willan, also from Kendal.[93] Taylor had clearly been appointed by Fell and worked at her behest. It is possible that he knew her initially in a professional rather than a religious capacity, as the Fells operated an iron forge.[94] His letters show that he also sent domestic supplies like cabbage seed and 'cotton weave' to Swarthmoor.[95] The letters and accounts kept by Thomas Willan and George Taylor are an excellent source for the develop-ment of the Quaker movement, underlining the significance of ministerial organisation, and shedding unique light on Quaker book distribution.[96]

The Kendal fund was established as part of the national campaign of the summer of 1654.[97] The first accounts, drawn up at the end of 1654, were backdated to June 1654, and show that £12 15*s.* had been collected from local Westmorland meetings at Grayrigg, Preston Patrick, Sedbergh, Shapp and Kendal, including an individual donation of £1 2*s.* from Margaret

---

[93] Although Willan's occupation is not clear, he subsequently had connections with the book trade, possibly gained in the course of his work in the 1650s with George Taylor. In 1661, a book printed in Rotterdam was 'To be enquired for at Thomas Simmons, and Robert Wilsons in London, and also at Thomas Willans in Kendal'; Wing STC E3419. The name Thomas Williams of Kendal also appears on a list of dispersers of Quaker literature drawn up by the government in 1664; PRO SP 29/109 fol. 44 [1664]. I would like to thank Michael Frearson for this reference.

[94] Young Kunze, *Margaret Fell*, pp. 101–28.

[95] Taylor and Willan to Fell, 26 February 1655, Sw Mss 1: 214; Taylor and Willan to Fell, Sw Mss 1: 238 [1655].

[96] The letters are mainly to be found in the Swarthmoor Manuscripts at Friends' House. Other letters are to be found in the Portfolio, William Caton, and Spence manuscripts.

[97] The Kendal Fund is mentioned by Braithwaite, *Beginnings of Quakerism*, esp. pp. 135–37. The best treatment is in Arnold Lloyd, *Quaker social history, 1669–1738* (London, 1950), pp. 157–63, which stresses that the Kendal Fund was the most important of a number of local funds for the movement in the Commonwealth period; and argues that 'national' funding of the movement, based in London, was a product of the Restoration.

Fell herself.[98] The 'Fund' at this stage was running at a deficit; payments to Quaker missionaries ran to £14 18s. 7d.[99] Expenses recorded were for individual ministers 'goeing forth' on journeys; for groups of prisoners in Norwich and Appleby; for shoes or items of clothing for travelling ministers; and also for books. By March 1655, the annual income had risen to over £17, with outgoings reaching £15 9s., 'soe that as neare as wee can yet tell wee have in our handes but about thirtie two shillings'.[100] At this stage Taylor and Willan also provided a statement of their own role in the movement, which was to support the work of their 'friends in the south':

theire care is for the whole... that none shuld want or bee burthensome, and ours is to be answerable to them here that they may receive from us upon the first notise what as shall bee laide out for anie friends surplie in the service.[101]

The same letter also made it clear that the system of supply and finance was expanding, and that Willan and Taylor were operating under instructions from Anthony Pearson as well as from Margaret Fell. Subsequent accounts show that Pearson sent donations worth £15, collected from Yorkshire; and that between June and September 1655, Taylor and Willan received and disbursed over £44.[102] By August 1655, a meeting at Sunderland was also making collections; in 1656, an important general meeting at Skipton organised regular collections from meetings in all northern counties and suggested that southern counties do the same.[103]

The expenses recorded in the accounts of the Kendal Fund were thus the expenses incurred by a national preaching ministry, most of whose members came from the surrounding counties of Lancashire and Westmorland. Over a period of some seventeen weeks, between December 1654 and April 1655, Taylor and Willan recorded that £1 6s. 6d. had been spent 'for postage'.[104] This was a considerable sum, at a time when a single letter from London cost between one and three pence by post, and when there was increasing competition within the postal service for the lowering of rates.[105] Even so, the Kendal treasurers rejected the postal service in favour of carriers, on the grounds not of security but of cost. In November 1654 Thomas Willan wrote to Margaret Fell complaining at high postal charges: 'truely the post

---

[98] Bonnelyn Young Kunze states that Fell probably 'contributed liberally' to the fund between 1654 and 1657, *Margaret Fell*, p. 153.

[99] Taylor and Willan to Fell [1654], Sw Mss 1: 208.

[100] Taylor and Willan to Fell, 24 March 1655, Sw Mss 1: 206.   [101] *Ibid.*

[102] Taylor and Willan to Fell, 1 September 1655, Sw Trs 3: 547.

[103] William Caton to Margaret Fell, 28 August 1655, Sw Mss 1: 375; Lloyd, *Quaker social history*, p. 157.

[104] 'George Taylors Accounts for 1654', 29 April 1655, Sw Mss 1: 215.

[105] Howard Robinson, *The British post office: a history* (Princeton, 1948), pp. 40–46. Craig Horle states that Anthony Pearson's brother became postmaster for Cumberland and Westmorland: *BDBR*.

master of London doth use much opreshon upon us'. In response, Willan had written to fellow Quakers, 'that they may send all by the Carrier, unless it be some thinge of Consernement for the Carrier comes Every weeke, and I shall have as much brought me for 2*d*. as I pay to post 2 or 3*s*. for'.[106]

In addition to funding itinerant preachers and postage, the accounts of George Taylor and Thomas Willan show that they received and forwarded books. Different consignments of books arrived in bundles of various sizes: ten dozen of one title, five dozen of another, fifty copies of another. They were in direct contact with Calvert, and frequently knew in advance about the books they expected to receive: 'I have three or four sorts of bookes that will come to me this weeke', Thomas Willan informed Fell in September 1654.[107] Their regular contact with Calvert is highlighted most effectively when the system broke down. In 1655, Thomas Willan wrote to Fell, explaining that a variety of books had been sent to him unexpectedly, which he had not ordered himself. Among them was another edition of George Fox's tract, *Sauls errand to Damascus*, which had been reprinted:

but by whose order I doe nott know, but he hath sent me fiftie of Ether sortt, and I doe nott know wheare to putt any of them, for theire is noe friends heare that I can putt anie of them tow, and they are wearie of Receiveinge any of the new ones and the people of the world att present will nether looke of bookes nor papers.[108]

George Taylor and Thomas Willan's accounts of how Quaker books were distributed reinforce the organisational strength of the early Quaker movement, and also demonstrate that books were integrated into the overall organisation for the campaign. The role played by Taylor, Willan and Fell shows that considerable control was exercised over the distribution of books: it was the responsibility of ministers to identify reliable contacts and carriers, to finance the sale or distribution of books, and to ensure that books were supplied to appropriate audiences as necessary.

READERSHIP

The records of the Kendal Fund enable an examination of how Quaker books were read by audiences. We know very little about reading practices among ordinary people in early modern England. Margaret Spufford usefully highlighted the difficulties in measuring literacy, and argued that the ability to read was probably far more widespread than the (historically measurable) ability to write: Spufford's 'deaf old fen woman', who became a Quaker on reading one of their tracts, underlines the power of print even in the

---

[106] Willan to Fell, 26 November 1654, Spence Mss 3: 7.   [107] *Ibid.*
[108] Willan to Fell [1655], Sw Mss 1: 213.

hands of very humble readers.[109] Barry Reay argued that Quakerism took hold among occupational groups which demanded unusually high levels of literacy.[110] Increasingly, however, studies show that oral and literate culture were intrinsically linked. So-called print culture was incorporated into an oral culture: books were read or sung aloud; ballads were pinned up on walls for decoration; at the same time, as Adam Fox has shown, aspects of oral culture increasingly required transmutation into written record or print.[111]

Two aspects of Quaker book production reinforce that their books were used publicly, and integrated into an essentially aural reception. First is the relatively small numbers of books with which Taylor and Willan were dealing. Second, is the fact that responsibility for the distribution of books lay often with the preaching ministers themselves. Far from books 'flying thick as moths' up and down the country, there were relatively few, whose distribution was carefully controlled by the Quaker leadership.

Quaker books were published in relatively small numbers. Three hundred copies of one of the first, *False prophets and false ministers described*, were printed in November 1652. Three hundred more of *A brief discovery of a threefold estate of Antichrist* were published in February 1653.[112] As their titles suggest, these were general works proclaiming the inner light of Christ, which would be used liberally in convincing the world, and were handed out at Thomas Aldam's trial in York in March 1653. More geographically specific works may have been printed in even smaller numbers: Richard Farnworth requested in October 1654 that 100 copies of an account of a dispute in Staffordshire should be printed.[113] The size of print runs grew with the movement: in 1656 it was decided that 600 copies of every book be printed; in 1657, one author claimed that 500 copies of her book had already been printed and that there was to be another run of 500, and called 'them that love the truth be at charge (by a copy) to print 1000 or more of the same, that they may go into all parts of England'.[114]

[109] Margaret Spufford (ed.), *The world of rural dissenters, 1520–1725* (Cambridge, 1995), p. 64.

[110] Barry Reay, 'The social origins of early Quakerism', *Journal of Interdisciplinary History* 11: 1 (1980), 62.

[111] Margaret Spufford, *Small books and pleasant histories: popular fiction and its readership in seventeenth-century England* (Athens, Ga., 1982); Tessa Watt, *Cheap print and popular piety, 1550–1640* (Cambridge, 1991); Adam Fox, 'Ballads, libels and popular ridicule in Jacobean England', *Past and Present* 145 (1994), 47–83.

[112] Richard Farnworth to Margaret Fell, Balby, December 1652, Sw Mss 3: 45; Thomas Aldam to Amor Stoddard, York, 19 February 1653, A. R. Barclay Mss 1: 15, fol. 50.

[113] Richard Farnworth to Francis Howgill and Edward Burrough, Swannington, October 1654, Portfolio 32: 56.

[114] *Journal of George Fox*, vol. I, p. 267, cited in Lloyd, *Quaker social history*, p. 153; [Jeane Bettris], *Spiritual discoveries to the overthrow of popery root and branch* 2nd edn (London, 1657), *STC* B2086, p. 1.

In his study of civil war newsbook production, Anthony Cotton showed that it was possible to produce a print run of 250 copies of a newsbook profitably.[115] In all probability, Calvert and his printers were reimbursed for their services to the Quaker movement. The small print runs produced were used with great precision, and demonstrate close collaboration between Quakers and printers. In 1656, Margaret Fell wrote to a friend in London, John Stubbs, with a manuscript which she asked him to take to Thomas Simmonds, 'and see it truly Sett in the Press'. She requested Stubbs to oversee the proof corrections, and then directed him: 'they may goe forth amongst freinds as the Rist of Books does, the same Quantety to Every place, and as they are Called for soe they may bee prented in Quantety'.[116] Thus, a standard quantity of books was distributed to local meetings on a regular basis, but with the implicit understanding that if there were higher demand, more would be printed. Such a system had been operating since the summer of 1654, when Thomas Aldam sent some books to Fox informing him that he had run out of books at York, 'but I have sent for more to London of severall sorts; which I doe Expect shortly, and if any write to mee I shall send part of such as comes to me'.[117]

While relatively small quantities of books were produced, their distribution was controlled by sedantry co-ordinators like Fell and Aldam. Willan and Taylor, working for Fell, distributed books to ministers as they were about to set off on their journeys all over England and abroad. In October 1654, prior to his journey to London and thence to Plymouth, Thomas Salthouse of Ulverston, bailiff to the Swarthmoor estate, received twenty-four copies of one title (at 2*s*. 6*d*.) and eighteen of another (at 1*s*. 6*d*.). The following month, November 1654, he was sent eighteen copies of yet another title, this time costing 2*s*.[118] It is likely that some of his books were intended for preaching as he travelled; others may have been for more local ministry. The quantities of books sent to Margaret Fell at Swarthmoor Hall (where travelling ministers went to recuperate between missions, and where local meetings were held) were also relatively small: 'one dozen of Francis Howgills at 2*s*.9*d*. three of the Answer to Gilpins booke at 9*d* and three of the answer to Sauls Errand at 10*d*' were sent in a typical package to Margaret Fell in 1655.[119]

---

[115] Anthony Cotton, 'The London newsbooks in the Civil War', p. 8. This calculation was worked out on the basis of a single folio sheet newsbook, produced under some pressure for weekly publication.

[116] Margaret Fell to John Stubbs [1656] Spence Mss 3: 40.

[117] Thomas Aldam to George Fox, York Castle, [July] 1654, Sw Mss 3: 44.

[118] Taylor to Fell, 14 October 1654, Sw Mss 1: 209; Taylor and Willan to Fell, annual account 1654, 1: 208.

[119] Taylor to Fell, 1 February 1655, Sw Mss 1: 213.

As has been seen, books were sent directly and as a matter of course to local meetings. These could be books which recounted events specific to the area. Twenty-four copies of *The persecution of them people they call Quakers in . . . Lancashire* were sent to Manchester, and twelve more to a meeting in Freckleton and Plumpton, Lancashire.[120] Books, or sections of books, were read aloud at meetings: this was certainly implicit in some of the tracts discussed in Chapter 1. Some form of private, individual reading did take place, as William Dewsbery's suggestion for a lending library for the inhabitants of Crayke, implies. Some books were individually priced: *The persecution of them people they call Quakers in . . . Lancashire*, for example, cost $1^{1/2}d$.[121] Quakers were also arrested for selling books on the streets in London and Beverley. Private sales and loans show that Quaker books were read for private edification.

There is far more evidence in the records, particularly those of Taylor and Willan, that books were used publicly, and were read aloud by the Quaker ministers, or handed out in situations in which the ministers could control their reception. Despite the commonly held perception that the written word was anathema to Quakers, their books were read aloud in marketplaces and in churchyards, very much like prepared sermons. Describing the impact of one of the first printed tracts in December 1652, Richard Farnworth wrote exuberantly to Fell:

> frends is made soe bould that they goe and Reeds them in the steeple house yarthes After they have done and in the marketts on the Crosse on the markett dayes, and some souldiers is made to goe Alonge with them and stand by them whilst they are Reeding, And the priests is all on fier.[122]

Books were also distributed in advance of major public events concerning Quakers. In March 1655, Thomas Aldam went to Whitehall in an attempt to deliver a 'paper' to Cromwell and members of the Council of State. He was not allowed to meet with Cromwell, but reported that on his way home, he 'did give Bookes to the Keepers of the gaurds' and managed to address some soldiers. Later he was rescued by Major Packer from angry crowds trying to tear up his books: Packer kept one of the books for himself, but let

---

[120] Taylor to Fell [1655], Sw Mss 1: 234.

[121] *Ibid.* The pricing of this book is evidence that Quaker books were sold for profit, and were not subsidised in any way by Giles Calvert or other publishers. As a sixteen-page book printed on two folio sheets, *The persecution of them people they call Quakers in . . . Lancashire* exactly reflects the price suggested by Francis Johnson, of 3/4 of a penny per folio sheet. Francis R. Johnson, 'Notes on English retail book-prices, 1550–1640', *The Library*, 5th ser., 5: 2 (1950), p. 90.

[122] Richard Farnworth to Margaret Fell, 2 December 1652, Sw Trs 2: 15–16; 2: 19. The books in question were probably Thomas Aldam's *False prophets and false teachers described* [n.p., 1652], *STC* A894BA.

Aldam take the rest away with him.[123] The point is that Aldam travelled, for a 'private' meeting with Cromwell, with books for distribution to crowds of soldiers and onlookers. He expected his appearance to provoke public interest; and used printed books to reinforce the impact of his presence. Similarly, books were distributed with great care to major trials involving Quakers. Trials were important focal points for the Quakers' protest against any form of prosecution for religious beliefs.[124] In August 1653, Willan and Taylor sent George Fox eighteen shillings' worth of books (amounting to anything between seventy and two hundred books), while he was awaiting trial for Blasphemy in Carlisle.[125] Robert Widders asked George Taylor in Kendal to send him books 'as soon as thou canst before the Asises' at Lancaster.[126] The public interest generated by trials was purposely made a focal point for the distribution of Quaker books.

Even on itinerant preaching missions, Quaker ministers integrated books and papers into their work. In 1655, Richard Clayton and James Lancaster travelled to the north of Ireland, provided with fifteen shillings' worth of books from the Kendal fund.[127] In a letter sent back to Margaret Fell, Clayton described his use of 'papers' as a part of his public preaching. At a garrison of soldiers, Clayton 'read a paper Amongest them and spoke some words Amongest them as the Lord gave uterance'; the effect was sufficiently striking that 'they were all silent', and more significantly agreed that 'they would lett there felow soulders see . . . the paper which I left with them'. Clayton's speaking 'as the Lord gave uterance' was therefore performed from the written paper; the value of this was that he could leave a copy of it with the garrison. Following his success among the soldiers, Clayton travelled onwards to Lurgan, 'and upon the Market day I went into the market and spoke through it, . . . and they were all quiet which was sarviceabell and did strengthen frinds to see there spirits bound and brought under'.[128]

Once again, the silence of the audiences was taken as a sign of convincement and acceptance of the Quakers' message; and as a sign that the arguments could be presented in writing: 'and soe upon the next market day', Clayton explained, 'I did put up a paper which did stey up 3 or 4 houers and many people reed it'.[129] Having established meetings in Lurgan, Clayton travelled nine miles to another market town, Legacurry, where, he reported: 'I was moved of the lord to put up a paper in it which did stay up most part of the day and I was moved to speake Amongest the people up and downe the market and receved noe persecution.'[130]

---

[123] Thomas Aldam to George Fox [March 1655], Sw Mss 3: 38.
[124] See below, Chapter 7.   [125] Taylor to Fell [1654], Sw Mss 1: 218.
[126] Robert Widder to George Taylor and Thomas Willan [Lancaster, 1655], Sw Mss 1: 307.
[127] Taylor to Fell [1655], Sw Mss 1: 233.
[128] Richard Clayton to Margaret Fell [1655], Sw Mss 1: 27.   [129] *Ibid.*   [130] *Ibid.*

In this case, Clayton was primarily 'moved' to put up his paper in the marketplace; and his preaching followed on from the paper. He attributed as much divine inspiration to pinning up a piece of writing as he did actually to speaking; he measured his success by how long the paper remained publicly visible. Thus the 'reading' of Quaker tracts or papers was directed by the ministers themselves and considered an integral part of their preaching. They physically controlled – sometimes with soldiers on hand – the ways in which their books were read.

It has been shown that travelling ministers used a variety of titles, or 'sorts' of books: John Stubbs and William Caton asked for twelve 'of some sorts of bookes' to be sent to them in Dover; Margaret Fell was promised 'three or four sorts of bookes that will come to me this weeke'.[131] When he travelled to Holland, William Ames carried a number of different tracts with him, the variety of which enabled him to select books appropriate to his audience. The members of one English church he visited in Amsterdam seemed to him 'to be zealous in theire way', but after a while he was moved to speak to them, at which, he wrote, 'they seemed to be astonished and owned my words and desired me to stay and heare theire minister but I having severall bookes about me which sufficiently declared what theire minister was and all his generation I left them amongst them and departed'.[132] It was the variety of books carried by Ames which he thought allowed denunciation of the minister to the gathered church in Amsterdam. Quaker ministers were very aware of different 'sorts' of books, and therefore were aware that they could be used in different circumstances.

The readership of Quaker tracts was controlled, and controlled effectively, by the ministers themselves. While tracts were not scattered up and down the country, as their enemies perceived, they were distributed in such a way as to reach the largest possible audience. Quaker ministers were concerned above all to proclaim the message that Christ's inner light was in everyone: their message therefore had potentially to reach everyone.[133] Their tracts were read in contexts where they would have maximum reinforcement from external sources. They were read aloud and delivered like sermons. They were handed out by Quaker speakers in the course of public meetings. The speakers were often themselves the authors, who were therefore in a position

---

[131] John Stubbs and William Caton to Francis Howgill and Edward Burrough, Dover, 19 March 1655, Sw Mss 3: 151; Thomas Willan to Margaret Fell, 26 September 1654, Spence Mss 3: 7.

[132] William Ames to Margaret Fell [1656 or 1658], A. R. Barclay Mss 1: 3, fol. 11.

[133] This contrasts with the purpose of writing in some of the Calvinist churches, where the recording of one's religious experience was undertaken to signify membership of an elect congregation, and where the audience, potentially, therefore was very limited and localised. See Patricia Caldwell, *The puritan conversion narrative: the beginnings of American expression* (Cambridge, 1983), pp. 45–55.

to explain their content, and also to assess the likely attitudes of the audience to the tracts. Quaker tracts could also be used to reinforce a spoken delivery. They were left behind as the preachers moved on, to enable audiences to consider what they had heard in greater depth. Sometimes these were hostile audiences, like the congregation addressed by William Ames in Amsterdam. More frequently they would be newly formed 'Quaker' groups. That books were delivered explicitly to 'meetings' reinforces that they were read aloud, as part of the meeting.

The strategies for Quaker book distribution underline the very blurred distinction between orality and literacy in seventeenth-century England. The Quakers' concern was to reach the widest possible audience. That they did this in large part through the medium of print suggests strongly that illiteracy was not deemed a major obstacle. Although private, individual readings of the tracts took place, Quaker books were the tools of preaching ministers, which amplified and preserved their message. The argument that the written word was 'anathema' to early Quakers needs to be revised in the light of this.[134] It is clear that Quaker public speaking was deemed to be a spontaneous outburst, inspired by the movings of the divine. That the use of print in such public speaking was not considered a problem or a contradiction by the ministers themselves needs emphasising: it suggests a familiarity with print, and reinforces the central role of the Quaker authors in organising and leading the movement.

The evident organisation behind Quaker publishing is impressive, and very important. The confidence and authority of a few authors probably enabled others to contribute writings which otherwise would never have made it to the press. This would certainly explain the relative prevalence of women authors. The leadership exercised over book production and distribution was also a feature of the wider movement; an understanding of how Quakers used their books provides new insight into how a relatively small number of men and women could spread their ideas so far and so rapidly. The following chapter presents a short case-study of how printed tracts were used in the genesis of a nationally coherent movement.

---

[134] Richard Bauman, *Let your words be few: symbolism of speaking and silence among seventeenth-century Quakers* (Cambridge, 1983), p. 11; Barbour and Arthur Roberts (eds.), *Early Quaker writings*, p. 14; Thomas N. Corns, '"No Man's Copy": the critical problem of Fox's Journal', in Thomas Corns and David Loewenstein (eds.), *The emergence of Quaker writing: dissenting literature in seventeenth-century England* (London, 1995), p. 99.

3

A national movement: pamphleteering in East Anglia[1]

On 13 November 1654, Richard Hubberthorne wrote a letter to George Fox describing his missionary work in Norwich: 'I am caled . . . amongest A people wheare the gospell hath not been preached nor noe man hath Layd A foundation to build upon but are all aliants and strangers to the life of god', he lamented. He noted further that although there were some newly convinced Quakers in the countryside, in the city of Norwich itself things were bleak.[2] During the same week, on the other side of England in Bristol, Richard Hubberthorne's fellow missionary Edward Burrough reported a far happier story of successful proselytisation, with meetings attended by 3,000 people, and Quaker ranks swelled by the significant defection of members of the Broadmead Church.[3]

The contrasting experiences of Hubberthorne and Burrough are indicative of the different ways in which Quakers were received as they travelled up and down the country. They reinforce that the Quakers' campaign was conducted on a national basis after mid-1654, with ministers preaching in major cities, market towns and the rural hinterland, and encountering considerable hostility as well as attracting significant support. This chapter offers a case-study of how Quaker ideas were introduced into a specific region, East Anglia. It will argue that the Quakers' use of print contributed towards the creation of a nationally homogeneous and coherent movement.

There are various explanations for the growth of Quakerism. Scholars like Rufus Jones or Geoffrey Nuttall located the origins of Quakerism within an intellectual or theological context, Rufus Jones arguing for strong links between continental mysticism and Quaker ideas; Nuttall that the Quakers were part of the spectrum, albeit the 'fag-end', of English puritanism, although Nuttall also identified important links with Familism and

---

[1] An earlier version of this chapter appeared in David Chadd (ed.), *Religious dissent in East Anglia III* (University of East Anglia, 1996), pp. 141–65.
[2] Richard Hubberthorne to George Fox, Norwich gaol, 13 November 1654, Sw Trs 2: 567.
[3] Edward Burrough to Margaret Fell, Bristol, 15 November 1654, Caton Mss 3, p. 190; W. C. Braithwaite, *The beginnings of Quakerism* (Cambridge, 1955), p. 170.

the Quakers.[4] These studies provide an important context in which to interpret the beliefs of Quaker leaders like James Nayler and George Fox, but
do not necessarily explain their wider appeal to Quaker followers. Other
explanations of the rise of the Quaker movement locate it within the context
of the English revolution, and as such study the social origins of Quaker followers. In 1957, Alan Cole found that Quakers came from the 'urban and
rural petite bourgeoisie', and argued that support for Quaker ideas came
from those 'sections of the population which found their economic position
threatened and their political demands frustrated by the political and social
upheavals of the seventeenth century'.[5] Yet Cole's findings, and his terminology, have been questioned by more sophisticated analyses of the social
structure of the early Quaker movement.[6] Most recently, interest has focused
on the social origins and composition of early Quakers within the context
of religiosity and religious dissent, concentrating on arguments about the
nature of popular religious experience.[7] Such studies by their very nature are
local.[8] Studies for East Anglia, as for elsewhere, suggest that seventeenth-
century Quakers were well integrated into local communities: they were
successful traders and artisans, associated with the cloth trade; they held
local offices; and were sightly wealthier and slightly more respectable than
the average religious conformist.[9] Yet local studies of the social composition
of the Quakers do not throw much light onto the issue of the origins of the

---

[4] Rufus Jones, *Spiritual reformers in the sixteenth and seventeenth centuries* (London, 1914);
Geoffrey Nuttall, *The holy spirit in puritan faith and experience* (Oxford, 1946), Jones, *The
puritan spirit. Essays and addresses* (London, 1967); Jones, 'James Nayler: a fresh approach'
JFHS Supplement 26, 1954.

[5] Alan Cole, 'The social origins of the early Friends', *JFHS* 48 (1957), 117, 118; Barry Reay,
'The social origins of early Quakerism', *Journal of Interdisciplinary History* 11: 1 (Summer
1980), 55–72.

[6] See Richard Vann, 'Quakerism and the social structure in the interregnum', *Past and
Present* 43 (1969), 71–91; Vann, *The social development of English Quakerism, 1655–1755*
(Cambridge, Mass., 1969); Barry Reay, 'The social origins of early Quakerism', 55–57, 62.

[7] Editor's introduction to Margaret Spufford (ed.), *The world of rural dissenters, 1520–1725*
(Cambridge, 1995).

[8] Alan Cole, 'The social origins of the early Friends', 99–118; Richard Vann, 'Quakerism and
the social structure', 71–91; Barry Reay, 'The social origins of early Quakerism', 55–72.
Although all these studies disagree as to whether the early movement consisted predominantly
of the upper or lower 'bourgeoisie'; depend on diverging definitions of the 'middling sort',
the gentry, and 'plebian'; and are even unclear as to whether early Quakers were a rural or
urban phenomenon, they all maintain that those most receptive to Quaker ideas were involved
in literate and mobile occupations. The majority of early Quakers were retail or wholesale
traders, artisans and yeomen.

[9] T. A. Davies, 'The Quakers in Essex 1655–1725' unpublished D Phil. thesis, University of
Oxford, 1986, ch. 7 *passim*; W. Stephenson, 'The economic and social status of protestant
sectarians in Huntingdonshire, Cambridgeshire and Bedfordshire (1650–1725)', unpublished
Ph.D thesis, University of Cambridge, 1990; Barry Reay discusses Essex Quakers in 'The social
origins of early Quakerism'; Richard Vann discusses Norfolk Quakers, *Social development
of Quakerism*. I am grateful to Adrian Davies for permission to refer to his thesis.

national Quaker movement, nor explain why it apparently spread so rapidly. The rich demographic information which exists for the Quakers was compiled, by definition, once Quaker communities were well established, and had begun to keep their own records. This state of affairs occurred only after the Restoration in 1660, when governmental persecution required the Quakers to develop a national, organised church structure.

This chapter will describe that part of the national campaign through which Quaker ideas were introduced and established in East Anglia in 1654 and 1655. In order to do this, it will focus not on the records of the local, East Anglian Quaker laity, but on the letters and tracts generated by the itinerant Quaker ministers who were initially responsible for the spread of Quaker ideas into East Anglia and indeed across the whole country. Adrian Davies has recently argued convincingly that the role of the local laity in the spread and tenacity of Quakerism is often ignored or underestimated by historians. While Davies's views are in no way disputed here, it is the argument of this and other chapters in this book that 'Quaker' ideas were clearly imported into new localities by itinerant ministers and their books, where they were taken up with varying degrees of success. This chapter examines the role of print in the dissemination of Quaker ideas in one area, as part of a much wider, national campaign.[10]

Quaker ministers, when they arrived in London in June 1654, were strangers. Richard Vann has written, rather quaintly but probably accurately, that 'it was obvious from their accents that most of them were from the north of England'.[11] In pamphlet warfare, both Quakers and their opponents played up their northern identity. Quakers referred to themselves in print as the 'Northern Army', or as the seed of God raised up in the northern parts of the nation; while one satirist of the Quakers published a tract entitled *The Quakers terrible vision: or, the Devil's Progress from the North of England to the City of London*.[12] The stylistic emphasis on their northern roots was significant. The itinerant ministers who exported and instilled Quaker beliefs into local communities were strangers. The fact that they were outsiders affected how Quaker ideas were spread, and how they were received.

---

[10] Adrian Davies, *The Quakers in English society 1655–1725* (Oxford, 2000), pp. 81, 107, 129.

[11] Richard Vann, *The social development of early Quakerism*, p. 8.

[12] Francis Ellington, *A true discovery of the ground of the the imprisonment* (London, 1655), STC T2683, p. 3; Anthony Pearson, *To the Parliament of the Common-wealth of England* [London, 1653], STC P992, sig Ar; *The Quakers terrible vision: or, the Devil's Progress* (London, 1655), STC Q33, sig Ar. Another alarmed puritan minister from Hereford pretended in response to a Quaker tract that he had never heard of Kendal. Edmund Skipp, *The worlds blazing starr* (London, 1655), STC S3949, p. 11.

In Cambridge, the imminent coming of the 'northern army' had been ominously heralded by the arrival of two northern women in the town in December 1653. It is likely that these two women, Mary Fisher and Elizabeth Williams, had travelled south with Gervase Benson, who was in London.[13] Although the two women did not apparently announce themselves as Quakers, they nevertheless caused the considerable foment and division which would be typical of their later co-religionists. On their arrival in Cambridge they 'fell into discourse' with scholars from Sidney Sussex College, telling them that 'they were Antichrists, and that their Colledg was a Cage of unclean Birds, and the Synagogue of Satan'.[14] For this, they were not surprisingly hauled before the mayor, William Pickering, who demanded of them 'whence they came, and where they lay the last night?' The Quakers were typically enigmatic in their replies:

> They answered him, they were strangers, and knew not the name of the place; but paid for what they called for, and came away. The Mayor asked them what was their names? they answered, their names were written in the book of life. Again he asked them, What was their husbands names? they answered, they had no husband but Jesus Christ, and he sent them.[15]

Following this interview, the mayor William Pickering concluded that the two women were whores and ordered them to be whipped at the market cross, so that 'their bodies were cut, and slashed, and torn, as never were the bodies of any rogues, or thieves, or whores, . . . as those poor Christians were'.[16] Finally, the women were thrown out of the town, although we should note in passing that Elizabeth Williams had gained a taste for university, and went later to Oxford, where she was ducked.[17]

The impact of the visit of Mary Fisher and Elizabeth Williams was greater than this one event. Their story was published in a tract: unusually, not by the Quaker women themselves, but by a sympathetic 'Eminent Hand' from Cambridge.[18] A significant postscript to the tract gave notice to all men, 'That none of the Justices of the Town had any hand in this barbarous and unlawful act, saving Mr. William Pickering Mayor'. Mary Fisher and Elizabeth Williams had gained the invaluable sympathy of local justices, which would be crucial to the later experience of Quakers in Cambridge. It is even more significant to the growth of the movement that Quakers in the north of England were made aware of the sympathy of the Cambridge justices. The same account of the whipping which was printed was sent in a private letter to a 'Christian friend' in London; and this letter found

---

[13] Gervase Benson to Margaret Fell, London, 29 November 1653, Sw Mss 4: 32.
[14] *The first new persecution* (London, 1654), STC F977, p. 4.   [15] *Ibid.*, p. 4.
[16] *Ibid.*, p. 5.   [17] Braithwaite, *Beginnings of Quakerism*, p. 159.
[18] *The first new persecution.*

its way into the hands of Quakers Gervase Benson and Anthony Pearson, who immediately incorporated it at the end of a tract by James Nayler, and subsequently circulated it in the north of England.[19]

Quakers coming from the north of England in the summer of 1654 were able to build on this first visit as they began a more sustained infiltration of Quaker ideas in Cambridge. The first of the itinerant Quaker ministers to arrive in the summer of 1654 were James Parnell and Ann Blaykling, travelling from Yorkshire to Cambridge.[20] Knowledge that Mary Fisher and Elizabeth Williams had already stirred up the town may have been behind their impulse to travel directly there, although James Parnell, a very young Quaker minister from Nottinghamshire, was perhaps disingenuously passive in his account of his journey to Cambridge:

> when I was betwixt 17. and 18. years of age, I was moved in my spirit to go to a place about fifteen miles from my outward dwelling place (southward) amongst a people, to whom the Lord was making known his truth, not knowing when I went out of going farther than that place; but when I was there, I was moved of the Lord to come on to *Cambridge*, and in obedience unto the Lord, I came to see what he had to do for me, not knowing one foot of the way, but as I was directed, neither knowing when I came there where to be received, but had heard before of two of my friends that was there whipped .[21]

Parnell's account of his journey appeared in another tract, which aimed to convince readers of the harshness of the authorities' response to an innocent and hapless spiritual wanderer; but in it Parnell nevertheless provided evidence both that fellow Quaker ministers suggested the journey to him; and that the story of the first Quaker visitors was commonly known. James Parnell stated in another tract that while in Cambridge he stayed in the house of a local justice, James Blackley. It is not improbable either that Parnell had known of Blackley's attitude from the accounts of the first Quaker visit in December 1653.[22]

Contact between Quaker ministers was an important dynamic in the sustained build-up of a national Quaker movement. The northern ministers

[19] *The first new persecution*, sig. A4r; James Nayler, *Churches gathered against Christ* (London, 1654), STC N267, pp. 20–21.

[20] The only account of their journey is that found in the pamphlet by Richard Hubberthorne, James Parnell [and Ann Blaykling], *The immediate call to the ministry of the Gospel* (London, 1654), STC H3225, pp. 1–13. There is no evidence from contemporary correspondence that either travelled to London first.

[21] James Parnell, *The fruits of a fast* (London, 1655), STC P530, sig. A3–A3v.

[22] Richard Hubberthorne and James Parnell, *The immediate call to the ministry of the Gospel* (London, 1654), STC H3225, p. 8. Blackley was known as a Quaker sympathiser, and was removed from office in 1657 under the increasingly intolerant Protectorate: Barry Reay, 'Early Quaker activity and reactions to it', p. 80; see also Laurel Phillipson, 'Quakerism in Cambridge before the Act of Toleration (1653–1689)', *Proceedings of the Cambridge Antiquarian Society* 76 (1987), 1–25.

travelling over the summer of 1654 were well informed about each others' movements. Thomas Ayrey, at the end of a gruelling journey from Lancashire to London which took in Bristol, Exeter and Plymouth, arrived in the capital on 2 August 1654. After a week of meetings with Seekers and Baptists, Thomas Ayrey was reported to have left for Ely. Meanwhile, Richard Hubberthorne, travelling from Lancashire to London through Oxford, arrived in London on 11 August, and by the 20th had left the capital to travel 'eastwards'.[23] By the end of August, it was reported that Hubberthorne was in Cambridge, and that Thomas Ayrey was travelling to meet him there.[24]

That Cambridge became an early focus for itinerant Quaker ministers is in part explained simply by the fact that it formed part of a national campaign which so far had concentrated on the north, west and centre of England. Richard Hubberthorne was particularly well equipped for a mission to Cambridge, having just published a pamphlet attacking Oxford University. The final section of the pamphlet included a discovery of 'The lewdness of those two great Mothers, who have brought forth so many Children, and never had a Husband', which denounced jointly the universities of Oxford and Cambridge, and the ministers educated there.[25]

The most immediate cause for Hubberthorne and Ayrey to set off for Cambridge, however, was probably the news that Ann Blaykling and James Parnell had been imprisoned in Cambridge. The initial role of James Parnell and Ann Blaykling was to publicise Quaker ideas in the town, announcing the coming of Christ and his universal light in all people; and warning people of the necessary battle with the forces of antichrist. As was typical in other towns, one way of doing this was to challenge a local minister. Accordingly, Ann Blaykling had incensed Philip Johnson, whom she denounced as a 'minister of the World', by claiming among other things that the Scriptures were not sufficient means to find Christ, and that all men were equal and ought not to acknowledge superiors.[26] James Parnell, meanwhile, had sought a wider audience for Quaker beliefs by pinning up a paper in the marketplace on market day. For this both Quaker ministers were arrested almost immediately.

The initial publicising of Quaker ideas led to the intensification of the local campaign. This again was dependent on outside support. Richard Hubberthorne soon joined them; and recorded that, after a few days of

---

[23] *Audland's Journal*, pp. 29–31.

[24] Gervase Benson to Margaret Fell, Cinderhill Green, Derbyshire [25 August 1654], Sw Trs 1: 199. This date is assigned as the earliest possible by Geoffrey Nuttall, EQL, p. 113. Audland's Journal (p. 31) records that Hubberthorne left London for the east on 18 August 1654.

[25] Richard Hubberthorne, *A true testimony of the zeal of Oxford-professors and university-men* (London, 1654), STC H3240.

[26] *The immediate call to the ministry of the Gospel*, pp. 10–13.

public meetings 'from house to house', he too was imprisoned by the mayor. The news of the imprisonment of Hubberthorne led to the arrival in Cambridge of Thomas Ayrey, who was arrested almost immediately by a now incensed William Pickering who commanded that Ayrey be imprisoned in isolation.[27]

It was at this stage, as was typical in patterns of Quaker missionary work, that the imprisoned ministers publicised events in Cambridge through a printed pamphlet. Here again, the intensification of the Quaker campaign in Cambridge incorporated the support of itinerant ministers in London and Swarthmoor Hall in Lancashire.

From the Quakers' own account of their arrests, the fact that they were outsiders was of enormous concern to the Cambridge mayor. William Pickering tried to indict Richard Hubberthorne on three separate occasions as a 'wandering person, and a rogue', which Hubberthorne steadfastly denied, pointing out that he had received no money from the parish, and had enjoyed the willing hospitality of people in Cambridge who were also independent of parish relief.[28] Pickering also failed to gain the support of his justices to indict Hubberthorne for cursing him. The primary aim of Pickering was not imprisonment, but to rid Cambridge of the itinerant Quakers. Hubberthorne's account of his interview with the mayor purposefully emphasised the frustration of William Pickering in trying to remove the Quakers, as Pickering accused Hubberthorne, 'thou dost not follow the examples of the Apostles, for when they were persecuted in one City they fled into another, but we cannot get thee out by no meanes'. At this, Hubberthorne claimed that the mayor had 'owned himself to be of the same generation that persecuted the Apostles', and remarked that he would leave the town only when the word of God had told him to do so.[29] William Pickering then offered Hubberthorne the choice of leaving the town of his own free will, being whipped out, or being imprisoned. In reply, Hubberthorne pointed out in all self-righteousness that to leave would in itself be unlawful, for, if Pickering thought he was in breach of any law, he should not be given liberty to leave without due punishment.[30]

The account given in the pamphlet was highly typical of those written from gaols across the country, arguing that Quakers were imprisoned and punished unlawfully. Hubberthorne had already rehearsed the arguments in manuscript and print, from gaol in Chester, and in Oxford.[31] Despite its typicality, the pamphlet also served to shift the status of Quakers in Cambridge from passing troublemakers to part of a sustained attack on the town. James Parnell's account of his arrest centred upon the paper he had pinned up in the

[27] *Ibid.*, pp. 2–3.   [28] *Ibid.*, pp. 3–5.   [29] *Ibid.*, p. 3.   [30] *Ibid.*, p. 4.
[31] Richard Hubberthorne to Margaret Fell, Chester gaol, November 1653, Sw Trs 2: 539; Richard Hubberthorne, *A true testimony of the zeal of Oxford-professors.*

market square. The mayor accused him that the paper denounced the ministers and magistrates of Cambridge. Parnell refuted this: his paper, he said, had merely attacked 'corrupt Magistrates, and heathenish Priest, wheresoever they are'. By assuming that the magistrates and ministers concerned were from Cambridge, Parnell argued, it was the mayor himself who admitted they were indeed corrupt and heathenish.[32] The paper which Parnell had brought to Cambridge, then, was a general denunciation of ministry and magistracy by which the Quakers had sought to gain attention and public debate. The pamphlet itself, published nearly three months later, consolidated the attack by naming the mayor and describing the Quakers' harsh and unlawful treatment in the town itself.

Moreover, the publication of the tract brought further itinerant ministers into Cambridge. Two more Quakers from Lancashire, Miles Halhead and James Lancaster, travelled down to London in September 1654. They met up with Edward Burrough, who was staying in Moorfields, and in regular contact with Hubberthorne, and then went straight to Giles Calvert's shop. With money provided from the Kendal fund they picked up 20 shillings' worth of books and left for Cambridge. It is likely, from the date of the tract, the date of their visit, and their subsequent destination, that they carried copies of the Cambridge pamphlet with them.[33] The arrest and imprisonment of James Parnell and Ann Blaykling in July had culminated, three months later, in the presence of six Quaker ministers, all from the north, and possibly more than one hundred copies of a printed tract circulating in the town.

In the ministers' initial accounts of events in Cambridge, the response of local would-be converts was hardly described. In the published tract, the sympathy of James Blackley and other justices was alluded to, as were the few public meetings of Hubberthorne, and the apparent willing hospitality he received in the town. Private letters between ministers named no local sympathisers and made no mention of local attitudes. From the viewpoint of the itinerant ministers, it was only after the initial blaze of publicity in the town that they began to consolidate local sympathy. This too was highly orchestrated by ministers from outside. As was typical in all local campaigns, the targets for the Quakers were Baptist and Independent congregations, and local notable figures. In Cambridge itself, the Quakers reported much opposition. In April 1655, Ann Blaykling and James Parnell were joined in Cambridge by Edward Burrough and Francis Howgill for a prearranged

---

[32] *The immediate call to the ministry of the Gospel*, p. 9.
[33] Francis Howgill to Robert Widders, London, 23 September 1654, Sw Trs 2: 486; Richard Hubberthorne to Edward Burrough, Cambridge gaol, 27 September 1654, Sw Trs 2: 564; George Taylor and Thomas Willan to Margaret Fell, Kendal Accounts 1654; Sw Mss 1: 208. *The immediate call to the ministry of the Gospel* was purchased by George Thomason on 26 September 1654. Twenty shillings would have paid for about 160 copies of the tract.

public debate with the local Baptists. The debate was bungled, both sides finding themselves locked out of the church they had booked for the dispute, and harassed by a 'rude multitude' of angry scholars. Burrough and Howgill, fearing that 'the truth should have suffered', sent for Quakers from the outlying area and held a meeting at a friend's house in Cambridge.[34]

Outside the town, they had more success. The next day, they held a large and successful meeting in Littleport, and then rode back to Ely where they reported a meeting of about seven hundred people. This was attended by two Independent ministers, who reported the meeting to Colonel Russell, a relative of Cromwell, who invited the Quakers to a meeting at his house. Here, Burrough reported in a letter to Margaret Fell, they were received 'cheerfully' and the Colonel's wife was 'struck down' by the truth of their arguments. Russell then organised a further dispute before the local Independent congregation, where the Quakers 'spoke powerfully', and the ministers hung their heads in shame, and the 'peoples hartes was raysed up in Love to us'.[35]

Despite the initial concentration of activity in Cambridge itself, the subsequent consolidation of Quaker meetings thus drew much more specifically from Independent churches and gathered congregations from the outlying areas. These were now frequently visited by itinerant ministers, and duly featured in their publications. James Parnell returned to Littleport in May 1655, where a meeting of Quakers held in an orchard was interrupted by three Baptist preachers from Wickhambrook in Suffolk. The Baptists were intent on the excommunication of former elders from their church who had gone to Littleport to join the Quakers. Events in Littleport had now reached such a pitch that Parnell published an account of the meeting in a tract, naming both the new Quaker recruits, and the forsaken Baptists.[36] Edward Burrough and Francis Howgill returned to meetings in Ely and Cambridgeshire in June 1655; and were followed there in July by George Fox who visited the area on his way to Derbyshire.[37]

From Cambridge gaol, James Parnell had also sent queries into Huntingdonshire, to Thomas Drayton, the 'perfectionist' minister of Abbots Ripton, and to the Baptist leaders of Fenstanton.[38] He was released from Cambridge gaol in March 1655, and went to Fenstanton to follow up the dispute, staying with a local sympathiser and disputing with the Baptist preacher. Both the

---

[34] Francis Howgill and Edward Burrough to Margaret Fell, London, 30 April 1655, Caton Mss 3, pp. 152–54.

[35] *Ibid.*

[36] James Parnell, *The watcher: or, the stone cut out* (London 1655), STC P541, sigs. F3r–G3r.

[37] Edward Burrough and Francis Howgill to Margaret Fell, London, 1 July 1655, Sw Mss 1: 86; Braithwaite, *Beginnings of Quakerism*, p. 201.

[38] For Thomas Drayton as a 'Perfectionist' see Geoffrey Nuttall, 'James Nayler: a fresh approach', 7–8.

Fenstanton and the Abbots Ripton disputes were subsequently published by Parnell, again naming the new recruits and denouncing their former congregations.[39] In June 1656, Richard Hubberthorne, travelling with Ann Wilson and Elizabeth Coward on their way to Rutland, retraced Parnell's route, holding meetings in Kings Ripton and claiming great success there.[40] Gradually, at the initiation of the itinerant ministers, local meetings of Quakers were established across Cambridgeshire. They were maintained by a careful flow of visits from itinerant ministers, orchestrated from London and from Swarthmoor Hall, and by tracts published by ministers describing the critical local disputes by which members of new Quaker meetings were formally distinguished from their previous co-religionists.[41]

The national network of Quaker ministers which sustained the infiltration of Quaker ideas in Cambridge and its surrounding areas operated with equal intensity as Quaker ministers moved north and east into Norfolk and Suffolk. The tactics of Quaker ministers in Norfolk, indeed, sustain the argument that the spread of Quaker ideas was achieved through a national campaign.

Richard Hubberthorne travelled towards Norwich straight from Cambridge in October 1654, and was arrested before he got there, for preaching in the church at Wymondham just outside Norwich. His arrival in this church may have been fortuitous: Wymondham is on the road between Cambridge and Norwich; but it was also apt. The minister there was a typical Quaker target: a former leader of a Congregational church at Norwich, who had been installed as minister in the new church at Wymondham formed in the parochial reforms of 1652.[42] Hubberthorne was arrested for speaking after the sermon, and taken to Norwich.

From prison in Norwich, Hubberthorne wrote to George Fox and James Nayler asking for reinforcements.[43] These came initially from ministers

---

[39] James Parnell, *The watcher, or the stone cut out* (London, 1655), STC P541, pp. 27–41; [Thomas Drayton], *An answer according to truth* (London, 1655), STC D2147; James Parnell, *Goliah's head cut off with his own sword* (London, 1655), STC P531, pp. 1–85.

[40] Richard Hubberthorne to Margaret Fell, Kings Ripton, 21 June 1656, Sw Trs 2: 595.

[41] Laurel Phillipson has pointed out that Quakers, rather than seeking recruits from Baptist and Independent churches alike, were actually in competition with Baptists to win over faltering Independent congregations. If this is so, it reflects in an interesting way in the records of the Quakers. Internal letters certainly suggest success amongst Independents like Colonel Russell; while it is striking that the published Quaker tracts focus almost exclusively on Baptists and their defection to the Quakers. This would indeed suggest that Quaker 'propaganda' was deeply concerned to convey the impression that Baptists were succumbing to Quaker ideas. Laurel Phillipson, 'Quakerism in Cambridge before the Act of Toleration', 1–25.

[42] Hubberthorne stated that he was arrested for speaking after the service at Wymondham in a tract of his sufferings published soon afterwards: Richard Hubberthorne, James Lancaster and Christopher Atkinson, *The testimony of the everlasting gospel witnessed through sufferings* [?Norwich], (1654), STC H3237, p. 2. The vicar of the church, John Money, is identified in A. G. Matthews (ed.), *Calamy revised* (Oxford, 1934), pp. 351–52.

[43] Richard Hubberthorne to George Fox, Norwich gaol, 13 November 1654, Sw Trs 2: 567; Hubberthorne to Fox, Norwich 25 June 1655, Sw Trs 2: 685.

already in the locality. By November he had been joined by James Lancaster, travelling from Cambridge; and by George Whitehead and Christopher Atkinson, two Westmorland preachers, both of whom travelled to Norwich from London. Hubberthorne also asked Margaret Fell in Swarthmoor Hall, Lancashire, to organise reinforcements. On 24 January 1655, two more itinerant Quaker ministers, Dorothy Waugh and George Fell, son of Margaret and Thomas, both arrived directly from Kendal, the expenses incurred in their journey being duly noted in the Kendal accounts.[44]

The support network for Quaker ministers in Norwich stretched from Lancashire to London. As in Cambridge, Richard Hubberthorne and fellow ministers endured considerable hostility in the city itself. The only Quaker converts in Norwich, according to Hubberthorne, were 'ranters and astroligers' who quickly turned away from the light and back to 'filthy reason'.[45] More successful inroads were made into gathered churches in the outlying areas. Before his imprisonment, Hubberthorne had clearly secured the sympathy of Captain John Laurence in Wramplingham, just outside Norwich. A local Norwich weaver, Thomas Symonds, had already heard, and warmed to, the Quaker ideas propounded by Ann Blaykling at Stourbridge Fair, and was thus both a sympathetic recipient to Quakers in Norwich, and could direct Quakers to other likely communities in the area. Ann Blaykling visited specific communities in the west of Norfolk: when she was arrested she was found to be carrying papers which included information about local roads and the names of contacts.[46] George Whitehead and Christopher Atkinson travelled to Norwich from London through Essex and Ipswich, stopping over in Woodbridge and Mendlesham on the way. Here, they visited a local community of Seekers, headed by Thomas Symonds's brother-in-law, where they left Quaker tracts and also initiated a dispute with a local preacher in Mendlesham which was later published.[47]

The modest inroads made by itinerant Quaker ministers in the counties of Norfolk and Suffolk contrasted nevertheless with their reception in the city of Norwich.[48] Here, Hubberthorne reported that the local priests and

---

[44] Richard Hubberthorne noted their arrival in a letter to Margaret Fell, 1 February 1655, Sw Trs 2: 580; George Taylor and Thomas Willan, Accounts, 1654, Sw Mss 1: 208.

[45] Richard Hubberthorne to Margaret Fell, Norwich, 1 February 1655, Sw Trs 2: 579.

[46] Vann, *Social development of English Quakerism*, pp. 10–11.

[47] For Thomas Symonds, see Vann, *Social development of Quakerism*, p. 13. Atkinson, Whitehead and Hubberthorne conducted a dispute with Frederick Woodall, the Fifth Monarchist congregational pastor of Woodbridge, Suffolk. Christopher Atkinson *et al.*, *Davids enemies discovered* (London, 1655), STC A4126; Richard Hubberthorne, *The innocency of the righteous seed of God* (London, 1655), STC 3226. Woodall was reputed to be 'A strict Independent, and zealous for the fifth monarchy', Walker, *Calamy revised*, pp. 542–43. William Braithwaite stated that prior to his arrival in Norwich, George Whitehead convinced a community of Seekers in Woodbridge, led by two Suffolk members of the Nominated Parliament, Robert Duncon and Edward Plumstead. Braithwaite, *Beginnings of Quakerism*, pp. 163–64.

[48] Richard Vann estimates that there were 41 Quakers in Norwich in 1662, compared to 217 in the rest of the county. This contrasts with 265 Quakers in Colchester, and a total of 1,283

magistrates were 'very darke and sottish', and that the citizens of Norwich were 'the most wrangelinge mischefous envious malitious people that ever I came amongest'.[49] As in Cambridge, the Quaker ministers used their writings to supplement their preaching, and to communicate their ideas to a wider audience than they could reach in person. The importation of books and papers was an important part of the Quakers' ministry. When James Parnell ventured into Essex in the summer of 1655, he was found on his arrest to be carrying 'heretical, false, scandalous papers, writings and pamphlets'.[50] From prison in Norwich, Hubberthorne's ministry depended on writing. When 'the deceipt got up' in one would-be convert in the city, Hubberthorne sent for him,

but his wife was in rage and watched him and would not suffer him to come out and sent for prists . . . and when I could not get to speake to him I wrote to him: to Judge the false prophet which was gott up in him but before it gott to him the deceipt had gott him out of his condition . . . and now is led by the will of sattan to render the truth odious.[51]

In addition to ministerial aid, Hubberthorne also requested books. Prior to his journey to Norwich in November 1654, Christopher Atkinson collected books worth £3 10s. from the bookseller Giles Calvert, and carried them with him.[52] From these, there stemmed pamphlet disputes in Mendlesham, Woodbridge and Norwich itself; while local Quakers in Mendlesham later claimed that Quaker books had been an important part of their conversion.[53]

Following the influx of books and ministers into Norwich, the Quaker campaign in the city again followed familiar lines. One by one the ministers were arrested and imprisoned: Hubberthorne for refusing to take off his hat in court; Atkinson for holding an illegal Quaker meeting on a Sunday; James Lancaster for speaking in the market square. Three days after her arrival in the city, Dorothy Waugh was arrested for speaking publicly in the market square.[54] As before, the series of ensuing court appearances and

---

Quakers in the county of Essex, in the decade 1655–1664. Vann, *Social development of Quakerism*, p. 93; T. A. Davies, 'The Quakers in Essex 1655–1725', p. 35.

[49] Hubberthorne to Fell, Norwich, 1 February 1655, Sw Trs 2: 579; Hubberthorne to Fell, Norwich, 15 March 1655, Sw Trs 2: 581.

[50] T. A. Davies, 'The Quakers in Essex', pp. 164–65.

[51] Hubberthorne to George Fox, Norwich gaol, 13 November 1654, Sw Trs 2: 567.

[52] More accurately, he borrowed £3 10s. from Calvert, who was later reimbursed from the Kendal Fund. George Taylor and Thomas Willan to Margaret Fell, Kendal, 14 October 1654, Sw Mss 1: 209; Taylor and Willan Accounts, 1654, Sw Mss 1: 208.

[53] George Whitehead, *The Christian Progress of . . . George Whitehead* (London, 1725), p. 31.

[54] Richard Hubberthorne to 'friends at Swarthmoor', Norwich gaol, 21 December 1654, Sw Trs 2: 571–72; Hubberthorne to Margaret Fell, Norwich gaol, 1 February 1655, Sw Trs 2: 580.

confrontations were compiled by the incarcerated ministers into a published tract.[55]

Even more than in Cambridge, the ministers depended on external support for the publication of their sufferings. A major objection of the authorities in Norwich, as in Cambridge, was that the Quakers were outsiders. Christopher Atkinson and James Lancaster were both closely questioned on their grounds for coming to Norwich, and the extent and nature of their 'outward means'.[56] If the prisoners were without financial support, they could be forced to leave the town as vagrants. Rather than trying to get the ministers to leave Norwich altogether, however, the authorities seemed intent on keeping them incarcerated. According to Hubberthorne, their grounds for doing so were weak. Several letters passed from Norwich to Swarthmoor and Kendal with accounts of the legal charges against the Quakers, which were unclear to the Quaker ministers, and certainly not elucidated by the city authorities. Following the Quarter Sessions of January 1655, Richard Hubberthorne informed Fell that his case had been postponed to the next hearing; and remarked that the authorities 'plott and devise how to keepe us in prison'.[57] In addition to the legal advice of Judge Thomas Fell, the prisoners were also financially supported from Swarthmoor.[58] When James Lancaster and George Whitehead were released from gaol, the authorities charged them board at a rate of seven shillings per week for the time they had spent in prison. Consultations between Norwich, Swarthmoor and Kendal resulted in the sum of £2 being sent to them to help pay the bill.[59]

The plight of the Norwich prisoners was complicated by the fact that communications between Swarthmoor and Norwich were difficult, Thomas Willan in Kendal reporting that Hubberthorne's letters had been tampered with by the postmaster.[60] Eventually letters were sent via London, and carried to the Norwich prisoners in person by Quakers from the capital.[61] The contact between London Quakers and the Norwich prisoners led to more intensified resistance to the Norwich authorities. The London Quakers promised to take copies of the indictments to London to publish them in the 'face of the nation wheare it is like our adversaries would be

---

[55] Richard Hubberthorne *et al.*, *The testimony of the everlasting gospel* [Norwich], (1654), *STC* H3237. This is remarkably consistent with their manuscript accounts.

[56] *The testimony of the everlasting gospel*, pp. 4–7.

[57] Richard Hubberthorne to Margaret Fell, 17 January 1655, Sw Trs 2: 577; Hubberthorne to Fell, 1 February 1655, Sw Trs 2: 579.

[58] *Ibid.*; Sw Trs 2: 550–51.

[59] Richard Hubberthorne to George Fox, Norwich, 2 April 1655, Sw Trs 2: 549; George Taylor and Thomas Willan to Margaret Fell [1654/5?], Sw Mss 1: 218; George Taylor, Kendal accounts, 29 April 1655, Sw Mss 1: 215.

[60] Thomas Willan to Margaret Fell, 1654, Sw Mss 1: 222.

[61] Richard Hubberthorne to Margaret Fell, Sw Trs 2: 579–80.

ashamed to appeare'.[62] At the same time, the London Quakers met both privately and in court with the magistrates at the April Sessions. Shortly thereafter, Hubberthorne too was released from gaol and continued his ministry in Norwich and its hinterland, indicating that the city authorities had been forced to back down considerably.

It is significant, in this context, that the tract produced by the Norwich prisoners, as well as recording their harsh treatment in Norwich, made a very open appeal to the government in London:

> Now these things being acted in the name of the Law, and the present government, and Lord Protector, and Rulers and heads of the Nation, being ignorant of what tyranny and persecution is acted privately in their Names, Therefore I am moved of the Lord to declare it Publictly [*sic*], that the heads and Rulers of the nation may see and consider whether any such tyranny be Protected to be set up in the Nation instead of the Law of justice: for the innocent doth cry for equity and justice in their Courts and Sessions, but in stead thereof tyranny, persecution, and cruelty, so having discharged my duty in clearing my conscience to you before the Lord: the sin lyes at your doores, who hath a power put into your hands.[63]

The experience of the Norwich prisoners in 1654 and 1655 provides ample evidence that they were part of a much wider national campaign. They received legal and financial support from Lancashire; and very significant advice and reinforcement from London. There was a steady flow of Quaker ministers into Norwich throughout the period of their imprisonment. Yet the geographical scope of Quaker involvement with events in Norwich is not merely a reflection of a national campaign able to support its ministers in the harsher cities. The Norwich pamphlet, which may unusually have been printed in Norwich, clearly did more than announce the presence of Quakers to the city itself; it also contributed to a wider Quaker plea to the Protectorate and the national government to strengthen its reform of the provinces.[64] There was thus a two-way process of homogenisation of the Quaker movement. Quakers coming from outside carried, in their tracts and preaching, a coherent and uniform message to localities; their experiences in the localities in turn were formative to the national profile of the Quaker movement.

The infiltration of Quaker ideas into East Anglia was orchestrated as part of a national campaign by itinerant Quaker ministers who were simultaneously active in an area bordered by Scotland, Devon and Kent. By the summer of 1655, Quakers were in Yarmouth on their way to Holland; and

---

[62] Richard Hubberthorne to George Fox, 2 April 1655, Sw Trs 2: 550.
[63] *The testimony of the everlasting gospel*, p. 3.
[64] The second edition of Wing's *STC* states that *The testimony of the everlasting gospel* was published in Norwich, although there is no reference to this on the copy of the tract in the Thomason Tract collection.

in Bristol on their way to Ireland. The sources generated by the itinerant ministers in the course of their ministry highlight the priorities of the campaigners. They recorded their routes, and their whereabouts. They asked for legal and financial aid, for reinforcement from other Quaker ministers, and for printed books. In East Anglia, as elsewhere, they developed a consistent body of ministers: Richard Hubberthorne, George Whitehead, James Lancaster, Ann Blaykling, James Parnell, Elizabeth Coward and Christopher Atkinson – all northerners – conducted the bulk of the Quaker ministry in East Anglia. The targets of the Quakers were clear: Baptist and Independent churches, and congregational ministers, found in the hinterland of the local urban headquarters from which the ministers operated. Yet the response of the East Anglian Quaker laity is missing. This in itself is significant. We know from later records that Quaker meetings were successfully established in the 1650s in Essex, Suffolk and Norfolk; and that these meetings continued to grow into the 1680s. We also know from the work of Adrian Davies that there was a strong continuity between religious dissenters in the 1630s and '40s, and subsequent Quaker convincement. That these people remained absent from ministerial accounts of their work denotes a highly systematic missionary campaign which focused on disseminating ideas, and establishing an organisational framework to enable the sustenance of local meetings. The use of printed tracts was a key element in the process of generating a national movement. Ministers presented a coherent and homogeneous message to audiences across East Anglia, preaching from papers and leaving books behind them. In due course, the East Anglian experiences of Quaker ministers, and new local recruits, were themselves incorporated into Quaker publications, and hence into the machinery of the national preaching ministry.

Part II

Identity and discipline

4

'The Quakers quaking':[1] the printed identity of the movement

Printed tracts were instrumental to the rapid establishment of a visible 'Quaker' movement in the early 1650s. The tracts proclaimed an unambiguous 'Quaker' identity, under which the main body of authors was assimilated, and common beliefs were reiterated. The most striking way in which this coherent identity was achieved was through constant printed references to 'Quakers' and 'quaking'. Quaker authors at a very early date appropriated their own nickname, and explored the meanings behind it at great length in their publications. Combined with the extensive itinerant preaching and meticulous organisation which underpinned the movement between 1652 and 1656, the sheer bulk of printed tracts which disseminated the notion of a 'Quaker' movement played a central role in establishing so rapidly that Quakers were a national movement and a force to be reckoned with.

   This self-promulgation had a profound effect in consolidating the history of the Quakers. As early as 1659, Edward Burrough claimed that his movement had first begun seven years earlier in 1652, the date when the first tracts were published.[2] Early eighteenth-century dictionary references to 'Quakers' dated the movement's origins quite precisely to 1650 or 1652.[3] The presbyterian bookseller Thomas Underhill estimated that there had been as many as 150,000 Quakers in the year 1655.[4] The movement's solid origins are

---

[1] A version of this chapter appeared as an essay in Susan Wabuda and Caroline Litzenberger (eds.), *Belief and practice in Reformation England: a tribute to Patrick Collinson by his students* (Aldershot, 1998), pp. 250–67. The 'Quakers quaking' was actually from the title of a tract published against the Quakers in 1656: Jeremiah Ives, *The Quakers quaking and their foundations shaken* (London, 1656), STC I1103. Many other tracts made similar play on the nickname: see for example Ralph Hall, *Quakers principles quaking* (London, 1656), STC H423; Ellis Bradshaw, *The Quakers quaking principles examined* (London, 1656), STC B4147.

[2] Edward Burrough, in George Fox, *The great mistery of the great whore unfolded* (London, 1659), STC F1832, sig. b4v.

[3] R. S. Mortimer, 'Some notes on early dictionary references to Quakers', *JFHS* 43 (1951), 29–34.

[4] Thomas Underhill, *Hell broke loose: or, an history of the Quakers both old and new* (London, 1660), STC U43, p. 14.

reflected too in historical assessments of its importance.[5] Part of this certainty about the importance of the Quaker movement undoubtedly stems from its subsequent survival, and from the Quakers' chronicling of their own history. But it is also clear that from 1652 onwards Quaker leaders sought to establish a coherent and recognisable 'Quaker' identity through the medium of their tracts. This chapter will examine how the printed tracts contributed to a systematic and self-conscious development of the 'Quaker' movement, epitomised by the appropriation of the very term 'Quaker' as a collective name.[6]

The importance of arguing that the Quakers' own tracts contributed to the rapid formation of a 'Quaker' identity lies in the current historical concern over the identity of the Ranters, whom some hostile contemporaries portrayed as the precursors of the Quakers.[7] In 1986, Colin Davis argued that the Ranters were an historical 'myth', invented by contemporaries, in particular by the royalist yellow press, seeking to manipulate popular fear and dissatisfaction with the Commonwealth government. The main evidence for the existence of the Ranters, Davis argued, came from publications explicitly denouncing them as dangerous misfits: the writings usually considered

[5] For Aylmer the Quakers are 'the most serious and remarkable' of the sects G. E. Aylmer, *The interregnum: the quest for settlement 1646–1660* (London, 1974), p. 13; for Morrill, they are the 'most important', John Morrill, *The nature of the English revolution* (London, 1993), pp. 25–26; Derek Hirst states that 'more than any other group, the Quakers made a reality of the sectarian challenge', *Authority and conflict: England 1603–1658* (London, 1986), p. 344; Ronald Hutton also thought that the Quakers 'more than any other' were the cause of political unrest. Ronald Hutton, *The British republic, 1649–1660* (London, 1990), p. 70.

[6] Strictly speaking, the term 'Quaker' should appear in inverted commas throughout this chapter. However, since the whole thesis is concerned with the developing historical identity of the 'Quaker movement', it seemed arduous and ultimately unnecessary always to refer to them within inverted commas. I therefore use the term 'Quaker' when explicitly referring to its constructed identity, and dispense with the inverted commas when using the term in an adjectival sense.

[7] Henoch Howet, *Quaking principles dashed in pieces* (London, 1655), STC H3152, p. 18; Thomas Ledger juxtaposed Quakers and Ranters: George Bateman, *An answer to vindicate the cause of the nicknamed Quakers* [n.p., 1654], STC B1094, p. 14; Edmund Skipp described the 'uncomfortable fraternity of Quakers and Ranters' as the progenitor of the Seekers: Edmund Skipp, *The world's wonder, or, the Quakers blazing star* (London, 1655), STC S3949, pp. 59–63. In 1655, the Lichfield congregational leader Thomas Pollard denounced Quakers and Ranters together with all other 'Reproachers of God': Thomas Pollard and Henry Haggar, *The Holy Scripture clearing itself of scandals* (London, 1655), STC P2775. See also Ralph Farmer, *The great mysteries of godlinesse and ungodlinesse* (London, 1655), STC F441, p. 29. Richard Baxter thought Ranters and Quakers were almost identical, except that the Quakers practised 'austere morality' while the Ranters exercised 'all abominable filthiness of Life': cited in J. C. Davis, *Fear, myth and history: the Ranters and the historians* (Cambridge, 1986), p. 92. Thomas Underhill considered that the Quakers had risen in the Ranters' stead after the latter had been broken by the Blasphemy Act: Thomas Underhill, *Hell broke loose: or, an history of the Quakers*, p. 15. The author of the fifth edition of Ephraim Pagitt's *Heresiography* considered that Ranters and Quakers were contemporaries, both 'of the same puddle', *Heresiography* (5th edn, London, 1654), STC P188, p. 143.

to be by 'Ranters', he claimed, were a sketchy and an incoherent collection of ideas, produced by a body of men whose association was uncertain.[8]

The very concrete nature of the 'Quaker movement' historically makes the study of the labelling of the movement an interesting exercise: the label 'Quaker' corresponded to a coherent movement, and yet the relationship between the label and the movement has not been established. While 'Ranters' were nebulous, and arguably abstract, historical identities, Quakers were far more tangible: historians have very few qualms even when it comes to counting them.[9] Because the existence of 'Quakers' is apparently incontrovertible, the process of their labelling can be examined. As with puritans, Ranters and Levellers, 'Quaker' was a pejorative term appended by their enemies. What is striking is that the Quakers themselves embraced this pejorative nickname with alacrity; and, furthermore, that it is this self-labelling which allowed both contemporaries and historians to identify the movement, its leaders and its ideas with such clarity.

Quaker historiography has paid surprisingly little attention to the actual development of the term 'Quaker'. Although the Temporary Subject Catalogue at Friends' House Library considers in some detail the first usage of the more sober term 'Society of Friends', which dates from the late eighteenth century,[10] for the term 'Quaker' it cites only from the *Oxford English Dictionary*. This is a reference to a letter of intelligence from Secretary Nicholas, dated 1647, which records a 'sect of woemen' at Southwark who 'come from beyond sea, called quakers; and these swell, shiver and shake'. The women were thought in this state to have been conversing with Mohammed's holy spirit, and when they came to afterwards they were said to

---

[8] Davis, *Fear, myth and history*. This book received a number of critical reviews, which are listed and responded to in J. C. Davis, 'Fear, myth and furore: reappraising the "Ranters"', *Past and Present* 129 (1990), 79–103. The debate continued in *Past and Present* 140 (1993), 155–210.

[9] Attempts to count the Quakers are strongest for the period following the Restoration, when Quaker meetings and records of membership were established. Barry Reay, however, has made a retrospective study from these records, and from the Hearth Tax returns, to assess the numbers of Quakers in the 1650s: Reay, 'Early Quaker activity', pp. 218–20. See also Richard Vann, *The social development of English Quakerism, 1655–1755* (Cambridge, Mass., 1969) and R. T. Vann and David Eversley, *Friends in life and death: the British and Irish Quakers in the demographic transition* (Cambridge, 1992). An impressive local study exists in the work of William Stephenson, 'The economic and social status of protestant sectarians in Huntingdonshire, Cambridgeshire and Bedfordshire (1650–1725)', unpublished Ph.D thesis, University of Cambridge, 1990.

[10] The Temporary Subject Catalogue at Friends' Library (under the heading 'Friend') cites from the General Epistle of the Yearly Meeting of 1781, which referred to 'every humble member of our religious society'; and notes that the first official use of the term 'Religious Society of Friends' is thought to be in the 1793 address to George III. The Temporary Subject Catalogue also notes that the terms 'Children of light' or 'Children of God' were the earliest collective names used when addressing the outside world.

preach what the spirit had delivered to them.[11] William Braithwaite believed that this was not a reference to 'Friends', presumably because, as we know, the 'real' Quaker movement began in the Midlands and north of England with the followers of George Fox.[12] Nevertheless, these early female Quakers were reported in a letter which also described the 'anti-monarchical' sentiments of the army at the Putney Debates, and the upsurge in sectarian activity during the Commons' vote on toleration.[13] 'Quakers' made their first historical appearance at one of the more politically charged moments of English history, when fears of sectaries were very high. It is clear that the term 'quaker' could be generically applied to anyone who engaged in ecstatic religious worship, and that the word was not specifically coined to describe Fox and his followers.

The successful appropriation of the term by Quaker leaders, and its importance in establishing their own significance, is illustrated by a rather bizarre entry in George Fox's *Journal*. The *Journal* was compiled in the 1670s and 1680s, and published posthumously in 1694: it consists not merely of Fox's narrative account, as Fox dictated to his step son-in-law Thomas Lower, but is also interspersed with extracts from Fox's own contemporary writings and edicts.[14] The first of these extracts concerns an occasion in October 1650, when Fox and his followers were reputedly first labelled as 'Quakers'. Having spoken at length after a public lecture in Derby, Fox was examined and subsequently imprisoned by two Derby magistrates, Gervase Bennett and Nathaniel Barton: during the examination, Gervase Bennett reputedly called Fox and his companions 'Quakers' because of Fox's insistence that they should tremble at the name of the Lord. William Braithwaite agreed

---

[11] Bodleian Library, Clarendon State Papers 2624, MSS Clarendon vol. xxx, fol. 140r. This is remarkably similar to the spiritual ecstasy of the Quakers, who were also thought by contemporaries to be conversing with Mohammed: Thomas Welde and William Cole *et al.*, *The perfect pharise under monkish holines* (London, 1654), STC c5045a, p. 42.

[12] W. C. Braithwaite, *The beginnings of Quakerism* (Cambridge, 1955), p. 57. The fact that the reference was to a group of women may also have convinced Braithwaite that these could not possibly be his own 'Quakers', although from what is known about the preponderance of women in both the Quaker movement and other religious sects of the time, it would not be safe to conclude positively that they had nothing to do with the subsequent Quaker movement. A short article by Henry Cadbury discusses the reference, and concludes that it is indeed the earliest reference to 'Quaker': H. J. Cadbury, 'Early use of the word "Quaker"' *JFHS* 49:1 (1959), 3–5.

[13] MSS Clarendon vol. xxx, fols. 139r, 140r.

[14] Edmund T. Harvey's Introduction in *The Journal of George Fox*, ed. Norman Penney (2 vols., Cambridge, 1911), vol. I, pp. xxxi–xlii; *The Journal of George Fox*, ed. John L. Nickalls (London, 1975), pp. vii–xxxvii. Much has been written about the literary structures and devices which shaped Fox's *Journal*; Thomas Corns most recently has convincingly cautioned against attributing too much literary strategy to it: Corns, '"No man's copy": the critical problem of Fox's Journal', in Thomas Corns and David Loewenstein (eds.), *The emergence of Quaker writing: dissenting literature in seventeenth-century England* (London, 1995), pp. 99–111.

with Fox that this was a decisive moment in Quaker history: 'the derisive name at once came into vogue'.[15]

Fox and his co-religionists were not entirely passive in the process of making 'Quakers' modish. A paper sent by Fox to Gervase Bennett, denouncing him and his imprisonment of Fox, is included in the *Journal;* dated 1650, Fox's paper establishes without doubt that enormous significance was attached to Bennett's phrase:

oh man what has thou sowen in the nation how many Reprochers scoffers and mockers through Every towne in the nation, hast thou begotten . . . for thou was the first man that gave the children of god that name of quakers, and soe it was spread over the nation.[16]

It is clear that this address to Gervase Bennett was not written in 1650. Bennett alone could not have been responsible for the spread of the term 'through Every towne in the nation', and certainly not by October 1650. The inclusion and mis-dating of Fox's address in the *Journal* is indicative of the fact that it was a retrospective compilation of documents relating to Fox's participation in the Quaker movement over a period of forty years. It is more probable that the letter to Bennett was written in 1653 or 1654, just as Quaker pamphleteering and the movement were gaining momentum and acquiring national significance. That Fox and his Quaker followers had caused a stir in the Midlands in 1650 was suggested by the Cheshire congregational leader Samuel Eaton. Writing in late 1653, Eaton confirmed that 'about three years since' he had travelled through Nottingham, where he had met with 'many reports respecting a People who are called Quakers, concerning Sorcery and witchcraft that should be among them'.[17] Another hostile pamphleteer, the Westmorland minister Francis Higginson, also harked back to 1650 when he described the Derby trial in a pamphlet published in 1653.[18] In 1653, then, memories of Fox's Derby trial were current, and undergoing a revival in print. In response to Higginson's tract of 1653, two Lancashire Quakers, Robert Widders and James Taylor, travelled to Derby in order to collect their own slanderous accounts of Justice Gervase Bennett (which now were added a certain political piquancy as Bennett was a member of the Barebones Parliament), as well as a copy of the 1650 *mittimus*. Their account of this journey, and the *mittimus* by which Fox had been arrested, were included in a subsequent tract, published in 1654, the main body of which

---

[15] Braithwaite, *Beginnings of Quakerism*, p. 57. See pp. 53–57 for Braithwaite's account of the incident at Derby.

[16] Fox, *Journal of George Fox*, ed. Penney (Cambridge, 1911 edn), vol. I, p. 6.

[17] Samuel Eaton, *The Quakers confuted* (London, 1653), STC E125, sig. A4v.

[18] Francis Higginson, *A brief relation of the irreligion of the northern Quakers* (London, 1653), STC H1953.

was actually a response to Samuel Eaton.[19] It is more than likely that this was the occasion on which Fox saw fit to denounce Gervase Bennett as the 'father of mockers scoffers and scorners' who had 'first' used the Quakers' derisive nickname.[20] Given the hindsight with which Fox was writing, this is an important example of the appropriation of the term 'Quaker' by the movement's leaders. At least two hostile pamphleteers identified events in the Midlands in 1650 as a significant landmark in the history of 'Quakers': George Fox emphasised its significance by drawing attention to the derisive nickname.

The use of nicknames to identify sects or movements in the context of early modern religion is usually seen as an indicator of the attitudes of early modern society as a whole. All participants in the 'Ranter' debate agree that the terms 'Ranter' or 'ranting' were in origin hostile, generic and essentially ambiguous, attributed to people or ideas which were understood as threatening to social norms.[21] Patrick Collinson has shown that the term 'puritan' is deeply problematic, applied at different times and in different circumstances to different people. Labelling of groups identified as outsiders or representing 'otherness' is understood as the prerogative of the majority who stood outside those groups. English society expressed itself in terms of binary oppositions: the appearance of puritans, 'papists' and ranters reveals more about society at large than about the nature or coherence of the supposed groupings themselves.[22]

What, therefore, is interesting about the Quakers is their own, concerted response to their nickname. Quaker authors argued persistently that the donning of a nickname confirmed that they were the 'people of the Lord': it enhanced their status as true prophetic figures who were bound to be rejected by the profane and the ungodly. In their tracts, Quaker authors devoted considerable time and effort over the significance of their denunciation as 'Quakers'. Furthermore, although the term 'Quaker' already had some currency from 1647 or 1650, the initiative in publicly applying it to the people and ideas associated with Fox and his co-religionists clearly came from Quaker authors themselves. In his paper to Bennett, Fox was

---

[19] [John Camm], *An answer to a book which Samuel Eaton put up to the Parliament* (London, 1654), *STC* c389, pp. 51–55.

[20] Other details in Fox's paper suggest that it was written just after the end of the Barebones Parliament, which also fits in with the chronology of the printed exchange with Samuel Eaton. Fox, *Journal of George Fox*, ed. Penney, vol. I, pp. 5–7.

[21] Davis, *Fear, myth and history*, pp. 17–21; Davis, 'Fear, myth and furore', *Past and Present* 140 (1993), pp. 155–56, 165, 172, 179–80, 192, 195–96.

[22] Patrick Collinson, *The puritan character: polemics and polarities in early seventeenth-century English culture* (William Andrews Clark Memorial Library, Los Angeles, 1989); Peter Lake, 'Anti-popery: the structure of a prejudice' in Richard Cust and Ann Hughes (eds.), *Conflict in early Stuart England* (London, 1989), pp. 72–106.

insistent that the nickname was innovative, but not the phenomenon to which it referred, reminding Gervase Bennett that 'Long before thou In scorne called them quakers', the 'people of the Lord god' had been well known around 'Mansfield Notingham, and sume parts of Lester sheare, and ther Abouts'.[23]

There is a very strong sense of community expressed between Quaker leaders from the first surviving letters. Although it is known that significant links between Quaker leaders existed before the summer of 1652, when Fox travelled to Swarthmoor Hall, it is nevertheless this momentous journey, and Fox's account of his own spiritual wanderings beforehand, which form the traditional narrative for the beginnings of 'Quakerism'. In part, this is an archival beginning. Over the summer of 1652 two Quaker leaders, Margaret Fell at Swarthmoor, and Elizabeth Hooton in York gaol, began to keep copies of their letters and papers. By the end of the year, the first pamphlets had been printed. The survival of these documents is in itself suggestive of a growing sense of group cohesion. In the letters themselves, the unity between Quaker leaders is very clear: 'Praise my dearest thou art mine and I am thine, lett us live together, I am with thee and thou art with mee, none cann break the Unyon', wrote Farnworth to Fox; on another occasion Farnworth sent his 'deare love to all deare babes and Lambes And faithfull Frends' at Swarthmoor Hall.[24] The words used by the Quaker leaders to describe their own brethren are most often 'fellowship', 'union', 'family' and 'friends': 'You are all deare to me in the grace of god which hath united us together and given us feloship one with another', wrote Richard Hubberthorne from Chester to Margaret Fell and friends at Swarthmoor Hall, going on to ask for letters to be sent to him which would reinforce his sense of 'the power of my father in you'.[25] Richard Farnworth instructed James Nayler and friends in Balby to 'walke in humblenes, before the lord, and to be of the household of god, even of the famillie of love'.[26] 'To you all the deare famaly of love my love is rune into you all,' wrote Richard Hubberthorne in the summer of 1652, 'you are my relations: father, mother, sisters and brothers, which I must now own: and dwell with in unitie and love.'[27] Such a sense of 'family' unity with his co-religionists compares strikingly with the sentiments of William

---

[23] Fox, *Journal of George Fox*, ed. Penney, vol. I, p. 7.

[24] Richard Farnworth to George Fox and James Nayler, Sedburgh, November 1652, Sw Mss 3: 58; Farnworth to Margaret Fell, Balby, 8 June 1653, Sw Mss 3: 46.

[25] Richard Hubberthorne to Margaret Fell, Chester prison [January 1654], Sw Trs 1: 340.

[26] Richard Farnworth to James Nayler and others, Balby, 6 July 1652, Sw Mss 1: 372. The term 'family of love' occurs more than once in the private correspondence between Quakers to describe their own unity. William Caton, in a letter to Fell in the troubled summer of 1656 (in the lead up to Nayler's 'fall'), wrote 'when I am with our beloved, in the injoyment of him, I enjoy thee & the rest of the famelly of love, of which he is the head' (Sw Mss 1: 313).

[27] Richard Hubberthorne to G[eorge] F[ox], [June/July 1652], Sw Mss 4: 4.

Dewsbery towards his actual family members, who reported to Margaret Fell in the summer of 1654 that his own work in the Lord had gone from strength to strength 'sinc my desposing of the Famally that was on mee in the outward'.[28]

The sense of themselves as 'Quakers' clearly arises from their perception of their relationship with the outside world. In August or September 1652, Richard Farnworth described a visit to York in a letter to George Fox and James Nayler. 'Friends', he wrote, 'are close shutt up in prison' and Farnworth had not been allowed to see them. Although one friend in particular, John Leake, was 'at Liberty again', Farnworth reported that there was 'another simple heart with Thomas Aldam', and '2 or 3 more in prison about Tithes', as well as 'one Mr Sikes at Knollingley . . . a great man of 3 or 4 hundred a yeare' who had 'proclaimed against Tythes, in his proclamation he calls them theeves and Robbers and he sent a maid about to cry against them'.[29]

Farnworth's letter describes a relatively fluid group at York, with the allies of Thomas Aldam and his fellow prisoners being defined in terms of their stance on tithes rather than mentioned by name or proclaimed as 'Friends'. In the letter, Farnworth went on to describe how Sikes had been urged by the authorities to renounce his proclamation against tithes in order to secure his release. Sikes refused to do this, stating, in Farnworth's account, that he would not pay so much as sixpence for his release, unless tithes were abolished, he himself compensated, and, significantly, 'his freinds called Quakers sett at Liberty'.[30]

This is the earliest instance of which I am aware of the use of the term 'Quaker' in the correspondence at Friends' House. Given the fluidity of the relationships between the prisoners at York, it is interesting that Sikes was aware of a specific group of 'Quakers', to whom he felt allegiance, although Farnworth's letter is ambiguous as to whether Sikes was counted as one of their own.[31] The fact that Farnworth had been allowed to see Sikes in prison, but not his closer 'Friends', also suggests that the authorities were well aware of the peculiar identity of the Quaker prisoners. By the summer

---

[28] William Dewsbery to Margaret Fell [August 1654], Sw Mss 4: 133.

[29] Richard Farnworth to George Fox and James Nayler, August or September 1652, Sw Trs 2: 42. In this I follow Geoffrey Nuttall's dating, Nuttall, EQL, VI, p. 83.

[30] Farnworth to Fox and Nayler, Sw Trs 2: 42.

[31] It may be significant that Farnworth 'named' Sikes in his letter to Fox, while the other 'simple hearts' remained anonymous. It was not uncommon for Quaker leaders to mention important new recruits by name; and Sikes would have been important because of the wealth he represented, as well as his public testimony against tithes. This is a typical example of the establishment of the early networking between Quaker leaders. Although Sikes does not appear again in the correspondence, the fact that people like him were made known to other itinerant Quakers would mean that potential allies, leaders or sponsors of the growing movement were literally 'put on the map' for future reference.

of 1652, therefore, Quakers were a visible, separate group, at least in York. The letter about Sikes reinforces the impression that the term was applied by outsiders to a known, tangible, group of 'Quakers'.

The consolidation of the term 'Quaker' in print occurred initially in the Quakers' own tracts; and it was their use of the term which gave rise to subsequent printed denunciations of the 'Quakers'. Over the next four years of publications, there is a clear textual dynamic in the spread of the term. This is not to argue that 'Quakers' were purely an invention of their own literature, nor of the literature of their opponents; but rather that there was a sustained textual development of the term which interacted concurrently with the oral dissemination of 'Quaker' ideas. That this was at the initiative of the Quaker leaders themselves is deeply revealing about the nature of the development of the Quaker movement, and the role of print in its consolidation. It is this phenomenon which this chapter will now explore.

A discussion of 'quaking' took place in one of the earliest extant publications of the Quaker movement. This was a broadside, published under the name of George Fox, which proclaimed itself to be 'An exhortation to you who contemne the power of God, and speak evil of it; As of Trembling, and Quaking, to beware what you doe'.[32] This broadside was concerned, as the title suggests, to rebuke hostile criticisms of Fox and his followers. Given the lack of published attacks on 'Quakers' or Fox's co-religionists at this point, it seems that Fox was responding to oral or unpublished attacks on him and his followers. Much of the broadside dealt with scriptural precedents for 'trembling', and argued that those who despised 'trembling' were turning away from those people who were witnessing the presence of God: what Fox was responding to was an apparently common denunciation of the ecstatic worship with which they were associated, and the concomitant accusation that they were 'Quakers'. It is a significant publication as it introduces most of the key references to biblical 'quaking' which other Quaker authors later embraced in their own justifications of their movement's identity. Fox's first point, from the Old Testament prophet Isaiah, was that 'trembling' was a sign of openness to God and of one's prophetical status, 'for (saith the Lord) This is the man that I do regard, he that is of a broken heart, and a contrite spirit and trembleth at my Word'.

Moreover, Fox argued, the prophet Isaiah had made clear that such 'tremblers' were bound to be denounced by the ungodly; and just as 'trembling' established one's prophetical status, so the denunciation of those who trembled was a sign of profanity:

---

[32] George Fox, *An exhortation to you who contemne the power of God* [n.p., 1652], STC A161A. This date is attributed in Wing's *STC*, and at Friends' House Library. The broadside itself contains no date; and the tract does not appear in the Thomason Collection.

and him do you despise now, that trembleth at the word of the Lord; but it makes manifest that you have the Letter but in notion, neither have you the spirit that was in Isaiah . . . for saith he, *Hear the word of the Lord, ye that tremble at the Word; when your brethren hate you and cast you out, and say, let him be glorified, he shall appear to your joy when they shall be ashamed*, and do ye not call them out now, as they did then? was it the power of the Devill that made these to tremble?

Fox then elaborated on further examples of divine revelation which led to 'trembling':

when the Lord spoke to Moses, . . . and said he was the God of Abraham, the God of Isaac and the God of Jacob; then Moses trembled and durst not behold him: will you say that this was the Devill that made Moses to tremble, and durst not behold him?

As would be a central theme in many subsequent publications, Fox then demanded his audience compare scriptural examples of quaking with their own experiences:

The same power now makes to tremble, and throws down proud flesh: you never read that any of the holy men of God scorned trembling, or them that trembled at the word of the Lord; but it is the unholy and ungodly proud Priests and Professors that must be scorning, that knows not the power of the Lord, and God scorns such.

It was the same power, Fox went on, which made David 'to tremble'; and he reasserted the similar religious experience of Quakers and the Old Testament prophets:

if he were here now, would you not say it was the power of the Devil? they wagged their heads at him, and made songs of him, and waited for his halting, and so doe ye now where the same power is made manifest, and so ye shew that ye are of the same generation which was against David and against the same power.

Fox completed his illustration with Daniel, who 'trembled, and his breath and strength was gone, and he did scarce eat any meat for three weeks together'; and with Habakkuk, who, 'when he heard of the power of the Lord his lips quivered, and his belly shoke, and rottenesse entred into his bones'. 'If you should see one now', Fox continued, 'their lips quiver, their bellies shake and tremble, would you not say they were bewitched, and it was the power of the Devil, and it was the voice of the Devil? . . . here you shew forth your blasphemies against the Holy Ghost, and against the power of the Lord.'

At the end of his broadside Fox turned around the status of his readers and introduced a new scriptural precedent for quaking: that of trembling in the fear of God and of man's sin. When Paul came to the Corinthians, 'he was with them in weakness, and fear, and trembling, that their faith might not stand in the wisdome of words but in the power of the Lord'; Joel was sent to blow his trumpet in Zion 'to sound an alarum in my holy mountain', and to 'let all the Inhabitants of the earth tremble'. As has been shown in earlier chapters, a major concern for Fox and the Quakers was to counter prevailing Calvinist ideology, and to argue instead that Christ's inner light was in all men. Whereas previously Fox's broadside had been addressed to 'you who contemne the power of God', and had assumed that the readers were 'of the same generation' as those who had despised the Old Testament prophets, at the end of his work Fox directed an appeal to his readers which allowed them to turn against their 'ungodly proud Priests and Professors', and towards his own movement:

Now if you should see a company of people trembling, your Teachers would call them fooles, and the Prophets of the Lord called them foolish people which did not tremble at the word of the Lord. So judge you all people, whether you have the power of the Lord, and the spirit which was in his people.[33]

Although this early broadside of George Fox's did not refer to 'quaking' other than in the opening sentence, it did establish the main scriptural justifications for trembling which would be used later by authors more directly with reference to 'quaking'. Moreover, it referred to a specific 'company' of people, just as Fox's *Journal* referred to the 'people of the Lord god' around Mansfield. Thus Fox was defining his co-religionists as a peculiar group of people; his lengthy insistence on the prophetical nature of their ecstatic worship, and the inevitability that they would be derided by the profane, ungodly outside world, further reinforced that those accused of 'quaking' or 'trembling' were the true spiritual successors of the Old Testament prophets.

Fox's broadside is significant for four reasons. It was a response to non-published, probably oral, accusations that he and his co-religionists quaked and trembled in their worship, and very probably had been called 'quakers'. The oral rebuke of 'quaking' was therefore current, and Fox's tract consolidated it before any of the printed attacks on 'Quakers' or quaking. It is notable, indeed, that all of the earliest published attacks on 'Quakers' included within them references to Quaker tracts which had themselves used the term.[34] Quaker leaders appropriated 'quaking' in their own literature. Secondly, Fox's tract established scriptural justifications for quaking,

---

[33] *Ibid.*

[34] The first 'anti-Quaker tracts' appeared in print in 1653. These all referred explicitly to 'Quakers'; and most of them identified the Quakers as a specifically northern phenomenon. Although most were apparently printed in London, it is interesting that the collector George Thomason did not obtain copies of many of them, either because they were distributed uniquely in the north; or more probably because the Quakers were not yet deemed significant in London. This means that dating the first hostile printed accounts of the Quaker movement is difficult; but the first ones were: Francis Higginson, *A brief relation of the irreligion of the northern Quakers* (London, 1653), Higginson, *A brief reply to some part of a very scurrilous and lying pamphlet [Saul's errand]* (London, 1653); Thomas Welde and William Cole *et al.*, *The perfect pharisee under Monkish holinesse* (Gateshead, 1653), STC C5045 (another edition of this was published in London for Richard Tomlins and dated by Thomason on the 14 January 1654, STC C5045A; see note 10 above); *Certain queries and*

which would be reproduced by Quaker authors subsequently and thus form a coherent and recognisable identity common to all Quaker authors. Thirdly, it established that oppression and taunts from outsiders were as important in confirming a distinctive 'Quaker' identity as were their own claims to be of the only true religion: the binary opposition between the godly and the ungodly was crucial to Quakers as well as to outsiders. And finally, it made clear that 'Quakers' were a specific company of people. All of these aspects were crucial to the public development of a peculiar identity.

Fox's broadside laid down the framework of scriptural justifications of quaking which were subsequently reiterated by a number of Quaker authors. Typically, these tracts were ones sent ahead of major Quaker infiltration of an area or town, which served to publicise the advent of Quakers and their ideas. Many of these were more elaborate versions of Fox's broadside: 'search the Scriptures, and you shall finde that the holy men of God do witness quaking and trembling, and roaring and weeping, and fasting and tears', exhorted James Nayler in 1653, and went on over four pages to recall the trembling of Moses, Daniel, Habakkuk and David.[35] This tract, in circulation in London in August 1653, well before any sustained Quaker presence in the capital, also assumed a 'Quaker' identity by its title, *The power and glory of the Lord shining out of the north*, a reference to the fact that Quakers in 1653 were a strange and distant northern phenomenon.[36] The title page of the tract also announced its identity in far more certain terms, stating it was written by 'one whom the Lord hath called out of this dark World, into the True Light, whom *Ismaels* brood calls a Quaker, whose name in the flesh is *James Nayler*'. Nayler implied that 'quaking' and a certain knowledge of the divine were intrinsically linked, promising to show his readers 'the way how all flesh comes to know the Lord and fear him, by his terrible shaking

---

　　 anti-queries, concerning the Quakers (so called) in and about Yorkshire (London, 1653), STC c1734a; Joseph Kellet, J. Pomroy and P. Glissen *et al.*, *A faithful discovery of a treacherous design* (London, 1653), STC f568 (dated by Thomason on 12 June 1653, but internally dated 11 February 1653); John Gilpin, *The Quakers shaken: or, a fire-brand snach'd out of the fire* (Gateshead, 1653), STC g769. Another edition of this was published in London for Simon Waterson, 1653, STC g770, and dated by George Thomason on 4 July 1653, by which date several Quaker tracts were obtainable in London.

[35] James Nayler, *The power and glory of the Lord shining out of the north* (London, 1653), STC n302, pp. 16–19.

[36] Thomason dated a copy of this tract 17 August 1653. In August there was considerable agitation over the trial of George Fox at Carlisle for blasphemy, with two notable Quakers, Anthony Pearson and Gervase Benson, petitioning the Carlisle authorities and members of the Barebones Parliament on Fox's behalf. This latter was probably done through William West, the Barebones member for Lancaster, who also distributed Nayler's tract himself. Although Nayler at the time of writing was in Westmorland, the tract's arrival in London would have coincided with possibly the first major awareness of Quakers in the capital, which would necessarily have been as northern strangers. For West's distribution of the tract, see above, Chapter 2, p. 75, n. 49. For the trial of Fox at Carlisle, see Braithwaite, *Beginnings*, pp. 117–19.

the earthly part in man, witnessed by the holy men of God in Scripture'.[37] Thus one of the first tracts aimed at a London audience, addressed to 'All People everywhere who profess that you love God', and including seven queries to those 'that are so much offended at perfection', explored various facets of Quaker identity: 'Quakers' were northern, spiritual inheritors of Old Testament prophets, likely to be scorned as such by the people of the world, but a means nevertheless of coming 'to know the Lord'.[38]

Other tracts which proclaimed Quaker ideas to an audience for the first time carried a far more abbreviated justification of quaking. *A message from the Lord* by Richard Farnworth in 1653 promised its readers a 'vindication by the Scriptures', 'that those whom the world scornfully call *Quakers* . . . are the only people of the Lord', and included by way of introduction the following summary of Fox's much lengthier account:

Moses quaked, *Hebrew* the 12 ver 21. Ezekiel was commanded to eat his bread with quaking. David did tremble, and there were with him that quaked. Job his bones did shake, and his flesh did tremble, *Job* 4.14. Habakkuk his belly did shake, and his lips quivered, and all his flesh trembled: See *Hab.* 3.16. David roared by reason of the powerfull workings of the Lord in him; and his bones did shake, and his flesh did tremble: See *Psal.* 38.8,9,10. and 22.1 *Psal.* 119, 120. Isaiah spoke to the people to heare the Word of the Lord, that did tremble at it, with many others, etc. And there were Mockers then as there are now: See *Job* 17.2, *Acts* 13.41, *Isa.* 28.22, *Isa.* 29.20, *Psal.* 50.2, 3.[39]

Pamphlets which vindicated quaking anticipated in advance the oral rebuke that they were 'Quakers'; and they provided the carrier of the tract with the means with which to respond to such rebukes.[40] 'Do not your People

---

[37] Nayler, *The power and glory of the Lord*, sig. A r. The phenomenon of 'quaking' was much maligned in tracts which recounted 'false conversions'. John Gilpin described how his need for fellowship had drawn him to the Quakers at Kendal, and after meetings with them and having read their books, recounted: 'I began (as I had formerly desired) to tremble and quake so extremely, that I could not stand upon my feet', John Gilpin, *The Quakers shaken* (London, 1653), p. 3.

[38] Nayler, *The power and glory of the Lord*, pp. 1, 25–26.

[39] Richard Farnworth, *A message from the Lord* (London, 1653), STC F491A, p. 3. Although there is no precise evidence for the circulation of this tract, it was one of a number of octavo tracts by Farnworth, described by Aldam as one of his 'little' books which were so effective in spreading the word. These books were still being circulated in 1654, and were distributed to the Quaker ministers as they set out on their national campaign in the summer of 1654. See Thomas Aldam to George Fox, York Castle [July] 1654, Sw Mss 3: 44.

[40] Another example of this can be found in a tract co-authored by Fox and Nayler, and obtained by George Thomason on 25 August 1654, at about the same time as the first Quaker preachers (although not Fox and Nayler) were arriving in the capital during their national campaign. This contained on its title page: 'a few words unto you that scorne Quaking and Trembling, which all the holy men of God that spake forth the Scripture, and also the holy men of God justified, and all you denied that scorneth such as witness such things now, as ever was in all the Generations of the Saints'. James Nayler and George Fox, *A word from the Lord* (London, 1654), STC F1991A, sig. A r.

cry, Stone thcm? Do not you wag your heads at them? Do not you gnash
your teeth at them which you call Quakers? Moses quaked, David quaked,
Jeremiah shaked, who cryed against the Priests', wrote Fox in a tract which
was circulated in London in April 1654, while Francis Howgill and John
Camm were there meeting with Oliver Cromwell.[41] These tracts primarily
rehearsed the argument that 'quakers' were prophets of the true religion and
coming of Christ; and as such were bound to be derided.[42]

The rebuke 'Quaker' was not only a verbal slur. The scriptural defence
of 'Quaking' was discussed also in tracts which were part of more formal
pamphlet debates with puritan opponents. In 1653, Thomas Welde and his
colleagues from Newcastle subjected the Quakers' treatment of 'quaking'
to their own lengthy exegesis.[43] They drew their evidence for the Quakers'
'quakings', not from their own first-hand experience, but from John Gilpin's
printed attack which graphically described the quaking and ecstatic worship
at Quaker meetings.[44] The authors were, nevertheless, keenly aware that
Quaker authors had developed their own interpretation of biblical quaking,
and spent some time countering their definitions: 'These last we mention', the
Newcastle authors wrote, 'lest they should charge us with passing over that
which they presume to make so much for them.'[45] James Nayler's reply to
the Newcastle ministers was equally revealing about the textual construction
of the 'quaking' identity of his movement. He first reproved the ministers
for equating 'quaking and trembling', with 'grovelling upon the ground, and
foaming at the mouth', which latter accusations (taken from Gilpin's tract) he
denounced as 'lyes and slanders' of the ministers' 'own inventing'; and then
asserted: 'but for *quaking and trembling* we owne it, as that which the Lord
hath said shall come upon all flesh'.[46] Nayler denounced the ministers for
speaking of tremblings in the Bible, 'but know them not within yourselves',

---

[41] George Fox, *The trumpet of the Lord sounded and his sword drawn* (London, 1654), STC
    F1969, p. 7. George Thomason dated a copy of this tract 8 April 1654.
[42] An early tract by Farnworth cited simply on its title page: 'And so terrible was the fight,
    that Moses said, I exceedingly fear and Quake. Hebr. 12.21.', see Richard Farnworth,
    Englands warning-peece gone forth (London, 1653), STC F482, sig. Ar. For further examples
    of descriptions of 'quaking', see George Fox and James Nayler, *A word from the Lord unto
    all the faithlesse generation of the world* (1654), STC F1992, pp. 9–12; George Fox, *A paper
    sent forth into the world from them that are scornfully called Quakers* (London, 1654), STC
    F1872, pp. 5–6; Richard Farnworth, *The brazen serpent lifted up on high* (London, 1655),
    STC F471, pp. 24–27; James Nayler et al., *Several petitions answered that were put up by
    the priests of Westmorland* (London, 1653), STC N316A, pp. 26, 35–36.
[43] Thomas Welde and William Cole et al., *The perfect pharise under monkish holines* (London,
    1654), pp. 41–44.
[44] Welde and Cole et al., *The perfect pharise*, pp. 41, 43; Gilpin, *The Quakers shaken*.
[45] Welde and Cole et al., *The perfect pharise*, p. 44.
[46] James Nayler, *An answer to the booke called the Perfect Pharisee under Monkish Holinesse*
    ([London] 1654), STC N261, p. 25.

and argued that 'what ye speake by heare-say' should be discounted.[47] Nayler was at pains to discredit salacious accounts of foaming at the mouth, but at the same time appropriated 'quaking' as a significant experience of his co-religionists.

Just as James Nayler 'owned' quakings and tremblings, other authors also became more positive in defining themselves collectively as Quakers. 'Quaking we own, else we should lay waste the Scriptures, as you do,' wrote John Camm in a printed reply to tracts by Samuel Eaton and Joseph Kellett.[48] Edward Burrough wrote of the 'despised and contemned people, called Quakers (whom I do own as my Brethren in the sufferings of Jesus)'.[49] The political importance of such a statement is illustrated in its more defiant use by a group of soldiers in Robert Lilburne's regiment of horse in 1657. Following General Monck's instruction that lists of all Quaker soldiers be submitted to him, a group of soldiers issued a statement which declared that since the name 'Quaker' was the term given by the world 'in much scorne and derision' to the Children of the Lord, they dared not use it of themselves, but went on to note: 'quakinge and tremblinge according to what the scriptures declares of wee doe owne'.[50] To acknowledge directly the label 'Quaker', the soldiers recognised, was to accept the worldly connotations and political ramifications of the term; nevertheless, they reiterated the scriptural significance which they themselves attached to it.

Thus a significant number of early Quaker tracts included a scriptural justification of 'quaking' or 'trembling'. They are indicative of a response to public accusations that particular preachers or groups were 'Quakers'. The initiative was taken by the Quaker authors themselves, and not by their opponents, in developing a lengthy explanation of the term's significance, and applying it to themselves. The qualified 'owning' by Quaker authors of their nickname was a public acknowledgement that those denounced as 'Quakers' did indeed form a visible group of people.

James Nayler's careful distinction between accusations of 'quaking' and of 'foaming at the mouth' is also important in this context. Other 'badges' of the Quakers associated with their ecstatic worship, such as swelling stomachs, writhing on the ground and speaking in tongues, were propounded

---

[47] *Ibid.*, p. 26.

[48] John Camm, *An answer to a book which Samuel Eaton put up to the Parliament* (London, 1654), STC c389, p. 45.

[49] Edward Burrough, preface to Christopher Atkinson, *The standard of the Lord lifted up* (London, 1653), STC a4128, sig. a3v. On another occasion Burrough also wrote that the inner light of Christ would show the 'poor people amongst you', called Quakers, to be the servants of God, 'whom I do own as my Brethren in the sufferings of Jesus'. Edward Burrough, *A warning from the Lord to the inhabitants of Underbarrow* (London, 1654), STC b6057, p. 20.

[50] Sw Mss 4: 237, cited in M. E. Hirst, *The Quakers in peace and war* (London, 1923), pp. 530–31.

initially by hostile observers of the Quakers.[51] Much of the evidence for the ecstatic worship, and particularly for glossolalia, or speaking in tongues, of the early Quakers, comes from hostile sources: a point which their ethnographer failed to emphasise.[52] Most frequently, as James Nayler's tract shows, these accounts were denounced as slander by Quaker authors. The authors did attempt to justify important symbolic acts, such as going naked, the wearing of sackcloth and ashes, the use of thee and thou, and the performance of other 'signs and wonders', as further evidence of their particular prophetical status: and Kenneth Carroll suggests very plausibly that the justification of these in print by key Quaker authors was instrumental in the repeated instances of such behaviour in the 1650s and 1660s.[53] Printed justifications for 'going naked' thus functioned in a similar way to the lengthier and more common justifications for 'quaking'. Propounded by an authoritative group of leading authors, the hostile epithet was developed into an accepted term which was understood to refer to an acknowledged and coherent body of people, accorded authority by their very persecution.

Such alacrity on the part of the Quaker authors in owning 'quaking' was central to the rapid perception of a 'Quaker' movement. The use of the term 'Quaker' in their tracts was far more widespread than the prosaic discussions of quaking. The small body of authors very rapidly began to subsume their individual names beneath their collective identity as 'Quakers'. This is a crucial distinction from Ranters, who never described themselves as such in their publications, and thus provoked much of the recent anxiety about the true nature of a Ranter text or Ranter beliefs.[54] Quaker authors wrote very

[51] Higginson, *A brief relation of the irreligion*, sig. a3r, pp. 10–23, 28–30; Gilpin, *The Quakers shaken, passim*; William Prynne, *The Quakers unmasked, and clearly detected* (London, 1655), STC P4045, sig. Ar, pp. 3–4, 6–7; H3152; *The Quakers dream* (London, for George Horton, 1655), STC Q22, p. 3; *The Quakers fiery beacon* (London, for George Horton, 1655), STC Q25, *passim*; Ralph Farmer, *The great mysterie of godliness and ungodliness* (London, 1655), STC F441, pp. 81–82; Cole and Welde *et al.*, *The perfect pharise*, pp. 41–45.

[52] Richard Bauman, *Let your words be few: symbolism of speaking and silence among seventeenth-century Quakers* (Cambridge, 1983), pp. 80–83.

[53] Important justifications for the use of 'thee' and 'thou' are found in Richard Farnworth, *The pure language of the spirit of the truth* (London, 1655), STC F494; Farnworth, *A call out of Egypt and Babylon* (London, 1653), STC F474, sigs. E2r–v; George Fox and James Nayler, *Several papers, some of them given forth by George Fox.* [n.p.], (1653), STC F1903, p. 10; James Nayler, *A few words occasioned by a paper lately printed* ([London], 1654), STC N279, p. 13; James Parnell, *The trumpet of the Lord blowne* (London, 1655), STC P539, pp. 1–2. For justifications of going naked and of the performance of other signs, see Farnworth, *The pure language of the spirit of the truth.*; Farnworth, *The spirituall man judgeth all things* (London, 1655), STC F505, p. 25; Francis Howgill, *A woe against the magistrates, priests and people of Kendall in Westmorland* (London, 1654), STC H3189, pp. 1, 3, 5. Kenneth Carroll, 'Sackcloth and ashes, and other signs and wonders', *JFHS* 53: 4 (1975), 314–25; Carroll, 'Quaker attitudes towards signs and wonders', *JFHS* 45: 2 (1977), 70–84.

[54] Davis, *Fear, myth and history*, pp. 17–75; Davis, 'Debate: Fear, myth and furore', 167–70, 175–76, 179–94, 202–03, 208–10.

definitely as 'Quakers', and as such produced an immediately recognisable body of tracts through which their beliefs were easily identified.

Just as the appropriation of biblical 'quaking' was highly nuanced, to invoke both their prophetical status, and the inevitable persecution that followed, so their description of themselves as 'Quakers' was also carefully qualified and a number of meanings attached to it. William Dewsbery declared his work to be 'From the Spirit of the Lord, written by one, whom the people of the world calls Quaker, whose name in the flesh is William Deusbery, but hath a New Name, the World knows not, written in the Book of Life'.[55] The authorial device rehearsed the argument that the epithet 'Quaker' was applied by ignorant people to the true servants of God and as such was an intrinsic indication that the Quakers were a peculiar and godly people.

The transcendence by Quaker prophets of their worldly identity was an important feature of their public prophecy, and served to underline their separate status from the rest of the world. Quakers preached and wrote not as ordinary mortals, but as spiritual servants of God. James Nayler described one of his tracts to be written 'By a Servant of the Lord, reproached by the world, and carnall worshippers, under the Name of a Quaker; whose Name in the Flesh is James Nayler'.[56] In September 1654 Edward Burrough was 'moved to write to the English army in England, Scotland and Ireland', emphasising that 'to them all it is the word of the Lord. My name in the flesh is Edward Burrough, one of them whom the world calls Quakers.'[57]

Edward Burrough's relatively stark dichotomy between his 'fleshly', mundane identity and the spiritual status of his work demonstrates that the authors proclaimed themselves to be 'Quakers' in order to underline their separation from the rest of the world.[58] The insistence that Quaker authors enjoyed a hidden, spiritual identity was not always linked to the fact that they were called 'Quakers', and sometimes related more simply to the 'carnal', worldly name of the author. Edward Burrough referred to himself in his tracts as 'a labourer in the Vineyard, who is not known to the world; (though named of the world) E D W A R D   B U R R O U G H'.[59] On another occasion he described his authorship as 'By one whose name is truly known by

---

[55] William Dewsbery, *The discovery of mans returne to his first estate* (London, 1654), STC D1259, sig. Ar.

[56] James Nayler, *A few words occasioned by a paper lately printed* [London, 1654], STC N279, sig. Ar.

[57] Edward Burrough, *For the souldiers and all the officers of England, Scotland and Ireland* [London, 1654], STC B6003, sig. Ar; dated by Thomason 26 September 1654.

[58] Another tract by William Dewsbery, written 'From the spirit of the Lord' declared itself to be 'by one whose name in the flesh is William Deusbery, called Quaker with the people of the world, who live in their perishing nature'. Dewsbery, *A true prophecy of the mighty day of the Lord* (London, 1654), STC D1279, sig. Ar.

[59] Edward Burrough, *A warning from the Lord to the inhabitants of Underbarrow* (London, 1654), STC B6057, sig. Ar; Burrough, *Truth defended: or certain accusation answered*

the children of the same birth, but unknown to the world, though by it called EDWARD BURROUGH'.[60] Other epithets were more concise, but still made the same point: 'By one known to the world by the name of Richard Farnworth'; or by one 'whose name in the flesh is Anne Audland'.[61] This was an important, if abbreviated, feature of the Quakers' insistence on the presence of the spirit in everyone; and the point was not lost on their critics: 'We are satisfied', wrote one, 'that this expression is meerly to cloake their pretence to an equality with God.'[62]

Accounts of trials of Quakers suggest that in their public dealings with magistrates and ministers there was a sustained insistence by Quakers that their 'worldly' identity was very different from their spiritual identity. John Camm, describing the Carlisle trial of George Fox, described the actions in court of 'A friend of them whom the world calls Quakers':

> when he was brought before the Rulers and Magistrates, they asked him what was his name, and he said it was hid from the world, and the world knew it not, and they asked him what his name was, and he said they should never know it.

His refusal to acknowledge his worldly identity was a specific factor in the prisoner's subsequent speaking: 'and then he was free to tell them what the world called him, else he saw their deceit'.[63]

A published account of the trial of William Dewsbery and others at Northampton in July 1655, 'Witnessed by the righteous seed, whom the world in scorn calls Quakers', indicates an almost formulaic public insistence that the Quakers' mundane identity had nothing to do with their spiritual one. In the account of the trial, the justice Thomas Atkins was subject to a set-piece exchange:

I.A. [Judge Atkins] What is thy name?
W.D Unknown to the World.
I.A. Let us hear what that name is that the world knows not.
W.D. It is known in the Light, and not any can know it but him that hath it; but the Name the World knows me by is William Dewsbery.
I.A. What Countreyman art thou?
W.D. Of the Land of Canaan.

(2nd edn, London, 1656), STC B6050, sig. Ar. In the first edition of *Truth defended* (published in 1654) Burrough desscribed himself simply as a 'servant of the Lord, whose Name in the flesh is, Edward Burrough'.

[60] Edward Burrough, *A trumpet of the Lord sounded out of Sion* (London, 1656), STC B6048, sig. Ar.

[61] Richard Farnworth, *Truth cleared of scandals* (London, 1654), STC F512, sig. Ar; Ann Audland, *A true declaration of the suffering of the innocent* (London, 1655), STC A4195, p. 2.

[62] Thomas Welde *et al.*, *A further discovery of that generation of men called Quakers* (Gateshead, 1654), STC W1268, p. 7.

[63] J[ohn] C[amm], *A true discovery of the ignorance, blindness, and darkness of those who are called Magistrates about Carlile in Cumberland* (London, 1654), STC C393, p. 19.

I.A. That is afar off.

W.D. Nay it is near, for all that dwells in God is in the holy City, New Jerusalem: which comes down from Heaven, where the Souls is in rest, and enjoyes the love of god in Jesus Christ, in whom the union is with the Father of Light.

I.A. That is true, but are you ashamed of your Countrey, is it a disparagement for you to be born in England?

W.D. Nay for the Truths sake I am free to declare according to the Knowledge of the World, my naturall Birth was in *York-shire*, nine Miles from *York*, towards *Hull.*[64]

In accounts of earlier trials at Northampton, in January and March 1655, Dewsbery described very similar exchanges. Asked at his first trial where he lived, Dewsbery responded: 'I live in the Lord', although he conceded that 'I have a wife and three children at Wakefield in Yorkshire.' At his trial in March, he answered the same question: 'My natural Birth was in Yorkshire', prompting the following exchange:

J.W. [Judge Windham] Dost thou begin to cant, is there any other Birth?

W.D. Yea except ye be regenerated, and born again, they cannot enter the Kingdom of God; which birth I witness.

J.W. At what place in Yorkshier wast thou born?

W.D. My natural Birth was at a Town called Alliethorp, nine miles from *York*, towards *Hull.*[65]

These published dialogues between Quakers and magistrates demonstrate a sustained initiative by Quakers to emphasise publicly that they acted as servants of the 'Most High God', 'for the testimony of Jesus Christ'.[66] Part of this public insistence on their prophetical identity, which would necessarily remain hidden from their unregenerate opponents, was the refusal to accept that their proper names had any real significance.

William Dewsbery's dialogues with the Northamptonshire judges, he claimed, were 'as near as remembred the substance' of what was said during the trials.[67] If this were indeed the case, William Dewsbery displayed considerable acumen when confronted with officers of the English legal system.[68] Yet regardless of whether the actual exchanges were as adept as the Quaker transcript suggests, their significance lies in the fact that these were the published accounts of the trials. Thomas Corns has shown from published accounts of Lilburne's trial that the use of dialogue and differing voices was a literary device which allowed readers to juxtapose conflicting ideological positions and therefore permitted a relatively free reading of

---

[64] [William Dewsbery, John Whitehead *et al.*], *A true testimony of what was done* (London, 1655), *STC* T3123, sig. Ar, pp. 1–2.

[65] William Dewsbery, *A discovery of the grounds from whence the persecution did arise* (London, 1655), *STC* D1266, pp. 5, 11.

[66] *Ibid.*, p. 1.   [67] *A true testimony of what was done*, sig. Ar.

[68] For a more detailed discussion of published accounts of Quaker trials, see below, Chapter 7.

the text.[69] There was a strong didactic element to Dewsbery's and similar accounts of trials, which demonstrated the Quakers' emphasis on the spirit, but also perhaps enabled readers to repeat Dewsbery's replies during their own examinations. Dewsbery sent manuscript and printed copies of what 'was doon at the asizes' to Margaret Fell, asking that 'it may be Read amongst frinds': his account was intended as much for fellow Quakers as for people in Northampton.[70] Such a formulaic denial of one's 'worldly' identity could occur both in print and in court rooms. The recording of such exchanges could be both descriptive, and prescriptive, of what actually occurred during trials of Quakers.

William Dewsbery was not merely concerned to emphasise his hidden, spiritual identity in the account of his trials. One of his specific complaints against the Northamptonshire justices was that on the warrant for his arrest 'there was not any name; but for one whom he in scorn called a Quaker'.[71] Dewsbery had been arrested, literally, for being a Quaker: something fundamentally at odds with the relatively tolerant tone of the Protectorate's Instrument of Government. Dewsbery argued that it was 'the Liberty of the Laws in the Nation, that all that profess the faith of Christ Jesus, may walk in uprightness to their faith in him, without any Breach of the Law'; yet in the eyes of the Northamptonshire justices, Dewsbery's status as a 'Quaker' had been sufficient to justify a warrant for his arrest.[72] The use of the 'Quaker' epithet by hostile authorities summed up the nature of his persecution. For the Quakers, it was a neat slogan which encapsulated their ungodly and unjust persecution; by qualifying themselves as 'Quakers so called', they reaffirmed their spiritual separation.

In this context, the use of the qualifying epithet on the title pages of tracts which described the author as 'known in the flesh' or 'one in scorn named a Quaker' acquires a number of meanings. It rehearsed the notion that Quakers were prophets, whose worldly identity was transcended by their spiritual status. It reiterated the argument that those who could only recognise the Quakers by their nicknames were necessarily blind to the light of God. And it suggested that those who referred to Quakers as 'Quakers' or by their proper names were by that very act persecuting them, and underlining their own unregenerate status.

---

[69] Thomas Corns, 'The freedom of reader-response. Milton's *Of Reformation* and Lilburne's *The Christian Mans Triall*', in R. C. Richardson and G. M. Riddens (eds.), *Freedom and the English Revolution* (Manchester, 1986), pp. 105–08.

[70] William Dewsbery to Margaret Fell, Northampton gaol, 3 September 1655, Sw Mss 4: 139; Dewsbery to Fell, Northampton Gaol, 5 August 1655, Abraham Mss [2]. Copies of Dewsbery's tracts were also sent from London to George Taylor and Thomas Willan in Kendal, who would have been responsible for their wider distribution. George Taylor to Margaret Fell, Kendal, 25 August 1655, Sw Mss 1: 294.

[71] Dewsbery, *A discovery of the grounds*, p. 6.   [72] *Ibid.*, p. 12.

The definition of authors as 'Quakers' primarily gave their pamphlets a clear collective status: they were writing not as individuals, but under the auspices of their religious movement. The promulgation of this collective identity was orchestrated by a tiny number of the movement's leading authors. As in so many aspects of Quaker publication, Richard Farnworth, by far the most sophisticated and prolific of the early Quaker pamphleteers, seems to have given the lead in propounding the use of the term 'Quaker'. His first use of the phrase, in a tract which he dated 1652, is also the most elaborate. The fact that it rhymes is further evidence of the performative nature of Quaker tracts:

> Written from the Spirit of the Lord, by one whom the people of the
>   world calles a Quaker,
> but is of the Divine nature made partaker:
> whom the world knows not, that are in their old nature,
> and so mock and deride:
> but *wo to the wicked, it shall be ill with them*.[73]

Farnworth's other early pieces also made use of the device in more abbreviated tones: 'This was written by One the World calleth a Q U A K E R, in March 1653' he proclaimed in one tract; another of his title pages pronounced it to be: 'Written by one whom the people of the world call a Quaker, whose name is R I C H A R D   F A R N W O R T H'.[74] Other early tracts by Farnworth developed the theme of prophetical status and the separation of spiritual and worldly identities: one tract was 'Written in the time of Israels Captivity, by one whom the people of the World call a Quaker; By name, R I C H A R D   F A R N E W O R T H';[75] another, similar phrase which added that his name was 'written in the Book of Life', went on to list the biblical sources for his claim: Revelation 12.17, Daniel 12.1,2,3; Ezekiel 18,19; Daniel 10 and Hebrews 12.[76]

Between them, Farnworth and Aldam at this time were busily propounding to their fellow ministers the value of printing as a means of spreading the 'truth'; their own zealous application of the 'Quaker' epithet has a certain resonance with this enthusiasm for effective use of the press. Thus, although the adoption of the authorial device clearly reflected central theological aspects of the Quakers' beliefs, its widespread use also had individual proponents, like Farnworth, whose influence over early Quaker publications was very strong.

---

[73] Richard Farnworth, *A discovery of truth and falshood* (London, 1653), STC F479A, sig. F3r.
[74] Richard Farnworth, *A brief discovery of the kingdome of Antichrist* [1653], STC F472A, sig. Ar; Farnworth, *A call out of false worships* (1653), STC F474A, sig. Ar.
[75] Richard Farnworth, *A voice of the first trumpet* [1653], STC F512B, sig. Ar.
[76] Richard Farnworth, *Moses message to Pharaoh* [1653], STC F491B, p. 1.

Apart from Farnworth's persistent early use of the term, there is no fixed pattern for authors emphasising their Quaker status over their own individual status. Fox and Nayler apparently felt it sufficient sometimes to use their proper names on the title pages of their tracts, without further need to define themselves as 'Quakers'. When John Audland and Thomas Ayrey arrived in Bristol on their journey south in July 1654, they were sent to the house of one Abraham Morris, who, they were told, would be able to 'discerne' whether they were of God. The decisive question put to Audland and Ayrey to discover their authenticity was whether they knew Fox or Nayler.[77] The fame of Fox and Nayler had very probably spread through their books: their names, like the term 'Quaker', were synonymous with their movement. The collector George Thomason sometimes added the epithet 'Quaker' to tracts in his possession by Quaker authors, apparently habituated to the practice of the authors themselves.[78]

Notable new recruits to the movement used the device to signal their newfound allegiance: although well established as an author and politician, in his first 'Quaker' publication, the Bristol Quaker George Bishop claimed it was:

Given forth for the sake of the honest-hearted, and in witness of the Truth, as it is in Jesus, every where spoken against, scorned, and persecuted, under the Reproachful Name of Quaking. George Bishop.[79]

Anonymous or composite works also used the device to identify themselves explicitly with the Quaker movement: *A Declaration of the marks and fruits of the false prophets* (1655) announced itself to be 'From them who in the World in scorn is called *Quakers*, which suffers for the Righteous Seed sake'.[80] This is indicative of the kind of literary influence exercised by authors like Farnworth over 'Quaker' tracts, written by new recruits under the auspices of the movement. An anonymous collection of papers, 'from them who in scorn are called Quakers', and which argued for the right of Quakers to meet, and the illegitimacy of their prosecution by magistrates and people, asserted 'There is a people in England, whom they call Quakers; the name is right, a Scripture name, and we own it.'[81]

---

[77] Audland's Journal, p. 26.

[78] See, for example, Thomason's copy of James Nayler's *A lamentation over the ruins of this oppressed nation* (London, 1653), STC N292, BL E727(9). On at least one occasion, however, Thomason deviated from this, and labelled George Fox 'ye Goose' instead. See George Fox, *A message from the Lord to the Parliament* (London, 1654), STC F1863, BL E812(2), sig. Ar.

[79] George Bishop, *Jesus Christ, the same today as every day* (London 1655), STC B2995, sig. Ar; for his earlier publishing career, see J. W. Martin, 'The pre-Quaker writings of George Bishop', *Quaker History*, 74: 2 (1985), 20–27.

[80] *A Declaration of the marks and fruits of the false prophets* [London, 1655], STC D711, p. 1.

[81] *Some papers given forth to the world* (London, 1655), STC S4547, p. 32.

On occasions authorship under the collective 'Quaker' title was obviously intended to assert group authority. In February 1655, following a series of meetings attended by large numbers of Quaker leaders, Ranters, and army officers, George Fox was detained in Leicestershire and in March taken to London under military escort for a personal interview with the Protector.[82] Official concern about Quakers was expressed in a proclamation of 15 February 1655, specifically aimed at Quakers and Ranters, and prohibiting their disturbance of ministers during public service.[83] At the same time, Giles Calvert, who had been present with Fox and the Quaker leaders in Leicestershire, and had been under government surveillance, had his shop ransacked and manuscripts of Quaker books in his possession removed by the authorities.[84] Resulting public interest in Quakers in London gave rise to a flurry of scurrilous attacks on the Quakers by London newsmongers.[85] Some of these were published by George Horton, the man who had been responsible for some of the 'yellow-press' attacks on Ranters four years earlier; and indeed Horton used the same woodcut depictions of Ranters to portray the Quakers.[86] The spring of 1655 therefore marked the first concerted attacks on Quakers in London's popular press, similar to Davis's 'Ranter sensation' of 1650–51. Hitherto, printed attacks on Quakers had been based on direct, localised experiences in the provinces, and most frequently had been incorporated into individual pamphlet disputes between Quakers and their individual opponents: from March 1655, a number of London newspapers carried a variety of scurrilous reports about Quakers from all over England.[87]

---

[82] Braithwaite, *Beginnings of Quakerism*, pp. 177–82.

[83] *A proclamation prohibiting the disturbing of ministers and other Christians* (London, 1655), 15 February 1655, BL 669.f.19 (68).

[84] George Taylor and Thomas Willan to Margaret Fell, 26 February 1655, Sw Mss 1: 214; J. S. T. Hetet, 'A literary underground in restoration England: printers and dissenters in the context of constraint, 1660–89', unpublished Ph.D thesis, University of Cambridge, 1987, p. 130.

[85] *The Weekly Post*, Tuesday 17 April to Tuesday 24 April, 1655, no. 123; *The Faithful Scout*, 'A true relation concerning the Quakers', no. 224 (April 1655); *The Faithful Scout*, March 2–9, 1655. See also Donald Lupton, *The Quacking mountbanck; or the Jesuite turned Quaker* (London, 1655), STC L3493, dated by Thomason 24 May 1655.

[86] Horton's publications included: *The Quakers dream, or the Devil's pilgrimage in England* (London, 1655), STC Q22, dated by Thomason 26 April 1655; *The Quakers terrible vision, or the devils progress in the city of London* (London, 1655), STC Q33, 4 May 1655; *The Quakers fiery beacon; or the shaking Ranters* (London, 1655), STC Q25, 24 June 1655. For Horton's role in publishing anti-Ranter sensational material, see Davis, *Fear, myth and history*, p. 108.

[87] *The Weekly Intelligencer* no. 7 (27 February – 7 March 1655); *Mercurius Fumigosis* no. 40 (28 February – 7 March 1655); *The Faithful Scout*, no. 217 (2–9 March 1655); *Mercurius Fumigosis* no. 42 (14–21 March 1655); *Perfect Proceedings of State Affairs* no. 290 (12–19 April 1655); *Mercurius Fumigosis* no. 51 (16–23 May 1655).

The 'Quaker' response to the yellow-press attacks on them was remarkable. It was initiated by the heavy-weight exponent of Quaker publishing, Thomas Aldam, by now released from York gaol and in London for interviews with the Protector in connection with George Fox's arrest.[88] Aldam's work, *The searching out the deceit*, clearly drew attention to its Quaker status on the frontispiece, and reminded those journalists attacking 'Quakers' that 'Moses the Judge of all Israel he exceedingly feared and Quaked.'[89]

Aldam's tract tells a remarkable story about his own view of the power of print and its importance to the Quaker movement. In response to newspaper reports casting slanders on George Fox and Margaret Fell ('an honorable woman in the Lord, whose being is in the North, one who is called Colonell Fell's wife'), two Quakers, Henry Clark and William Wilson, 'went to the Printer' to find out the basis for the stories. They discovered that Henry Walker 'had given those things in to be Printed', and struck up a bargain with Walker. If Henry Clark and William Wilson could obtain from Fox an absolute denial of the reports, given under Fox's own hand, then Walker undertook to name his sources and prove his stories to be true. When three Quakers, including Aldam, presented themselves the following day with Fox's written denial, Walker allegedly broke his promise, 'denied to prove it there, and said he would not mention any ones name'.[90] Aldam was infuriated, provided a lengthy summary of the stories Walker had published, and dared Walker in print:

Now Walker we do demand of thee who hast given out these unsavory expressions, and hast given them forth to print into the Nation, to declare to us what is the name of this Gentlewoman, and the maid, and the name of her husband, the Country they dwell in, and what towne they dwell in, and the place where these things was done, and who saw it, and where they dwell.[91]

Aldam's tract was followed by two works, both of which were written under the collective name of Quakers. The first, *A declaration from the children of light (who are by the world scornfully called Quakers)*, was written by London Quakers John Boulton, Simon Dring, William Rayman and Richard Davis, and published in May 1655. The authors attacked the 'false reports, scandals and lyes' published by Henry Walker, Robert Wood and George

---

[88] Thomas Aldam to George Fox, Sw Mss 3: 38. Nuttall dates this letter mid-March 1655: Nuttall, EQL 136, p. 136. See also Geoffrey Nuttall, *Studies in Christian enthusiasm* (Wallingford, Penn., 1948), pp. 33–35.

[89] Thomas Aldam, *The searching out the deceit* ([London], 1655), STC A894C, p. 3 and *passim*. This cannot be dated precisely since Thomason did not possess a copy, although from the subsequent publications it was probably published in March or April 1655.

[90] Aldam, *The searching out the deceit*, pp. 1–2.   [91] *Ibid*., p. 4.

Horton. They went on to pronounce dire warnings to all 'Ballad-makers', 'Image-makers', and those 'that print and sell them'.[92] This publication was followed by an anonymous broadside, published in June, *Slanders and lyes being cast upon the Children of Light*, which further denounced the publications of Henry Walker, Robert Wood and now Robert Ibbotson, and declared itself to be 'From them whom the world calls QUAKERS scornfully; but Moses who quaked and trembled, said, To him Reproaches was great Riches.'[93]

In the anti-Quaker publications of the spring of 1655, there are very clear parallels with the 'Ranter sensation' of 1650–51.[94] Just as the Ranters were reviled in the press following the legislation against them in the Blasphemy Act of August 1650, so the salacious stories about Quakers appeared after Cromwell's proclamation, and after official fears about the Quakers' connections with antigovernment plots led to Fox being brought to London. Blair Worden argued that the hostile stories appeared with some degree of approbation by the Protector, who did not try to prevent them.[95] Newspaper stories about the Quakers included reports of Quaker preaching in Whitehall, but more commonly focused on Fox's alleged seduction of Margaret Fell, instances of sorcery and eccentric behaviour, and the prevalence of Ranters among Quakers. As with the Ranters, there was similar confusion about the exact nature of the threat they posed.[96] *The Faithful Scout* believed the Quakers were papists; Henry Walker in the more serious *Perfect Proceedings of State Affairs* argued that plots against the government came not from the Cavaliers, but from Quakers, Ranters and Anabaptists, whose sword 'would put ten thousand to flight'.[97]

In contrast to the Ranters, however, there was a clear, concerted 'Quaker' response to this journalistic attack. That the authors chose to write as 'Quakers', as well as under their favoured collective title, the children of

[92] *A declaration from the Children of Light* (London, 1655), STC D589, sig. Ar, pp. 4–6.

[93] *Slanders and lyes being cast upon the children of light* [London, 1655], STC s3956. For careers of Horton, Walker, Wood and Ibbotson, see Joseph Frank, *The beginnings of the English newspaper, 1620–1660* (Cambridge, Mass., 1961), pp. 236–52; J. B. Williams, 'Henry Walker, Journalist of the Commonwealth', *The Nineteenth Century and After* 63 (March 1908), 454–64.

[94] Davis, *Fear, myth and history*, pp. 76–83; J. F. McGregor, 'Fear, myth and furore' Comment 1, 155–64. Aylmer suggests that there were similar 'sensations' in the sudden and widespread usages of the terms 'Leveller' in 1647, and 'Brownist' in 1641–42. G. E. Aylmer, 'Did the Ranters exist?', *Past and Present* 117 (1987), 217.

[95] Blair Worden, 'Toleration and the Cromwellian Protector', *Studies in Church History* 21 (1984), 212.

[96] Davis, *Fear, myth and history*, pp. 80–82.

[97] Thomas Aldam, *The searching out the deceit*, p. 4; *Perfect Proceedings of State Affairs*, no. 290 (12–19 April 1655), p. 4593.

light, demonstrates that the Quaker leaders attributed much authority to the collective term, significantly when the character of the whole movement was under scrutiny. Moreover, they turned their ire against the journalists and publishers themselves: they attacked the source and nature of the scurrilous publications, but at the time reinforced the real collective identity of the 'Quaker' movement. Publishing as 'Quakers' in this instance was very adept, and highly pertinent to the purpose behind the publication.

The 'Quaker' identity of authors and tracts affected the nature of public responses to them. In December 1652, a petition from the gentlemen and freeholders of Worcestershire, undoubtedly on the initiative of Richard Baxter, was presented to Parliament, decrying the proliferation of religious sects and demanding improvements to England's ministry.[98] By February 1653, a response to this specific petition had been published by three of the Quaker prisoners at York, Thomas Aldam, John Harwood and Benjamin Nicholson.[99] Baxter issued his own rapid response, in *The Worcestershire petition . . . defended*, published in May 1653.[100] Baxter was keen to respond to queries laid down by Aldam and his colleagues in their own tract, believing that they were 'the mouth of Divel'; and that the extreme nature of their attack on the national ministry would convince any remaining stragglers of the necessity of Baxter's petition.[101] Baxter was unaware of the precise status of his opponents: 'The Authours are many, not worth the naming, some subscribing one part, and some another: and sometimes daring thus to subscribe, Written from the spirit of God.'[102] In his autobiography, Baxter admitted 'I knew not what kind of Person he was that I wrote against, but it proved to be a Quaker, they being just now rising, and this being the first of their Books (as far as I can remember) that I had ever seen.'[103] The York prisoners had not written under their collective epithet, and as a consequence had been recognised by Baxter as part of a generic attack on the national ministry.

The perception that there were Quakers was determined by the Quaker authors' own, deliberated appropriation of the name. In 1655 Richard Baxter acknowledged to his readers that he should not trouble himself with 'so wilde

---

[98] *The humble petition of many thousands . . . of the county of Worcester* (London, 1652), STC B1285.

[99] Thomas Aldam *et al.*, *A brief discovery of the threefold estate of Antichrist* (London, 1653), STC A894B.

[100] Richard Baxter, *The Worcestershire Petition to the Parliament for the ministry of England defended . . . In answer to . . . A brief discovery of the threefold estate of Antichrist* (London, 1653), STC B1455.

[101] *Ibid.*, sigs. A2r, A3v.   [102] *Ibid.*, sig. A2v.

[103] *Reliquiae Baxterianae*, ed. Matthew Sylvester, part 1, pp. 115–16, as cited in N. H. Keeble and Geoffrey Nuttall, *Calendar of the correspondence of Richard Baxter* (2 vols., Oxford, 1991), vol. I, p. 94.

a Generation as the *People called Quakers* are'; John Bunyan referred to 'those pained hypocrites *called Quakers*'.[104] Henry Haggar wrote a response to a book by Richard Farnworth, 'who is commonly called a Quaker'; and included some queries 'concerning those people called Quakers'.[105] One of the earliest publications against the Quakers was a set of queries 'concerning the Quakers (so called) in and about Yorkshire'.[106] None of these publications directly addressed the issue of the Quakers' name, nor the Quakers' insistence that their being so named was evidence of their prophetical status. That the critics themselves adopted the qualifier when using the hostile epithet underlines that the Quakers' self-presentation was widespread and deeply influential.

One contemporary at least was deeply offended by the Quaker authors' device. In the fifth, posthumous, edition of Ephraim Pagitt's *Heresiography* (1654), which added the 'Quakers or Shakers, and the Ranters', the author was so outraged by the fact that they 'owne the title of Quakers . . . that it may appeare a name imposed by themselves', that he began his description of 'The Quaker or Shaker' with a discussion of this phenomenon.[107] James Nayler's citations 'from all the places of the Scripture which mentions either trembling or shaking' were, he argued, 'impertinent and farre from the purpose'.[108] The work of Richard Farnworth, 'another of this sanctified brotherhood', was in the eyes of the author even worse, for in his 'Easter reckoning (another piece of rambling sopperie)' Farnworth's claim to be a Quaker appeared as a rhyming ditty, which was transcribed in order to reveal the extent of Farnworth's blasphemy.[109] In his careful citations from the works of Farnworth, Nayler and Thomas Aldam, the author of *Heresiography* had detected that Quakers were deliberately playing on their nickname, and was accordingly outraged. This was apparent to a heresiographer, who self-consciously drew his description of the Quakers from a comprehensive reading of their own writings, while critics like Baxter and Bunyan, perhaps more concerned with immediate confrontations with the Quakers, unconsciously repeated the exploitation of the nickname. It is indicative that Quaker pamphlets, used to effect by Quaker ministers in

---

[104] Richard Baxter, *The Quakers catechism* (London, 1655), STC B1362, sig. A3r; John Bunyan, *Some gospel truths opened, according to Scriptures* (London, 1656), STC B5598, p. 213 (my italics).

[105] Thomas Pollard and Henry Haggar, *The holy scripture clearing itself of scandals* (London, 1655), STC P2775, sig. Ar.

[106] *Certain queries and anti-queries, concerning the Quakers (so called) in and about Yorkshire* (London, 1653) STC C1734A.

[107] Ephraim Paggit, *Heresiography*, 5th edn (London, 1654), p. 137.

[108] *Ibid.*, p. 137. Cf. James Nayler, *The power and glory of the Lord shining out of the North* (London, 1653), STC N302, pp. 16–19.

[109] *Heresiography*, p. 137.

public confrontation, were influential and to some extent internalised by the puritan critics of the movement; when their tracts were studied alone, for a different purpose, the Quakers' deliberate self-presentation was apparent to an observer as early as 1654.

An important consequence of authors defining themselves as 'Quakers so called' is that it alerted readers (and subsequently historians) to the fact that they were reading a Quaker tract. The authorial device therefore contributed to the notion that Quakers were a recognisable and coherent body: it was all the more effective because it most often appeared on the title pages of their tracts. This practice is in quite specific contrast to publications by other religious groups. Baptist 'confessions' tended to be issued in the name of specific congregations or regional associations; otherwise, radical religious writings appeared most frequently in the name (sometimes contrived) of individual authors.

The description of the authors as 'Quakers' on title pages was exploited further by the fact that the word itself could appear in large capital letters on the front of the tract, confirming to readers and would-be purchasers of tracts that they were the specific publications of an organised, identifiable group. The earliest instance of this was also one of the most influential publications, *Saul's errand to Damascus*, the first publication to be organised by Margaret Fell in February 1653. It was dated by Thomason on 12 March 1653, the first date on which Thomason recorded any tracts by Quakers.[110] *Saul's errand* referred to 'Quakers' in capital letters, and invited a number of anti-Quaker publications (Plate 1).[111] Subsequent publications which marked a new stage of the development of the movement also made similar, deliberate reference to 'Quakers'. The arrival of John Camm and Francis Howgill in London in March 1654 was marked by a number of 'Quaker' tracts circulating in the capital (Plate 2). This impulse was even more evident as the Quaker ministers began converging on London in August 1654 (Plates 3 and 4).

It has been important to cite at length from the Quakers' own use of the term to demonstrate the similarities in phraseology in the Quaker tracts. Quaker authors remained in close touch with one another; they circulated papers and letters among themselves, checked each others' manuscripts prior to publication, carried each others' manuscripts to London for printing, and organised the publication of composite works. They relied heavily on Giles

---

[110] George Fox, James Nayler, John Lawson and W[illiam?] W[est?], *Saul's errand to Damascus* (London, 1653), *STC* F1894.

[111] An immediate reply to *Saul's errand* was by Francis Higginson, *A brief relation of the irreligion of the northern Quakers* (London, 1653), *STC* H1953 and *A brief reply to some part of a very scurrilous and lying pamphlet* [*Saul's errand*] (London, 1653), *STC* H1954. Its content was also dealt with at length in William Cole and Thomas Welde's *The perfect pharise under monkish holines* (London, 1654) *STC* C5045A, and noted by Ralph Farmer, *The great mysteries of godlinesse and ungodlinesse* (London, 1655), *STC* F441.

SAUL's

ERRAND

To

D A M A S C U S:

WITH

His Packet of Letters from the High-
Priefts, againft the difciples of the Lord.

OR,

A faithful Tranfcript of a PETITION
contrived by fome perfons in *Lancafhire,*
who call themfelves Minifters of the Gofpel,
breathing out threatnings and flaughters againft a
peaceable & godly people there, by them nick-named

QUAKERS.

Together with the Defence of the perfons
thereby traduced, againft the flanderous and
falfe fuggeftions of that Petition , and other
untruths charged upon them.

Publifhed to no other end , but to draw out the bowels of tender
compaffion from all that love the poor defpifed fervants of Jefus
Chrift, who have been the fcorn of carnal men in all ages.

Matth 5.10,11,12. *Bleffed are they which are perfecuted for righteoufnefs ; for
theirs is the kingdom of heaven. Bleffed are ye , when men fhall revile you,
and perfecute you , and fhall fay all manner of evil againft you, falfly, for my
fake. Rejoyce, and be exceeding glad ; for great is your reward in heaven :
for fo perfecuted they the Prophets which were before you.*

London, printed for *Giles Calvert,* at the black Spread-Eagle
at the weft-end of *Pauls.* 1 6 5 3.

Plate 1. Title page to George Fox *et al.*, *Saul's errand to Damascus* (London, 1653),
STC F1894.

THE

TRUMPET.

Of the

LORD

SOUNDED,

And his Sword drawn,

And the Separation made between the

Precious and the Vile;

AND

The Vineyard of the Lord dreſſed by his own Husbandmen, and the dead trees cut down, and all the myſtery of Witchcraft diſcovered in all Profeſſions:

By them who have come thorow great tribulation, whoſe garments have been waſhed in the blood of the LAMB; who are accounted as the off-ſcowring of all things for Chriſts ſake, ſcornfully called by the World

QUAKERS.

And the angel thruſt in his ſickle into the earth, and gathered the vine of the earth, and caſt it into the great wine-preß of the wrath of God. And the wine-preß was troden without the city, and blood came out of the wine-preß even to the horſe bridles, by the ſpace of a thouſand ſix hundred furlongs. Rev.14.19,20.

London, Printed for *Giles Calvert,* at the black Spread-eagle neer the Weſt-end of *Pauls.* 1654.

April: 4. 1654

Plate 2. Title page to George Fox, *The trumpet of the Lord sounded and his sword drawn* (London, 1654), STC F1969, circulated in London prior to the Quakers' arrival there.

A Word
From the Lord,

TO ALL THE

W O R L D,

AND ALL

PROFESSORS

IN THE

W O R L D;

Spoken in PARABLES:

Wherein all may come to read themfelves through the PARABLES, and fee
where they are ; Alfo a word to all Profeffors, who
caft the pure Law of God behind their backs, and
turn the grace of God into wantonnefs, and defpife the day
of their vifitation; with a dreadful voice to all the children of
darknefs, who hate and deny the light; that all may come to
fee themfelves, and repent, before the fierce wrath of the Lord,
which is kindled in *England*, fweep you all away : by them who
are redeemed out of the curfe, to ferve the living, called

QVAKERS.

Aug. 25   *K Friends, For*

London, Printed for *Giles Calvert*, at the Black *fpread-
Eagle*, at the Weft end of *Pauls*, 1654.

Plate 3. Title page to George Fox and James Nayler, *A word from the Lord to all
the world, and all professors in the world, spoken in parables* (London, 1654), STC
F1991A, dated by Thomason 25 August 1654, and hence in circulation as
Quaker ministers congregated in the capital.

A DECLARATION

Againſt all

PROFESSION

AND

PROFESSORS

THAT

Have not the Life of what they Profeſs,
from the Righteous ſeed of God, whom
the World, Prieſts, and People,
ſcornfully calls

QUAKERS,

Who are in that Life that the holy Men
of God were in, and witneſs that power
that made them to Tremble and quake,
and ſhook the earth, and threw it down;
which the World, Prieſts, People, and
Profeſſors, having the words declared
from this power and life, but not it,
ſcoffs and ſcorns at, but this is our
Riches.

Aug: 28

London, Printed for *Giles Calvert* at the Black.
ſpread Eagle at the weſt end of *Pauls.1655.4*

Plate 4. Title page to [George Fox], *A declaration against all profession and professors* (London, 1654), *STC* F1784, dated by Thomason 28 August 1654, circulated as Quaker ministers congregated in the capital.

Calvert and later on Thomas Simmonds to publish their works, whose printers would have been habituated to the format of 'Quaker' pamphlets. The consequence was a remarkable homogeneity of expression and presentation. The use of the term 'Quaker' epitomises the cohesive nature of their publications.

The utilisation of the term 'Quaker' or 'quaking' in the printed tracts presents us with a number of features of Quaker publishing. At its most mechanical, the numerous references to 'Quakers' signalled a cohesive series of authors and publications, which presented audiences with the notion of a collective body of ideas and people. In the wider context of how the tracts were read and received, the exploitation of the term 'Quaker' also served to summarise many aspects of Quaker belief: 'Quakers' were prophets, servants of God, and destined to be mocked and derided by the outside world, which was by its very nature unable to recognise them. The significance of the term was presented through the lengthy discussions of scriptural 'quaking' in the tracts, and also through the more frequent appropriation of the term 'Quaker' by authors. Above all, the concerted use of the term underlines that Quaker pamphleteering was an active process, intended self-consciously to foster and promote the movement, and to make it instantly recognisable to literate and illiterate audiences across the country. The response of contemporaries and historians alike testifies to the authors' success in so doing.

5

'Women's speaking justified': women and pamphleteering[1]

In October 1655, two Quakers, Priscilla Cotton and Margaret Cole, while imprisoned in Exeter gaol, wrote a warning to the priests and people of England. They sent it up to London for printing. In it, they levelled the following bitter accusation against England's ministry:

> thou tellest the people, Women must not speak in a Church, whereas it is not spoke onely of a Female, for we are all one both male and female in Christ Jesus, but it's weakness that is the woman by the Scriptures forbidden . . . Indeed, you your selves are the women, that are forbidden to speak in the Church, that are become women; for two of your Priests came to speak with us; and when they could not bear sound reproof and wholesome Doctrine, . . . they railed on us with filthy speeches, . . . and so ran from us.[2]

This short and fascinating tract may well have been sold and passed around the southwest of England by Priscilla Cotton's husband, Arthur, who certainly distributed other Quaker books in the area.[3] He may also have regretted it. The following year, in the wake of the turmoil surrounding Martha Simmonds and Hannah Stranger in the Nayler affair, Arthur Cotton wrote to George Fox, requesting more Quaker missionaries for the two counties of Devon and Cornwall. His letter was unusually specific, asking Fox for ministers, 'which power and wisdom Guids,' and then elaborating: 'and Rather men Friends For they doe nott Care to here any women Friends'.[4]

Printed tracts have played a very specific role in shaping our understanding of the role of women in the early Quaker movement. Quaker women

---

[1] A version of this chapter has appeared in Robert Swanson (ed.), *Gender and Christian religion: studies in church history*, vol. xxxiv, Ecclesiastical History Society (Woodbridge, 1998), pp. 205–34.

[2] Priscilla Cotton and Mary Cole, *To the priests and people of England, we discharge our consciences* (London, 1655), STC c6474, pp. 6–8. George Thomason dated his copy on 16 October 1655.

[3] Arthur Cotton to George Fox *et al.*, Sw Trs 1: 628, 20 February 1656. In 1664, one Nicholas Cole of Plymouth was named as a distributor of Quaker books: PRO, sp 29/109 fol. 44. I am grateful to Michael Frearson for this reference.

[4] Arthur Cotton to George Fox, Sw Trs 1: 630, 18 November 1656. The Nayler affair is discussed fully in Chapter 8.

were extremely active participants in the early movement, acting as ministers, undertaking vast itinerant missions and publishing a number of Quaker
tracts. In the organisational developments of the movement after the Restoration, separate meetings for women were established, the first of their kind
in protestant churches. Pamphleteering was an important part of this female
public role in the 1650s. Patricia Crawford has shown that nearly half of
all women's published writing was produced by Quaker women during the
1650s.[5] This fitted well with the argument, first voiced by Keith Thomas in
a seminal article published in 1958, that the civil war sects, and the Quakers
in particular, provided unusually active public roles for women.[6] Quaker
literature also included some of the earliest justifications for women's public
speaking, and for their spiritual equality with men.[7]

The kind of conflicts described in the opening cameo were important in
shaping the development of women's public roles in the Quaker movement.
As has been shown, Quaker pamphleteering was a strategic and sophisticated part of the Quakers' campaign to establish themselves as a national
movement. From a very early date, leaders of the movement published a
series of ambiguous arguments about the status of women which served to
legitimate and limit their presence in the Quaker movement. The ongoing
attitudes of men like Arthur Cotton were central to the very early establishment of internal discipline structures. The perceived need to curb and control
unruly women contributed in a very important way to the development of a
highly organised movement. This chapter will argue that a doctrinal position,
on the spiritual equality of women, and on their fitness for public ministry,
was very carefully presented in print, while at the same time strategies were
developed for controlling their public roles. Pamphleteering in the Quaker
movement was a dynamic process which helped to shape perceptions of the
movement, both for contemporaries and for historians.

Quaker women have for a long time been a celebrated part of women's
history. Hailed as 'Mothers of Feminism'[8] and 'incipient feminists',[9] the public preaching, itinerant ministry, prolific writing and defiant acts of protest
of Quaker women in the seventeenth century have been described time and

[5] See Patricia Crawford, 'Women's published writings 1600–1700' and Richard Bell and Patricia
Crawford, 'Statistical analysis of women's printed writings 1600–1700', in Mary Prior (ed.),
Women in English society 1500–1800 (London, 1985), p. 269.

[6] Keith Thomas, 'Women and the civil war sects', *Past and Present* 13 (1958), 42–62.

[7] Elaine Hobby, 'Handmaids of the Lord and Mothers in Israel: early vindications of Quaker
women's prophecy', in Thomas Corns and David Loewenstein (eds.), *The emergence of
Quaker writing dissenting literature in seventeenth-century England* (London, 1995), pp. 88–
98.

[8] Margaret Hope Bacon, *Mothers of feminism: the story of Quaker women in America* (San
Francisco, 1986).

[9] Christine Trevett, *Women and Quakerism in the seventeenth century* (York, 1991), p. 10.

again by historians. One of the reasons for this is that Quaker women are more accessible to historians than other women. Because of the unusually conscientious approach of early Quakers to recording their own history, we have access to the autobiographies, spiritual testimonies and printed tracts of early Quaker women. Accounts of their trials and imprisonments are recorded in Quaker books of sufferings; they wrote, and appear in, hundreds of Quaker letters still preserved at the Friends' House Library.[10]

The traditionally strong public role of Quaker women is reflected in their compelling presence in denominational histories. Mabel Brailsford wrote the first narrative history of seventeenth-century Quaker women in 1915, shortly after Braithwaite's study of the beginnings of the movement as a whole was first published in 1911.[11] In 1922, the first account of the social origins of early Quaker ministers included an analysis of the social status of women ministers: a subject which has not been attempted subsequently.[12] Margaret Fell, the 'Mother of Quakerism', has been the subject of substantial biographies; and the individual lives of other early Quaker women have also been chronicled.[13]

More recent studies of Quaker women reflect the changing discipline of women's history, and there is an increasing tendency to remove Quaker women from their immediate denominational context and to study them instead as female activists.[14] They have been studied as radical participants of the English revolution, threatening to 'shake patriarchy's foundations'.[15] Their published writings have been singled out and studied by feminist

---

[10] The role of women in recording Quaker history is in itself interesting, from Elizabeth Hooton and Margaret Fell keeping copies of their letters from 1652, to Emily Jermyn and Charlotte Fell Smith transcribing the Swarthmoor and Abram Barclay manuscripts in the nineteenth century.

[11] Mabel Brailsford, *Quaker women 1650–1690* (London, 1915); W. C. Braithwaite, *The beginnings of Quakerism* (1st edn, London, 1911).

[12] Ernest E. Taylor, 'The first Publishers of Truth: a study', *JFHS* 19 (1922), 66–81. Compare with Barry Reay, 'The social origins of early Quakerism', *Journal of Interdisciplinary History* 11:1 (Summer 1980), 55–72; and also Reay, 'Early Quaker activity and reactions to it, 1652–1664', unpublished D Phil. thesis, University of Oxford, 1979, pp. 37–38. Phyllis Mack argues that Quaker women from London tended to be of higher social status than those from the north of England: Phyllis Mack, *Visionary women: ecstatic prophecy in seventeenth-century England* (Berkeley, 1992), 186–96.

[13] Isabel Ross, *Margaret Fell, Mother of Quakerism* (York, 1984 edn); Bonnelyn Young Kunze, *Margaret Fell and the rise of Quakerism* (London, 1994); E. Manners, *Elizabeth Hooton: first Quaker woman preacher (1600–1672)*, *JFHS* Supplement series 12 (London 1914); Lucy Hodgkin, *A Quaker saint of Cornwall: Loveday Hambly and her guests* (London, 1927); Brailsford, *Quaker women*.

[14] In 1991, Christine Trevett felt the need for a new feminist study on Quaker women in the seventeenth century, and, in her own words, wrote it, 'because no-one else had'. Trevett, *Women and Quakerism*, p. vii.

[15] Dorothy Ludlow, '"Arise and be doing": English preaching women, 1640–1660', unpublished Ph.D dissertation, Indiana University, 1978; Ludlow, 'Shaking patriarchy's foundations', in Richard L. Greaves (ed.), *Triumph over silence* (London, 1985); Thomas, 'Women

literary critics.[16] Most recently, Quaker women have been studied as examples of seventeenth-century female spirituality and self-consciousness.[17]

Women were active participants of many radical movements in the 1640s and 50s. The sects and gathered churches which proliferated in the period provided a unique opportunity for women, and sometimes quite humble women, to play a significant public role.[18] Patricia Crawford's work on women's published writing shows a sharp rise in the number of women's publications, which addressed broad political and religious issues.[19] Patricia Higgins has examined women's petitions to parliaments and the political demonstrations mounted by women in London; and Phyllis Mack, Dorothy Ludlow and Patricia Crawford have examined the activities of radical female sectaries.[20] This was the period of 'the world turned upside down'; 'when women preach and cobblers pray'. Arguments differ as to how far, or whether, these activities were challenging of patriarchal society, and whether they had any lasting effect on the status of women.[21] Women justified and qualified their behaviour by affirming the inferiority of their sex, or claimed that their authority to act was based on spiritual, rather than actual worldly, equality with men.[22] They thus reinforced patriarchal assumptions that women, as women, should not behave in this way.

Discussions of female participation in the early Quaker movement also emphasise the spiritual impulse behind the women's extraordinary

---

and the civil war sects', 42–62; Phyllis Mack, 'Women as prophets during the English civil war', *Feminist studies* 8: 1 (1982), 19–45; and (more cautiously), Patricia Crawford, 'Sex and power in the early Quaker movement: the case of Martha Simmonds', in Crawford, *Women and Religion in England, 1500–1720* (London, 1993).

[16] Patricia Crawford, 'Women's published writings, 1600–1700', identified Quaker women's printed writings in the context of all works published by women over this period, in Prior (ed.), *Women in English society*; Elaine Hobby, *Virtue of necessity: English women's writing, 1649–88* (London, 1988); Margaret Ezell, 'Breaking the seventh seal: writings by early Quaker women', *Writing women's literary history* (Baltimore, 1993), pp. 132–60.

[17] Elaine C. Huber, ' "A woman must not speak": Quaker women in the English left wing', in Rosemary Reuther and Eleanor McLaughlin (eds.), *Women of spirit: female leadership in the Jewish and Christian traditions* (New York, 1979), pp. 154–81; Mack, *Visionary women*.

[18] Crawford, *Women and religion in England*, esp. pp. 119–182; Crawford, 'The challenges to patriachalism: how did the revolution affect women?', in John Morrill (ed.), *Revolution and restoration: England in the 1650s* (London, 1992), pp. 112–28.

[19] Crawford, 'Women's published writings 1600–1700', p. 269.

[20] Patricia Higgins, 'The reactions of women, with special reference to women petitioners', in Brian Manning (ed.), *Politics, religion and the English civil war* (London, 1973), pp. 179–222; Ludlow, ' "Arise and be doing": English preaching women, 1640–1660'; Ludlow, 'Shaking patriarchy's foundations'; Mack, 'Women as prophets during the English civil war'; Crawford, *Women and religion in England*, chapters 6–8.

[21] Patricia Crawford, echoing the question posed by Joan Kelly, 'Did women have a Renaissance?', wonders whether women in mid-seventeenth-century England had a revolution; and seems to think not. Crawford, *Women and religion*, p. 5; see also Crawford, 'The challenges to patriachalism', pp. 112–28.

[22] Mack, 'Women as prophets during the English civil war', 19–38.

behaviour, and recognise it as equally limiting. Christine Trevett wrote in 1991: 'this was no brand of radical feminism which was being offered, revolutionary though it was in its way . . . It was *spiritual* equality which was being held out to [Quaker women].'[23] Phyllis Mack argued that the ecstatic prophecy and public preaching of Quaker women was based on a negation of gender which was implicit to the whole of Quaker theology: both women and men in the Quaker movement insisted that they preached as 'disembodied spirits' in the Light of God, rejecting any worldly or carnal identity. At the same time, she argued that the non-spiritual, day-to-day existence of Quaker women was shaped by a celebration of women as 'nursing mothers of Israel'; and that the perception of them as providers and nurturers fed directly into the organisational and institutional developments in the Quaker movement as a whole.[24]

While mainstream historians of the Quaker movement have had no difficulty in identifying early Quakers and their beliefs as radical and democratic, historians of Quaker women are less inclined to make the same analysis. This is partly because women's historians extend their assessment of the Quaker women's religious activities well into the 1660s and 1670s, when their role became defined far more by formal women's meetings, with the specific tasks of organising marriages, education and the discipline of other women.[25] The focus on female religiosity or spirituality has also had the effect of divorcing early Quaker women from the immediate political context of the early Quaker movement. To some extent, non-denominational historians of Quaker women deny them any agency in the development of Quaker ideas and fail to see them as active participants in the movement's growth. Recent works on Quaker women by Mack, Christine Trevett and Elaine Huber all studied the 'Quaker doctrines' which shaped the women's spirituality as an established, immutable and homogeneous mass. A major factor in the spiritual empowerment of women is seen to be George Fox himself. Christine Trevett is in no doubt that George Fox in 1648 was the first Quaker proponent of women's public speaking; Elaine Huber argues that George Fox should be credited for 'insisting on leadership roles for women'; Phyllis Mack wonders why Fox was 'so receptive to the authority of women'.[26]

Thus the argument is that Quaker women were at once empowered by the liberty they derived from their spirituality; and at the same time limited

---

[23] Trevett, *Women and Quakerism*, p. 52.   [24] Mack, *Visionary women*, pp. 134, 236–61.

[25] For accounts of the development of women's meetings, see Arnold Lloyd, *Quaker social history, 1669–1738* (London, 1950), pp. 107–19; Mack, *Visionary women*, pp. 265–304; Young Kunze, *Margaret Fell*, pp. 143–68; Isabel Ross, *Margaret Fell*, pp. 283–302.

[26] Trevett, *Women and Quakerism*, pp. 13–14, 47–48; Huber, ' "A woman must not speak", p. 160; Mack, *Visionary women*, p. 240. Mabel Brailsford also devoted the whole of the first chapter of her book to the influence of the teachings of George Fox on the women of the Quaker movement: Brailsford, *Quaker women*, chapter one.

in the degree of female awakening this involved because the Quaker notion of spirituality was essentially un-gendered. Yet the emphasis on spirituality alone as an explanation for the proliferation of women in the movement is problematic. The activities surrounding pamphleteering present a useful context in which to reassess the public role of women in the movement. Pamphleteering was, first and foremost, an activity in which women participated, as authors, messengers and distributors.[27] More than this, it was through the Quakers' publications that the framework of ideas was presented by which women's public ministry was justified and discussed. The extent to which women participated in the development of these ideas will reveal something about their wider role in the movement.

Although they are rightly celebrated as prolific female authors of the mid-seventeenth century, Quaker women did not dominate Quaker pamphleteering as a whole; only a handful of early Quaker authors were women. Women wrote more frequently as contributors to tracts than as authors in their own right.[28] The most prolific of the women authors, Margaret Fell and Martha Simmonds, were not quite in the league of the leading corpus of authors. The fact, nevertheless, that both of these women held positions of considerable authority in the movement, Fell as its chief co-ordinator, and Simmonds as a charismatic leader whose authority in London rivalled James Nayler's, underlines the argument that writing was equated with leadership.[29] It also shows that Fell, and less surprisingly Simmonds, did not exercise the same degree of authority as the likes of James Nayler, Edward Burrough or Richard Farnworth.

Printed Quaker tracts in the 1650s which discussed the rights of women to preach constituted only a very small proportion of Quaker literature. Of the three hundred or so Quaker tracts printed between 1652 and 1656, only four addressed the issue at any length.[30] Although Quaker women were active ministers and remarkably prolific female authors of their time, none of them addressed the argument herself.

---

[27] Maureen Bell, 'Mary Westwood, Quaker publisher', *Publishing History* 23 (1988), 5–66.

[28] Ten women contributed to tracts; and some of these, like Margaret Braidley and Ann Blaykling may have been the subject of a tract rather than the actual authors. Others, like Elizabeth Hooton, Jane Holmes and Mary Fisher, appeared as signatories rather than as authors of separate sections of tracts. Six women – Margaret Fell, Martha Simmonds, Ann Audland, Ann Gargill, Priscilla Cotton and Hester Biddle – wrote tracts in their own names and as the sole author. See Peters, 'Quaker pamphleteering and the development of the Quaker movement, 1652–1656', Cambridge Ph.D thesis, 1966, p. 27.

[29] Crawford, *Women and religion*, pp. 160–82; Christine Trevett, 'The women around James Nayler, Quaker: a matter of emphasis', *Religion* 20 (1990), 249–73.

[30] The texts are: Richard Farnworth, *A woman forbidden to speak in the church* (London, 1654) *STC* F514, reprinted 1655, *STC* F515; Ann Audland *et al.*, *The saints testimony finishing through sufferings* (London, 1655), *STC* S365; Priscilla Cotton and Mary Cole, *To the priests and people of England* (London, 1655), *STC* C6474; George Fox, *A woman learning in silence* (London, 1656), *STC* F1991.

Despite this, the very existence of an argument in favour of women's speaking is rightly perceived as significant and has contributed to the view that the early Quaker movement was empowering of women.[31] The argument over Quaker women's speaking has been dominated by the fact that the case was very famously propounded by Margaret Fell, in 1666. This pamphlet, *Women's speaking justified, proved and allowed of by the Scriptures*, has attracted much attention from women's historians. An edition of it was reprinted in 1989. Moira Ferguson counted it a piece of feminist religious polemic. Isabel Ross, the Quaker biographer of Margaret Fell, hailed it as the first book to be written by a woman since the Reformation which argued for the spiritual equality of women.[32]

It is problematic to equate Fell's work, written in 1666, with the emerging Quaker movement of the early 1650s. Margaret Fell was, by 1666, established as a major leader of the movement. Her wealth and social status were considerable: as wife and later widow of Judge Thomas Fell, Margaret Fell oversaw a substantial farming estate and maintained her lower-middling gentry status; after the Restoration she met with Charles II to discuss religious toleration with him.[33] In 1669 she married George Fox, and together in the 1660s and 70s it was their work which consolidated the Quaker movement into a respectable and disciplined church. Fell's gentry status was very important in establishing the respectability of the Quakers; indeed on occasion more important than her gender as a significant counterweight to the perceived humble status of George Fox.[34] Fox and Fell collaborated over the establishment of separate women's meetings in the 1660s, in the face of serious internal opposition by other Quaker leaders; and both the Fox–Fell marriage, and the publication of *Women's Speaking justified*, were part of the attempt to defend the meetings.[35] Seen in this context, *Women's speaking justified* has been described as 'cautious', and lacking in the 'charm and wit' of other Quaker women's writing.[36] Elaine Hobby, who has made a useful

---

[31] But note the important caveat that seventeenth-century texts about the role of women are frequently misread by historians: 'because they can so readily be situated in the context of gender politics, they are never fully situated in the political and discursive specificities of the early modern period'. Diane Purkiss, 'Material girls: the seventeenth-century woman debate', in Clare Brant and Diane Purkiss (eds.), *Women, texts and histories 1575–1760* (London, 1992), p. 70.

[32] Margaret Fell, *Women's speaking justified, proved and allowed of by the Scriptures* (London, 1666), STC F642, reissued by Pythia Press, London, 1989; Moira Ferguson (ed.), *First Feminists: British women writers 1578–1799* (Bloomington, Ind., 1985), p. 114; Ross, *Margaret Fell, Mother of Quakerism*, p. 201.

[33] Young Kunze, *Margaret Fell*, pp. 65–82, esp. pp. 78–79. Thomas Fell died in 1658.

[34] Bonnelyn Young Kunze, 'Religious authority and social status in seventeenth-century England: the friendship of Margaret Fell, George Fox, and William Penn', *Church History* 57: 2 (1988), 170–86.

[35] Young Kunze, *Margaret Fell*, pp. 154–55.   [36] Trevett, *Women and Quakerism*, p. 54.

study of women's writing between 1649 and 1688, considered it 'far more careful and conservative' than the actual preaching activities of women over the preceding decades.[37]

There are clear parallels between Fell's work and the handful of texts which actually posited the right of women to preach in the 1650s. In many ways Fell's work of 1666 was a summary of these texts, and can be seen, like them, as part of an attempt by the Quaker leadership to normalise and legitimate the potentially disruptive public preaching of women in the Quaker movement.

The first Quaker pamphlet which posited the right of women to speak was written by Richard Farnworth. It was circulating in London in the first half of January 1654, and so was probably written around the end of 1653; by all accounts, it can be counted as a significantly early Quaker tract.[38] It was called, rather perversely, *A woman forbidden to speak in the church*, but despite the title was a case well argued from scriptural texts. Indeed, Farnworth rather modishly took on race, class and gender on the frontispiece, quoting from Galatians (3.28.): 'There is neither Jew nor Greek, there is neither bond nor free, there is neither male nor female, for ye are all one in Christ Jesus.' The point of the tract was to counter the argument from the Pauline edicts that a woman should not speak in the church; and that she should learn from her husband in silence and all subjection.[39] The central justification used by Farnworth for women's public speaking came from the Book of Joel: 'And it shall come to pass, in the last dayes, saith the Lord, I will pour out my Spirit upon all Flesh; your Sons and Daughters shall prophecy.'[40] (See Plates 5 and 6.)

Farnworth began his tract, in a way typical of early Quaker writing which challenged and subverted the worldly meanings placed on words, by arguing about the term 'church': for Farnworth, it was not a physical, or rather 'carnal' building, but 'is made all of living stones, elect and precious [1 Pet. 2 5.], and the Saints, their Bodyes are made fit Temples for the Holy Ghost to dwell in [2 Cor. 6.16.]'.[41] By defining a church as the people who comprise its congregation, it would become more acceptable that women should be allowed to speak 'in the church': it established that women spoke as elect saints first and foremost. From this, Farnworth very rapidly went

---

[37] Hobby, *Virtue of necessity*, p. 45. Elaine Hobby is also quite correctly at pains to make mention of the earlier visionary Quaker works which vindicated women's preaching in far more extravagant terms before the Quaker 'official stance on the subject became ever more guarded' (p. 45).

[38] Richard Farnworth, *A woman forbidden to speak in the church* (London, 1654), *STC* F514. The stationer George Thomason obtained a copy on 18 January 1654.

[39] Cf. 1 Cor. 14. 34; 1 Tim. 2. 11.   [40] Cf. Joel 2. 28; and also Acts 2. 17–18.

[41] Farnworth, *A woman forbidden*, p. 2.

LG

A WOMAN

forbidden to speak
IN
the Church,

The grounds examined, the Myſtery
opened, the Truth cleared, and the
ignorance both of Prieſts and
Peeple diſcovered.

Written by a friend of the Truth, whoſe name in
the fleſh is RICHARD FARNEWORTH.

And Jeſus anſwering, ſayd unto them, Do ye not therefore erre,
becauſe ye know not the Scripture, neither the power of God, Mark
12. 24

For as many of you as have been baptized into Chriſt, have put
on Chriſt : There is neither Jew nor Greek, there is neither bond nor
free, there is neither male nor female, for ye are all one in Chriſt Ieſus, Gal. 3. 27. 2*.

Ieſus anſwered and ſayd, My Doctrin is not mine but his that
ſent me : If any man will do his Will, he ſhall know of the doctrin
whether it be of God, or whether I ſpeak of my ſelf, John 7.16.17.

LONDON,
Printed for *Giles Calvert* at the Black Spread Eagle,
at the Weſt End of *Pauls.* 165*4* 1653

Plate 5. Richard Farnworth, *A woman forbidden to speak in the church* (London,
1654), STC F541, sig. A1r.

The VVoman learning in Silence : 8

OR, THE

MYSTERIE

OF THE

Womans Subiection

TO HER

HUSBAND.

As also,

The Daughter prophesying, where-
in the Lord hath, and is fulfilling that he spake
by the Prophet *Joel*, *I will poure out my*
Spirit upon all Flesh, *&c.*

Given forth by *George Fox.*

Quench not the Spirit.
Despise not Prophesying.

march: 22   *LONDON,*   *1655*
Printed for *Thomas Simonds*, at the sign of the *Bul*
and *Mouth* neer *Aldersgate.* 1656. 5

Plate 6. George Fox, *The woman learning in silence, or, the mysterie of
the woman's subjection to her husband* (London, 1656), STC F1991,
sigs. A1 and A2r.

on to dismiss gender as a significant criterion in determining who should be allowed to speak in the 'church':

> that which is flesh is flesh, and that knoweth not the things of God, neither in male nor female, but is adulterated from God, but that which is spirit is spirit, and is born of God, either in male or female, that knoweth him, and that is permitted to speak in the Temple.[42]

Farnworth also cited examples of female prophets from the Bible to underline that women were likely to serve well as messengers of holy spirit. Paul 'writ to the Romans to receive Phebe, which was a Servant or Minister to the Church at Conchrea'; he had likewise commended Priscilla and Aquila; and also Mary 'who bestowed much labor on us'. Farnworth paid particular attention to Tryphena and Tryphos, 'delicious or delicate, two godly women, and beloved of the Lord, who laboured with Paul in the Gospel'.[43] Farnworth gathered all of his examples of female ministry from chapter sixteen of Romans, and so did not over exert himself in his case-study. His broader discussion conflated an attack on worldly wisdom and professional ministry with a justification of female ministry, arguing that spiritual identity superseded gender:

> Let all carnal Wisdome in Male as well as in Female keep silence, for that is not permited [*sic*] to speak, it is adulterated from God; and the natural man knowes not the things of God.

From this, it was a short step to arguing that women's weaker natural state lent itself to their greater receptivity to God:

> all the Wisdom of the world it knoweth not God, who is a Spirit, and he chuseth the weak things of this world to confound the things which are mighty, 1 *Cor*.1.27.28.29. and the Woman is counted the weaker Vessel, but the Lord is filling that Vessel full of his Wisdom, and ruleing it by his holy Spirit he dwelling in his Temple.[44]

Farnworth's argument appeared more pragmatic at the end of his tract when he finally returned rather neatly to his original dichotomy of the carnal and spiritual definition of the church. He now provided – again referring to two biblical female prophets – a much more immediate and recognisable justification for the necessity of women to speak in the church, and one which referred to the actual nature of early Quaker worship:

> But to *Aquila* and *Priscilla* salute me, and to *the Church that is in their house*, 1 *Cor*.16.19, and let her speak by the Spirit of the Lord the things of God made manifest unto her, for if she be not permitted to speak in the Church, and the Church be in her house, she must not speak, but go out of her house.[45]

---

[42] *Ibid*., p. 3.   [43] *Ibid*., p. 7. Compare with Romans 16.   [44] *Ibid*., p. 4.   [45] *Ibid*., p. 8.

Farnworth's conclusion was based on the fact that Quaker women held an important role in the early Quaker movement: of hosting Quaker meetings in their houses. The first pamphlet expounding the Quaker doctrine of 'allowing women to speak' was based on ideas of the spiritual equality of women and men, but also responded to a need to legitimate the existing functions carried out by Quaker women.

Farnworth's pamphlet was reprinted the following year, in 1655. In 1656 George Fox also published a tract which discussed the rights of women to speak. Like Farnworth's, this carried the similarly perverse title, *The woman learning in silence*; and Fox spent his first page citing almost verbatim from the Pauline edict forbidding women to speak without apparently contradicting it.[46] Yet once under way, Fox's pamphlet reiterated the arguments of spiritual equality, scriptural precedent and the fact that any preaching essentially denied any worldly identity, first expounded by Farnworth to defend the right of Quaker women to speak. The intellectual presentation of spiritual equality, in Quakers' published writings, was thus clearly based, as Mack argued, on a negation of 'worldly' gender; the right of women to prophecy did not empower women, as women, with any worldly agency.

Placed in the context of other contemporary Quaker writings, these two tracts also, however, contributed to the construction of a wider argument that placed other limitations on women. Earlier, in April 1653, Richard Farnworth had written a tract which dealt with the position of women in the Quaker movement. This tract, entitled *An Easter-Reckoning*, after a lengthy account of the wrongdoings of England's ministry, contained a section called 'The Lords free love-offering to his own people', or 'How everyone is bound in duty to be in subjection to the Lord, and to walk in obedience to his commands'.[47] This outlined the proper societal relations between God's own people in a godly commonwealth, beginning with children's 'dues or duty' to parents, servants' duties to their masters, magistrates' duties to God, and ending with instructions to alehouse keepers and warnings to 'whoremongers and adulterers'.[48] Under the heading 'Wives dues or duty to their husbands', Farnworth exhorted:

Wives, be in subjection to your own husbands, and love them in the Lord, walking in obedience to his commands, and be not angry, nor proud, nor stubborn, nor cross, nor hasty, nor peevish, nor perverse, do not scold, nor braul, nor lye, nor swear, for God doth forbid it; but be loving, and meek, gentle, and lowly minded, and be in subjection to the Lord, and live in love one with another; let not the woman usurpe authority over the man, but be in subjection, as Sarah was, who obeyed Abraham,

---

[46] George Fox, *The woman learning in silence* (London, 1656), STC F1991.
[47] Richard Farnworth [and Thomas Aldam], *An Easter-Reckoning* (London, 1653), STC F480, sig. Ar.
[48] *Ibid.*, pp. 17–20.

and called him Lord; and be chast, and sober minded, and stay at home, and waite
upon the Lord, and give glory to his name, in yeelding obedience to his commands,
that he may be honoured and glorified for ever.[49]

To the husbands, Farnworth was less exacting in his recommendations:

Husbands, love your wives, as Christ loved his Church, and gave himself for it, and
be loving and gentle to them, according to the command of the Lord.[50]

An Easter-Reckoning is an astounding tract because it appeared so early
in the history of the Quaker movement, and yet established rules for the
maintaining of Quaker discipline. It has been seen already from the private
Quaker correspondence that Farnworth and other Quakers frequently circulated letters to be read at the local Quaker meetings which were springing
up across the north of England. These similarly amount to a sort of early
Quaker church discipline; yet for two reasons Farnworth's printed tract is
more remarkable. First, the private manuscript exhortations between early
Quakers more frequently related to forms of worship, urging friends not
to lose their faith, and to meet together for worship. Farnworth's printed
tract, which was strongly reminiscent of the more common Christian conduct books, was concerned with very real issues of social hierarchies and
patriarchal control.[51] Secondly, Farnworth's tract was intended for a wider
audience than isolated Quaker meetings. At least one hostile reader encountered the tract, for he referred to it in a printed work of his own attacking
the Quakers; and we can be certain that other readers outside the Quaker
movement would have seen the tract.[52] *An Easter-Reckoning* was a very
early statement of Quaker conduct, intended to publicise Quaker doctrines
to an audience who would undoubtedly be hostile, and in particular hostile
to the predominance of unruly, outspoken women in the Quaker movement.

If the link between *An Easter-Reckoning* and Farnworth's later publication of *A woman forbidden to speak* seems tenuous, George Fox made it
abundantly clear. In his own tract, *The woman learning in silence*, he abandoned on page two his account of the wonders worked by women prophets
in the Bible, to expound boldly on seventeenth-century patriarchy:

Husbands love your Wives, and be not bitter against them. Wives submit your selves
first to your Husbands as unto the Lord: The Husband is the head of the Wife, even
as Christ is the head of the church, and is the Saviour of the body: Therefore as the
church is subject to Christ, so let the Wives be subject to their own Husbands in
everything. Husbands love your Wives, even as Christ loved the church, and gave
himself for it, that he might sanctifie and cleanse it by the washing of water by the

---

[49] *Ibid.*, pp. 18–19. Cf. Ephesians 5. 21 and Colossians 3. 18–25; 4. 1.   [50] *Ibid.*, p. 19.
[51] For a discussion of the genesis of the wider, but very similar 'protestant family', Patrick
Collinson, *The birthpangs of Protestant England* (London, 1988), pp. 60–93.
[52] Luke Fawne *et al.*, *A second beacon fired* (London, 1654), STC F565.

Word, that he might present it a glorious church, without spot or wrinckle, or any such thing, that it should be holy without blemish.[53]

In Fox's view, then, Quaker women, like all wives, were to be cleansed, and sanctified. They were to have their spots, wrinkles and blemishes removed. There were thus very clear limitations to his 'receptivity of their authority'; and he states them in the very tract in which he justifies their role as prophets.

The other printed Quaker tract of the early 1650s which defended women's public speaking affords a greater insight still into the influence of Quaker men in propounding the argument that the women's right to speak was entirely spiritual. Because it was written jointly by men and women, and described a series of events at a Quaker trial, it provides evidence of the very differing attitudes of men and women in the Quaker movement to the activities of women, and to the perceived need to justify them to a hostile public.

The tract, called *The saints testimony finishing through sufferings*, was written by a group of Quaker prisoners at Banbury in 1655: usually, it is associated with the authorship of the Quaker Ann Audland, although in fact many Quakers contributed to it.[54] The tight chronology leading up to the publication of the tract is important.

Ann Audland was wife of John Audland (*c.* 1630–1664), a yeoman from Crosslands (also described as a linen draper), who had served in the army in the civil war, and had been a preacher to the Seeker group at Preston Patrick from 1650.[55] Ann Audland herself, born in Kendal in 1627, had been educated for a time in London where she made contact with gathered churches, before returning to Kendal and the Preston Patrick Seekers, marrying John Audland in 1650.[56] In September 1654, John Audland and John Camm travelled to Bristol through Banbury and Oxford. Once they arrived in Bristol they sent a letter to Giles Calvert to be forwarded to their wives, Ann and Mabel, probably asking them to undertake a preaching mission to Banbury.[57] Ann Audland, leaving her young child at Kendal, travelled to Banbury with Mabel Camm and Mabel Camm's servant Jane Waugh, arriving there on 13 January 1655; shortly afterwards, Ann Audland and Jane Waugh were imprisoned for assaulting the local minister and using blasphemous words.[58] Ann Audland took issue with the grounds of her imprisonment, which she

---

[53] Fox, *The woman learning in silence*, p. 2. Cf. Ephesians, 5. 25–27.
[54] Ann Audland *et al.*, *The saints testimony finishing through sufferings* (London, 1655), STC s365.
[55] For John Audland, see *BDBR*.   [56] *DNB*; *DQB*.
[57] John Audland and John Camm to Edward Burrough and Francis Howgill, 13 September 1654, A. R. Barclay Mss 2: 157; see also Audland's Journal, pp. 32–34.
[58] Braithwaite, *Beginnings of Quakerism*, p. 199. Ann Audland requested of Burrough and Howgill: 'Let mee heare how the childe at Kendall doth' in a letter from Banbury. Ann Audland to Edward Burrough and Francis Howgill [?6 April 1655], A. R. Barclay Mss 2: 175.

argued were unlawful; and on 5 February 1655 she explained why in her first tract, written in prison, and called *A true declaration of the suffering of the innocent*. It was published in London and in circulation by early March.[59] As has been seen, the recording of Quaker sufferings and trials in print was already an established genre of Quaker writing; Ann Audland would in all probability have seen many similar accounts, and was evidently confident of her purpose in writing:

This [she explained to the local Justice of the Peace] was I moved to write to clear my conscience of thee, and leave thee without excuse, that when the Book of *Conscience* is opened, thou mayest remember that thou wast warned in thy life-time.[60]

In this first tract, of which she was the sole author, she made little reference to her gender, sticking to the legal injustices wrought upon her, and by extension upon the nation. She subsumed her female identity as author under that of her identity as a Quaker, as did her male colleagues: the frontispiece states that it was written: 'By *Anne Audland*, whom the world scornfully calls QUAKER'. The word Quaker appeared in large capitals on a single line, the largest word on the page.

Here we see the practical implications of the doctrine that it was through the spirit rather than the flesh that men and women were to prophecy. By emphasising that she was known only to the world as Ann Audland, she was clearly implying that she had another, spiritual identity which remained hidden from those who knew no better. The similarities with her male co-religionists must be stressed: Ann Audland would certainly have encountered the stylistic affectation of insisting that they are known by their names only 'in the flesh'. Ann Audland was more explicit than her male contemporaries in her use of this device as an excuse for, or rather negation of, her gender, as the frontispiece sported the citation from Acts 2.18:

And on my servants and on my handmaidens, I will poure out in those dayes of my Spirit, and they shall prophesie.

Inside the tract, she also stated that Christ 'is one in the male and in the female'.[61] Beyond referring to these biblical texts, however, Ann Audland developed the argument no further. If we can consider the brief reference to these texts as a justification for her behaviour as a woman, it was based on the negation of the significance of her gender, rather than on an attempt to qualify or normalise it.

Perhaps as a result of Ann Audland's alacrity in publishing an account of her sufferings, and also because of the very sophisticated news network

---

[59] Ann Audland, *A true declaration of the suffering of the innocent* (London, 1655), STC A4195. George Thomason obtained a copy on 3 March 1655.
[60] *Ibid*., p. 2.   [61] *Ibid*., p. 5.

of Quaker correspondence, events at Banbury rapidly became a focal point for other Quaker missionaries, just as they did for Richard Hubberthorne and his colleagues in Norwich and Cambridge.[62] Quaker ministers, including Richard Farnworth and Robert Rich, as well as more women, Sarah Tims and Margaret Vivers, came to Banbury from Bristol, Gloucestershire, Berkshire and elsewhere; and over the course of the summer of 1655 each was imprisoned in turn.[63] An account of their imprisonments, and trial at Banbury Quarter Sessions in September 1655, was published in November. It was this jointly authored work, *The saints testimony finishing through sufferings*, which proffered a further justification of women's public speaking. In this tract, indeed, there was a much greater sense that hostility to the Quakers was born out of an hostility to women: when Sarah Tims was called to the bar, apparently well versed in Quaker legal tactics, the tract stated:

she desired to know by what Law they committed her; and one *Iohn Austine*, called Mayor, answered, *that sweeping the house, and washing the dishes was the first point of law to her* (or words to that effect) so sent her back again to the Prison, she not being charged with any breach of the Law.[64]

Margaret Vivers had apparently posed more of a problem to the court, and the tract claimed that the court officials had:

confessed that they had *Margaret Vivers* (who had spoken to the Priest in the *Steeple-house* . . .) there, neither for whoredome, felony, nor theft, . . . yet it was the Mayors mind that she should be there, but whether she had committed any offence or no, they could not tel . . . the man that had kept her in custody, did object against a woman speaking in the church; it was asked whether the Spirit of God might not be permitted to speak in the Temple of God, yea or nay; the which by some was answered and granted that it might.[65]

At this point in the tract, the account of the trial was suspended, and there followed a by now familiar section proving the spiritual equality of men and women, and the biblical precedent for women prophets.[66] It is only later

---

[62] News of Ann Audland reached Kendal and thence Margaret Fell: Thomas Willan to Fell, 10 May 1655, Sw Mss 1: 235; William to Fell, Sw Mss, 1: 247. John Audland sent news of his wife to Edward Burrough and Francis Howgill in London: A. R. Barclay Mss 1: 116; 2: 175. Audland also informed John Wilkinson and John Storey of the prisoners in Banbury just as they were about to set off for London from Wiltshire in early April: John Audland to John Storey and Wilkinson, 1 April 1655, A. R. Barclay Mss 1: 28. As has been seen, both London and Swarthmoor were crucial centres from which the national campaign was co-ordinated.

[63] Audland, *The saints testimony*, p. 2. See also John Audland to Margaret Fell, 1 October 1655, Sw Mss 1: 391, who noted that Bristol heavy-weights Captain Edward Pyott, Dennis Hollister, Thomas Gouldney, Walter Clement, John Camm and Robert Rich had gone to Banbury for the assizes.

[64] Audland, *The saints testimony*, mispaginated, sig. Bv.

[65] *Ibid.*, pp. 14–15.   [66] *Ibid.*, pp. 15–16.

in the tract, when Richard Farnworth's trial was recorded, that it becomes clear that it was he who spoke in court on the right of women to prophecy:

> there was a few words spoken concerning the Objection of the womans non-permission, . . . and when it was asked them on the Bench, if the Spirit of God might not speak in the Temple, they were then put to a stand, or partly silent about the same; and *R.F.* then and there said, if any of them would deny it, he would by plain Scripture prove that the Spirit of God might speak in his Temple (meaning either in the body of male or female).[67]

The presence of so many women in court had clearly raised the hackles of the authorities. It is not surprising that their response was to silence and ridicule them. But the response of Farnworth was more interesting. On one level, he was defending his silenced fellow prisoners' right to speak publicly, reiterating the by now well-rehearsed argument for spiritual equality which he himself had first published in 1654.[68] But on another level he was legitimating, and attempting to normalise, the behaviour of his female co-religionists to an angry court house. The exchange on the subject of the 'Women's non-permission' took place between men. Farnworth was already concerned with the public presentation of the position of women in the Quaker movement, as has been seen not only in *A woman forbidden to speak*, but also when he had set out 'The wives dues or duty to their husbands' in 1653. It is in this context that his public defence of their behaviour in court should best be understood.

In contrast to carefully argued printed tracts of Farnworth and Fox, the references by women to their public speaking are very different. When Ann Audland first recorded her experiences in February 1655, she had felt apparently no need to justify her behaviour as a woman at any great length, either in court or in her written account. In her account of the trial in *The saints testimony*, she was concerned not with any scriptural defence of her behaviour, but instead reproved the judge indignantly for telling Sarah Tims to sweep the floor.

It is necessary to modify Phyllis Mack's argument that Quaker women's preaching was based on a negation of their gender. Certainly, the scriptural justifications used implied such a negation, but Quaker women like Ann Audland were still very aware of the gendered consequences of their public speaking. The highly gendered pamphlet by Priscilla Cotton and Mary Cole was an angry outburst at a minister who had forbidden them to speak: 'Indeed, you your selves are the women, that are forbidden to speak in the

---

[67] *Ibid.*, p. 24.
[68] The Quaker doctrine of spiritual equality was by now being discussed in Quaker meetings in Edinburgh. The puritan minister of Terling, John Stalham, who had visited Edinburgh in March 1655, was well versed enough in the argument to be able to relay it in his tract, *Contradictions of the Quakers* (Edinburgh, 1655), *STC* s5184, p. 7.

Church, that are become women.'[69] There is also some evidence that women were more likely to express their behaviour as gendered verbally than they were in their printed works. One of the earliest, and possibly the first, printed tract, and possibly the first such, which attacked the Quakers, included the following story:

One Williamsons wife . . . when she came to see [the minister] at Appleby, said in the hearing of divers there . . . that she was the Eternal Son of God; And when the men that heard her, told her that she was a woman, and therefore could not be the Son of God, she said no, you are women, but I am a man.[70]

John Stalham also suggested that he had come across similar ideas expressed at a Quaker meeting in Edinburgh.[71]

There is evidence that women did argue with men about their right to speak; that they did encounter considerable male opposition to their behaviour as women; and that they responded in highly gendered language. It would be highly unlikely if this were not the case. Quaker women were necessarily made aware of the implications of their behaviour, and responded in kind. But they did not participate in the eloquently argued, printed tracts of Farnworth, Fox and later Margaret Fell, which justified, normalised and limited their behaviour.

Quaker leaders orchestrated the presentation of scriptural evidence in favour of women's speaking; and they did so out of a desire to contain and literally to justify the activities already being carried out by their female co-religionists. Their arguments did not as such enable the women to preach but were reacting to a *fait accompli* of Quakerism – the presence of a large number of highly visible and articulate women. The construction by men like Fox and Farnworth of a wholly spiritual argument for women's speaking served not only to limit their female contemporaries, but has also contributed to an overemphasis by women's historians on the insufficient argument that Quaker women were spiritually empowered to the detriment of their worldly agency.

If we turn to evidence beyond the published arguments defining or justifying women's right to speak in public, it is clear that women played a very important part in the early Quaker ministry. Whatever the problems of historians in explaining their active participation in the movement, it is

---

[69] Priscilla Cotton and Mary Cole, *To the priests and people of England, we discharge our consciences* (London, 1655), *STC* c6474, pp. 6–8. George Thomason dated his copy on 16 October 1655.

[70] Francis Higginson, *A brief relation of the irreligion of the northern Quakers* (London, 1653), *STC* H1953, pp. 3–4. The fact that this is an anti-Quaker tract means we cannot take Higginson's report at face value; but clearly indicates the fear of female activity associated with the Quaker movement.

[71] Stalham, *Contradictions of the Quakers*, p. 7.

nevertheless irrefutable that they were an accepted and even pre-existing component of the membership. They provided each other with considerable support networks and financial backing. Nevertheless, men in the Quaker movement increasingly saw them as problematic and felt the need to constrain their behaviour; and the very first aspects of internal Quaker organisation grew out of a need to curb their behaviour and enforce discipline on the movement.

Internal correspondence between Quakers describes an early movement in which women were active and accepted participants. The Quaker schoolmaster Thomas Taylor wrote to George Fox from Leicestershire in 1655, describing how he had met up on his travels with the Yorkshire Quaker, Margaret Killam (*sic*), who had been holding a meeting at Swannington, and how they had 'walked downe in the morning to Nun Eaton to see frends', where he reported 'a pretty convincement upon some women there, and a young man or two, but none come forth but shee that was formerly'.[72] Recruiting in this case, then, came largely from women. As interesting as this was the apparent acceptance with which Thomas Taylor viewed Margaret Killam's missionary work, explaining: 'But at Nun Eaton we stayed not long, for shee M:K: was to be next day . . . at Barrow at a meeting.'[73] This attitude was very common. Women were very often described on the road, travelling from town to town, arranging meetings, and sending news and greetings to their fellow missionaries.

This kind of acceptance occasionally extended to a clear welcoming of women. Francis Howgill spoke of an important conversion in Ireland of:

> the most emenent house in the towne and they are of the treue seed. She was a baptiste and they Cast her out for heresy . . . a nouble woman she is, she declare agaynst the prest in publicke and was moved to declare agaynest the baptists and one day the markett day toke a load of Bookes of the highest prestes in the nation and burned them In the street, and these things are a good smell.[74]

William Dewsbery, writing to Margaret Fell with news that the servant-turned-minister Mary Fisher had reached Barbados, in addition welcomed the contribution made by a number of women: 'Justice Crook's wife is prichous in her Measur and many of the handmads of the lord is very betyfull in ye power of our god; who is Carying on his work all over.'[75]

---

[72] Thomas Taylor to George Fox, Lichfield, 16 March 1655, Sw Mss 3: 30.   [73] *Ibid*.
[74] Francis Howgill to Margaret Fell, *c*. January 1656, A. R. Barclay Mss 1: 65, fol. 192.
[75] William Dewsbery to Margaret Fell, 15 October 1655, Sw Mss 4: 141. Mary Fisher was a servant in the household of Elizabeth and Richard Tomlinson at Selby, Yorkshire, and seems to have been convinced with them in 1652. As well as being imprisoned in York with Elizabeth Hooton and Thomas Aldam, she travelled with Elizabeth Williams to Cambridge in 1653. She travelled to Barbados and thence to New England in 1655, with another minister Ann Austin: they were suspected of witchcraft and forced to leave. After returning to England early in 1657, Mary Fisher travelled with other ministers to Turkey to warn the Sultan. Phyllis Mack, *Visionary women*, pp. 168–70.

A very good reason for the acceptance by Quaker men of the participation of women in their movement is that they were already there. The term 'Quaker', it is often asserted, was first used with reference to a group of women in Southwark, who were reported to 'swell, shiver and shake'.[76] The rapid growth of the Quaker movement was achieved essentially by the linking up from around 1652 of established groups of radical sectarians and Seekers, whose ideas already reflected more or less the newly publicised Quaker beliefs. Among these were groups of women sectaries. An early centre in London to which northern Quakers first travelled was a meeting at the house of Simon Dring in Moorfields, where there was 'none but two women' who were preachers; and the link with them was probably the northern woman Isabel Buttery, a friend of James Nayler and other northern missionaries, and who distributed some of the first Quaker tracts in London.[77]

This female network may well have extended beyond the Quaker movement.[78] In 1654 the prophet and Fifth Monarchist Anna Trapnel published an account of her journey from London to Cornwall. Women featured heavily in the account: before she left, Anna Trapnel conferred with her 'sisters' about the necessity of her going; on the way, she dined at an 'old disciples house' in Exeter, belonging to Widow Winters, who frequently entertained travelling 'saints'. She also stayed with the former Barebones MP Colonel Robert Bennett in Devon, and his wife and daughters travelled on with her for part of her journey, as far as the house belonging (as she described it) to the sister of Captain Langdon. She stayed, indeed, in a number of households where the women featured heavily. Upon her arrest and return to Bridewell in London, she described once again how her 'sisters' visited and stayed with her in prison.[79] The encountering of so many women, on a journey which was apparently spontaneous and ordered by the will of God, is in itself interesting. Two years later, however, two Quaker women from Bristol, Sarah Bennett and Mary Prince, travelled to Cornwall, passing through Devon. They too stopped off to see Colonel Bennett and his wife, and expected to find Anna Trapnel there. On their confrontation with Colonel Bennett, Mary Prince described how: 'love rose in him and he owned my words to be true and was brought tender', and they left some of their books with him. The two women had less success with Mrs Bennett, who listened, they reported, to 'all that was saide but theare is A hie sperite in her,' which they attributed to the enduring influence of Anna Trapnel.[80] What is nonetheless clear is that there were known households which the itinerant godly of the 1650s would visit; that the women in these households were important targets; and

---

[76] Clarendon State Papers 2624, MSS Clarendon vol. xxx, fol. 140r.
[77] Alexander Delamain to Thomas Willan, 1654, Sw Mss 3: 93.
[78] Mack, *Visionary women*, pp. 146–47.
[79] Anna Trapnel, *Anna Trapnel's Report and Plea* (London, 1654), STC T2033.
[80] Mary Prince and Sarah Bennett to George Fox [June, 1656], Sw Mss 3: 116.

that other women knew about them. It is out of exactly this milieu that the Quaker movement grew.

More evidence of a sense of solidarity between Quaker women comes from their own correspondence. Letters between women typically salute exclusively women: the barely literate Sarah Bennett, probably of Bristol, sent greetings to Margaret Fell, daughters, John Camm's wife and Ann Audland in a letter.[81] She had probably met Ann Audland at her trial in Banbury, and Mabel Camm and the daughters of Margaret Fell when they had travelled to Bristol; but it is highly unlikely that she had met Margaret Fell herself, whose name and reputation had clearly permeated south.[82] Ann Audland herself wrote to Margaret Fell: 'Blessed art thou amongst all women the standard of righteousness.'[83] Ann Dewsbery, a woman we hear little of otherwise, although her husband William was an active Quaker missionary, wrote in rapture to Margaret Fell after meeting her for the first time: 'blesed be the time that ever I saw thy face'. At the end of her letter, she gave news of her husband and explained: 'but I did not aquant him that I was to writ to you'.[84] Quaker women ministers corresponded autonomously with each other; and openly encouraged and inspired one another.[85]

The organisation of the early movement supported women in other ways. In 1654 Margaret Fell initiated the setting up of the central Quaker fund at Kendal, into which local groups from the northwest of England made donations of money. The accounts of money disbursed from the Kendal fund show a number of women receiving money for journeys and clothes. Ann Dixon from Grayrigg was given ten shillings in April 1655 for going to London 'or into the south parts as moved', and thus was not only free to travel independently, but was clearly expected to travel where and how she wanted.[86] The Yorkshire minister Barbara Pattison, who was imprisoned in Plymouth gaol where she published a tract with Margaret Killam, received £1 5s. for clothes and 'other nessessaries';[87] in December 1654, Alice Birkett received 2s. 6d. for a pair of shoes, and 3s. for going to hear a Quaker

[81] Sarah Bennett to Margaret Fell, Bristol [1656], Sw Mss 4: 71.
[82] Margaret Fell's daughters Margaret and Sarah were in Bristol in June or July 1655: John Audland to Edward Burrough and Francis Howgill, 2 July 1655, A. R. Barclay Mss 1: 58.
[83] Ann Audland to Margaret Fell [1655], Sw Mss 1: 22; cf. Luke 1, 28.
[84] Ann Dewsbery to Margaret Fell, 1 March 1656, Sw Mss 4: 142.
[85] Phyllis Mack makes the important point that men also wrote to Margaret Fell, the main recipient of Quaker correspondence, in equally enthusiastic terms. This does not exclude the fact that Quaker women ministers had a unique role model in Margaret Fell. Mack, *Visionary women*, pp. 153–54.
[86] George Taylor to Margaret Fell, 29 April 1655, Sw Mss 1: 215.
[87] Sw Trs 3: 543 [1655]; Margaret Killam (*sic*) and Barbara Pattison, *A warning from the Lord to the teachers and people of Plimouth* (London, 1656), STC K473. George Thomason dated his copy 29 December 1655.

trial at the Quarter Sessions in Cheshire.[88] Rebecca Ward borrowed twenty shillings from William Gandie of Frandley, Cheshire, and, when her father refused to pay him back, she arranged for William Gandie to be paid from the Kendal fund. She also asked for some money to be given to her impecunious father who 'was much burthened with friends passing upp and down', relying on his Welsh hospitality as they waited for a crossing to Ireland.[89] The servant Dorothy Waugh, sister of Jane Waugh, took off on a journey with Agnes Wilson which aroused indignation on the part of George Taylor and Thomas Willan, for she 'never Accquainted us of her Jorney and hath taken six or seven shillings of a friend and Bidd him tell us of it'. They found this particularly galling as Agnes Wilson had already been given three shillings for the journey.[90] The accounts of the Kendal Fund are very revealing about the public activities of women. That money was given to women as well as men underlines the acceptance of women's missionary work within the movement, but also, more importantly, provides very real evidence as to how these women were given (and were sometimes bold enough to borrow in advance) the means to travel about the country.

In many ways, then, the early Quaker movement was very accommodating of women. Yet despite the expectation by men that women could and did act as missionaries and preachers, there was frequently a sense that their presence was also fraught with difficulties. Much of the wariness of Quaker men, as has been seen in the printed tracts on the position of women, stemmed from the fear that women provided an easy target for public ridicule of the movement. In 1653 the Quaker Thomas Lawson was ordered by Fox to write a paper to 'send among friends' to clear his name of some rumours being 'tattled' about him. The rumour had sprung, apparently, from his interruption of a preaching minister with an unnamed Quaker woman, who had been denounced by the congregation as a whore and the two of them had been accused of sexual depravity. Lawson – not apparently the woman – was asked to explain the allegations made against him. In the paper he duly submitted to Margaret Fell, Lawson, as well as denying any impropriety on his part, was very concerned to describe how the rumour had spread:

the outward minde standing on looked forth at the reports of the world, and being at liberty tatled them abrode, without any ground, but onely by heresay, so things spread abrode, and are carried up and down'.[91]

Quaker men also responded in kind, and very rapidly, to the printed attacks on women in the movement. One of the earliest puritan attacks on Quaker principles, indeed, was that they held the doctrine 'of community in worldly

[88] George Taylor to Margaret Fell 1654, Sw Mss 1: 215.
[89] George Taylor and Thomas Willan to Margaret Fell, [1655], Sw Mss 1: 238.
[90] *Ibid.*   [91] Thomas Lawson [1653] Sw Mss 1: 246.

things', which some of them, '(did they speak out) extend to break marriage bonds'.[92] Yet Quakers less often responded to this kind of allegation than to direct slanders of individuals, as when Thomas Aldam challenged the publishers of newsbooks to substantiate allegations of adultery between Margaret Fell and George Fox.[93]

It is ironic, given the subsequent controversy surrounding Nayler, Martha Simmonds and other women in London, that James Nayler was zealous in countering reports of sexual transgressions or the subversion of patriarchal norms in the early Quaker movement.[94] While he was in prison at Appleby in the winter of 1652–53, James Nayler wrote to Fox that he had been visited by his wife, whose 'comeinge over' was 'very servisable, and hath stopped many mouths, and hath convinced them of many lies thay had raysed and was beleeved in the contrye'.[95] Nayler, whose sudden convincement at the plough had led him spontaneously to abandon his family and livelihood, had been discussed at his recent trial, was subsequently scorned in print as 'dissembling separation from the world':

James Nayler being asked, how he left and gave away his Estate, when he entered into this way [Quakerism], said, in the publick Sessions at Appleby, He gave it to his wife. A pretty shift.[96]

Thus Nayler's primary concern was that his wife's visit be of public value in countering the derision of his discredited household and patriarchal authority. In his private letter to Fox, Nayler went on to suggest a degree of marital harmony beyond the fear of scandal: he had 'had great refreshment by hir Cominge, for she came and returned with much fredome and great Joy, beyond what I in reason could expect'. But the limits on Nayler's expectations of his marriage are very clear: 'she was sent of my father and fitted by him not to be in the least a hinderer, but a fartherer of his works'.[97]

James Nayler was conscious of the need to refute public or published allegations of sexual impropriety in the movement. When William Cole and Thomas Welde sneered at Christopher Atkinson's 'very immodest familiarity (to say no more) with a woman of his way, in the sight of a godly Minister at Kendale', James Nayler took up the taunt in his reply: 'to make a ground

[92] Joseph Kellett *et al.*, *A faithful discovery of a treacherous design* (London, 1653), STC F568, p. 42.
[93] Thomas Aldam, *The searching out the deceit* (London, 1655), STC A894C, pp. 1–4. See above, Chapter 4.
[94] Ann Hughes discusses similar tactics in Leveller literature: Ann Hughes, 'Gender and politics in Leveller literature' in Susan Amussen and Mark Kishlansky (eds.), *Political culture and cultural politics in early modern England* (1995).
[95] James Nayler to George Fox, Appleby gaol [January 1653], Sw Mss 3: 66.
[96] Thomas Welde and William Cole *et al.*, *The perfect pharise under monkish holines* (London, 1654), STC C5045A, p. 51.
[97] Nayler to Fox [January 1653], Sw Mss 3: 66.

for your slander, ye say (to say no more) but why, to say no more? if ye know more, why doe you not speake the truth, but slander in secret?'[98] Within months of this confident refutation of the accusations against Atkinson, more reports of his sexual misdemeanours were circulating, this time in private letters between Quaker ministers with an undisputed ring of truth. In consequence, Atkinson was formally ejected from the Quaker movement by a gathering of ministers at Norwich.[99] Substantiated, internal reports of licentious behaviour were taken seriously; while publicly they were refuted or diffused whenever possible.

Phyllis Mack argues that the Quakers were bound by an extraordinary sense of community in which the role of women as nurturers and providers of the household was cherished and extended to the organisation of the movement as a whole.[100] But in the concern of the early Quaker men to protect the movement, there is also a sense that women could do very real damage. In the wake of the turmoil of James Nayler's trial in December 1656, Richard Hubberthorne wrote to Fox with an account of a highly troubled meeting:

yesterday wee had A meetinge at the bull and mouth and mildred was there in all Impudence and I haveinge spokne somthing in the livinge power of the lord to the people shee was tarmented and shee resolved soe to speake as that I should not speake any more to them and when she had spokne untill her naturell brith [birth] was spent she againe still did strive to speake and often tould the people that they should not heare A word from mee stay as longe as they would together for she intended to speake as longe as they stayed and in the livinge power of the lord I was cept and moved to stay: the meetinge begun at the 3 hower and wee stayed almost untill midnight for I was to stay and much of the lord was found in it for she did soe strive in her wickednes untill all her naturall parts was spent and her sences distracted that she was even realy mad and truth reaigned in pure dominion and in the life of truth was all freinds refreshed to see the deceipte to wast and destroy itselfe till it retained noe streingth and freinds in the life weare kept and reioyced over it: and the world was satisfied Concerninge it and Could see it and Judge it yet she said that the next meeting shee would Come in more power and we should not speake A word but the next meetinge shee did not come at all for shee hath soe destroyed her naturall parts that shee is soe horsie that shee Cannot speake at present: and it is like gods Judgments will Come upon her sudainly.[101]

This account suggests the intensity of the leadership struggle between Hubberthorne and 'Mildred'; the very clear distinction between the natural parts

[98] Cole and Welde *et al.*, *The perfect pharise*, p. 49; James Nayler, *An answer to the Booke called the perfect pharisee* ([London], 1654), STC N261, p. 27.
[99] Richard Hubberthorne to George Fox and James Nayler, 10 December 1654, Sw Trs 2: 569; Richard Clayton to Margaret Fell, 12 July 1655, Sw Trs 1: 564; George Taylor to Margaret Fell, 14 July 1655, Sw Mss 1: 239. See also above, Chapter 1, p. 33.
[100] Mack, *Visionary women*, pp. 228–35; 236–61.
[101] Richard Hubberthorne to Fox, 20 March ?1658, Sw Trs 2: 593. I am grateful to Rosemary Moore in the dating of this letter.

of the woman, which were wicked and distracted, and the spiritual responses of others at the meeting epitomises the distinction between carnal and spiritual, which in print Richard Farnworth had attributed to 'male' and 'female' in the opposite sense. Hubberthorne's letter is also very important because 'Mildred in all Impudence' was clearly known to Fox, and Hubberthorne was keeping him informed. In the same letter, Hubberthorne reported that Francis Howgill's sister Mary, for the past six months 'hath been much in these Counties of Essex suffolke and norfolke wheare she hath done hurt for she ministereth Confusion amonge freinds'. Hubberthorne's solution to the problem, he informed Fox, was to hold a general meeting in the area to reassure friends shaken by Mary Howgill's preaching.[102] We thus see emerging an early form of church discipline, with recognised leaders like George Fox and Margaret Fell, and intermediary scouts who reported on any ministerial deviance, and even implemented temporary structures to counter the ill-effects on the movement.

There are frequent examples of this kind of early internal group discipline. Thomas Aldam, imprisoned in York Castle, was particularly meticulous: in 1652 he called in Richard Farnworth and William Dewsbery on two separate occasions to speak to his fellow prisoner Jane Holmes, who had fallen, he said, into 'pashon and Lowdnesse': not a common problem reported among male Quaker preachers. But she refused to 'come to Judgement', and took a separate room in the prison, with Mary Fisher. Thomas Aldam described the situation very gravely in a letter to Margaret Fell, and asked, scrupulously, that any money sent to the prisoners should be expressly directed to one group or the other as they no longer ate together.[103] Two years later, still in York Castle, Aldam sent another woman, Agnes Wilkinson, to Margaret Fell, who, Aldam said, had 'acted contrary to the light, in filthynes', and was 'cast out of the light with them who was partakers with her'. Aldam asked Fell to set a watch over her and 'keepe her out from Amongst Frends' until she repented.[104]

There were heightened fears about the role of women in the public ministry voiced around the time of the Nayler crisis, which Patricia Crawford has argued, centred around the assumption of leadership by Martha Simmonds as much as by James Nayler.[105] In July 1656 William Caton and George Fox discussed 'the women, or rather sisters', in Cornwall who had been

---

[102] Hubberthorne did not stop Mary Howgill preaching elsewhere. She went on to visit Cromwell in June 1656, and the town of Dover in July; and as a result published a piece of prophecy, *A remarkable letter of Mary Howgill to Oliver Cromwell, called Protector* (London, 1657).

[103] Thomas Aldam to 'Friends' [November 1652], Sw Mss 3:40; Aldam to Thomas Towndrowe [1652/3], Portfolio 36:114; Brailsford, *Quaker Women*, p. 22.

[104] Thomas Aldam to Margaret Fell, 30 October 1654, Sw Mss 4: 89.

[105] Crawford, *Women and religion*, pp. 173–80. The Nayler affair is discussed in Chapter 8.

'fellow helpers in the Gospell'; George Fox said little to it, but suggested 'that some of them might Cease'.[106] In August 1656 Richard Clayton, a Quaker missionary in Ireland, sent back to Margaret Fell 'a filthy decetfull wench' lest 'she should have cased the truth to have sufered'.[107] William Caton was paralysed in Sussex in early 1657, refusing to go to Amsterdam because of rumours there of a woman 'gone distracted'. Edward Burrough wrote to Fox in February 1657 concerned by a 'short little maide', and urging him to take her out of the ministry and find her a more suitable post as a servant-girl somewhere, as many friends 'hath ben burdened by her as by her ministery . . . and to some she was an offence in bedfordshire'.[108]

The majority of early cases of internal Quaker discipline revolved around the perceived need to temper the behaviour of women, or indeed to 'cast them out' of the still nascent movement. Much early discipline of men, as in the case of Christopher Atkinson who was eventually excommunicated, touched on sexual transgression with women, or on rumours of it. The leaders of the early Quaker movement made very real decisions about the propriety of the ministry for many Quaker women. Their monitoring and ejection of wayward women foreshadowed developments in the systematic holding of meetings and circulation of epistles which characterised the Quaker movement of the 1660s and beyond. Public refutations of accusations of sexual transgression in the movement were concerned with identifying and denying individual women; they did not rehearse and defend of the right of women to preach. Private letters also made very few references to the spiritual equality of women and men. It becomes all the more convincing, in this context, that the tracts by Fox and Farnworth were written not as impassioned pleas for the right of their sisters to preach, but as a careful appropriation and legitimating of their behaviour as women.

Quaker pampleteering about women did not occur in an intellectual vacuum, and it cannot be isolated from other aspects of the early movement. Elaine Hobby has shown that a number of women and men wrote about the spiritual equality of the sexes, and that they did so in a variety of ways.[109] In the same vein, a number of women published tracts which were remarkably similar in content to those of their male Quaker colleagues, which made little or no reference to their gender. This chapter has examined the development of one aspect of early Quaker belief – that women and men were

---

[106] William Caton to Margaret Fell, 23 July 1656, Sw Mss 1: 313.
[107] Richard Clayton to Margaret Fell, 5 August 1656, Sw Trs 1: 568.
[108] William Caton to Margaret Fell, Sw Mss 1: 314; 1: 366; Edward Burrough to George Fox, A. R. Barclay Mss 1: 36, fol. 100.
[109] Elaine Hobby, 'Handmaids of the Lord' and Mothers in Israel: early vindications of Quaker women's prophecy', in Corns and Loewenstein (eds.), *The emergence of Quaker writing*, pp. 88–98.

spiritually equal, and equally fitted to the ministry – within the wider context of Quaker pamphleteering. The arguments offered by Farnworth and Fox about the public ministry of women, stressing the importance of the spiritual over the worldly, were in complete harmony with other ideas developed in print at the same time. Farnworth and Fox accepted and justified the ministerial and public roles played by women (and we must not lose sight of just how unusual this was in the mid-seventeenth century); but they also believed that women's preaching was particularly prone to worldly, passionate outbursts. They therefore felt the need, in print, to reiterate accepted scriptural views about the proper relations between husbands and wives, and parents and children. There are strong parallels between the published positions of Fox and Farnworth (and later Fell herself), and the nature of internal discipline structures in the early movement. The evidence from letters reveals that women were integrated into the early movement and were active participants in its growth. They received money, support, shelter and inspiration from the very close network of Quaker missionaries. The same organisation developed, at a remarkably early stage, the mechanisms through which to constrain them.

What does this tell us about the role of print in establishing aspects of doctrine in the early movement? The leadership used the press to present a coherent argument about women which justified their public speaking to an audience which in all probability would be hostile. They published such ideas in response to the fact that women were active participants in the movement, and an integral part of its membership and leadership. The fact that they presented the argument in print owed much to the actual presence of preaching women. Just as women participated in the movement, so they also played a part in shaping the presentation of arguments which justified their ministry.

Part III

Religious and political debate

6

Pamphleteering and religious debate

The Quakers were active participants in debates about the further, final reformation of England. They were convinced that this was a matter affecting all members of society and therefore requiring everyone's participation. Quaker leaders sought to involve the largest possible number of people in the discussion and reform of the new godly commonwealth; and the role of pamphleteering in this was of paramount importance. Quakers employed a wide spectrum of printed tracts, from short, punchy denunciations of ministers used primarily at public meetings, to much lengthier and more intense exchanges with their puritan opponents, in order to engage people in religious discussion. Their tracts did not offer theoretical solutions; nor did they comment at length on the intricacies of religious reform. They established instead that everyone should partake in the moral and religious reform of England. Quaker pamphleteering enabled and demanded widespread participation in religious and political debate.

This chapter examines the role played by Quaker tracts in encouraging religious debate and protest, and in widening arguments against a national church and professional ministry. The Quakers' printed exchanges with puritan ministers, some of whom, like Richard Baxter, Thomas Goodwin, John Bunyan, Thomas Collier or Thomas Welde, were notable spokesmen in their own right, have often been described by scholars as a unique category or genre of tract, and have been studied separately in order to understand the nature of Quaker theology, or to define the Quakers in contradistinction to their puritan predecessors.[1] As such, the Quakers' pamphlet debates have been dismissed as lacking in any theological coherence or sophistication, and

---

[1] Richard Baxter, *The Quakers Catechism; or, the Quakers questioned* (London, 1655), STC B1362; Thomas Goodwin *et al.*, *The principles of faith, presented to the Committee of Parliament for religion* (London, 1654), STC P3496; John Bunyan, *Some gospel truths opened, according to Scriptures* (London, 1656), STC B1598; Thomas Collier, *A looking-glasse for Quakers* (London, 1657), STC C5290; Collier, *A dialogue between a minister of the Gospel and an enquiring Christian* (London, 1656), STC C5276A; Thomas Welde and William Cole *et al.*, *The perfect pharise under monkish holines* (London, 1654) STC C5045A (see n. 140); Welde, *A further discovery of that generation of men called Quakers*

153

the conclusion drawn has been that Quaker theology was only consolidated in the second generation of the movement.[2] The contention of this chapter is that printed exchanges were part of a much wider spectrum of pamphleteering, which was in itself an integral part of the Quakers' campaign to achieve universal religious participation.

The nature of the Quakers' religious beliefs demanded active proselytisation by its ministers and the universal participation of everyone else. A central feature was the force and urgency of the Quakers' millenarianism. Many tracts proclaimed in one way or another that Christ's kingdom on earth was being built. James Parnell announced that 'the Lord is come, and is coming to make war'; Edward Burrough warned the inhabitants of his native Underbarrow that 'the Lord is arising, whose Angel is gone forth Preaching the everlasting Gospel'; a number of tracts were likened to trumpet blasts from Sion.[3]

The Quakers were spiritual millenarians, believing that Christ's second coming occurred spiritually, within individual men and women.[4] Christ's presence, and his kingdom on earth, was an inward, spiritual presence within all men and women. The Quakers' millenarianism was mystical: the notion of Christ's earthly kingdom pervaded their prophecy, and provided a sense of urgency to their writing, but was not specifically defined. The second coming was an event which was experienced by individuals in their own time, and could be described in the past, present or future tense.[5]

The fact that the Quakers' millenarianism was spiritual and individual did not preclude the fact that the ultimate battle between the Lamb and the powers of the earth was deemed to be actually happening all around them,

(Gateshead, 1654), *STC* w1268. They were identified as a separate entity in David Runyan's typographical analysis of Quaker writings: Hugh Barbour and A. O. Roberts (eds.), *Early Quaker writings 1650–1700* (Michigan, 1973), pp. 567–73. For a classic distinction between Quakers and puritans, see Geoffrey Nuttall, 'Quakers and puritans', in his *The puritan spirit: essays and addresses* (London, 1967), pp. 156–76.

[2] Ralph Bohn, 'The controversy between puritans and Quakers to 1660', unpublished Ph.D thesis, University of Edinburgh, 1955; Hugh Barbour, *Quakers in puritan England* (New Haven, 1964), pp. 127–59; Barbour, *Early Quaker writings*, p. 14; Craig Horle, 'Quakers and Baptists, 1647–1660', *Baptist Quarterly* 26: 8 (1976), 350.

[3] James Parnell, *A shield of the truth* (London, 1655), *STC* p533, sig. ar; Edward Burrough, *A warning to the inhabitants of Underbarrow* (London, 1654), *STC* b6057, p. 16; Richard Farnworth, *A voice of the first trumpet* (London, 1653), *STC* f512b; George Fox, *The trumpet of the Lord sounded* (London, 1654), *STC* f1969; James Parnell, *The trumpet of the Lord blowne* (London, 1655), *STC* p539; Edward Burrough, *A trumpet of the Lord sounded out of Sion* (London, 1656), *STC* b6048.

[4] T. L. Underwood, 'Early Quaker eschatology', in Peter Toon (ed.), *Puritans, the millennium and the future of Israel: Puritan eschatology 1600–1660* (London, 1970), pp. 91–103. See also Barry Reay, 'Quakerism and society' in J. F. McGregor and B. Reay (eds.), *Radical religion in the English revolution* (Oxford, 1986), p. 146.

[5] Bernard Capp, 'The Fifth Monarchists and popular millenarianism', in McGregor and Reay (eds.), *Radical religion*, p. 165; T. L. Underwood, 'Early Quaker eschatology', in Toon (ed.), *Puritans, the millenium and the future of Israel*, p. 98.

witnessed every time a Quaker was persecuted by worldly forces.[6] The conflict between Quakers and puritan ministers was portrayed as the final battle between Christ and Antichrist, a 'signe that the Ruine of his Papall Monarchy the Antichristian ministry' was at hand.[7] Symptomatic of this was the religious confusion and proliferation of sects in England, foretold in the Book of Revelation: the deceivers and hypocrites prophesied of in the 'last days' had now emerged as the many-headed monster of 'religions and formes'.[8] The Quakers presented themselves as a single and simple manifestation of truth in the face of so many differing voices: now that Christ was 'arisen in his Saints, to reveale this man of sinne by his light', all 'formes of Religion' had 'joyned together to strike at this light'.[9]

Nor did the Quakers' spiritual millenarianism preclude the necessity for an extensive campaign to prepare England. Quaker prophets urged the people of England to be ready: 'this is the day of your Visitation, the mouth of the Lord hath spoken it', thundered Edward Burrough. 'Remember that you have been shewed the Deceits which you live in, and have been warned of the miserie and desolation that shall come upon you, except you lay these things to heart, and turn to the Lord.'[10] Martha Simmonds urged the 'wise virgins' of England that the time was come to 'make our bodies fit for himself to dwell in'.[11] Such exhortations also extended to the body politic. Shortly before the meeting of the Barebones Assembly in July 1653, Richard Farnworth addressed a tract to members of the Council of State: 'Rejoyce ye Saints and righteous ones; the beast hath but a short time to raign; the Lord is making his power known.'[12]

---

[6] Underwood, 'Early Quaker eschatology', p. 98.

[7] Martin Mason, *A check to the loftie linguist* (London, 1655), STC M926, p. 2.

[8] James Nayler, *A few words occasioned by a paper lately printed* [London, 1654], STC N279, p. 4.

[9] *Ibid.*

[10] Burrough, *A warning from the Lord to the inhabitants of Underbarrow*, p. 19.

[11] Martha Simmonds, *Oh England, thy time is come* [London, ?1656], STC S3793. For other examples of explicit warnings of the immediacy of Christ's second coming, see Richard Farnworth, *Englands warning piece gone forth* (London, 1653), STC F482; F., G. [George Fox], *A warning from the Lord* (London, 1654), STC F1980; George Fox, *A warning from the Lord to the Pope* (London, 1656), STC F1981; [George Fox], *A warning to all in this proud city called London* [London], (1654), STC F1982; George Fox, *A warning to the world that are groping in the dark after sects* (London, 1655), STC F1987; Ann Gargill, *A warning to all the world* (London, 1656), STC G259; John Harwood, *A warning from the Lord to the city of Oxford* [London], (1655), STC H1104A; John Harwood, *A warning from the Lord to the town of Cambridge* [London], (1655), STC H1105; Margaret Killam (*sic*) and Barbara Pattison, *A warning from the Lord to the teachers and people of Plimouth* (London, 1656), STC K473; John Rous, *A warning to the inhabitants of Barbados* [London], (1656), STC R2045; [Humphrey Smith], *A warning to the priests, magistrates, rulers and inhabitants of Exon* [n.p.] (1656), STC S4085; Christopher Taylor, *A warning from the Lord to this nation* [London] (1655), STC T267.

[12] Richard Farnworth, *Gods covenanting with his people* (London, 1653), pp. 33, 37. George Thomason dated a copy of this tract 29 June 1653. This will be discussed further in Chapter 7.

A second crucial force which shaped the Quakers' aggressive proselyti-sation was their renunciation of Calvinist predestinarianism. The insistence that the light of Christ 'lighteth every man that comes into the world' meant that Christ's kingdom was accessible to everyone. 'You pretend as to the Kingdom of God, but you are not seeking where it is', wrote Nayler to 'all People everywhere' in 1653; 'the Kingdom of God is within you, and the way to the Kingdom is within you, and the light that guides into the way and keeps in the way is within'.[13] The task of missionaries like James Nayler was to alert all people everywhere to 'stand still' in the light, and 'wait for the power of God'.[14]

The doctrine of reaching the inner light required active participation by all. As has been seen, the reading of Quaker tracts was discussed as part of this process, and was offered as a means of recognising the inner light.[15] It also fundamentally undermined the need for a professional preaching min-istry and formal religious worship and teaching. Turning to the light within promised certain knowledge of salvation, since the light of God itself pre-vented 'backsliding' into drunkenness, theft or adultery because it enabled these to be seen unequivocally as sins: the light 'will let thee see if thou dost [backslide], thou must not go unpunished'.[16] The responsibility lay emphat-ically with each individual, once he or she had been warned to follow the divine stirrings in their conscience: 'you that are called and perswaded by the light to obey and follow it', warned Richard Farnworth, 'if you will not obey and follow the same, but continue in their wilfulnesse, sinfulnesse, and rebellion', then damnation and condemnation would certainly follow.[17]

These two strands of Quaker belief entailed a proactive campaign which not only sought to inform and warn the entire population, but was also fundamentally at odds with the tenets of a national church supported by a beneficed ministry. The nature of the Quakers' proselytising would inevitably challenge members of an established church, who were perceived as inhibit-ing the spiritual preparation of the people of England. The fact that the national church was itself ill-defined, and in a state of doctrinal and organi-sational flux, escalated the nature of the Quaker challenge, and transformed them from opponents into participants in the debates.

It has been argued that there was a 'deliberate vacuum at the centre' of interregnum ecclesiastical policy.[18] Although Cromwell's national church was remarkably broad in the variety of advisers he appointed, there was

---

[13] James Nayler, *The power and glory of the Lord shining out of the north* (London, 1653), STC N302, p. 1.

[14] George Fox, *To all that would know the way to the Kingdom* [London, 1654], STC F1942, p. 18.

[15] See above, Chapter 1.   [16] Fox, *To all that would know*, p. 1.

[17] Richard Farnworth, *The brazen serpent lifted up on high* (London, 1655), STC F471, p. 9; Barbour, *Quakers in puritan England*, pp. 139–43.

[18] William Lamont, *Godly rule politics and religion, 1603–1660* (London, 1969), p. 143.

considerable difficulty in establishing a church which could be genuinely national, and include Presbyterians, Independents and even Baptists. A major problem was agreeing on a set of doctrines by which the national church could be defined, but which allowed for a workable distinction between the 'pretious' and the 'vile', or the godly and the ungodly. A key manifestation of this involved defining the extent of religious toleration, which would outlaw the kinds of persecution associated with the Laudianism of the 1630s, and yet would not allow religious libertinism and other associated dangerous ideas to flourish. The governments of the 1650s had in their legislation to 'define the boundaries of acceptable doctrine'; yet they had also to avoid imposing forms of worship, differences over which would prevent broad unity.[19]

The lack of central ecclesiastical policy in the 1650s was evident at parish level, where local ministers had practically to work within and strengthen the ill-defined presbyterian church established in 1646. One major problem was popular apathy. It is increasingly argued that the majority of people clung to traditional Anglican ceremony and forms of worship and were increasingly alienated by attempts to complete a puritan revolution. At the other end of the religious spectrum, people were no longer legally obliged to attend their parish church by the Act of September 1650: an act which undermined the authority of parish ministers.[20] The parochial ministry was crucial to the success or failure of England's godly commonwealth.[21] Their centrality was recognised by legislation under both the Commonwealth and Protectorate to strengthen and improve the state of the preaching ministry of England and Wales.[22] Yet puritan ministers remained in the minority. Most clergy retained their Anglican ideology and indeed their livings after the Restoration; few areas of the country successfully established a workable presbyterian system of worship.[23]

[19] Blair Worden, 'Toleration and the Cromwellian Protectorate', *Studies in Church History* 21 (1984), p. 205 and *passim*. See also Claire Cross, 'The church in England 1646–1660', in G. E. Aylmer (ed.), *The Interregnum: the quest for settlement 1646–1660* (London, 1974); Lamont, *Godly rule*; J. C. Davis, 'Cromwell's religion' in John Morrill (ed.), *Oliver Cromwell and the English revolution* (London, 1990), pp. 181–208; Anthony Fletcher, 'Oliver Cromwell and the godly nation', in *ibid.*, pp. 209–33; John Spurr, *The Restoration Church of England, 1646–1689* (New Haven, 1991); Christopher Durston, 'Puritan rule and the failure of cultural revolution, 1645–1660' in Christopher Durston and Jacqueline Eales (eds.), *The culture of English puritanism, 1560–1700* (London, 1996), pp. 210–33.

[20] William A. Shaw, *A history of the English church during the civil wars and under the Commonwealth 1640–1660* (2 vols., London, 1900), vol. II, p. 77; John Spurr, *The restoration church of England*, p. 5.

[21] Barbara Donagan, 'Puritan ministers and laymen: professional claims and social constraints in seventeenth-century England', *Huntington Library Quarterly* 47 (Spring 1984), 81–111.

[22] Shaw, *History of the English Church*, vol. II, pp. 248–52.

[23] Derek Hirst, 'The failure of godly rule in the English republic', *Past and Present* 132 (August 1991), 33–36', 46; John Spurr, *Restoration church of England*, pp. 4–14; John Morrill, 'The church in England, 1642–1649' in Morrill (ed.), *Reactions to the English Civil War, 1642–1649* (London, 1982); Claire Cross, 'The church in England'; Durston, 'Puritan rule and the failure of cultural revolution', pp. 210–33.

The fact that parish ministers were crucial to the success or failure of the puritan revolution is highly pertinent to the ways in which Quaker ministers conducted their own national campaign for radical religious reform. The Quakers' role in contributing to religious debate was firmly rooted at local level. In the course of their itinerant preaching, Quaker ministers routinely visited Baptist, Independent and Presbyterian congregations. As part of this, they argued with the religious leaders, the 'orthodox puritans', who were active in shaping the religious reform of republican England.

John Audland's manuscript account of his journey from Lancashire to London in June 1654 describes such behaviour as a regular feature of his work. Arriving in Hereford, by God's direction, as he claimed, on a Saturday night, Audland went the next morning to the minster, and his companion Thomas Ayrey to 'another great Steeplehouse'; in Bristol they attended a Baptist meeting in the morning and an Independent meeting in the afternoon; in Plymouth they again separated on a Sunday morning, Audland going to what he referred to as the 'Cathedral' while Ayrey visited the Baptists.[24] In most of the towns where they stayed, Ayrey and Audland made a point of speaking individually to all congregations and gathered churches.

The pattern of public debate and pamphlet exchanges with puritan ministers followed the geographical scope of the itinerant ministers. This could lead to enormous contrasts in the figures challenged. In the second half of 1653, Richard Hubberthorne published answers to a set of questions sent to him by Robert Lucas, a yeoman and elder of the *classis* of Kellet, Lancashire, the parish adjoining Hubberthorne's native Yealand.[25] From Kellet, Hubberthorne travelled south to Chester and Wales; sending as he went[26] a set of queries to Richard Sherlock, 'Priest at Borwick', and his patron Sir Robert Bindloss, an active protector of Anglican worship and

---

[24] Audland's Journal, pp. 24–29. Compare this manuscript account with the published tract by John Stubbs and William Caton, which described exactly the same tactics in Maidstone, where John Stubbs went to the 'steeplehouse', 'where a people called Presbyterians were' and William Caton to the place where 'a people called Independents were'. Earlier that morning they had already visited a Baptist meeting at Boughton Green nearby. John Stubbs and William Caton, *A true declaration of the bloody proceedings of the men in Maidstone* (London, 1655), STC s6072, p. 1.

[25] Richard Hubberthorne, George Fox *et al.*, *Truths defence against the refined subtilty of the serpent* [n. p.], (1653), STC F1970, pp. 89–106; 'Minutes of the Manchester Presbyterian Classes', ed. W. A. Shaw, part 1, *Chetham Society* n. s. 20 (1890), p. 11.

[26] Hubberthorne was imprisoned in Chester gaol in November 1653, and was probably still there in January 1654. The published account of Hubberthorne's queries, *The Quakers wilde questions objected against*, was entered in the Stationers' Company register on 30 January 1654. It seems likely that Hubberthorne's exchange with Sherlock happened as Hubberthorne was *en route* to Chester. For details of his journey see Sw Mss 4: 66; Sw Mss 1: 339; Sw Mss 1: 140; G. E. B. Eyre (ed.), *A Transcript of the registers of the Company of Stationers 1640–1708* (3 vols., London, 1913; repr. Gloucester, Mass. 1967), vol. I, p. 441.

ministers during the 1650s.[27] From Chester, Hubberthorne visited the Fifth Monarchist Vavasour Powell's congregation in Wrexham in late 1653, both sides publishing their own account of events.[28] In the space of a few weeks, Richard Hubberthorne had confronted a Presbyterian elder, an Anglican minister, and a Fifth Monarchist minister, and published accounts of all of them. Hubberthorne's disputes were rooted in the geographical scope of his ministry.

Ministers critical of the Quakers were drawn into debate with them as a result of the physical presence of the Quakers in their locality. The compilation of one of the tracts published by Hubberthorne as the culmination of extensive Quaker preaching in Lancashire, *Truths defence against the refined subtilty of the serpent*, provides evidence of this (see Plate 7). *Truths defence* contained an extensive collection of questions and answers which had passed between Quakers and a variety of 'men (called Ministers) in the North'. One set of queries had been 'occasioned by a Printed Paper of Richard Farnsworth, sent to be answered'. This was a remote debate: the Quaker authors noted that the queries had been sent anonymously, with 'no Name subscribed'.[29] There then followed 'Certain Queries given forth by a sort of high Professors that dwell in Farnez Fell in Lancashire', sent to George Fox; and the thirty-two queries sent by Robert Lucas to Richard Hubberthorne already mentioned.[30] Lucas had already enjoyed an exchange of kinds with the Quakers in 1652, when George Fox wrote him a letter which accused him of having 'poysoned the Towne with thy filthy envyousse, corrupt, crooked uncleane spirit', so that 'the people are like a company of distracted people', whose self-doubt was obvious, 'many of them chafeing and fretting themselves, gnawing their tongues like thy selfe'.[31] Lucas's queries thus built on a more specific and personal exchange with Quaker leaders. The more radical puritan minister of Staveley, Gabriel Camelford, had been subjected to the personal presentation of handwritten queries during his church service from the Quaker Thomas Atkinson, formerly one of his parishioners. Camelford had replied to the questions, and sent his own for the Quaker's attention. In the publication, all questions and answers were published,

---

[27] These were published in Richard Sherlock, *The Quakers wilde questions objected against* (London, 1654), STC s3254, pp. 1–7. Hubberthorne had sent a total of twenty-seven queries. John Spurr identifies Bindloss as one of the many gentlemen patrons of Anglicanism during the 1650s, who took in 'distressed divines' as tutors or chaplains: see Spurr, *The Restoration Church of England*, p. 14.

[28] Hubberthorne and John Lawson to Margaret Fell, Sw Mss 4: 66; Richard Hubberthorne, *Truth cleared, and the deceit made manifest* (London, 1654), STC H3241. Vavasour Powell wrote an account published in the newsbook *Severall proceedings*, to which Hubberthorne referred in *Truth cleared*, p. 1.

[29] Hubberthorne and Fox, *Truths defence*, p. 67.   [30] *Ibid.*, pp. 78–88, 89–106.

[31] George Fox to Robert Lucas [1652], Sw Mss 4: 227.

Truth's Defence 12

AGAINST

the Refined Subtilty

OF THE

SERPENT

Held forth in divers Answers to severall Queries made by men (called Ministers) in the North.

Given forth by the Light and Power of
God appearing in

George Fox
and
Richard Hubberthorn

And they watched him, and sent forth Spies, which should feign themselves just men, that they might take hold of his words, that so they might deliver him into the power and authority of the Governours. Luke 20.20.

Printed for *Tho: Wayt* at his house in the *Pavement* in *York.* 1653.

Plate 7. George Fox and Richard Hubberthorne, *Truth's defence against the refined subtilty of the serpent* ([n. p.], 1653), STC F1970.

and Camelford's original answers were subject to a lengthy exegesis by Atkinson himself. The exchange of queries, and the publication of a variety of debates, thus resulted from different types of contact between Quakers and their opponents, from the encountering of the Quakers' printed tracts, the sustained preaching of Fox in one area, to the formal exchange of written questions before a congregation.

At the end of *Truths defence*, Richard Hubberthorne denounced dry, academic debate as the preserve of an elitist and privileged ministry. In compiling answers to questions sent in response to localised preaching, he dismissed the exchange of questions. 'Now all you who are doting about Questions, and are Ministers of Questions, and not Ministers of Grace,' wrote Richard Hubberthorne in the conclusion of the tract, 'but are busi-bodyes, tempting, and laying Snares and digging Pits, ye are now fallen into the Pits which ye have digged for others.' The wise, he noted triumphantly 'are taken in your own craftiness'. In contrast, the Quakers' questions were 'received freely from the Lord', and, Hubberthorne declared, 'freely I have declared unto you without partiality, or having mens persons in admiracion, because of advantage . . . the Lord hath given us a mouth, and wisdom, which all our Gain-sayers are not able to resist . . . and our speech is with Grace, seasoned with salt, and we know how to answer every man'.[32]

THE ATTACK ON THE ORTHODOX MINISTRY

The form of Quaker exchanges with other religious leaders mirrored the actual content of the argument. Quaker authors dismissed the learned form of religious debate, based on the exchange of lengthy questions and answers. This was one aspect of a much wider assault on a professional ministry. In all of their confrontations with religious leaders, whether as part of a spontaneous address or a more formal debate, the major area of contention was the derivation of a minister's authority. It has been argued that the puritan 'ordination controversy', over the rights of laymen to preach, was overshadowed by the 'Quaker problem' after 1654.[33] It is more accurate to suggest that Quakers were active participants in this debate, although they may have changed its parameters. For the Quakers, the nature of the debate had to be practical rather than academic, involving the personal challenging of individual ministers in the course of their sermons. Accounts of public exchanges suggest the physical confrontations were highly charged, aimed at claiming the attention of the congregations. Richard Hubberthorne reputedly stood

---

[32] Hubberthorne and Fox, *Truths defence*, p. 107.
[33] Richard Greaves, 'The ordination controversy and the spirit of reform in puritan England', *Journal of Ecclesiastical History* 21: 3 (July 1970), 226.

up, defiantly wearing his hat, while Vavasour Powell was preaching, and asked him 'with what power he preached the Gospel?' Powell's defenders in the Wrexham congregation alleged that Hubberthorne had told Powell, rather more directly: 'thou speakest of a power thou hast not in thee'.[34] The dramatic impact of this event must have undermined Powell's authority, as much as Hubberthorne was actually questioning it. However, the substance of Hubberthorne's question, about the importance of spiritual authority over authority conferred by men, was repeated time and again in the written queries circulated by other Quaker ministers. The preacher to a congregational church in Cheshire, Samuel Eaton, was asked whether he had 'the same eternall Spirit which gave forth the Scriptures', and whether he had 'heard the voice of the living Lord God'.[35] Eaton's reply to the latter, that he had neither heard the immediate voice of God nor waited for it, provoked the conclusion from his Quaker opponent that he was 'no Minister of God' but a heathen: 'thou knows nothing of salvation but by heresay; and here thou shewest thy self to be a false prophet'.[36] The young Quaker James Parnell debated with Thomas Drayton, a 'Teacher of the world' in Huntingdonshire, over the immediacy of Christ's ministry: 'Those that have an inward call to the Ministry do not stay for an outward call by man, but goe forth in bedience [*sic*] to the word of the Lord', wrote Parnell.[37] For doubting whether Parnell was 'called either way', his opponent was roundly rebuked: 'if thou wast called and guided by the Spirit of the Lord, thou would'st know, without doubts, whether I was so called yea or nay'.[38] This particular debate over ministerial authority included the further tension of youth pitted against the wisdom of age. Thomas Drayton claimed he felt obliged to reply to the handwritten questions sent him by the 'Young Quaker', 'lest the Boy should be highly conceited of himself, and falsely boast, That he understandeth more then the Ancients'.[39] Parnell replied that even 'a Babe may comprehend thee, and tell thee of thy folly, and when thou thinkest of thy beard or age (as thou sayst) confusion of face may cover thee'.[40]

Beyond this type of point-scoring were serious issues about the status of ministers which were a long-standing feature of the reformation, and which were widely debated in the 1650s.[41] Quakers argued that ministerial

[34] Hubberthorne, *Truth cleared*, p. 4.
[35] Samuel Eaton, *The Quakers confuted* (London, 1654), STC E125, sig. B3r-v.
[36] [John Camm], *An answer to a book which Samuel Eaton put up to the Parliament* (London, 1654), STC C389, p. 16
[37] James Parnell, *Goliah's head cut off with his own sword* (London, 1655), STC P531, p. 6.
[38] Parnell, *Goliah's head*, p. 6.
[39] Thomas Drayton, *An answer according to truth, that trembles not, nor Quakes, nor quayleth* (London, 1655), p. 1. Parnell was nineteen.
[40] Parnell, *Goliah's head*, p. 12.
[41] John Morgan, *Godly learning: puritan attitudes towards reason, learning and education, 1560–1640* (Cambridge, 1986), esp. pp. 62–94.

authority derived immediately from God. Richard Farnworth told an Independent minister: 'the ministers of Christ and the gospel was not made by the will of man, but of God were they ordained, and was sent by Christ Jesus and the holy Ghost'.[42] This extended to discussion of the structure of church government. Farnworth reminded one opponent, Andrew Trusterom of Clent, Worcestershire, that Trusterom had been ordained 'from the old (wicked) Bishops', which the minister could not deny without denying his very 'call and ordination'. The minister's claim that he had been chosen by elders was equally dismissed by Farnworth: church elders who were vested with their power by men, were not true elders: 'Elders of the flock of Christ . . . were not called to that work by the will of man, but were called and made overseers by the holy Ghost.'[43] James Nayler was equally dismissive of ministers 'who are either called by the cursed Bishops, or by earthly Magistrates, or else you call one another by your own wills, but no appointment of God nor gift of the holy Ghost, is witnessed amongst you'.[44] Nayler did not reject church government out of hand, but insisted that the spirit alone should be the guiding force:

Church-government, we own, and Jesus Christ the head and governour of his Church, to whom we submit, but deny your Classes, Assemblies, and Masterships, by which you rule and govern in your own wills: and the Ministers we own, which is of Jesus Christ and immediate call to it, and deny all whose call is mediate, and are made ministers by the will of man.[45]

It was within the context of true ministerial authority that the Quakers questioned the rights of ministers to claim tithes, the validity of their university training, and the propriety of their heightened social status.[46] These, for the Quakers, were all signs of worldly, not spiritual, calling. Quaker opposition to tithes, privileged learning and social hierarchy has often been emphasised as evidence of their political egalitarianism: social protest was at the root of the Quaker ideology. Barry Reay rejected as 'misleading' the suggestion that the principal objection to tithes was scriptural, and stated that Quakers offered a 'wide range of economic and social objections to tithes . . . which reflected a deep hostility towards the social order and a rabid anticlericalism'.[47] The argument that the Quakers' radicalism stemmed from a long-standing tradition of 'popular social protest', while not disputed here,

---

[42] Richard Farnworth, *The brazen serpent lifted up on high* (London, 1655), STC F471, p. 40.
[43] Farnworth, *ibid.*, p. 41.
[44] James Nayler, *A discovery of the man of sin* (London, 1654), STC N274, p. 38.
[45] *Ibid.*, p. 12.
[46] For the currency of these debates see Morgan, *Godly learning*, and Greaves, 'Ordination controversy'.
[47] Barry Reay, 'Quaker opposition to tithes 1652–1660', *Past and Present* 86 (1980), 105. See also Alan Cole, 'The Quakers and the English revolution', *Past and Present* 10 (1956), 43; Margaret James, 'The political importance of the tithes controversy in the English revolution, 1640–60', *History* (June, 1941), 15–16; Leo Damrosch, *The sorrows of the Quaker Jesus:*

should not obscure the immediate relevance of Quakers' debates with their contemporaries over the proper course of religious reform.[48]

The debate over the authority of the national ministry touched on very practical, political issues. In his dispute against Thomas Welde and four other Newcastle ministers, Nayler rounded on them for their former role in the Commission for the North:

> And whereas you deny that the late commission did ever pretend to put any in the Office of a Minister, here all the North may witness against you, that you care not what you say to excuse your selves and accuse others, though never so false. Did not you and those that were in commission call them before you, and examined and appointed whom you would, and denied whom you would at will and pleasure? and your partiality in it, the North can witness; and now you deny it: be ashamed and confounded before all men, you shameless creatures.[49]

A second, related element in the exchanges over the religious state of England was the Quakers' attack on Calvinism. All Quaker tracts proclaimed the universal inner light of Christ and as such were representative of part of a move away from Calvinist doctrines among other radical thinkers of the period.[50] The Quakers criticised puritan teachers and ministers in particular for preaching that salvation was limited and unknowable. James Nayler accused them of 'upholding of the kingdom of sin, making people beleeve they shall never be free from it, while they are on the earth'.[51] In so doing, they opposed 'the end of Christs coming, which was to take away sin and

---

James Nayler and the puritan crackdown on the free spirit (Cambridge, Mass., 1996), pp. 50–52.

[48] Christopher Hill, *The world turned upside down* (Harmondsworth, 1987), pp. 231–58, esp. p. 247.

[49] Nayler, *A discovery of the man of sin*, p. 38.

[50] This has been discussed for the early Stuart period by Nicholas Tyacke, 'Puritanism, Arminianism and counter-revolution', in Conrad Russell (ed.), *The origins of the English civil war* (London, 1973); Peter White, 'The rise of Arminianism reconsidered', *Past and Present* 101 (1983); Nicholas Tyacke, *Anti-Calvinists: the rise of English Arminianism c. 1560–1640* (Oxford, 1987). For an account of the rise of Arminianism among radical congregations in the 1650s, see Ellen More, 'The New Arminians: John Goodwin and his Coleman Street Congregation in Cromwellian England', unpublished Ph. D thesis, University of Rochester, New York, 1979, esp. pp. 162–234. The categorical rejection of Calvinism by Quakers is made clear in a French version of George Fox's tract, *To all that would know the way to the kingdom*. The English version included a set of questions addressed to all 'who denies the teachings of God in Spirit, and would keep people in the teachings of men from the Letter, ever learning, but never able to come to the knowledge of the truth'. The French version addressed the same questions more succinctly to those 'of the reformed religion, who follow the teachings of Calvin'. George Fox, *To all that would know the way to the kingdom* [London, 1654], *STC* F1943, p. 14; [George Fox], *A tous ceulx qui voudroyent cognoistre la voye au Royaume* (London, 1655), *STC* F1739, p. 17. The French version is addressed 'à ceux qu'on appelle de la Religion reformée, qui soutiennent les Ordonnances qui jadis furent baillées par Calvin'.

[51] Nayler, *A discovery of the man of sin*, p. 4.

to set free from it, and to present perfect unto the Father without spot or blemish'.[52]

Puritan ministers were criticised for preaching that salvation and sin were ultimately unknowable because it disempowered their audiences and, therefore, undermined active religious participation. Nayler accused ministers of persuading people 'to leave the work of redemption and freedom till after death, or you know not when . . . and thus encourage people to spend their days in folly, and leave the world with torment and horror at their death'.[53] Preachers who claimed that salvation was unknowable were denounced as fraudulent or ineffectual. In his confrontation with Richard Hubberthorne, Vavasour Powell denounced the Quakers for boasting of 'a gift of discerning', and promising their audiences that they could know salvation and reject sin. In response, Hubberthorne suggested that Powell's confession of his ignorance of salvation undermined his own credibility as a minister:

you have cleared your selves from the spirit of discerning, that the Scripture speaks of, and hath showed forth your nakedness and folly, for to some was given a spirit of discerning, which now is witnessed with some, but not with you.[54]

Furthermore, Hubberthorne questioned the spiritual authority of Powell's preaching, reportedly asking the members of the congregation:

which of them could witness they were convinced or converted by his [Powell's] preaching unto them, and who had forsaken their sins; but none there could witness any such thing, but pleaded for sin, and that they could not be free from sin, and it was plainly made manifest in the Congregation to all those whose understandings was enlightened, that thou was one who ministered for Satan.[55]

In contrast to this, James Nayler boasted of his own certainty and thus of his integrity: 'that which I know, declare I unto you, and the way I know where I have found my beloved, my Saviour, my Redeemer, my Husband, my Maker'.[56] Another author promised his readers that if they 'Reade without prejudice', they would 'receive Instruction, and not increase thy owne misery'.[57] To the Muggletonian John Reeve's publication, claiming that a vision had enabled him to discern the elect, Edward Burrough and Francis Howgill were deeply dismissive: 'call not thy own imaginations his Word, but thou who hast a dream, tell thy dream for a dream, and he that hath the Word of the Lord, let him speak it faithfully'.[58]

---

[52] *Ibid.*   [53] James Nayler, *The power and glory*, p. 21.
[54] Richard Hubberthorne, *Truth cleared*, p. 3.
[55] *Ibid.*, p. 4.   [56] Nayler, *The power and glory*, p. 25.
[57] A. P. [probably Anthony Pearson], in James Nayler, *A few words occasioned by a paper* [London, 1654], sig. A2v.
[58] Edward Burrough and Francis Howgill, *Answers to severall queries* (London, 1654) STC B5984, p. 9.

The attack on Calvinism meant that Quakers did not particularly distinguish between Independents, Particular Baptists and Presbyterians, and
even Fifth Monarchists. Richard Hubberthorne's dispute with Vavasour
Powell touched on the exclusive nature of Powell's saints. Debates with Fifth
Monarchists Vavasour Powell, Frederick Woodall and Christopher Feake all
suggest that a crucial element was the Quakers' dislike of the elitism of the
Fifth Monarchists, compounded by the role of Powell in heading the Committee for the Propagation of the Gospel in Wales. Powell was dismissed by
Hubberthorne as 'one of the chief Priests in Wales'.[59] Frederick Woodall, an
ordained minister and after 1652 a pastor to a congregation in Woodbridge,
Suffolk, was dubbed 'the High Priest' by Christopher Atkinson.[60]

THE CONDUCT OF RELIGIOUS DEBATE

Having established that debate was firmly rooted in the Quakers' itinerant
preaching, and having discussed the issues of contention between Quakers
and their puritan opponents, the chapter can now show how Quaker ministers sought to gain the widest possible audience participation through
their publications. The whole spectrum of their preaching campaign, which
included their publications, aimed at mobilising people to participate in the
final establishment of Christ's kingdom on earth.

Very simple publications, which were probably used as part of the
Quakers' initial public preaching, involved basic attacks on ministers and
their doctrines. These were tracts which carefully defined 'false' prophets or
'false' ministry', and which argued by the same token that the Quakers were
the only true prophets.[61] As with the definitions of 'quaking', discussed in

---

[59] Hubberthorne, *Truth cleared*, sig. A*r.
[60] Christopher Atkinson, *David's enemies discovered* (London, 1655), STC A4126, p. 11. For
Woodall, see Bernard Capp, *The Fifth Monarchy Men* (London, 1972), p. 269. Compare
with the hostility of Nayler towards Thomas Welde and William Cole, both Commissioners
for the north, cited above.
[61] All of the following tracts indicate by their titles that they are denunciations of the puritan
ministry, or of other religious professions. I have excluded from this list the many publications which are specific attacks on particular ministers, or responses to hostile tracts. *A brief
discovery of the kingdom of Antichrist* (STC F472A); *A call out of Egypt* (STC P378); *A call
out of Egypt and Babylon* (STC F474); *A call out of false worships* (STC F474A); *A character
whereby false christs may be known* (STC F475); *A declaration against all profession and
professors* (STC F1784); *A declaration of the difference of the ministers* (STC F1790); *A
declaration of the marks and fruits of the false prophets* (STC D711); *A description of the
prophets, apostles, and ministers of Christ* (STC C4453); *A discovery of some fruits of the
profession* (STC F1795AA); *A discovery of the priests* (STC P188); *A publicke discovery of
the open blindness of Babel's builders* (STC N305); *A true tryall of the ministers and ministry
of England* (STC B1903); *A word from the Lord to all the world, and all professors in the
world* (STC F1991A); *A word from the Lord, unto all the faithlesse generation of the World*

Chapter 4, definitions of 'false prophets', derived from both the Old and New Testaments, were laid down in the very earliest of Quaker publications, and subsequently reiterated by other authors. The first extant publication which gave an account of 'false prophets' was that written by the prisoners in York Castle in 1652, entitled *False prophets and false teachers described*.[62]

The involvement of the audience in identifying false prophets was a primary feature of this and other tracts. In *False prophets and false teachers described*, readers were invited to draw comparisons with their own ministers and those false prophets of the Bible. The argument against the 'false prophets' began with the book of Isaiah: the 'watchmen' of the wicked rulers of Israel were 'blind and cannot see, they are dumb doggs, yea greedy doggs that can never have enough, every one looks for his gain from his quarter'.[63] Jeremiah's prophecy against Jerusalem followed: 'A horrible and a filthie thing is committed in the Land, the Prophets prophesie false things, and the Priests bear rule by their Means, and the people love to have it so.'[64] The tract then added its own comment, clearly aimed at audiences other than learned ministers:

It was so then, but is it not so now? do not the Priests bear rule by their Means over you, and do not you love to have it so? O foolish people, that have eyes to see and cannot see, ears to hear and cannot hear, hearts and cannot understand . . . see if you hold not up this filthie thing which God sent his true Prophets to crie against.[65]

The prophet Ezekiel, continued the tract, 'spoke freely' (as, by implication, the present-day Quaker prophets did) 'against them that spoke for the Fleece'.[66] Again, the Old Testament prophecy was sharpened by a more contemporary exhortation: 'Now the Lord is comming to teach all his freely, . . . and they that are taught of the Lord deny all teaching without: if you would be taught of the Lord, cease from your Hirelings.'[67] The tract made use of the prophet Micah, who had warned against the complacency of false prophets: 'The prophets divine for money and the Priests preach for Hire, and they

---

(*STC* F1992); *A word of reproof to the priests and ministers* (*STC* T1855); *False prophets and false teachers described* (*STC* A894BA); *False Prophets, antichrists, deceivers* (*STC* F631); *Spiritual discoveries to the overthrow of popery* (*STC* B2086); *Spirituall wickedness, in heavenly places* (*STC* N319); *The arraignment of poperie, being a short collection taken out of the chronicles* (*STC* F1750A); *The boasting Baptist dismounted* (*STC* M924); *The lying prophet discovered and reproved* (*STC* H1103A); *The priests ignorance and contrary walkings* (*STC* F492); *The Ranters principles and deceipts discovered* (*STC* F501); *The teachers of the world unvailed* (*STC* F1924); *To the priests and people of England* (*STC* C6474).

[62] Thomas Aldam, Elizabeth Hooton, William Pears, Benjamin Nicholson, Jane Holmes and Mary Fisher, *False prophets and false teachers described* [1652], *STC* A894BA.

[63] *Ibid.*, p. 1; cf. Isaiah 56. 10, 11, 12.   [64] *Ibid.*, p. 1; cf. Jeremiah 5. 30, 31.

[65] *Ibid.*, p. 1.

[66] *Ibid.*, pp. 1–2; cf Ezekiel 34. The passage is apparently a summary of the whole chapter.

[67] *Ibid.*, p. 2.

lean upon the Lord, and say, Is not the Lord amongst us?' More pertinent still from Micah was the accusation that the false prophets of Jerusalem were greedy and belligerent: 'Put into their mouths and they cry peace, peace; but if you put not into their mouthes, they prepare war against you.'[68]

The central New Testament texts came from the gospel of Saint Matthew, and from Paul's second letter to Timothy. Christ's warning against the pharisees in the Sermon on the Mount was directly incorporated into the Quakers' own text as part of another plea for the readers to judge their own ministers:

Do they not sit in the same Seats that the Scribes and Pharisees had? they had the chiefest place in Assemblies, have not your Priests so now? they had the uppermost rooms at Feasts, have not your Priests so now? they went in long Robes, do not your Priests so? they were called of men Masters, are not your Priests so now, do they not hold the same things that they did, and yet say they are sent of Christ?[69]

The letter from the apostle Paul to Timothy listed the defining characteristics of the false teachers who would come in the last days, which were used time and again by Quaker authors:

Of this sort are they (saith he) proud, covetous, self-lovers, boasters, heady, high-minded, railers, false-accusers, incontinent, fierce, despisers of those which are good, lovers of pleasures more than lovers of God; having a form of godlinesse, but denying the power thereof; from such turn away.[70]

This passage was used in direct juxtaposition to another part of the Sermon on the Mount and Christ's warning against false prophets, who would come in sheep's clothing, but 'inwardly they are ravening wolves': 'By their fruits ye shall know them: for every Tree is known by its fruits'; 'First look at the Trees, and then at the fruits,' implored the Quakers, 'and see if this sort of men be not such now.'[71] The tract then returned to Paul's warning against false teachers:

those that have eyes may see, that this sort of men preach now, and that for Hire, which is contrary to the Doctrine of Christ. Do not proud men Preach? Do not

---

[68] *Ibid.*, p. 2; cf. Micah 3. 11, 3. 5.

[69] Thomas Aldam *et al.*, *False prophets and false teachers described*, p. 3. This description of 'false teachers' or 'false prophets' became a central feature of the Quaker authors' denunciation of the national ministry of England: the objection to being 'called Master' in particular was a frequent cry in the Quaker tracts. See, for example, John Camm, *An answer to a book which Samuel Eaton put up*, pp. 38–41; [Richard Farnworth and James Nayler], *A discovery of faith* (London, 1653), STC F479, pp. 6–7; Richard Farnworth, *Englands warning piece gone forth* (London, 1653), STC F482, p. 5; Martin Mason, *The proud pharisee reproved: or, the lying down orator laid open* (London, 1655), STC M933, p. 4; James Nayler, *A few words occasioned by a paper lately printed* ([London], 1654), STC N279, p. 13.

[70] Thomas Aldam *et al.*, *False prophets and false teachers described*, p. 5; cf. 2 Tim. 3. 1–6.

[71] *Ibid.*, pp. 4, 5; cf. Matt. 7. 16–20; Luke 6. 43–44.

covetous men Preach? Do not self-lovers Preach? Do not high-minded men Preach? Do not railing men Preach? Do not false-accusing men Preach? Do not men that are despisers of those that are good Preach? Do not men that live in pleasures Preach?[72]

The final section of *False prophets and false teachers described* was a description of the true ministers of Christ, largely taken from the New Testament letters of the apostle Paul advising on the structures and practices of the church. The true ministers of Christ had held themselves to be examples for others to walk by, 'blameless as the stewards of God', 'that people were taught by their godly conversation to walk accordingly'.[73] Moreover, they ministered for free: 'neither did we eat any mans bread for nought, but wrought with labour and travell night and day, that we might not be chargeable to any'.[74] The true ministers of Christ:

gave no occasion of offence in any thing, that their Ministerie should not be blamed . . . But in all things approved themselves as the Ministers of God, in much patience, in aflictons, in necessities, in distresses, in stripes, in prisons, in tumults, in watchings, by fastings, by puritie, by knowledge, by long suffering, by kindnesse, by the Holy Ghost, by love unfeigned, by the world of truth, by the Power of God.[75]

The persecution endured by the Quakers was a sign of their status as 'true' ministers; as was their insistence that they received no money for their itinerant preaching. Such characteristics, the tract insisted, were not to be found in the 'Ministers that the world sets up', who were 'patterns of ungodlinesse, walking on in Hypocrisie, and persecuting the Saints of the most high God'.

This very simple tract provided accessible and familiar definitions of true and false ministry, and asked its audiences to use them in judging their ministers. Occasionally, tracts suggested stronger action by their readers. A tract written by George Fox 'on behalf of a people called Quakers', declared 'the grounds and reasons why they deny the Teachers of the World'. After eight pages of scripturally based denunciation of a paid preaching ministry, Fox instructed 'All people that read these things, never come more at the Steeple-house, nor pay your Priest more Tythes, till they have answered them.' Moreover, he warned his readers that their action on reading his tract was imperative: 'for if ye do [pay tithes], ye uphold them in their sins, and must partake of their plagues'.[76] A copy of this tract was dated by George Thomason in March 1654, as John Camm and Francis Howgill were making the first serious attempts to establish a Quaker presence in the capital: this

---

[72] *Ibid.*, p. 5.   [73] *Ibid.*, p. 6; cf. Titus 1. 6–8.   [74] *Ibid.*, p. 6; cf. 1 Thess. 2. 9; 2 Thess. 8.
[75] *Ibid.*, p. 8; cf. 2 Cor. 6. 3–10.
[76] George Fox, *A paper sent forth into the world* (London, 1654), STC F1872, *passim*, esp. p. 8.

kind of straightforward denunciation, with encouragement to action, was the opening salvo in the Quakers' onslaught in a new area.

The correspondence shows that these types of tract were used orally in public meeting places. In a letter to Margaret Fell dated 1653, Thomas Aldam described a large meeting at Ackworth, Yorkshire, at which some of Farnworth's followers had been:

> moved to goe to the steeple house and cleamed [i.e. pinned] up two Papers one on the Steeple house dore and Another not far off, Concerning the priests Errors. Many people were made to Reede them and convinced it was truth and proved by Scripture and confessed to our frends it was truth.[77]

The paper concerned was very probably Richard Farnworth's *A call out of Egypt and Babylon*, or a manuscript version of it, which offered 'six and twenty Errours of the Priests discovered'. These reiterated, very simply, objections against the practices of ministers who were 'made of Oxford and Cambridge'. The citation of a few of them demonstrates their aptitude for oral presentation:

> *The teachers of the world* sing David's quakings, tremblings, cryings, praises, prayings, and prophecies, in meter; and have a glass to preach an hour: and when they read the Psalms, hats must be on; when they sing them, hats must be off: . . . The apostles did not so when they spoke to the world. These act contrary to the Scriptures, *and have the spirit of errour.*
>
> *The teachers of the world* have the chiefest places in the assemblies, are called of men Masters, laying heavie burthens upon the people . . . contrary to Christs commands and practice; so shewing themselves to be Antichrists, Seducers, and Dissemblers, *and have the spirit of errour.*
>
> *The teachers of the world* say, men shall never be perfect, when the Scripture saith, Be ye perfect, even as your heavenly Father is perfect: . . . Here they deny the scriptures, *and shew the spirit of errour.*[78]

Farnworth went on in the pamphlet to describe how the ministers took money for funerals and marriages, for churching women, for tithes; and how they emphasised the importance of the scriptures over the power of God. The fact that they were presented in very short points which were ideal for reading aloud, ending and beginning with the same phrase, is very suggestive that the tract was used orally. That Aldam mentioned it to Margaret Fell as especially effective is evidence that attacks on puritan ministers were not aimed at them but presented to their congregations and wider audiences. At the height of the Quaker expansion into the south of the country in the summer of 1654, Aldam sent George Fox copies of a very similar paper by

---

[77] [Thomas Aldam] to Margaret Fell, 1653, A. R. Barclay Mss 2: 159.
[78] Richard Farnworth, *A call out of Egypt and Babylon* (London, 1653), STC F474, mispaginated pp. 34–29, sigs. E4v–F2r. (The italics are mine.)

Farnworth, *A call out of false worships*, urging him: 'Let them bee spread abroad in the contry.'[79] (See Plate 8.)

A primary stage of Quaker campaigning therefore involved disseminating short, accessible tracts and papers which drew the readers' attention to the shortcomings of a national ministry. These public denunciations were not aimed directly at the ministers themselves, but at members of congregations and even passers-by in marketplaces, who were then urged to 'judge' or question their own ministers.

The pattern of audiences publicly questioning their ministers was also established in Quaker tracts. Some tracts included printed questions which allowed readers to ask more complex questions of their ministers, about the nature of their authority and their fitness to preach.[80] The Quakers' critics were well aware that they were subject to a systematic campaign of questions. Edmund Skipp, preacher at Bodenham in Herefordshire, noted how the 'railing and clamorous words, and unjust accusations', sent by the Quakers to most professors of religion, were remarkably similar in the language they used, regardless of the religious leanings of the recipient: 'which maketh me note,' Skipp commented, 'that they are exemplary one to another in their writing, taking up the same form of words'.[81] A very early printed attack on the Quakers by Fifth Monarchist sympathisers accused 'these preaching Anti-preachers' of making allegations 'hand-over-head against all that mention the name of God in the publick Assemblies of the Nation'.[82] Anyone in possession of a suitable Quaker tract would be able to ask searching questions of a preaching minister (see Plate 9).

The exchange of questions seems most often to have occurred in public, during the sermons of the Quakers' critics. Once again, then, the challenging of a minister's authority was done publicly, for the edification of the audience. Gabriel Camelford, curate of Staveley, adjacent to Ulverstone, was particularly aggrieved that Thomas Atkinson had presented him with a set

---

[79] Thomas Aldam to George Fox, 1654, Sw Mss 3: 44.
[80] See, for example, Richard Farnworth, *An Easter-Reckoning, or, A Free-will Offering* (London, 1653), STC F480, pp. 1–9; George Fox et al., *A declaration against all poperie, and popish points* [London], 1655, STC F1783, sig. Br; Fox et al., *Several papers, some of them given forth by George Fox* [n.p.] (1653), STC F1903, pp. 30–35; Fox and Nayler, *To all that would know the way to the kingdom* (3 edns, London, 1654 and 1655), STC F1942A, F1943, pp. 14–17; James Nayler, *The power and glory of the Lord shining out of the north* (London, 1653), STC N302, p. 25; Nayler, *The railer rebuked, in a reply to a paper subscribed Ellis Bradshaw* ([n.p.], 1655), STC N306, pp. 7–8.
[81] Edmund Skipp, *The world's wonder, or, the Quakers blazing star* (London, 1655), STC S3949, p. 10.
[82] Joseph Kellet et al., *A faithful discovery of a treacherous design* (London, 1653), STC F568, p. 47. For the Quaker responses generated by this tract, see *A return to the priests about Beverley* (London) (1654), STC R1185; Richard Farnworth, *Light risen out of darkness* (London, 1654), STC F490; *A short answer to a book set forth by seven Priests* (London, 1654), STC P36.

34

The Priests Ignorance, or contrary walkings to the Scriptures, or the practise of the Apostles, who were the true Ministers of Jesus Christ.

Together, with

Six and twenty Errours of the Priests discovered.

2 John.4,9.
Isai. 8. 20.

THe teachers of this world profess the Scripture to be their rule, and touchstone to try withall, and he that walks contrary to the Scriptures is a Seducer, and hath the spirit of errour.

2 Pet.1.11.
Gal.1.11.
Ezek. 3.1.
&c. 33.33.
& 22.

That which makes a minister of the world is *Oxford*, and *Cambridge*, and they are so long there, give so much for their learning, and when they have done, they have so much for their preaching: the Prophets and Apostles did not so, Christ gave no so such command: and here they act contrary to the Scriptures, and have the spirit of errour; and they will let none preach but themselves, and such as come from *Oxford* and *Cambridge*; here they act contrary to the Scripture faith, *Yee may all prophesie one by one, and if any thing be revealed to him that stands by, let the first hold his peace,* (Hereby some take holy one of Israel, and shew the spirit of errour.

1 Cor. 14. 30.

1 Cor.6.6.
Act.10.33.
1 Pet. 5.2.
Mat. 5. 40.
Deut. 4.2.
Pro. 30.15.
6.
Rev. 22. 18,19.

The teachers of the world have a set man of the world: and if any man refuse them, they sue them at the law: the Prophets and the Apostles did not so; these act contrary to the Scripture, and have the spirit of errour.

The teachers of the world take a text, raise doctrines, uses, points, trialls, motives, and have a Clark to say *Amen*: the Apostles did not so: these act contrary the Scripture, and shew the spirit of errour.

The

35

The teachers of the world sing *David's* quakings, tremblings, cryings, washings, prayses, prayings, and prophecies, in meeter; and have a glass, to preach an hour: and when they read the Psalms, hats must be on; when they sing them, hats must be off: but the Priest hath one or two caps on his head. The Apostles did not so when they spoke to the world. These act contrary to the Scriptures, and have the spirit of errour.
Psa.6.
Cor.14.15.
Cor.14.40.

The teachers of the world cry, *Let us sing to the praise and glory of God,* and give the ignorant praphane people words to sing, as, *I am not purs in minde, I have no sorrful eye,* whereas they are put in minde, and have scornful eyes. Herein they dishonour the Lord, causing people to lye, shewing the spirit of errour.
Psa.131.11.
1 joh.2.21.

The teachers of the world have the chiefest places in the assemblies, are called of men Masters, laying heavie burthens upon the people, stand praying in the Synagogues. Jesus Christ forbad such things: the teachers of the world now act such things, contrary to Chrifts commands and practise; so shewing themselves to be Antichrifts, Seducers, and Defembers, and have the spirit of errour.
Mat.23. 6, 7,8,9,10, 11.
Mat.6.5,7 8,9.
1 joh.2.21.

The teachers of the world hold up outward temples, calling them Churches. Whereas the Church is *in God,* 1 Thef.1.1. and calls it the house of God, and thus act contrary to the Scriptures, having the spirit of errour.
1 Cor.1.10 Act.17.24, 25.

The teachers of the world sprinkle infants, telling people it is an Ordinance of God; which is contrary to the Scriptures, never commanded by the Lord: but the behold it up, and so bewitch the people, and are seducers, having the spirit of errour.
Gal.3.
Luke 11.42, 63.

The teachers of the world call people unto a Sacrament, for the which there is no Scripture. Here they act contrary to the Scriptures, teaching lyes, contrary to the Scripture, a declaration of God. Here they are seducers, and shew forth the spirit of errour.
Gen.11.3.
Gen.19.38 Gen.10.

The teachers of the world marry people, and take money for it. The Apostles did not so. Here they act contrary to the Scriptures, shewing the spirit of errour.

The Teachers of the world take money for burying the dead, the Apostles did not so; here they act contrary to the Scripture, shewing the spirit of errour.
Mat.10.8.
Mat.8.11.

The Teachers of the world take Money for Churching women. The Apostles did not so. Thus these act contrary to the Scripture, shewing the Spirit of errour.

F

The

Plate 8. Typical objections to the puritan ministry, circulated in print: Richard Farnworth, *A call out of Egypt and Babylon* (London, 1653), Thomason 29 June 1653, STC F474, sigs E4v–Fr.

the plagues and woes written, are thy Portion? As thou liest in sinne, thou shalt drinke the dregs thereof, and wring them out, except thou Repent.

Queries.

1. WHether Jesus Christ be not that Covenant of light, spoken on in the Scriptures, promised by the Father, to enlighten and leade all that will owne and follow him out of the dark world, up to God, the Father of light, yea, or no?

2. Whether that be not the light of Christ which enlightens the Conscience, witnessing there against all sin and unrighteousnesse, which convinceth and sheweth the deeds of darknesse, and exerciseth the Conscience in purity and holinesse of all that will follow and obey it, yea, or no?

3. If you say that be not the light of Christ, then how is Christ the light of the world? and how doth he lighten every one that commeth into the world? and how doe you distinguish between the light of Christ, and that which you call a naturall light? and doth the light of Christ enlighten the creature any other way then by shining into the Conscience, yea or no?

4. Whether the light of Christ be not a sufficient guide to all who receive and follow it, to bring out of darknesse unto the Father, and reveale him to the creature without adding to it any other humane helps, and was not he given to all the ends of the earth for this very end, yea, or no?

5. Whether those that are in Scripture called the Children of light, be not onely such as are gathered out of darknesse by this light, and into it walking in it in measure; and those which are called the Children of darknesse, be not such as whose understandings are darkened, by following the Prince of darknesse, to seek out other lights from their imaginations, setting up Persons, Formes, Customes, Times, Dayes, Places, Let-

ter, and other visible carnall things to get light from, which are not the spirit of Christ, yea, or no?

6. Whether it was not by the same light of the spirit of Christ, that all the holy men of God in all ages were Inspired, had their Revelations, and by which they spoke forth what is written in Scriptures, in a mystery to all the Children of darknesse: and whether the light of Christ be not the same now, that ever it was, to every one that have received in their severall measures, yea, or no?

7. Whether all those who are not onely ignorant of this light, but also enemies to it, rendring it under odious termes, as unable to leade out of darknesse, be not Ministers for the Prince of darknesse, and against Christ the true light, and so are Ministers of Anti-Christ, and upholders of the Kingdome of darknesse, which Christ came to destroy, yea, or no?

More Quaries.

1. WHether can the Scriptures be Read and Understood by any other spirit then that which gave them forth, yea, or no?

2. Whether that spirit be excluded from manifesting it selfe in the Saints, now in the same power and manner, as formerly it hath done, yea, or no?

3. Whether that spirit where it is, be not infallible, and judge of all truth, and all deceipts in its measure, as it is manifested, yea, or no?

4. Whether those who have not the spirit, which is the infallible judge, have any true ground to passe the censure of excommunication, or to judge of blasphemy in others, yea, or no?

5. Whether that which is spoken by that spirit where it is, be not the very word of God, yea, or no?

6. Whether the spirit of the world, by their carnall laws, grounded upon humane wisdome and reason, have any power from God to judge that spirit where it is? and have they not in all Ages, when they have attempted it, passed the censure of Blasphemy

Plate 9. Prepared queries circulated in a tract in November 1653. [George Fox, James Nayler and Anthony Pearson], *Several papers, some of them given forth by George Fox* (1653), STC F1903.

of queries 'in the face of the Congregation'.[83] The Cheshire congregational leader Samuel Eaton claimed that he had been spurred into writing against the Quakers after one of them had presented nineteen queries to Eaton 'in the face of the Congregation', and had voiced his ideas on the perfectibility of mankind 'in the presence of all that were assembled'. A private exchange of letters had been going on between Eaton and the Quaker for two months, one of the Quakers being former members of Eaton's own church. It was the public challenge which propelled Eaton to respond in print.[84]

Puritan ministers could be goaded into print against the Quakers by the presentation of questions, the local circulation of Quaker tracts, or simply by a sustained Quaker presence which threatened their own following. Once their critics had ventured into print, however, Quaker authors responded in kind as part of their proselytising ministry, with their own followers in mind, and steadfastly maintained that they were not partaking in any dry academic debate. In July 1655, Edward Burrough wrote a letter from London to his colleague John Audland, who was conducting his ministry in Bristol. Burrough drew Audland's attention to a book which had been published in reply to one of Audland's tracts, and he suggested that Audland write a response in his turn. Audland was unenthusiastic about the value of the exchange. The book in question, he thought, 'doth not answer mine', and although he intended to write 'a little to it', he complained to Burrough that 'its soe silly few doth regard it'. Moreover, Audland was sure that 'onely the filthy spirit from whence it Cam' would be at all interested in the publication of the exchange: 'amonge the Children of Light it will not stand'.[85]

Audland was referring to a book written by a Bristol schoolmaster, George Willington, entitled *The gadding tribe reproved*.[86] Audland had already tackled a series of works provoked by the Quaker presence in Bristol, by William

[83] Richard Hubberthorne and George Fox *et al.*, *Truths defence against the refined subtilty of the serpent* ([n. p.], 1653), STC F1970, p. 3. Gabriel Camelford is listed in *Calamy revised* as the curate of Staveley, Lancashire by August 1649; and later as the pastor of a church of Independents and Baptists at Tottleton, Colton in Furness, in 1669.

[84] Samuel Eaton, *The Quakers confuted* (London, 1654), STC E125, sig. B2r.

[85] John Audland to Edward Burrough, Bristol, 14 July 1655 [poss. 1656], A. R. Barclay Mss 2: 177, fol. 151.

[86] Audland initially wrote a reply to three books: Ralph Farmer, *The great mysteries of godlinesse and ungodlinesse* (London, 1655), STC F441, copy dated by Thomason 23 January 1655; William Prynne, *The Quakers unmasked, and clearly detected* (London, 1655), STC P4045, copy dated by Thomason on 19 February 1655; and Samuel Morris, *A looking-glass for the Quakers or Shakers* (London, 1655), STC M2810, copy dated by Thomason on 20 March 1655. John Audland's response was *The innocent delivered out of the snare* (London, 1655), STC A4196, copy dated by Thomason on 9 April 1655. This seems to have provoked George Willington, *The gadding tribe reproved by the light of the scriptures* (London, 1655), STC W2802, copy dated by Thomason on 9 April 1655; a reply by John Audland, *The schoolmaster disciplined* (London, 1655); and another, even more hyperbolic version of William Prynne's *The Quakers unmasked, and clearly detected* (London, 1655), STC P4046, copy dated by Thomason on 19 June 1655.

Prynne, the Bristol presbyterian minister Ralph Farmer, and by a Bristol man, Samuel Morris, in a work entitled *The innocent delivered out of the snare*; and for as reticent an author as Audland, the book by Willington had clearly not inspired any desire for further exchange. The major criteria for Audland's unwillingness to contribute further to this dispute was the fact that he perceived no need for it. The book did nothing to damage the 'increase' of the truth in Bristol and its environs, which Audland reported to be growing steadily; and those interested in the reply were not likely to be sympathetic to the Quaker movement.

Audland's reserve contrasts strikingly with the attitude of his colleague Richard Farnworth, a far more prolific author. In April 1655, Farnworth was conducting his ministry in Herefordshire and Worcestershire. In a letter to Fox, Farnworth described meetings he had held, in the otherwise 'dead and darke' city of Hereford, with 'a few Prety hearts', formerly members of Edmund Skipp's congregation. Farnworth reported that he was hindered in his work by the impact of a recent book attacking the Quakers by Edmund Skipp, *The world's wonder*, which, Farnworth reported, 'doth much harm'. Farnworth had already written a counter-attack, which was currently in the press; and he was confident that 'if my Answer to it were downe and abrod,' it 'would be usefull'.[87]

Even allowing for the very different authorial profiles of Audland and Farnworth, these two letters epitomise the Quaker authors' attitudes to the publication of pamphlet disputes. While in Bristol John Audland felt that Willington's book would not 'stand' with the 'children of light', and therefore presented no threat, in Herefordshire Farnworth had already identified the followers of Skipp, as well as some Baptists living just outside Hereford, as requiring some response to an attack on the Quakers. Both Audland and Farnworth wrote to a potential audience, likely to 'owne the truth', and who would be helped by the publication of a Quaker tract. Quaker authors regarded printed exchanges between themselves and their critics as primarily instrumental for spreading the truth and increasing the following of the Quaker movement: they did not debate with puritan adversaries as a matter of principle or for the sake of it.

Concern with audience is also clear in the arrangements made by Farnworth for the distribution of a published account of a more formal public disputation with Baptists in the Midlands. Farnworth told his London contacts, Francis Howgill and Edward Burrough, that the 'Baptists are sore

---

[87] Richard Farnworth to George Fox, Bromyard, Herefordshire, 26 April 1655, Sw Mss 3: 55; Skipp, *The world's wonder*, copy dated by Thomason on 28 February 1655. Farnworth's response, co-authored with Humphrey Smith, appeared as *Antichrist's man of war apprehended* (London, 1655), STC F470. A copy of this tract was dated by Thomason 20 June 1655.

Broken and Squandered and much troubled' following 'great opposition' between them and the Quakers. He told Howgill and Burrough to print the account of his disputes against the Baptists, and to arrange for 100 copies to be distributed within the locality where the dispute had happened, and for another 100 to be sent to friends in Yorkshire, 'because so many [Baptists] is Amongst them'.[88] An account of a local dispute could be used in an environment far removed from the original exchange, and was not, as far as Farnworth was concerned, valid only among the audience who had originally witnessed the disputation or who knew the participants. This underlines that the arguments Farnworth raised against Baptists could be employed by other Quakers in parallel confrontations in the north. Quaker tracts were intended to enable active religious participation.

The debate about the future of the national church and further reformation was conducted through a wide spectrum of different media. The participation of the audience was of primary importance. Authors went out of their way to emphasise the importance of immediate participation, and distanced themselves from the holding of scholarly debate for its own sake. Between 1653 and 1654, James Nayler maintained an unusually lengthy pamphlet exchange with five Independent Newcastle ministers, Thomas Welde, William Cole, Richard Prideaux, Samuel Hammond and William Durrant. When they complained to him that his reply had not answered their accusations, Nayler rejected the format of their debate:

> To which I answer, That which moved me to write what I did in answer to the slanders in it, was not to satisfie your wils, nor wisdom, nor any who stand in their own wils or wisdom for then had I become a man-pleaser . . . But that which moved me, was for the simple ones sake, lest he should come to be deceived by the sleights of your slanders, and by the envious serpent: And I know and am assured, it hath and shall accomplish the end for which it was sent forth.[89]

Ultimately, an account of a more formally staged debate might be published, not only in order to allow participants to re-live and rehearse their sides of the argument, but also to enable Quaker leaders elsewhere to initiate and direct similar debates with opponents elsewhere.[90] The Quaker attack on puritans

---

[88] Richard Farnworth to Francis Howgill and Edward Burrough [17 October 1654], Portfolio 32: 56. The book was probably Farnworth's *Truth cleared of Scandals* (London, 1654), STC F512, an account of a dispute between Farnworth and Baptists held at Harlaston, Staffordshire, in September 1654.

[89] James Nayler, *A discovery of the man of sin*, p. 1.

[90] See Ann Hughes, 'The pulpit guarded: confrontations between orthodox and radicals in revolutionary England', in Anne Laurence, W. Owens and Stuart Sims (eds.), *John Bunyan and his England, 1628–88* (London, 1990), pp. 44–48, for a discussion of the publishing of religious disputation in this period. This argument is developed by Hughes in '"Popular" Presbyterianism in the 1640s and 1650s: the cases of Thomas Edwards and Thomas Hall', in Nicholas Tyacke (ed.), *England's long Reformation, 1500–1800* (London, 1998), 235–59.

was systematic: as one opponent put it: 'its not any person or circumstance so much that is aimed at, as the Ministry it self, or all outward Teachers'.[91] Yet the clear emphasis on the importance of the audiences demonstrates that the Quakers' campaign was conducted through congregations and audiences. Ann Hughes has argued that the holding of public disputations by relatively lowly, unordained religious leaders in the 1650s is evidence of the participatory, even 'popular', nature of religion in the interregnum.[92] The spectrum of Quaker pamphleteering reinforces this, but suggests further that religion was debated more widely than through formal disputations alone. From direct, simple denunciations of a preaching ministry to more complex debate and exchange, Quaker leaders had their eye on the responses and attitudes of the wider readership, not of the puritan ministers themselves.

THE PURITAN RESPONSE

It has been remarked that orthodox puritan ministers had more to lose than the Quakers by stooping to dispute formally with them.[93] The pamphlet warfare launched against the Quakers demonstrates that orthodox puritans saw pamphleteering as a form of participation in wider religious debate. It also underlines the very different views about the nature of participation held by Quakers and their critics. Puritan ministers had two purposes in engaging with the Quakers in print. Many claimed they did so with the pastoral care of their and other congregations in mind, in an attempt to prevent defections from their church. A second motivation for publishing against the Quakers was to participate in wider political arguments over the nature and extent of religious toleration. Examples of local disruption caused by the Quakers were related to the problem of national religious legislation: and the problem was directly or indirectly laid at the door of the government. The Quakers were thus a foil for wider religious debate.

Many opponents of the Quakers claimed that they were entering into debate with them against their better judgement; and that they did so only with the interests of their congregations at heart. An important sub-plot in Samuel Eaton's work against the Quakers was that one of his former congregation was in danger of being beguiled into joining a Quaker meeting, and Eaton was thus 'necessitated to appear in Print against them'.[94] Eaton claimed he had long resisted taunts from the Quakers: 'though I have been often sollicitted to confer with them', he wrote, he had 'perpetually declined it, because I looked upon them as a People not only deluded, but given over

---

[91] Joseph Kellet *et al.*, *A faithful discovery*, p. 50.
[92] Hughes, 'The pulpit guarded', pp. 48–49.   [93] *Ibid.*, p. 36.
[94] Samuel Eaton, *The Quakers confuted*, sig. Bv.

to the power of Satan'.[95] It was the exercise of his pastoral duty which drove him, he claimed, to publish. Similarly, Richard Baxter, well known for his pastoral zeal, included in one of his anti-Quaker works a letter written 'to a young unsetled Friend, who before inclining strongly to Anabaptistry, at last fell in with the Quakers, and desired my thoughts of them and their waies'.[96] Baxter claimed that he had been more or less forced into print. His Quaker opponents, who were probably Richard Farnworth and Thomas Goodaire, were portrayed as unsuitable disputants, arriving on a day 'when it pleased God to confine me to my Chamber by sicknesse', and Baxter's inexperienced assistant 'avoided publicke disputing with them'. Following a subsequent 'unprofitable verball discourse with an unreasonable railing fellow', which Baxter did not choose to describe in print, he described how he had resolved instead to debate with them through manuscript questions and answers.[97] It was the threat of the publication of these by the Quakers, Baxter claimed, which led him to publish his own answers to the manuscript queries: 'I chose rather to tell the world of these Passages between us, then leave them to their reports; especially hearing . . . that the ignorant have need of some plain Information to prevent their Apostasy and perdition.'[98] Baxter claimed to write first and foremost with the interests of the laity at heart.

Some of the Quakers' opponents believed that public confrontation or disputation was a valid way to combat the Quaker threat, and they themselves initiated debate. In the summer of 1656, Edward Burrough reported to James Nayler that 'priests' in Oxfordshire had 'challenged' the Quakers to a dispute; Ralph Josselin pledged in his diary to 'make opposicon to their wayes in defence of truth'.[99] Quaker tracts describing public disputations also gave the impression that it was belligerent puritan ministers who interrupted Quaker meetings to force public debates: 'when we came at the meeting house, we found you 2 Priests got peaking up [*sic*] Pharisee like, and had been labouring to incense the people against us', Farnworth accused two ministers in Worcestershire; earlier he reproached the Baptist Thomas Pollard for coming to a private Quaker meeting 'of purpose to cavill, to oppose the Truth'.[100]

Puritan ministers were more likely to favour formal debate than the Quakers, because they reflected with the learned and professional status associated

[95] *Ibid.*, sig. Br.
[96] Richard Baxter, *The Quakers catechism* (London, 1655), STC B1362, sig. B3r-C4r.
[97] *Ibid.*, sigs. A3r-A3v.   [98] *Ibid.*, sig. A4r.
[99] Edward Burrough to James Nayler, 12 July 1656, Portfolio 1: 43; Josselin, *The diary of Ralph Josselin 1616–1683*, ed. Alan MacFarlane, British Academy Records of Social and Economic History New Series III (London, 1976), p. 348.
[100] R[ichard] F[arnworth], *The brazen serpent lifted up* (London, 1655), STC F471, p. 27; Farnworth, *Truth cleared of scandals* (London, 1654), p. 5.

with a formal ministry. Public disputations were carefully orchestrated formal occasions with established rules and procedures, which drew on the oral debating skills acquired through grammar school and university education.[101] They were anathema to Quakers who claimed to speak when moved by God, and not by formal rules of debate. At Chadwich in Worcestershire, the two ministers who gate-crashed Farnworth's meeting laid out the proper format for a debate, suggesting 'that all the people would be silent' so that Farnworth and they 'might speak together'.[102] Farnworth could not agree to this: 'I was not free in my spirit to have the spirits of others tyed up' and he reiterated: 'I had appointed that meeting with the people, and had something from the Lord to declare to the people there, so be silent', he ordered the ministers, 'till I have done.' Even when his opponents agreed to his terms, Farnworth emphasised the divine instruction behind his speaking which was an obvious bar to formal disputations: 'So after that silent, I stood a while, and a woman bad me to speak and speak up aloud, but I to her answered and said, woman, I am not to be commanded by thee, but by the Lord, and as he pleaseth, so I shall speak.'[103]

The Quakers' opponents emphasised their pastoral responsibilities and professional status in battling against the Quaker threat. They claimed to be acting in the interests of their own flocks; and in so doing underlined their own professional status and expertise. Nevertheless, their readiness to counter the Quakers in print is not sufficiently explained by this: pastoral duties were more traditionally exercised in good sermons and adept disputing. The transition to print, for puritan ministers, necessarily involved a wider audience than their own congregations. Very frequently, as will be shown, this wider audience was implicitly or explicitly political.

Published accounts of local confrontations with Quakers often included pleas for further religious reform. Often the very fact of publication required the author to justify why he had turned to the press, and such preambles very often referred to the wider context of national religious policy. Some anti-Quaker authors were clearly critical of the abilities of England's preaching ministry to deal with the Quakers. One dispute was published after a local man heard of a contest at Worcester at which a local beneficed minister, Mr Baker, 'non-plust his [Quaker] opposite, and substantially proved his Calling and his Ministry true and Divine'. The news of a victory against a Quaker so impressed the man that he asked the 'reporters' of the dispute how Mr Baker had won the argument. He was frustrated: none present was able to remember 'how, or by what Scriptures or Arguments he did so prove it'. He then intreated Mr Baker himself, 'to hear from you the full truth' for across

---

[101] Hughes, 'The pulpit guarded', pp. 34–37.
[102] F[arnworth], *The brazen serpent lifted up*, p. 27.   [103] *Ibid.*, p. 28.

the nation 'our best and ablest Ministers, are at so greate a loss, and so hard put to it' to answer the Quakers successfully.[104]

Quakers were represented as agents of antichrist, who portrayed themselves as exceptionally godly in order to allure elect congregations, and thus were presented as a threat to the new godly order. Edmund Skipp prefaced his work from the gospel of Matthew: 'There shall arise false Christs and false Prophets, and shall shew great signs and wonders, in so much that (if it were possible) they shall deceive the very elect.'[105] Puritan ministers from Beverley (with the help of Fifth Monarchists Christopher Feake, John Simpson, George Cokayne and Lawrence Wise) published a 'Letter to the Faithful in and near to Beverley', which warned that in 'this Apostatizing age', the 'devil hath transformed himself into an Angel of light', and noted that 'whensoever God hath drawn neer unto any Countrey or City in the light of his Gospel, to dispel Popish and Antichristian darkness, the Devil hath usually . . . raised up a sort of new and spiritual Antichristians'.[106] The message of these pamphleteers, in February 1653, was that the Quakers were a warning to members of the Rump Parliament to reform the ministry and abolish tithes: 'we plead not for the ignorant, ungodly, persecuting men Called Ministers,' they wrote, 'but do sadly bewail that after all the Petitions from the Nation, Declarations of the State, and Proposalls from the wise hearted', nothing was being done 'to withdraw the Publick incouragement from the corrupt Ministry with whom God hath a controversie'.[107]

Other opponents of the Quakers focused on the national threat they posed to the national church and the security of the English Commonwealth. William Prynne argued that the Quakers were the 'spawn of Romish frogs, Jesuits, and Franciscan Popish Freers', witnessed by the fact that they came from the Catholic north, by their 'several Missions and Directions into all parts . . . from their Generals and Superiors of their respective Orders', by their sudden trances, visions and raptures, and by their attacks on ministers, tithes and presbyterian government: 'they are Anti-magistraticall and well as Anti-ministeriall'.[108] Other writers were less emotive, but still warned that the national church was threatened by the Quakers. 'I humbly beseech you that ye be not soone shaken in mind, by this upstart generation of quaking seducers', implored the Bristol schoolmaster George Willington to the

[104] *A copy of a letter, with its answer, concerning a contest at Worcester* [n.p., 1656], STC c6167, sigs. Ar–Av.

[105] Skipp, *The worlds wonder*, sig. Ar; cf. Matt. 24.24.

[106] Joseph Kellet *et al.*, *A faithful discovery*, sigs. A2r–A2v.

[107] *Ibid.*, p. 50. Cf. Hos. 4.1, whose prophecy of God's sentence against Israel (or England) was used by preachers earlier in the seventeenth century. Patrick Collinson, *The birthpangs of Protestant England: religious and cultural change in the sixteenth and seventeenth centuries* (London, 1988), p. 20.

[108] Prynne, *The Quakers unmasked, and clearly detected* (London, 1655), pp. 2–7.

inhabitants of Bristol and London. 'I am afraid that the Lord hath a controversie with the Church of England', he continued, for God suffered the Quakers to seduce people not only in their 'private meetings, and conventicles', but also 'in the Presse by scandalous and lying pamphlets, which is the way to make our Magistrates and Ministers to be in contempt of the people'.[109] The Quakers threatened to undermine the newfound liberties of the Republic. 'O that my counsell might be acceptable unto you!' he wrote to the 'Sons of the Church of England': 'have not itching eares, forsake not your old teachers to follow new lights: for the good way is an old way'.[110]

Another disputant claimed that he was forced to write because the quality of attacks on the Quakers was so poor. 'Thou may think it high presumption for so weak and unable a person, to ingage against such a Sect, when so many able and learned men, the sons of the Churches, have come off with loss', confessed Thomas Winterton to his reader, but continued: 'the grounds on which these Rabbies opposed them on were as unsound as the Quakers were; so as they but clash their errors together'. This, moreover, was the reason for the Quakers' success: 'a new Opinion that doth but equally defend it self always gets ground; and upon this score, I am confident, that they have gained a multitude'.[111] Thomas Winterton argued that the Quakers were not being adequately countered; and assumed that his own contribution to the fight against Quakers would stop their rapid spread.

Thus published attacks on the Quakers were presented in the name of the national church; or in criticism of a national puritan ministry, incapable of countering the Quaker threat. The attacks on Quakers were part of a wider political debate, and authors directly confronted national government and the issue of religious legislation. Some made a direct connection between the rise of the Quakers, and the dangers of legislation for religious liberty. Writing in the late spring of 1653, the former New England minister of Kirkby Stephen in Westmorland, Francis Higginson, directly addressed the government in his tract, informing its members that his account of the Quakers was intended to demonstrate to them 'what ill use these men make of that Libertie, permitted to dissenters in Religion'. Religious liberty, Higginson maintained, was:

pleaded only for, and I believe intended to be conceded only to tender Consciences: and that is not Liberty, but Libertinisme, that some men seek after: viz. That they may be as wicked as they will without controul.[112]

---

[109] George Willington, *The gadding tribe reproved* (London, 1655), *STC* w2802, pp. 13, 18–19.
[110] *Ibid.*, p. 20.
[111] Thomas Winterton, *The quaking prophets two wayes proved false prophets* (London, 1655), sig. A2r.
[112] Francis Higginson, *A brief relation of the irreligion of the northern Quakers* (London, 1653), *STC* H1593, sig. A2r.

Higginson then warned the Government that 'uncurb'd Licentiousness' and 'blasphemous heretical seducers through the Nation' would dismay supporters of the Commonwealth:

many honest Christians now look upon the present times as ill boding times, who a few years ago were raised in their expectation, to see better dayes then any age ever produced.[113]

The rise of the Quakers was thus identified, in Higginson's eyes, with the fundamental problem of religious legislation. Higginson implored the Government, 'that by their Authoritie they would cause the truth to be brought to Light'. 'The God of Heaven', he implored, 'make us all willing and able to move in our proper Orbes for the interest of his Sonne Jesus Christ, and his glorious Gospel': the proper 'Orbe' of the Council of State, was unambiguously to curb the proliferation of the Quakers.[114]

Turning to the press politicised the nature of the criticisms levied against the Quakers. Some tracts against Quakers had an explicitly political agenda, like Francis Higginson's. Others carried political dedications: Ralph Farmer dedicated his tract to the secretary of state John Thurloe.[115] As will be seen, many anti-Quaker tracts originated as petitions against Quakers or in favour of tighter religious controls: there was a fine line between theological debate and political petitioning.

In order for the Quakers to be used as a political tool by the new puritan orthodoxy, they had to be presented as a national, homogeneous threat to religious liberty and to the success of the reformation. In print, puritan ministers necessarily generalised their experience of the Quakers. Many stated clearly that they were not primarily interested in debating with the Quakers, who were universally condemned as antichristian, but were more concerned to publicise the dangers represented to the rest of society by the Quakers. Although they might, in their printed attacks on Quakers, choose to reply to manuscript queries, to Quaker literature, or to publish an account of their own confrontations with Quakers, their major aim was to caricature the Quakers for their own polemical purposes.

This factor is very important in giving shape to the printed works which appeared against the Quakers. In referring the 'seduced followers' of Nayler and Fox to the 'Errors of your Sect', Francis Higginson explained:

it is not my intent in this discourse to debate them with you, or to undertake a confutation of them. To those that are not Children in knowledge, the very nomination of them is a sufficient confutation: such cleer opposition is there between them and the

---

[113] *Ibid.*, sig. A2v.   [114] *Ibid.*, sig. A2v.
[115] Farmer, *The great mysteries of godlinesse*. Samuel Eaton's answer to some queries from the Quakers included a 4-page address to Barebones Parliament, 'the supream Authority of the Nation'. Eaton, *The Quakers confuted*, sigs. A2r–A4r.

word of Truth. And for your selves, I suppose private and moderate reasonings (if you would admit of them) would be more praevalent to reclaim you, then Writings.[116]

Higginson's desire to restrict himself to 'the very nomination' of Quaker ideas is the key point. Contemporaries who were worried by the Quakers believed that the way to stem their rise was primarily by cataloguing and publicising their heretical beliefs. In the genre of later heresiographies of the Quakers, Francis Higginson, whose work was probably the first to be published against the Quakers, suggested to his readers that his account would reveal that the origins of the Quakers lay in the excesses of the Münster anabaptists:

> When you have read it, you will be ready to dream (if you be acquainted with the History of the last Century) that you behold the turbulent Exorcists of Germany, redivive in England, and acting their old Tragick parts over again.[117]

In order to prove this, Higginson promised in his tract a discovery of their 'horrid principles and Practises, Doctrines and Manners'.[118] These covered their 'Blasphemies', 'damnable Heresies', and 'lying Doctrines', as well as their 'Diabolicall Trances and Raptures', 'railing Language' and 'great swelling words of vanity', 'their boasting of Perfection, and Voices, and Revelations, and immediate Inspirations from the Spirit'; and finally 'their unchristian, immodest, unhumane Incivilities, and Impudencies'.[119] The political purpose behind Higginson's writing explains much about his content. Higginson wanted state action to tighten up on religious liberty: he therefore had to prove their outrageous behaviour.

Caricatures of the Quakers, if they were to be politically meaningful, had to prove that Quakers were beyond the bounds of toleration. In this context, the Blasphemy Act of 1650 was important in shaping some of the earliest and most influential criticisms levelled against the Quakers. The Blasphemy Act of 1650 prescribed imprisonment for those claiming equality with God, denying the existence of heaven or hell, or maintaining the propriety of swearing, drunkenness, adultery, incest or murder.[120] It is contentious among historians for its role in the repression or otherwise of the Ranters: Colin Davis argued that it was directed primarily against atheists and anti-formalists; Frank McGregor, on the contrary, that it was formulated with Ranters specifically in mind. Both argued implicitly that the terms of the legislation represented to some degree the actualities of religious radicalism in August 1650.[121] By 1652, however, the terminology of the Blasphemy Act

---

[116] Higginson, *A brief relation*, sig. A2r. [117] *Ibid.*, sig. A2r.
[118] *Ibid.*, sig. Ar. [119] *Ibid.*, sig. A2v.
[120] C. H. Firth and R. S. Rait (eds.), *Acts and Ordinances of the Interregnum* (3 vols., London, 1911), vol. II, pp. 409–10.
[121] J. C. Davis, *Fear, myth and history: the Ranters and the historians* (Cambridge, 1986), pp. 114–20. Gerald Aylmer was especially critical of this view, arguing that denunciations

was itself used to formulate descriptions of the Quakers. Before its repeal under the terms of the Instrument of Government of December 1653, the Blasphemy Act was an important means of prosecuting Quakers, and was fundamental in James Nayler's appearance before Parliament in 1656.[122] Contemporaries were aware of its significance. In a set of petitions drawn up by ministers in Westmorland against the Quakers in January 1653, the petitioners thanked Members of Parliament for:

what has been done by them in the cause of God, as their Acts against Adulteries, Fornication, Swearing, Drunkenness, Sabboth-breaking, Ordinances against Promoters of Heretical Doctrines, Acts against Ranters or Blasphemers.[123]

The Blasphemy Act was formative in shaping a number of early publications against the Quakers. This is made very clear from a study the genesis of the first anti-Quaker tracts, produced by ministers from Lancashire, Westmorland and eventually Newcastle. Francis Higginson's *Brief relation of the irreligion of the northern Quakers*, and his *Brief reply to . . . Saul's errand to Damascus*, and the Newcastle ministers' *Perfect pharisee under Monkish holinesse* were all extremely influential publications against the Quakers, read and used by puritan ministers in Bristol, London and Edinburgh.[124] All stemmed from attempts to prove the Quakers were legally guilty of blasphemy. The ways in which they were published reveal much about the nature of religious debate in the 1650s, and highlight the different approaches towards religious participation in Quaker and anti-Quaker publications.

In October 1652, after he had been preaching in the area for about six months, George Fox was accused of blasphemy by two Lancashire magistrates, John Sawry and Mr Toluson, for having claimed that he was equal with God. The original deposition accused Fox rather obliquely of having 'uttered severall blasphemies which are unfitting to bee mentioned' and suggested that the justices of the hundred of Lonsdale should 'heare' the

---

of atheists were esoteric, and not comparable to the broader, popular fear of Jesuits or Anabaptists. G. E. Aylmer, 'Did the Ranters exist?', *Past and Present* 117 (1987), 208–19, esp. 213–14; J. F. McGregor, 'Seekers and Ranters', in J. F. McGregor and B. Reay (eds.), *Radical religion in the English revolution* (Oxford, 1986), pp. 132–33.

[122] The various ways in which Quakers were prosecuted are discussed in Chapter 7 below; the James Nayler affair is discussed in Chapter 8.

[123] James Nayler *et al.*, *Several petitions answered, that were put up by the priests of Westmorland* (London, 1653), *STC* N316A, p. 23. J. C. Davis maintained that the so-called Blasphemy Act did not pertain to the Ranters specifically: J. F. McGregor clearly refutes this. 'Debate: Fear, myth and furore: reappraising the Ranters. Comment 1', *Past and Present* 140 (August 1993), 156–57.

[124] The works were cited by Bristol presbyterian, Ralph Farmer, *The great mysteries of godlinesse and ungodlinesse* (London, 1655), *STC* F441; and Essex minister John Stalham, *Contradictions of the Quakers (so called)* (Edinburgh, 1655), *STC* S5184.

attestations of several witnesses, 'and so proceede with this offender as the Law in such cases hath provided'.[125] A second note against Fox, however, 'thought good' to provide 'a narrative of such things as will bee made out against him'. These included, on the attestations of schoolmaster Michael Altham, that 'He did affirme that he had the divinitie essentially in him'; that 'both Baptisme and the lords supper were unlawfull'; and finally that he 'did disswade men from reading the Scripture tellinge them that it was carnall'. William Smyth and Nathaniel Atkinson added that Fox had claimed 'he was equall with god'; that 'god taught deceit'; that 'Scriptures was Antichrist'; that 'he was the Judge of the world'; and 'that he was as upright as Christ'.[126]

Fox, perhaps on the intervention of Judge Thomas Fell, never appeared at the Quarter Sessions held in Lancaster on 18 October 1652; instead, a private meeting was arranged between Fox and the Lancashire magistrates, at which several ministers were also present. After this meeting, it was alleged that Fox reaffirmed his equality with God; following this, the ministers, justices and gentlemen of Lancashire drew up a petition addressed to the Council of State which denounced Fox and James Nayler, as well as three others, Richard Hubberthorne, James Milner and Leonard Fell. The petition stated that the Blasphemy Act, with Fox and his followers in mind, had been confirmed at the sessions, and implored the Council of State, in the interests of the Commonwealth, to act against the men.

According to the account in Fox's *Journal*, the subscribers of the Lancashire petition ran out of money and were not able to publish, or present their petition to the members of the Council of State. The nascent Quaker movement, however, mobilised itself, publishing both a transcript of the hostile petition in their first major pamphlet, *Saul's errand to Damascus*, and an account of the private meeting between Fox and the Lancashire ministers, published as a letter from Nayler in one of the publications by the York prisoners.[127]

Before the publication of *Saul's errand* in March 1653, James Nayler and Francis Howgill were arrested in November 1652, in the market town of Kirkby Stephen, Westmorland, and were in turn tried for Blasphemy at the Appleby sessions in January 1653. The attempt to try the Quakers for Blasphemy failed here as it had at Lancaster, for lack of solid proof.

[125] Lancashire Record Office, Quarter Sessions Recognizances, 1652, QSB1.

[126] *Ibid.* William Smith of Over Kellet was a minister who signed the *Harmonious Consent* of Lancashire ministers in 1648. Michael Altham was the minister of Over Kellet in 1655 and 1659, 'Plundered Ministers Accounts', ed. W. Shaw, *Lancashire and Cheshire Record Society*, 34 (1896), pp. 142, 143, 189; A.G. Matthews (ed.), *Calamy revised* (Oxford, 1934; repr. 1988).

[127] George Fox *et al.*, *Saul's errand to Damascus* (London, 1653), STC F1894. Fox's meeting with the Lancaster justices and priests was recorded in a letter, dated 27 October, which was published as part of Thomas Aldam's *A brief discovery of a threefold estate of Antichrist*.

Howgill reported in a letter to Margaret Fell from Appleby gaol that, 'as for my Brother James, their is no question but he will be Cleared for theire weare many freinds that heard all the Discourse'.[128] A letter by Gervase Benson published subsequently stated that the magistrates had been unwilling to try Nayler for Blasphemy.[129] At the sessions, a petition addressed to the justices of the county was drawn up by the ministers and inhabitants of Westmorland against the 'Horrid Blasphemies', 'damnable Heresies' and 'dangerous Errors' of George Fox and James Nayler; requesting that they be expelled from the county, and that Howgill and other local Quakers be prevented from travelling 'except as private men about their own occasions'.[130] As with the Lancashire petition against Fox, the Quakers obtained a copy, and published a transcript of it, along with their own detailed exegesis, in *Several petitions answered*.[131] The victorious account of Nayler's Appleby trial, at which local justices Gervase Benson and Anthony Pearson were convinced of the truth, were published in *Saul's errand to Damascus*.[132]

According to the Quakers' own published accounts, their opponents had little success in prosecuting them under the Blasphemy Act. Nevertheless, the Blasphemy Act had been important in enabling the ministers from Lancashire and Westmorland to present a case against the Quakers, to urge their prosecution and to compile evidence against them. The minister of Kirkby Stephen, Francis Higginson, who had played an important role in the arrest of Howgill and Nayler and in their subsequent trial, was of primary importance in mobilising action against the Quakers. A few days before the beginning of the Quarter Sessions on 8 January, Francis Howgill wrote from Appleby gaol to Margaret Fell. The spectacle of the Quakers' detention, and their success in continued preaching, had attracted much attention. 'Many weake ones are much strenthened by our bouldness,' Howgill wrote, 'and all the prests heare abouts are . . . sending all the Cuntrey abrod for witnesses agaynst us'. Howgill and Nayler were fuelling the ministers' anxieties by maintaining a steady flow of writings from prison, 'which vexes them horably'. The response of the local ministers was to 'seke by all meanes to prove any thing agaynst us': and the ministers' final coup was to send 'to NewCastell to have us any way disposed of'.[133] The alarm of Francis Higginson had thus caused him to contact his colleagues in Newcastle, Thomas Welde, and more importantly William Cole. William Cole had been vicar of Kirkby Lonsdale in Westmorland, twenty-five miles south of Francis Higginson's parish in Kirkby Stephen before taking up a position as curate at St John's

---

[128] Francis Howgill to Margaret Fell, 5 January 1653, A. R. Barclay Mss 1: 74, fol. 218.
[129] James Nayler, Richard Farnworth, *et al.*, *Several petitions answered, that were put up by the priests of Westmorland* (London, 1653), STC N316A, pp. 51–52.
[130] *Ibid.*, p. 2.   [131] *Ibid.*   [132] Fox *et al.*, *Saul's errand to Damascus*, p. 26.
[133] Howgill to Fell, 5 January 1653, A. R. Barclay Mss 1: 74, fol. 217.

in Newcastle. He was also present at the trial of James Nayler and Francis Howgill in January 1653.[134] Between them, Higginson and Cole, with his Newcastle colleagues, converted their attempts to try the Quakers by law into a series of published tracts which attacked their religious and moral principles.

The political and religious activity involved in prosecuting Nayler, Howgill and Fox for Blasphemy was what lay behind the subsequent pamphlet denunciations of the Quakers. In the late spring of 1653 Francis Higginson published *A brief relation of the irreligion of the Northern Quakers* and *A brief reply to some part of a very scurrilous and lying pamphlet called Saul's errand to Damascus*.[135] A phrase in the preface suggests he was writing after the final expulsion of the Rump Parliament on 20 April, and before the calling of the Nominated Parliament on 4 July 1653: Higginson, requesting government intervention against the Quakers, addressed first 'those honourable Gentlemen that are in Authoritie', and then, as a pragmatic alternative, 'or any that it shall please the Lord in his Providence to call the Government of this Nation'.[136] At the time of writing, Francis Higginson had already encountered the Quakers' tracts *Saul's errand* and *A brief discovery of a threefold estate of Antichrist*, as well as another work by Aldam and the York prisoners, *False prophets and false teachers described*, and Richard Farnworth's *A call out of false worships*.[137]

---

[134] Matthews, *Calamy revised*; 'Minutes of the Committee of Plundered Ministers', ed. W. Shaw, Part, 2, pp. 216, 222, 270. William Durant was appointed lecturer at a number of Newcastle churches in the 1640s and was later a co-pastor of a congregational church there. Samuel Hammond was a lecturer at St Nicholas, Newcastle, in 1652. Richard Prideaux was a lecturer at All Saints, Newcastle, and is described by Calamy as 'of the congregational judgment'. He was also made an assistant to the Commission for the four northern counties in 1654.

[135] Francis Higginson, *A brief relation of the irreligion of the Northern Quakers* (London, 1653), STC H1593; Higginson, *A brief reply to some part of a very scurrilous and lying pamphlet called Saul's errand to Damascus* (London, 1653), STC H1954. In the copy held at Friends' House Library, London, the signation for the two books is continuous: *A brief relation* runs to 36 pages, sigs. A–F4v; *A brief reply* starts at sig. G1. Furthermore, *A brief reply* has a manuscript note 'A continuation of the last' on its title page. FHL Adv. Box H2, vol. 32: 12.

[136] Internal evidence in Higginson's tract also suggests that it was written in the early part of 1653. He recounts events which occurred in late 1652; and refers to the arrival of the Quakers in Westmorland 'the last summer' – i.e. 1652. Higginson, *A brief relation*, sig. A2r; p. 1. The book was not recorded by its publisher in the Stationers' Company registers.

[137] Higginson, *A brief relation*, sigs. av–a2r. Thomas Aldam *et al.*, *False prophets and false teachers described*. This tract is attributed the date 1652 by Wing's STC and evidence from the correspondence suggests that it was in circulation around Kendal and Westmorland by early January 1653, Richard Farnworth to Margaret Fell, 7 January 1653, Sw Mss 4: 83. It could have been in circulation as early as 2 December 1652; see Richard Farnworth to Margaret Fell, Sw Mss 3: 45. Richard Farnworth, *A call out of false worships* [1653], STC F474A, is not possible to date precisely. The fact that it was one of Farnworth's octavo pamphlets, which were rather crudely printed, and the fact that it cited no place

In his tracts, Francis Higginson reiterated verbatim the 'Blasphemies' of George Fox compiled by the Lancashire magistrates, referring to the account in *Saul's errand* in which Fox was accused of claiming equality with God, and referring also to more witnesses of Fox and Nayler's blasphemies: George Bickett, Adam Sands and Nathaniel Atkinson, who alleged that Fox professed himself to be the light of the world; and two witnesses from Kendal who affirmed that Nayler said 'he was as holy, just, and good, as God himself'.[138] He was also concerned to counter Nayler's 'misrepresentation' of his arrest and trial in *Sauls errand*, which he was able to do from his own knowledge of events.[139]

Francis Higginson's tract demonstrates the close links between political and religious activity. He wrote against the Quakers because of his own confrontations with them in his parish of Kirkby Stephen; because of the failed attempt to try Quakers for Blasphemy in Appleby; and because he perceived the need for tighter curbs on religious liberty. He collated evidence from his colleagues in the ministry, from the Quakers' own tracts, and from his own experiences. He presented the first hostile account of Quaker doctrines and practices to the outside world, and at the same time was involved in attempts to prosecute them under civil law.

The perfect pharisee under Monkish holinesse, written by the five Newcastle ministers, Thomas Weld, Richard Prideaux, Samuel Hammond, William Cole and William Durrant, made no explicit reference to its political roots.[140] It presented itself as a serious work which attempted to make manifest the 'folly' of the Quakers, 'so it may proceed no further'; and even presented the reader with a scholarly methodology: first to 'lay down their Doctrines'; secondly to 'prove them to be theirs from their own words and writings'; and finally, to 'confute them from the Scriptures'.[141] This work concentrated on seventeen 'Positions' of the Quakers, all carefully backed up with evidence from Quaker publications, or from attested evidence of personal confrontations with the Quakers.[142]

The collaboration with Higginson and his colleagues is very clear. The first Quaker 'doctrine' described by the Newcastle ministers was 'Equality with God'; the proof provided came from accounts of George Fox's meeting with magistrates and ministers at Lancaster, cited from the account in *Saul's errand* and from their own witnesses. They made full but unacknowledged

---

of publication, nor appeared in Thomason's collection, may suggest that it was an early publication, possibly printed in the north of England. It may well have been one of the books by Farnworth referred to by Aldam in a letter dated '1652'.

[138] Higginson, *A brief relation*, p. 3.   [139] Higginson, *A brief reply*, pp. 57–80.

[140] Thomas Welde and William Cole *et al.*, *The perfect pharisee under Monkish holinesse* (Gateshead, 1653), *STC* c5045. The later edition, *The perfect pharise under monkish holines* was published in London in 1654 (*STC* c5045A), and dated by Thomason on 14 January 1654 (see n. 1 above).

[141] Welde and Cole *et al.*, *The perfect pharise*, sig. Av.   [142] *Ibid.*, pp. 3–30.

use of Higginson's information, citing the evidence of 'Mr. George Berket', 'that George Fox did affirm himself to be the Judge of the World'; they also cited freely from discussions had between William Cole and Quakers.[143]

The perfect pharisee then listed rather more nebulous 'principles' and 'practices': the refusal to wear hats, honour men, or the tendency to quaking and 'rayling', for which the authors felt no need 'to produce any evidence' as they were 'so well known to all that know this sort of men'.[144] By the end of the tract, the authors included allusions to Christopher Atkinson's 'very immodest familiarity (to say no more) with a woman of his way', and a story of the wife of Edmond Adlington, who went naked through the streets of Kendal.[145] Such incidents, 'the very badge of their profession', were presented by the authors with a degree of stylistic distaste; and took up considerably less space than the more intricate doctrinal remonstrances. But nevertheless they appeared; and nevertheless they, too, were substantiated by attestations from witnesses. Furthermore, a follow-up publication by the same authors, written in response to James Nayler's reply to the tract, made great play of the fact 'that Nayler denyes not what we wrote about their going naked' and resolved to 'adde more, because some that have lesse aquaintance with these people, may seem to make question of it'.[146] After due elaboration on the theme, the authors also suggested that 'were it need-full to prove it', they could provide even more evidence 'by sending into places where these converse'. The nakedness of the Quakers was a significant factor in their denunciation by a collection of educated, professional puritan ministers.

The Newcastle dispute was formative. It gave rise to the first, cohesive and informed published exchange on a set of ideas which it identified as 'Quaker doctrines'. Although these stemmed in large part from abortive attempts to prosecute Quakers for blasphemy, the Newcastle ministers went on to identify perfectionism, the 'light within', and the spiritual basis of the scriptures; all crucial tenets of the Quakers' beliefs.[147] *A perfect pharisee* cited evidence from a wide range of sources, referring to Higginson's book as well as to an impressive number of the Quakers' own publications.[148]

---

[143] *Ibid.*, p. 4.
[144] *Ibid.*, p. 31. The practices listed were in fact arguably more concrete and to be more enduring than Quaker doctrines.
[145] *Ibid.*, sig. F4v.
[146] Thomas Welde and William Cole *et al.*, *A further discovery of that generation of men called Quakers* (Gateshead, 1654), STC w1268, pp. 83–84; see 83–88.
[147] *The perfect pharise*, pp. 3–31.
[148] The books they cited included *Saul's errand*, F1894, James Nayler, *The Power and the Glory* (STC n302); Nayler, *Several Papers set forth* (STC f1903), Farnworth, *A message from the Lord*; Nayler, *The generall good to all people*; Farnworth, *Gods covenanting with his people*, Farnworth, *A discovery of faith*; George Bateman, *An answer to vindicate the cause of the nick–named Quakers* (1653), b1094; *The Querers and the Quakers cause* (London, 1653), STC q163.

They also dipped freely into John Gilpin's lurid account of his 'false' Quaker conversion, *The Quakers shaken*, from which they drew accounts of ecstatic trances, foaming at the mouth and 'grovelling upon the ground'.[149]

More significant still was the response evoked in the Quakers. James Nayler responded with his own published reply, steadfastly denying that he was contending with 'what they call their confutation', but declaring instead: 'what is truth is owned, what is false is denyed'.[150] In effect, Nayler considered the 'Doctrines' put forward by the Newcastle ministers at great length, refuting some of their evidence and restating some of their positions in his own words and with justifications from the Bible. The Newcastle ministers responded rapidly with a 96-page rebuttle; within the month, Nayler published a further 50-page reply.[151] The effect was the publication of a thorough discussion of ideas posited by the Quaker authors.[152] These kinds of exchange, the majority conducted by Nayler himself, became a major form of publication.

The published exchanges between the Newcastle ministers and James Nayler also epitomise the different approaches to pamphleteering and the nature of religious participation. It has been shown that Quakers sought to undermine the authority of puritan ministers by attacking their chosen forms of debate as well as by attacking their actual status and authority. Nayler went out of his way to undermine the credibility of the Newcastle ministers, who based their accounts of the Quakers on indirect literary sources – including the Quakers' own books – rather than writing from their own immediate experience. The authors, he wrote: 'are all strangers to that sort of people called Quakers, except one, so thou may the rather perceive, what they have Written, is gathered by reports'.[153] Specific reports in *The perfect*

---

[149] Welde and Cole *et al.*, *The perfect pharise*, p. 164; John Gilpin, *The Quakers shaken: or, a fire-brand snach'd out of the fire* (London, 1653), STC G770. Gilpin's tract was highly influential in anti-Quaker propaganda, and appeared in Samuel Clark, *A mirrour or looking-glass both for saints and sinners* (London, 1671). Gilpin's work was also used as evidence against the Quakers in Bristol by Ralph Farmer, *The great mysteries*, sigs. M4r-Mv; and in Cambridgeshire by Thomas Drayton, *An answer according to truth*, p. 40. For the importance of Gilpin in forming a number of images associated with Quakers, see Chapter 4 above.

[150] James Nayler, *An answer to the book called The Perfect Pharisee* [n.p., 1654], STC N261, sig. AV. George Thomason dated a copy of this work on 9 May 1654.

[151] Welde and Cole *et al.*, *A further discovery of that generation of men called Quakers* (Gateshead, 1654), STC W1268; James Nayler, *A discovery of the man of sin*. George Thomason dated his copy of this last on 3 June 1654.

[152] Although Nayler was the main author, the Newcastle ministers drew on published works by Farnworth, Fox and their apologist George Bateman; John Audland and 'A. P.' co-authored Nayler's *Answer to the book*. Although Joseph Smith identified A. P. as Alexander Parker, it is more likely to be Anthony Pearson, who had his own connections with Newcastle.

[153] A. P., preface, in James Nayler, *An answer to the booke called The Perfect Pharisee* [London, 1654], STC N261 sig. AV.

pharisee were also disclaimed by the Quakers. William Cole's allegation, that one William Baldwinson of Underbarrow had heard Nayler confess he was 'as holy, just, and good, as God himself', was roundly denied by Nayler:

> As for William Baldwinson, whom you father this untruth on, I never had any private discourse with him, nor ever was I in company where he was, but once in Underbarrow, where was the house full of people that I have never seen before; and if he should affirme any such thing, they of his owne Towne shall all witnesse against him.[154]

In an article which examined a public disputation between James Nayler and Immanuel Bourne, parish minister of Chesterfield, Derbyshire, Rosemary O'Day observed that 'Nayler obviously felt himself to be cornered by the verbal quibbling in which Bourne and the rest engaged' and summarised his participation as 'emotional outburst'. Yet Nayler was not so out of his depth as O'Day supposed when she stressed his status as 'an uneducated and simple wandering preacher'.[155] Nayler's purpose was avowedly not to condone disputation; in his published works he repeatedly emphasised his dislike of 'striving for Master-hood in words or writing' and instead saw his writing as a means of awakening readers to their own inner light.[156] In the same vein, Richard Hubberthorne's boast that 'our speech is with Grace, seasoned with salt, and we know how to answer every man' was an attack on 'Ministers of Questions' whose disputations were a form of intellectual snobbery, 'having mens persons in admiracion, because of advantage'.[157] Nayler expressed the hope that his final publication against the Newcastle ministers would let the reader (emphatically not the authors) see: 'how unprofitably thou hast spent thy time in running from one man to another, (which call themselves Ministers),' and urged them, 'go not to any man ... but wait in the light which is in thy conscience'.[158]

Thus pamphlet disputes between Quakers and their critics were not a straightforward exchange of differing religious views. Although puritan and Quaker ministers did argue and debate with each other, the role of print in this process was not simply to publicise further the debate. The Quakers

---

[154] James Nayler, *An answer to the booke called The Perfect Pharisee* [London, 1654], STC N261, p. 5. Compare with *The perfect pharise*, p. 3; and also, for the same story, without William Baldwinson's name, Higginson, *A brief relation*, p. 3. In Higginson's account, the witness claimed that many others heard Nayler utter this particular Blasphemy, but 'being all followers of the *Nailer* and *Fox*, they will be unwilling to testifie it'.

[155] Rosemary O'Day, 'Immanuel Bourne: a defence of the ministerial order', *Journal of Ecclesiastical History* 27: 2 (April 1976), 113. In fact Nayler had probably received a grammar-school education, was an experienced preacher from the time of his service in the New Model Army and, according to his recent biographer, probably farmed a substantial amount of land: William G. Bittle, *James Nayler 1618–1660. The Quaker indicted by Parliament* (York, 1986), pp. 2–4.

[156] Nayler, *A few words occasioned*, p. 3.   [157] Fox, *Truths defence*, p. 107.

[158] Nayler, *A discovery of the man of sin*, sig. A2r.

produced tracts to encourage wider public engagement over the issues of the puritan ministry, which the Quakers perceived as privileged and elitist, and in need of reform. The form of the tracts mirrored this attack nicely as Quaker authors urged their audiences to question, and judge, their ministers for themselves. Published debates, seen in the context of other Quaker publications, appear as part of a spectrum of Quaker tracts which attacked the national church. The emphasis was placed on the participation of the audiences and congregations who would read the tracts and watch the disputes. In contrast, the new orthodox puritan ministry published tracts which emphasised their authority as religious leaders; and to exercise what influence they could over national religious reform.

The resort to print has important implications for our understanding of religious participation in the 1650s. The Quakers' anticlericalism touched on the future of the national preaching ministry of England, an area of enormous political concern to the Commonwealth and Protectorate governments, as well as the ministers themselves. The Quaker tracts aimed to involve as many people as possible in this debate, on a very local basis. The very appearance of these arguments in print homogenised the questions posed and the nature of the debate: as hostile observers pointed out, the same questions could be posed by well-primed audiences across the country. Print also led to the compilation of generalised, abstract definitions of the 'Quakers' which allowed them to be presented as a political problem by puritan ministers to the government. Locally experienced debate, once printed, entered the domain of national politics; pamphleteering was a political activity which was expected to achieve change. The following chapter examines the political dimensions to the Quakers' campaigning.

7

Print and political participation

Just as the Quakers used printed tracts to enable full participation in religious debate, so they also used print to encourage audiences to partake in the activities and debates surrounding the political achievement of religious settlement and godly reformation. It is often argued that the Quakers were a radical force without having a political agenda or offering any political solutions to the 1650s. Alan Cole, for example, suggested that the emphasis on the spiritual in Quaker belief prevented any real scope for political participation or for the kinds of compromise required of the Interregnum governments. More practically, John Morrill has pointed out that they offered nothing constructive towards constitutional reform.[1] Barry Reay went some way to showing the radical political origins of the Quakers, although like Alan Cole and Christopher Hill, Reay located the Quakers in the context of the failed revolution of 1647–49: as Hill commented, the rise of the Quakers: 'witnessed *both* to the defeat of the political Levellers *and* to the continued existence of radical ideas'.[2] Although large elements of Quaker belief were undoubtedly radical, such as their opposition to tithes and their championing of the poor, many scholars have argued that these stemmed from the Quakers' religious ideas and did not have a sound socio-economic or political basis; Barry Reay's assessment of the Quakers ultimately described them as troublemakers, significant more for the popular and political hostility they evoked than for their own ideas. Arguments which emphasise the alienation of Quakers from the worldly politics of the 1650s are thus based on an assumption that political participation involved the promotion of a coherent programme for comprehensive political and consitutional reform. Certainly it is true that in their pamphleteering the Quakers produced nothing like

---

[1] Alan Cole, 'The Quakers and politics, 1652–1660', unpublished Ph.D thesis, University of Cambridge, 1955, pp. 23–36; John Morrill, *The nature of the English revolution* (London, 1993), pp. 26–27.

[2] Christopher Hill, *The world turned upside down: radical ideas during the English revolution* (Harmondsworth, 1975, repr. 1982), p. 240. Cf. Hill, *The experience of defeat* (Harmondsworth, 1985).

the Levellers' *Agreements of the people*, nor any extended critique of the Interregnum governments. Furthermore, Reay and Cole both based their arguments largely on the printed tracts produced by Quakers during 1659, the year when the Quaker movement was arguably at its most politically influential, as leaders lobbied for the 'Good Old Cause' and the return of the Rump Parliament, and signalled their willingness to participate in a new regime through petitions and other political writing, as well as by submitting lists of Quakers who would serve the new regime as magistrates.[3] Both Reay and Cole, therefore, measured the Quakers' political activity largely in terms of their brief support for a thoroughly doomed government, against very traditional criteria of what constitutes political participation.

Much recent work on the culture of print in the English revolution, however, has suggested that the availability and use of print changed the nature of political participation, involving ever wider audiences in debate or political protest, and even ushering in notions of public opinion and political consent.[4] The pamphleteering activities of the Quakers are an excellent example of how men and women in the 1650s used print to encourage and sustain widespread political debate and engagement with issues of immediate relevance: religious toleration and the successful implementation of godly rule. This chapter will argue that, if we turn away from the content of the tracts alone, and focus on the contexts and processes involved in Quaker pamphleteering, it becomes apparent that the Quakers engaged in a very systematic way with issues which affected them and their rights to participate in the political nation from the outset of the movement in 1652–53. While their tracts may not have offered any single constitutional blueprint, their pamphleteering demanded and fostered a widespread, and deeply practical, understanding of the legal and constitutional issues underpinning the achievement of religious toleration and a godly commonwealth, which reveals much about the nature of political participation in the 1650s.

This chapter discusses, first, how Quakers used a combination of print, manuscript papers, preaching and public events such as Quarter Sessions trials to publicise the inadequacies of the English republic's religious settlement. This occurred at a very local level, but increasingly from 1654, was tightly co-ordinated as a nationwide and coherent campaign. Secondly, the chapter will show how print served to transform accounts of local prosecution into an explicitly political context, in the form of addresses to the government

---

[3] Cole, 'The Quakers and politics', esp. chs. 3 and 4; Barry Reay, 'The Quakers, 1659, and the restoration of the monarchy', *History* 63 (1978), 193–213.

[4] See the stimulating introduction in David Norbrook, *Writing the English Republic: poetry, rhetoric and politics, 1627–1660* (Cambridge, 1999), esp. pp. 8–14; David Zaret, 'Petitions and the "invention" of public opinion in the English Revolution', *American Journal of Sociology* 101: 6 (May 1996), 1497–1555; Dagmar Freist, *Governed by opinion: politics, religion and the dynamics of communication in Stuart London, 1637–1645* (London, 1997).

and calls for legislative reform. Here too, print was one facet of a complex campaign which involved personal, and occasionally secret, communication with politicians, the army and radical sectarian leaders. Ultimately, it was the use of print which signalled and facilitated widespread participation in the struggle for religious toleration.

LOCAL PROSECUTION OF QUAKERS

As has been seen, the Quakers' campaign of itinerant preaching exposed the flaws in the religious policies of Interregnum governments. Although many historians would now argue that religious apathy was a major factor in the failure of the puritan revolution, it is also undeniably the case that the framing of a religious settlement was a monumental task. Blair Worden and others have shown how the religious legislation of the Commonwealth and Protectorate foundered on identifying a workable distinction between religious error, considered an acceptable step in the process of salvation, and heresy, which was deemed to be no less than Satanic intervention.[5] The Quakers' views enraged their contemporaries on precisely this issue: the tortuous parliamentary debates on whether to accuse and convict James Nayler of blasphemy in December 1656, described by MP Thomas Burton in his *Diary*, illustrate the severity of the dilemma. While many MPs were eager to convict Nayler, more moderate MPs like Colonel Sydenham warned of 'the nearness of this [the Quakers'] opinion to the glorious truth, that the spirit is personally in us', and others baulked at the fitness of Parliament to define blasphemy in the first place.[6] Yet the appearance of James Nayler before Parliament was an extraordinary and unique event, which, as will be discussed in Chapter 8, had serious consequences both for the Protectorate and the Quaker movement. Behind Nayler's case, and the rather exalted problem of framing the legislation to enable religious settlement, lay the day-to-day difficulty of implementing the religious policies of interregnum governments, as magistrates up and down the country had to interpret for themselves loosely worded or ineffectual legislation. Well before James Nayler found himself

---

[5] Blair Worden, 'Toleration and the Cromwellian Protectorate', *Studies in Church History* 21 (1984), esp. 209–16. For views on the general apathy with which puritan reforms were greeted, see John Morrill, 'The church in England, 1642–1649', in Morrill (ed.), *Reactions to the English Civil War, 1642–1649* (London, 1982); Derek Hirst, 'The failure of godly rule in the English republic', *Past and Present* 132 (August 1991), 33–66; Christopher Durston, 'The failure of cultural revolution, 1645–1660' in Durston and Jacqueline Eales (eds.), *The culture of English puritanism, 1560–1700* (London, 1996), pp. 210–33; Anthony Fletcher, 'The godly divided: the end of religious unity in protestant England', *Seventeenth Century* 5: 2 (1990), 185–94. A rather more optimistic view of reforms in the 1650s is given by William Lamont, 'The left and its past: revisiting the 1650s', *History Workshop Journal* 23 (1987), 141–53.

[6] *The diary of Thomas Burton*, ed. J. T. Rutt (4 vols., London, 1828), vol. I, pp. 69, 56.

called before Parliament, Quaker leaders had engaged in a systematic and practical campaign to expose the inadequacies of the religious legislation of Interregnum governments, and to argue for the establishment of a truly godly magistracy.

The confrontations between Quakers and local ministers described in the last chapter were an intrinsic part of their proselytising mission. These confrontations did not always conclude neatly with the appearance of a printed tract describing a local dispute. Itinerant preaching involved the interruption of church services, followed sometimes by rowdy meetings in churchyards; it involved travelling to meetings on the Sabbath; and it involved Quaker ministers publicly declaring that they preached with the light of God in them, a message which could be, and was, interpreted under the terms of the 1650 Blasphemy Act. The Quakers' itinerant preaching exposed them to prosecution by local magistrates.

Throughout this period, Quakers were prosecuted under a wide range of laws, a fact which in itself highlighted the confused religious policy of the 1650s. The most serious was the Blasphemy Act of August 1650, which prescribed imprisonment, and banishment for subsequent offences, for those claiming equality with God, denying the holiness and righteousness of God, or maintaining the propriety of swearing, drunkenness, adultery, incest or murder.[7] As has been seen, Quaker beliefs could be interpreted as claiming equality with God, but many of the hostile pamphlets which accused Quakers of sexual promiscuity may also have been an attempt to label Quaker practices as blasphemous.[8] Cases of blasphemy were, in the absence of ecclesiastical courts, to be tried before the civil courts, although sometimes requiring the doctrinal opinions of the local minister: the intervention of ordained ministers in such cases was exploited by Quakers to argue that their puritan opponents were manipulating state powers for their own religious ends. Nevertheless, prosecutions of Quakers under the Blasphemy Act were rare.[9]

The Instrument of Government, which constitutionally underpinned the Protectorate from December 1653 to 1657, permitted any protestant religious worship as long as individuals professed faith in God by Jesus Christ, and did not disturb the public peace.[10] Here again, the religious terminology was debilitatingly vague – even MPs in the course of the Nayler debate admitted that he had professed faith in Jesus Christ – and it was easier

---

[7] C. H. Firth and R. S. Rait, *Acts and Ordinances of the Interregnum* (3 vols., London, 1911), vol. II, pp. 409–12.

[8] This was clearly the case in the Nayler debates. See also above, Chapter 6, p. 189, Chapter 4, pp. 114–15; Chapter 5, pp. 148–49 for accusations of sexual promiscuity.

[9] Barry Reay, 'Quakerism and society' in J. F. McGregor and B. Reay (eds.), *Radical religion in the English revolution* (Oxford, 1986), p. 157.

[10] Firth and Rait, *Acts and Ordinances*, vol. II, p. 822.

and more common throughout this period for Quakers to be tried on non-theological grounds for common disturbance of the peace.[11] Often they were prosecuted as 'strangers' or vagrants; on one occasion at least, two itinerant Quaker preachers were outraged to find themselves indentured by a local court to work under a master.[12] Writing in 1658, Edward Burrough complained about 'a late act for the taking up, and punishing of idle, loose and dissolute persons such as are vagrants, and wandering Rogues, vagabonds, and sturdy beggars'. While recognising that the law was good, if 'duly and justly executed upon such as are truly guilty herein,' he warned: 'take heed of judging any to be such, who are not really so; for many of the servants of the Lord now, as it was in generations past, are moved to leave their own Country and dwellings, and relations, and goe abroad in the Nations to preach the Gospell of Christ'.[13]

Another common means by which Quakers were prosecuted, or so they claimed, was a Marian Act which forbade the interruption of ministers during service.[14] Not surprisingly, this was controversial among Quakers, who protested at being prosecuted under a 'popish' law, and who asserted that its use by unscrupulous magistrates was widespread. As will be shown below, the legal status of the Marian Act was dubious: Quakers claimed that it had been repealed at the accession of Elizabeth I.[15] Despite its obvious propaganda value, however, the use of the Marian Act against Quakers does seem to have been widespread: many Quakers tried to avoid prosecution under the Marian Act by explicitly waiting until the end of the sermon before responding in kind to the minister.[16]

In February 1655, following the dissolution of the first Protectorate Parliament, Cromwell issued an explicitly anti-Quaker proclamation, *A proclamation prohibiting the disturbing of ministers*, which sought to end one of the more widespread and disruptive of Quaker tactics.[17] The

---

[11] *Diary of Thomas Burton*, ed. Rutt, vol. I, p. 59, Worden, 'Toleration and the Cromwellian Protectorate', pp. 199–233, Arnold Lloyd, *Quaker social history, 1669–1738* (London, 1950), p. 83; for the erratic prosecution of Quakers, see Barry Reay, *The Quakers and the English Revolution* (London, 1985), ch. 3, esp. pp. 52–53. For a useful analysis of the many ways in which early Quakers broke the law, much of which is relevant to the 1650s, see Craig Horle, *The Quakers and the English legal system, 1660–1688* (Philadelphia, 1988), pp. 7–14.

[12] John Stubbs and William Caton, *A true declaration of the bloody proceedings of the men in Maidstone* (London, 1655), STC s6072.

[13] Edward Burrough, *A measure for instruction to all the rulers, judges, and magistrates* (London, 1658), STC B6013, p. 23.

[14] 1 Mary, St 2 c. 3, *Statutes of the Realm*, vol. IV (1547–85), pp. 203–04.

[15] 1 Eliz. c. 2. *Statutes of the Realm*, vol. IV, p. 358.

[16] Barry Reay, 'Early Quaker activity and reactions to it, 1652–1664', unpublished D Phil. thesis, University of Oxford, 1979, p. 69.

[17] *A proclamation prohibiting the disturbing of ministers*, 15 February 1655 (London, 1655), BL 669.f.19.68.

Proclamation revived the spirit of the Marian Act, albeit now placed on a firmly magisterial footing, explicitly ordering that Quakers, Ranters or others who interrupted public preaching and worship should be punished as civil disturbers of the peace.[18] In July 1655, the puritan minister and diarist Ralph Josselin complained darkly that the clause in Cromwell's declaration 'not to disturbe the minister in exercise, was to hint to them, they might doe it after if they would, securely, for that is their practice'.[19] After April 1655, Quakers were also prosecuted under another proclamation which required suspected Roman Catholics to take an oath of abjuration renouncing papal authority, and which Quakers refused to take as part of their objection to swearing oaths.[20]

A reading of their tracts suggests that itinerant Quaker preachers were almost systematically arrested on their arrival in towns and villages: as was shown in Chapter 3, in localised pamphleteering, an account of a confrontation with a local puritan minister or congregation was often followed by an interview with local magistrates, and possibly by arrest, imprisonment and trial.[21] This process may not have been quite so systematic as the tracts themselves proclaimed, however. The rate and severity of Quaker prosecutions were determined by the attitude of regional magistrates, and Barry Reay

---

[18] *Ibid.*

[19] Josselin, *The diary of Ralph Josselin 1616–1683*, ed. Alan McFarlane (London: British Academy Records of Social and Economic History, New Series III, 1976), p. 348.

[20] S. R. Gardiner, *The history of the Commonwealth and Protectorate, 1649–1656* (4 vols., London, 1894–1903), vol. IV, p. 18; W. C. Braithwaite, *The beginnings of Quakerism* (Cambridge, 1955), p. 446.

[21] For published accounts of trials following on from itinerant Quaker preaching, see, for example, Thomas Aldam *et al.*, *A brief discovery of a threefold estate of Antichrist* (London, 1653), *STC* A894B; Ann Audland, *A true declaration of the suffering of the innocent* (London, 1655), *STC* A4195; John Camm, *A true discovery of the ignorance, blindness and darkness* (London, 1654), *STC* C393; William Dewsbery, *A discovery of the grounds from whence the persecution did arise in Northamptonshire* (London, 1655), *STC* D1266; Richard Farnworth, *God's covenanting with his people* (London, 1653) [no *STC* entry]; George Fox, *Saul's errand to Damascus* (London, 1653), *STC* F1894; Richard Hubberthorne, *The immediate call to the ministry of the Gospel witnessed by the spirit* (London, 1654), *STC* H3225; Richard Hubberthorne, *The testimony of the everlasting Gospel witnessed through sufferings* [1654], *STC* H3237; James Nayler, *A discovery of the man of sin* (London, 1654), *STC* N274; Nayler, *Several petitions answered that were put up by the priests of Westmorland* (London, 1653), *STC* N316A; James Parnell, *The fruits of a fast, or a declaration* (London, 1655), *STC* P530; [Humphrey Smith], *A representation of the government of the borough of Evesham* [London, 1655], *STC* R1104; Ann Audland, *The saints testimony finishing through sufferings* (London, 1655), *STC* S365; *Something in answer to a petition to Oliver Cromwell* (London, 1654), *STC* S4659; John Stubbs, *A true declaration of the bloody proceedings of the men in Maidstone* (London, 1655), *STC* S6072; Francis Ellington, *A true discovery of the ground of the imprisonment* (London, 1655), *STC* T2683; William Dewsbery, *A true testimony of what was done* (London, 1655), *STC* T3123; George Whitehead, *The path of the just cleared* (London, 1655), *STC* W1944; John Whitehead, *The enmity between the two seeds* (London, 1655), *STC* W1975; Miles Halhead, *The wounds of an enemie in the house of a friend* (London, 1656), *STC* W3665.

found wide local discrepancies in the application of laws against Quakers.[22] Quaker ministers' letters more often describe relatively easy passages from one town or village to the next, without detention by the authorities. Francis Howgill and Edward Burrough travelled for a month through Norfolk and Suffolk in the politically troubled summer of 1655, reporting meetings in Ipswich, Norwich and Bury St Edmunds, as well as many market towns: 'from towne to towne, all over, and many large and greatt mettings we had in those Counties day by day'. They were not entirely free from the fear of prosecution: 'many trapes was layd for us to have brought us into bondage but the lord preserved us for his owne worke'.[23] Quaker ministers were aware of the potential legal dangers they faced, and went to some lengths to avoid them: meetings were established on county or parish boundaries, where members might evade prosecution; as Reay and others have shown, the successful survival of the movement depended on the sympathetic attitudes of local magistrates.[24]

Nevertheless, the leading Quaker ministers were apparently eager, when the necessity arose, to challenge secular authorities over the legitimacy of their legal stance against the Quakers, and to enable their fellow brethren to do the same where necessary. The importance of attending trials is very clear from the correspondence. In October 1655, John Audland wrote a typical letter to Margaret Fell describing his travels around the Bristol area. Six friends, he reported, were in prison at Bristol, 'most for steeplehouses' (or interrupting sermons); two more were in prison at Ilchester, again 'for steeplehouses'. Audland had been travelling around the country and had had 'pretious meeteings' with 'severall Justeces, which are loveing and ownes truth and hath a desire after it'.[25] He had also just returned from the assizes at Banbury where his wife Ann had been on trial for blasphemy. Audland had not gone there alone: Bristol Quakers Captain Edmund Pyott, Denis Hollister, Thomas Gouldney, Walter Clement and others had travelled from Bristol with him, and had been 'bould and sarviseable'. Audland's letter reveals the centrality of court cases for the Quaker ministers. The same band of men who had travelled from Bristol to Banbury were about to set off again for the Northampton Quarter Sessions, where 'frinds are continued in prison'.[26]

There was thus a constant mapping of prisoners reported to Margaret Fell, sometimes with the grounds of their imprisonment, sometimes merely

[22] Barry Reay, 'Early Quaker activity', pp. 65–83.
[23] Francis Howgill to Margaret Fell, 1 July [1655], Sw Mss 1: 86.
[24] Barry Reay, 'Early Quaker activity', p. 53; pp. 65–74; Adrian Davies, *The Quakers in English Society 1655–1725* (Oxford, 2000), pp. 170–79.
[25] John Audland to Margaret Fell, 1 October 1655, Sw Trs 1: 89.   [26] *Ibid.*

with news of their arrest.[27] A major concern was to identify to Fell the laws under which they were charged, in order that they could challenge them. In May 1654, Richard Hubberthorne, imprisoned for speaking at the end of a puritan minister's sermon, told the justices of Congleton that they belonged to the generation of persecutors, 'and read them out of there owne law and they had nothinge to charge mee with according to there owne law'.[28] Often, it seems, Quaker ministers called on the legal advice of Judge Thomas Fell, Gervase Benson and Anthony Pearson to try to identify the validity of the charges against them. When he and John Lawson were arrested in Chester in late 1653, Hubberthorne asked Margaret Fell for the London addresses of Thomas Fell and William West so that they could correspond.[29] Accounts of their dealings with the magistrates at Chester are among the earliest suggesting informed legal tactics. John Lawson tried unsuccessfully to get hold of the mittimus, the document which would state the grounds of imprisonment, and the witnesses' examinations, in order to prove the weakness of the charges against the Quakers.[30] Richard Hubberthorne described in a letter to Fell how he had challenged the mayor of Chester to name 'the breach of any law' for which he could be properly indicted. When none was offered, it was suggested instead to Hubberthorne that, under the jurisdiction of the city of Chester, he would be set free if he agreed to leave the city. Hubberthorne's account of his reply echoed contemporary demands for reforms which would simplify the law, but also reinforced the inherent difficulties in prosecuting religious belief:

if the law of that Citie was contrary to the law of the nation then they might turne me out of the Citie into the nation but if the law of the Citie was one with the law of the nation they must either turne me out of that nation or not out of that Citie for I was as free in that Citie as in any part of the nation, not doinge any man any wronge nor beinge chargable to no man.[31]

The following year, Richard Hubberthorne and his colleagues once again required legal advice following their imprisonment in Norwich. In December 1654, prior to their trial, Christopher Atkinson, George Whitehead and James Lancaster wrote formally to the mayor and magistrates of Norwich

---

[27] Following an appearance at the York Assizes, Aldam wrote a letter which listed that John Killam had been imprisoned 'for speaking to the Priest of doncaster, in his preaching as they call it'; five others were imprisoned 'for speakinge to the people in the streets in Yorke'; and one other had been briefly imprisoned for 'throwinge Bookes into their Coaches'. Thomas Aldam [1654], A. R. Barclay Mss 1:113, fol. 325. For letters relating to the imprisonment of fellow Quakers, see Sw Mss 1:5, 1:12; 1:112; Markey Mss p. 98; A. R. Barclay Mss 1:110, fols. 317–18; Caton Mss 3:420; 3:423.

[28] Richard Hubberthorne to Margaret Fell, 29 May 1654, Sw Trs 2: 559.

[29] John Lawson to Margaret Fell, Chester gaol [November 1653], Sw Mss 4: 66.

[30] John Lawson to Margaret Fell [November 1653], Sw Mss 4:69.

[31] Richard Hubberthorne to Margaret Fell [4 December 1653], Sw Trs 2: 540, 541.

requesting information about the charges against them.[32] Hubberthorne reported in a letter to Fox that he was called to the Quarter Sessions, after three months' imprisonment, without being told of the charges against him: 'nothing for which I was Imprisoned was layd to my charge', and after Hubberthorne was moved to much 'declaringe of truth unto them . . . they indicted me for standing before them with my hat on'. After further discourse from Hubberthorne, the justices, he claimed, were 'made to confesse that they had noe written law for what they acted but the custom of the nation and when they could noe longer forbeare . . . to heare their deceipt laid open they sent me to prisson againe for another Quarter'.[33] The lack of formal indictment led Hubberthorne to contact not only Fox and Fell, but also friends in London, who undertook to provide legal advice on his imprisonment, and publicise the paucity of the Norwich indictments in the capital.[34] The three Quakers from London joined Hubberthorne at the next sessions, 'declared the law' to the justices, and explained 'how they acted contrary to it'.[35] It was 'declared' to the judge in the trial that 'the acte by which C. Atkinson was indicted was repealed'.[36] The judge 'could not deny but it was, yet saith he, "it is my Judgement that it is not, though many say it is: and I am Chefe in this place at this time," and soe the Juery durst not but fine [i.e. find] it'.[37] Hubberthorne's letter to Margaret Fell describing these exchanges made it quite clear that the Norwich judge was acting arbitrarily and unjustly: 'he makes his law either to imprison or to sett free at his will for the same thinge and so in his will doth rule in this Countrey and all both magistrate and people are subjects to his will and dare not acte contrarie to what he saith'.[38]

Trials, indeed, appear on occasion to have been seized as an opportunity for Quaker leaders to challenge judges on their judicial and constitutional authority. In August 1656 Thomas Aldam was to be tried for non-payment of tithes. Gervase Benson joined him in York for the trial, and appears almost to have engineered his own arrest in order to appear before the bar. His letter to Margaret Fell describing the confrontation between himself and the judges underlines the importance Benson attached to trials as an occasion

[32] Hubberthorne to Fell, 28 December 1654, Sw Trs 2:575.
[33] Hubberthorne to George Fox [1654], Sw Trs 2: 549.
[34] Hubberthorne to Fox [1654], Sw Trs 2: 550.
[35] Hubberthorne to Margaret Fell, 12 April 1655, Sw Trs 2: 555.
[36] It is not clear from the Quakers' own letters what the charge against Atkinson was. Initially, it was reported that he was arrested for being at a Quaker meeting on a Sunday; subsequent reports stated that he had been 'indicted' for disturbing a priest, possibly while Atkinson was in custody. Unless either of these involved disturbing the public peace, neither was strictly speaking illegal at this time. It is most likely that the 'repealed' law was the Marian Act. See Sw Trs 2: 549, 571; Sw Mss 1:218.
[37] Richard Hubberthorne to Margaret Fell, 12 April 1655, Sw Trs 2: 556.
[38] *Ibid.*, 2: 555–56.

for political rhetoric: 'then I sayd to the Jury and to all the people that I did witnes then that there was noe law in the Nation, that did enable him that sat there as Judge to give any priest tythes'. Benson continued to ask for legal proof of the judge's authority, demanding that the law be read out loud, 'that the people might witnesse with me or against me. It was sayd they had not the book there, then I sayd, let us read the law, wee have it in writeinge And I witnese it is a true copie for my selfe did write it forth of the statute.' Following the trial, Benson and Aldam 'went into the castle yeard and read the words of the statute amongst the people which was very servicable and gave some queries and coppyes of the words of the statute amongst them . . . Then our service was to goe alonge with the sheriffe and Judges and to them gave papers.'[39] Benson's tactics are very revealing about the importance of trials as public spectre for early Quaker leaders, and as a forum for legal, and ultimately constitutional, debate with both magistrates and bystanders.

Resentment at arbitrary justice formed one aspect of the Quakers' opposition to local magistrates. Another crucial area of contention was the collaboration between magistrates and ministers in the prosecution of Quakers. The role of magistrates, the Quakers argued at length in their tracts, was to protect the innocent from evil-doers, and to create a truly godly commonwealth, but emphatically not to control religious practice. They were incensed when they saw puritan ministers turning to local magistrates for legal help in quashing Quaker preaching. A constant theme of the Quaker campaign, evident both in the correspondence and their publications, was to highlight the inadequacies of a system in which magistrates sought to protect the puritan ministry. Imprisoned under the Blasphemy Act in Appleby in November 1652, Francis Howgill wrote to Margaret Fell, describing his arrest in terms which suggested confusion and disarray among the local magistracy: Howgill had been arrested when local ministers had seen him preaching in the high street of Kirkby Stephen, panicked, and 'ran back to the justis' who was apparently waiting 'in the high prests house'. Throughout the ensuing interview, Howgill avoided speaking with the magistrates and continued to question the ministers on the derivation of their authority. Eventually the magistrate bound him to appear at the next Quarter Sessions, and Howgill was then able to denounce the 'Tirany and Persecution' in his actions. At this the magistrate called all those present, 'to witness that I sayd the law was tiriny and opreson, and said I was guilty of treason: hereupon I sayd take heed what thou dost: I speake of thy actions and not of the law'.[40]

---

[39] Gervase Benson to Margaret Fell, 9 August 1656, Sw Mss 4: 156.
[40] Francis Howgill to Margaret Fell, 5 January 1653, A. R. Barclay Mss 1:74, fol. 218. See also A. R. Barclay Mss 1:18, fol. 59, 1: 29; Sw Mss 3:66.

Howgill's account is redolent of the confusion surrounding the prosecution of Quakers, and of the blurred line between ministerial and magisterial authority which they sought to expose. When he was arrested in Chester in November 1653, Richard Hubberthorne was questioned by the mayor. The questions were aimed at ascertaining whether Hubberthorne was a vagrant; when the mayor, according to Hubberthorne's account, 'had no satisfaction to his carnall mind' he 'bid the prest aske' questions on the 'principles of religion', presumably to see whether Hubberthorne could be prosecuted under the Blasphemy Act.[41] In this the priest 'was confounded' and could find nothing in Hubberthorne's replies 'whereof to accuse me'. Cries from the court room to indict him as a vagrant were responded to by Hubberthorne:

if there was any that could Accuse me for the breach of any law make it knowne and execute it upon me, or if ther was any that could lay any thinge to my charge, here I am, charge it upon me: some said they could not charge me with any thing: and the rest was silent.[42]

Thus in court rooms up and down the country, Quakers sought to highlight the inadequacies of laws which were used to govern religious practice and the practical difficulties in enforcing them. The fact that Howgill's and Hubberthorne's letters were unpublished reminds us of the blurred line between manuscript papers and published tracts in Quaker campaigning: the letters did not simply inform Margaret Fell of the whereabouts and circumstances of the prisoners, but were clearly intended to inspire, encourage and inform other itinerant Quaker preachers to challenge the legality of the charges against them. Hubberthorne asked for his letter, which provided a verbatim account of the answers he had given to the mayor, to be sent on to friends in Yealand and Kellet.

Very similar accounts of prosecutions appeared in print; the wider readership implicit in printed tracts signals an ever-increasing body of men and women able to challenge the actions of local justices. From an early date concern was voiced of the need to publish their sufferings. In November 1654 Thomas Willan requested information from Margaret Fell so that the 'book of sufferings' could be printed; the following year Gervase Benson and Anthony Pearson, in response to a paper from Margaret Fell, informed her that they were 'endeavouringe to gett togeather the sufferings of freinds in the North parts for Tythes . . . for laying open to the people the grounds of the payment of tythes and the ends for which people did give them; and how they have from tyme to tyme diverted them from the end for which they weare given'. Here again, trials are described as an occasion to air political grievances: 'soe farr as wee can see these Assizes may produce some thinge

---

[41] Hubberthorne to Fell, Sw Trs 2: 540. [42] *Ibid.*

that may be materiall', and they promised to send her an account as soon as possible.[43]

Although the compilation and publication of 'sufferings' form an important part of the Quaker denominational tradition, there was also an immediate practical purpose in the publication of 'sufferings' which has been insufficiently emphasised: examples of trials were published in order to rehearse the key issues of state interference in religion and to enable readers to raise concrete objections to their own prosecution. The tracts stressed the importance of ascertaining the precise reasons for imprisonment, and hence of obtaining a copy of the mittimus. William Dewsbery made a point of mentioning that neither the gaoler nor the justices would provide him with a copy of his mittimus; often, the mittimus was transcribed into the tract recording the prosecution, and its legality refuted.[44] Similarly, fines or other financial exactions were highlighted, illustrating the greed and iniquities of the legal system. In January 1653, Francis Howgill and James Nayler were committed to prison on the grounds of evidence presented in petitions of Westmorland ministers; and were told they would not be released until the petitions were answered. 'I was moved to answer them', stated the author of the tract which recorded the trial, but discovered that they would have to pay 4s. 6d. for copies of the petitions, 'which we know was oppression'.[45]

The Quakers' concern with the magistrates' interference in matters of religion was also integrated into printed accounts of trials. A note by Gervase Benson in the published account of James Nayler's trial at Appleby in January 1653 stated that it had been 'alledged that the words by [Nayler] spoken, were not within the Act against Blasphemy, nor against any Law'. As a result, Benson continued, the justices had decided to risk a fine by the

---

[43] Thomas Willan to Margaret Fell, 26 November 1654, Spence Mss 3: 7; Anthony Pearson and Gervase Benson to Margaret Fell, 1 August 1655, Sw Mss 4: 162. The following year Benson wrote to Fell with a long account of the trial of Thomas Aldam for his refusal to pay tithes; 9 August 1656, Sw Mss 4: 156. See also Anthony Pearson, *The great case of tythes truly stated* (London, 1657), *STC* P989. The 'book of sufferings' referred to in November 1654 seems either not to have been printed, or not to have survived, since Thomas Willan specifically referred to the 'sufferings' of Christopher Atkinson and Edward Burrough in Scotland and Northumberland, of which no record survives in print.

[44] William Dewsbery, *A discovery of the grounds from whence persecution did arise* (London, 1655), *STC* D1266, p. 3; for allusions to the terms of the mittimus, see J[ohn] C[amm], *A true discovery of the ignorance, blindness and darkness . . .* (London, 1653), *STC* C393, p. 3; James Parnell, *The fruits of a fast* (London, 1655), *STC* P530, pp. 10–12; Richard Hubberthorne et al., *The immediate call to the ministry of the gospel* (London, 1653), *STC* H3225, p. 8; [Humphrey Smith], *A representation of the government of the borough of Evesham* [1655], *STC* R1104, sig. Ar. In 1653, two Quakers from Lancashire travelled to Derbyshire to acquire a copy of the *mittimus* by which Fox had been imprisoned in Derby in 1650: see John Camm, *Something in answer to a book* (London, 1653), *STC* C389, p. 55.

[45] [James Nayler], *Several petitions answered, that were put up by the priests of Westmorland* (London, 1653), *STC* N316A, pp. 52–53.

Assize judges, and commit Nayler on the evidence of the ministers' petition alone '(though no oath of the truth of any particular therein contained was made)'. Benson also recorded that the justices had made their own order, at their own discretion, forbidding meetings of the people of God, ignoring the parliamentary legislation which allowed freedom of meeting.[46]

Quaker tracts also made a great deal out of the collaboration of ministers and magistrates in securing the arrest and trial of Quakers. The humiliation of ministers in court rooms was presented in such a way as to belittle both the ministers' recourse to the law, and to undermine the value of legal restrictions on religious practice. An account of the meeting between George Fox and the Lancaster justices in October 1652 described the anguish of the minister of Bolton le Sands, John Jacques, who, on hearing George Fox speak, 'was in such a rage, that he broke forth into many high expressions', and, among other things, said, 'That the letter and the spirit were unseparable'. At this, the account related, 'the Justices stood up and bid him prove that, before he went any further', but the minister was apparently unable to, 'and went down in a greater rage than before', subsequently telling enquirers that he had not been present at the meeting.[47] In the same tract, the trial of James Nayler at Appleby was described, including Gervase Benson's warning that Nayler could not be indicted for blasphemy. At this, 'The Priests began to preach against the Justices, and say they were not to meddle in these things . . . and are not pleased with the Law, because it is not in the Statute to imprison us, as the Priest that pleaded against us said; and the Justices bad him go put it into the Statute, if he could: he said it should want no will of his.'[48]

Thus both tracts and correspondence were full of accounts of bungled prosecutions which Quakers used to argue that the magistracy had no role in matters of religion. Their actions in court rooms, and their printed tracts, led contemporaries to insist that Quakers were 'anti-magisterial as well as anti-ministerial'.[49] Yet the published accounts of trials and discussion of the role of magistrates present a rather more complex picture. Quaker tracts exposed local magistrates who they claimed acted unlawfully, or who were themselves morally unfit to be magistrates.[50] But the attack was on individual

---

[46] *Ibid.*, pp. 51–52.

[47] Thomas Aldam *et al.*, *A brief discovery of a threefold estate of Antichrist* (London, 1653), STC A894B, pp. 11–12.

[48] *Ibid.*, p. 13.

[49] William Prynne, *The Quakers unmasked, and clearly detected* (London, 1655), STC P4045, p. 7; Thomas Birch (ed.), *A collection of the State Papers of John Thurloe* (7 vols., London, 1742), vol. IV, p. 508.

[50] See, for example, Ann Audland's warning to her own prosecutor: 'This was I moved to write to clear my conscience of thee, and leave thee without excuse, that when the Book of Conscience is opened, thou mayest remember that thou wast warned in thy life-time.' Ann Audland, *A true declaration of the suffering of the innocent* (London, 1655), STC A4195, p. 2.

magistrates, not on magistracy itself. On other occasions, magistrates were portrayed as open to the Quaker preaching of the inner light, as upholders of justice in the face of the manoeuverings of puritan ministers, and sometimes even undergoing conversion in the course of a trial.[51] And in general terms, Quaker authors consistently advocated their support for a truly godly magistracy. Edward Burrough's discussion of magistracy in 1658 is typical:

> It [magistracy] is an ordinance of God, ordained of him for the preserving of peace among men, for the punishing and suppressing of evil doers, and for the praise and safety to them that doe well; that mens persons and estates may be preserved from the violence and wrong dealing of evill men.[52]

Quaker tracts, therefore, also engaged with the proper function of magistracy, arguing that magistrates had a duty to enforce laws which protected the people of God, and to punish evil-doers. Like their Fifth Monarchist contemporaries and puritan forebears, Quaker ministers actively engaged with the issue of further 'godly' reformation, and with the proper role of the magistracy in the new English Commonwealth.[53]

This concern with the implementation of godly rule is apparent in the everyday workings of the movement, as well as in its publications. Gervase Benson and Anthony Pearson, themselves justices, were key spokesmen for further reformation. On one occasion they wrote jointly to a 'friend' with whom they had spent the previous evening debating. 'If thou be unsatisfied of our principles concerning Magistracy Government and Laws', they wrote, further queries should be sent to Colonel William West, to which they promised 'a clear plaine and positive answer' which would be according to the Scriptures and to the 'principles of good men in all ages' and would be 'such as upon noe other grounds the late warre can be Justifyed and our selves, amongst others who have been engaged against the publick Enemy, cleared from blood'.[54] Earlier, in 1653, Gervase Benson had addressed a paper to his fellow justices in Kendal.[55] In it, Benson acknowledged 'the great

---

[51] See the conversion of Anthony Pearson at Nayler's trial in *Saul's errand to Damascus*, p. 34; the report that Judge Fell and Justice Colonel West were 'much convinced of the truth' in Thomas Aldam, *A brief discovery of a threefold estate of Antichrist*, p. 12; the concern of Gervase Benson and Anthony Pearson over Nayler's trial for blasphemy in 1653 in James Nayler, *Several petitions answered*, pp. 51–52.

[52] Edward Burrough, *A measure for instruction to all the rulers, judges, and magistrates* (London, 1658), STC B6013, p. 1.

[53] Bernard Capp, *The Fifth Monarchy Men* (London, 1972), pp. 157–71; J. C. Davis, 'Gerrard Winstanley and the restoration of true magistracy', *Past and Present* 70 (1976); Patrick Collinson, *The religion of protestants: the church in English society 1559–1625* (Oxford, 1982), pp. 149–88.

[54] Gervase Benson and Anthony Pearson [1654], Sw Trs 1: 189. They subscribed it 'from them who are one with Justice and Equity and welwishers of Englands Commonwealth'.

[55] Gervase Benson [1653], Sw Trs 1: 183. A copy of the paper was addressed to Justices 'Coats' and 'Seponsan' at the Gryleswick Assizes. Gervase Benson was an alderman of Kendal in

oppressions' under which the Commonwealth laboured, which, he argued, were occasioned not 'by the evill of the lawes' but by 'mal-administration and execution'. Benson thought fit to provide his fellow justices with evidence of such corruption, citing in his own home town of Sedburgh the existence of fourteen alehouses, frequented by the local priest and the very men who were supposed to license them.[56] The Act of Parliament which prescribed the appointment of a registrar of marriages 'by publique and common vote' had been flouted, and a 'man put in by some men accordinge to their wills': 'and of what life and conversacion the man is might be serviceable to enquire', Benson noted darkly.[57] In short, 'both priest and Clerke are guiltie of those offences themselves they should reform in others', and they would be 'condemned by the righteous Judge who hath appointed a day wherein he will Judge all things'.[58]

Quaker leaders also went beyond the exposure of ungodly magistrates, and carried out their own attempts at godly rule. Aspects of internal Quaker discipline have already been examined as an intrinsic feature of the movement's development: wayward preachers were removed, and local meetings regulated by written instruction.[59] Yet concern with discipline was more profound than this, and went far beyond the immediate auspices of the movement. In August 1656, George Fox sent a note to Richard Farnworth, ordering him: 'See that friendes Be kept in Order; and search out the matter of Disorder, and that which Causeth itt.'[60] In early October, Farnworth wrote to Edward Burrough and Francis Howgill, informing them of his intention to travel into Lincolnshire 'to Enquier, into the Cause and matter of disorder, if any be, (According to G.F. his order or directions to mee etc.) that they being brought to light'.[61] A 'memorandum' of 'passages Examined etc. at Martine in Lincolnshire', by Richard Farnworth on 20 November, recorded how a group of friends came 'to Lay some Causes, before the Truth In mee; which was heard and determined'. These included the slandering of one John Hudson, accused, and cleared by Farnworth's investigation, of stealing pears; the acquittal of John Jessick of Ingham who had been charged with selling over-priced barley; and upholding the confession of John Jessicke's

---

1653: on 26 September, an attempt was made to vote him out of the corporation on the grounds that he had questioned its authority and refused to take part in a vote for the Mayor. Kendal Corporation Ms, *HMC* Appendix 12. I am very grateful to Dr Colin Phillips of Manchester University for this information.

[56] Gervase Benson, Sw Trs 1:183.   [57] *Ibid.*, 1:184.   [58] *Ibid.*

[59] See above, Chs. 1, 2 and 5.

[60] Richard Farnworth, 28 October 1656, Portfolio 36: 140v. It is important to note that Farnworth's activities coincided with the considerable unrest within the movement surrounding the controversial behaviour of James Nayler, Martha Simmonds and others, and their ultimate arrest and trial. The Nayler affair is discussed in more detail below, Chapter 8.

[61] Richard Farnworth to Francis Howgill and Edward Burrough, 4 October 1656, A. R. Barclay Mss 1: 38.

wife, 'that she had been forward and uttered words hastly Contrary to the Light'.[62]

The most complex case heard by Richard Farnworth concerned a blacksmith called John Wright and his daughter, who was a servant to one Thomas Craven. The case revolved around a group of 'wandering beggers, goeing abroad,' as the report put it, 'Contrarie to the Law of England'. Thomas Craven had ordered his servant to take the beggars to the local constable. This she duly did, but the constable was absent, so she sent the beggars on their way, and they were apprehended in the next town. Farnworth's report noted that the 'Law' provided a reward of two shillings for apprehending beggars, and that accordingly, John Wright, the servant's father, had gone to the constable to claim his daughter's reward. It was John Wright's action which caused offence. As Farnworth pointed out, the servant had been acting under Thomas Craven's orders, not her father's; furthermore she had failed in her duty by letting the beggars go free and therefore had no claim to the reward; and finally, John Wright had claimed the money without the consent or knowledge of Thomas Craven, whose reward, if anybody's, it surely was. John Wright accordingly was 'Convicted of an Errour' and 'Confessed that he had done wronge'. It was 'ordered' by Farnworth that by the light in his conscience which had allowed him to confess his error, Wright should now pay the money back.[63]

The cases of John Wright and the others present a number of issues. Beyond referring to them as a 'Certaine Company of Friends', the sectarian status of the individuals brought before Richard Farnworth was never mentioned and the possibility of their expulsion from the local meeting was not discussed. Indeed it is unclear whether all were members of the local Quaker meeting: the man who wrongly slandered John Hudson, for example, was never named. John Wright had clearly wronged Thomas Craven; yet we can be more certain that Wright was a Quaker than that Thomas Craven was. And while John Jessick's wife had spoken 'contrary to the light', and John Wright was made to see his errors by the 'light in his conscience', the other cases did not conclude by recourse to the inner light. There was thus a blurred line between the company of friends and the outside world. The action against the beggars was justified as a 'Law of England', as was the reward for their apprehension. The authority of the constable was upheld; the wrongdoing of the beggars never questioned. The servant–master relationship was respected by Farnworth, as was that of father and daughter. In a sense it did not matter whether Thomas Craven was a Quaker or not. Richard Farnworth was judging his brethren not on the terms of their fellowship, but on their ability to lead a godly, righteous life. Farnworth was putting into action his belief in

---

[62] Richard Farnworth, 20 November 1656, Portfolio 36:149.   [63] *Ibid.*, 149–50.

the need for a godly commonwealth, to be upheld by godly laws and godly magistrates.

Farnworth's activities as a self-appointed magistrate in Lincolnshire were never recorded in print, but they do not deviate from the attitudes towards local magistrates published by the Quaker leaders in the first half of the 1650s.[64] Magistrates were expected to uphold a just and true society; they derived their power from their own righteousness; they were to protect the innocent, and especially those who suffered religious persecution. Magistrates who deviated from this were exposed and denounced by the Quakers in public and in print, but the ideal of true magistracy was championed. Richard Farnworth's practical intervention in the everyday lives of the Ingham brethren provides a very important context in which to understand the printed rhetoric on the role of England's magistracy. Sustained pamphleteering against the ungodly practices of local magistrates complemented Quaker efforts to impose their own order on society. Quaker tracts often urged readers to 'be not sayers but doers': the unpublished activities of Farnworth, of Gervase Benson and others, demonstrate the practical implications of this. Their interventions in issues of local order reveal another side to the 'failure of godly rule' described by Derek Hirst. As local office-holders and ministers became increasingly reluctant or unable to carry out a puritan 'cultural revolution', Quakers were all the more inclined to implement their own, through direct intervention and the practical application of their beliefs, as well as through their own printed rhetoric.[65] Far from being alienated from worldly politics, they were involved in very practical and immediate ways. In this context, too, far from being an optimistic outburst, the list of Quakers eligible to serve as magistrates which was submitted to the Rump Parliament in 1659 can be located within a continuum in the Quaker campaign.[66]

Thus far it has been shown that, at a local level, Quaker leaders used a sophisticated combination of private correspondence, printed tracts and public events to inform audiences of the practical implications of enforcing England's religious settlement, and to urge active participation in the struggle to achieve a truly godly commonwealth. In so doing, they were able to address an impressive variety of audiences, from individual magistrates and bystanders at Quaker trials, to fellow Quaker leaders conducting preaching campaigns up and down the country. This allowed for the development of

---

[64] The classic example, indeed, is a tract by Richard Farnworth published in 1653, *An Easter-Reckoning* (London, 1653), *STC* F480, which discussed a whole range of proper societal relations, including a list of the magistrate's duties. See above, Chapter 5, pp. 135–36.

[65] Derek Hirst, 'The failure of godly rule', 33–66; Christopher Durston, 'The failure of cultural revolution', in Durston and Eales (eds.), *The culture of English puritanism*, pp. 210–33.

[66] Reay, 'The Quakers, 1659', 195–96; Anthony Fletcher, *Reform in the provinces: the government of Stuart England* (New Haven and London, 1986), p. 18.

a cohesive and co-ordinated strategy which contemporaries perceived as a serious attack on magistracy and order.[67]

QUAKER PAMPHLETEERING AND NATIONAL POLITICS

The culmination of such a concerted effort at local level was the emergence of a Quaker lobby addressed to the national governments of the Commonwealth and Protectorate. Here again, print played a central role as specific tracts were published, calling on government to repeal legislation, or act fast to foster a true reformation of manners. Yet once again it is important not to isolate the content of these tracts from the wider context of the Quaker campaign as a whole. The majority of tracts addressed to central government derived from the experiences of Quakers in the localities, as local examples of unfair prosecutions were presented as evidence of the need for legislative change. Such tracts were often written as prophecy rather than as direct pleas or petitions to the government: Quaker authors dismissed petitions as deferential and placing too much weight on worldly authority. Anthony Pearson was at pains to explain in a tract addressed to Parliament that his intention was not 'to clamour or complain, nor to petition any thing from you', but to warn them of the terrible consequences of persecuting innocent Quakers.[68] (See Plate 10.) It has been argued in the past that because Quaker writing was prophetic, it was less politically relevant, or effective than the works of their contemporaries, although more recent work has rightly stressed the political significance of prophecy in this period.[69] It is clear, in fact, that printed tracts addressed to central government were not intended to achieve specific legislative or political change, but rather addressed a broad audience, and aimed to promote widespread political involvement. As will be discussed below, Quaker leaders established quite effective communication with members of the body politic through private letters and meetings, in

[67] It is important to emphasise the practical context behind this type of pamphleteering activity. The themes of suffering and martyrdom are central to the protestant tradition: for Quakers in particular, the recording of sufferings is recognised as a means of witnessing their faith. For this reason, Quaker sufferings are often studied as an important literary genre of Quakerism which has particular significance for the establishment of the denominational tradition in the later seventeenth and eighteenth centuries. Joseph Besse's collection of sufferings is the classic martyrology of Quakerism, clearly compiled from some of the early published accounts mentioned in this chapter, which has been compared to Foxe's *Book of Martyrs*. Yet the recording of 'sufferings' was also an important part of the Quakers' campaigning which sought to effect widespread political participation. See Joseph Besse, *A collection of the sufferings of the people called Quakers* (2 vols., London, 1753); John R. Knott, *Discourses of martyrdom in English literature, 1563–1694* (Cambridge, 1993), esp. pp. 216–55.

[68] Anthony Pearson, *To the parliament of the common-wealth of England* [n.p., 1653], STC P992, p. 1.

[69] Alan Cole, 'Quakers and politics', pp. 35–36; Phyllis Mack, *Visionary women: ecstatic prophecy in seventeenth-century England* (Berkeley, 1992), esp. pp. 165–211.

(1·)

10

TO THE
PARLIAMENT
OF THE
Common-wealth
OF
ENGLAND.

Chriſtian Friends ,

I Am moved of the Lord to preſent this Paper to you, it requires your ſpeedy conſideration ; and therefore as you love your own ſouls defer it not : the crying ſin of perſecuting the righteous Seed of God, is now brought to your door, and you muſt account for every days delay ; ariſe, ſtand up and execute Juſtice and Judgement, that you may be hid in the day of the Lords fierce Wrath, which is at hand.

I come not to you to clamour or complain, nor to petition any thing from you, but to diſcharge my duty in obedience to the command of the Lord , in laying before you the afflictions and ſufferings of the innocent by the hands of your Miniſters and Servants, that ſo you may acquit your ſelves , left the guilt fall upon your own heads.

N the Northen Parts of this Nation, God hath raiſed and is raiſing up his own Seed in many people, according to his promiſes ; which hath layen in bondage in a ſtrange Land for many generations , and is daily encreaſing their number to the praiſe of his own name, which gathers their
A hearts

Plate 10. Anthony Pearson, *To the parliament of the common-wealth of England* [n.p., 1653], STC P992, sig. A.

which they requested specific action or reform. The Quakers' printed tracts, often addressed to the people of England and circulated at moments of high political drama, do not constitute a discrete programme for constitutional change, but do underline the Quakers' expectation that the legislative and political reforms necessary to effect godly rule would be established through popular political involvement and understanding, and that print was a highly effective medium through which to achieve this.

A close chronological study of early Quaker pamphleteering indicates a very clear correlation between the circulation of printed tracts and the engagement of the Quaker movement with events of national political significance. Many of the key organisational developments in the movement already discussed, such as the organisation of printing or the funding of the national preaching campaign, can also be linked to moments of high political drama. As much as the content of the tracts, therefore, the processes involved in their production, circulation and use suggest that the early movement emerged as a multifaceted political campaign which combined the private lobbying of political leaders with printed tracts urging widespread participation to achieve godly rule.

THE POLITICAL CHRONOLOGY OF THE QUAKER CAMPAIGN

The first evidence of early Quaker mobilisation, especially the links with London forged in early 1653, is linked to wider political events. Although it is well established that the early Quaker movement had its roots among the religious communities in the midlands and the north of England, it is important to modify the impression that these were isolated communities of Seekers. The army background of many of them is well known. Chapter 2 has already described how the Quakers grouped around Thomas Aldam and Richard Farnworth had links to the capital through Captain Amor Stoddard. As well as acting as a co-ordinator of the Quaker movement's publishing, Stoddard supplied Quakers with news and publications from the army. In January 1653, the army's Council of Officers issued a statement which called for a constitutional settlement on Parliament's status, and the establishment of regular parliamentary elections. On 28 January, this statement was circulated for consultation to all regiments in England, Scotland and Ireland, and swiftly published.[70] Amor Stoddard sent a copy of the Officers' letter to Aldam and his fellow prisoners in York. Aldam's rapid

---

[70] Gardiner, *Commonwealth and Protectorate*, vol. II., pp. 233–36; Austin Woolrych, *Commonwealth to Protectorate* (Oxford, 1986), pp. 50–52; Ian Gentles, *The New Model Army in England, Ireland and Scotland, 1645–1653* (Oxford, 1994 reprint), pp. 424–25. The letter was published as *A letter from the general meeting of the officers of the army*, dated by Thomason on 28 January 1653.

response strongly suggests that Stoddard was an established contact between Quakers and army officers: 'It did much rejoyce mee to heare my fathers voyce soundinge forth throughe you, as in the remonstrance of the chiefe Officers of the Armie', wrote Aldam to Stoddard, and went on to applaude the 'generall Convincement' in the army officers' letter.[71] He also expressed his own political frustrations, which closely mirrored the complaints of the army: 'the Cry of the pore oppressed Common wealth are greate, the cry is oppression, oppression, Injustice, Injustice, Corrupt men sett up to Judge the wayes of god'.[72]

The Officers' letter made further inroads into the nascent Quaker movement. Benjamin Nicholson, a fellow prisoner with Thomas Aldam at York, produced his own printed response.[73] James Nayler, imprisoned at Appleby, also read and welcomed the army officers' letter, commenting in a letter to George Fox: 'there is some good things propoundinge by the armie, ariseing from a true sence'. Nayler went on to explain that he would have passed it on to Fox, 'but it may be you will have them at large some other way'.[74] Contact with army officers, and engagement with army politics, was taken for granted among Quaker leaders.

At the same time as Stoddard was feeding army literature to Quakers in Yorkshire, Margaret Fell was establishing Quaker links with the political capital through her husband Thomas, and Colonel William West. In February 1653, as the future of the Rump Parliament was hotly debated in London, Margaret Fell asked her husband, who was then in London, to present a 'declaration that Coll: Benson and other Frends drew . . . to them that are in authoryty', and also sent him a 'note that George was moved to rise out of bed and writ[e] that should be shewed to any in Parlement that is afrend to the Truth'.[75] Margaret Fell was insistent that her husband should act quickly in contacting sympathetic Members of Parliament. 'I pray thee, doe not let it ley [at] they dore, but shew it to any that is anything . . . loveing to the Truth.' The same letter carried a number of manuscripts which Fell requested her husband to have printed, including the manuscript of *Saul's*

---

[71] Thomas Aldam to Amor Stoddard, 19 February 1653, A. R. Barclay Mss, fol. 50.
[72] *Ibid.*, fol. 51.
[73] Benjamin Nicholson, *Some returns to a letter which came from a general meeting of Officers of the Army* (London, 1653), STC N1106, p. 2.
[74] James Nayler to George Fox [January 1653], Sw Ms 3:66. Nayler's most recent biographer, William Bittle, believes that Nayler was responding not to the letter of the Council of Officers, but to another circular attributed to the Levellers. He does this purely on the basis that Nayler was more likely to sympathise with a 'Leveller' publication. Given that Stoddard sent the York prisoners the Council of Officers' letter, there is no reason to suppose that this was not the one referred to by Nayler. In any event, the key point is that army literature from London was finding its way to Quaker prisoners in York and Appleby. William Bittle, *James Nayler 1618–1660: the Quaker indicted by Parliament* (York, 1986), pp. 41–42.
[75] Margaret Fell to Thomas Fell, 18 February 1653, Abraham Mss [1].

errand to Damascus, with its account of Fox's and Nayler's prosecution for blasphemy in Lancaster and Appleby.[76] Margaret Fell was equally purposeful in prescribing the audience for these early printed sufferings: 'let them be printed,' she instructed, so that it 'may openly appear to the world what we live in'.[77]

Benjamin Nicholson's printed response to the officers' letter, and *Saul's errand to Damascus*, were the first Quaker tracts obtained by London stationer George Thomason, both dated by him on 12 March 1653, and were probably the first Quaker publications to circulate in the capital. The nature and timing of their production were explicitly integrated into wider political mobilisation by Quaker leaders, either responding to the army's initiative, or making contact with sympathetic Rumpers.

THE QUAKERS AND BAREBONES

The coincidence of pamphleteering and involvement in national political issues is reinforced by the Quaker publications circulated in the capital in the early summer of 1653. The Rump Parliament, which had overseen the execution of Charles I and the declaration of the republic in 1649, was forcibly dissolved by Cromwell's troops in April 1653 as the rift between it and the army became irreconcilable. In its place came the Nominated Assembly, or Barebones Parliament, an assembly of some 140 representatives, nominated by members of the Council of Officers, and generally greeted with millenarian enthusiasm by Fifth Monarchists and the radical protestant sects.[78] The first meeting of Barebones, on 4 July 1653, attracted sustained Quaker pamphleteering, and the first concerted effort by the movement to publicise its views in the capital. The use of print in this precise political context demonstrates how print enabled the circulation of ideas remotely: although the Quaker ministers continued to conduct their ministry in the north of England, they had not yet established a formal presence in London.[79]

---

[76] See above, Chapter 6, pp. 185–88.
[77] The books in question were *Saul's errand to Damascus* and *Several petitions answered.* Margaret Fell to Thomas Fell, 18 February 1653, Abraham Mss [1].
[78] Austin Woolrych, *Commonwealth to Protectorate*, esp. pp. 103–43, Blair Worden, *The Rump Parliament 1648–1653* (Cambridge, 1974).
[79] There was undoubtedly sustained contact with London and political events there, however, by virtue of the fact that William West, the close friend of Margaret Fell and her husband, was chosen to represent Lancaster at the Nominated Assembly; and that after May 1653, Anthony Pearson, a JP and clerk to the radical MP Arthur Haselrig, became an active member of the movement. For William West, see Woolrych, *Commonwealth to Protectorate*; pp. 229–31, 430; for Anthony Pearson, 9 May 1653, see Sw Mss 1: 87; Braithwaite, *Beginnings of Quakerism*, pp. 113–14; Amy E. Wallis, 'Anthony Pearson (1626–1666)', *JFHS* 51: 2 (1966), 77–95.

On 29 June 1653, the bookseller George Thomason obtained seven Quaker pamphlets, most of them written by Richard Farnworth and Thomas Aldam.[80] This constituted a very substantial acquisition: prior to this he had only obtained one assuredly Quaker tract since *Saul's errand* and Nicholson's *Return* to the army's letter.[81] Farnworth's bundle of tracts, written over the winter and spring of 1653, all drew attention to the fact that Quakers were imprisoned under the Marian Act which forbade the interruption of church services.[82] *A brief discovery of the kingdom of Antichrist*, written in March 1653, was an account of confrontations between Quakers and puritan ministers of Yorkshire, 'the greatest persecutors of the truth of God'.[83] After several accounts of the 'false prophecy' of the ministry in Yorkshire, Farnworth complained specifically about the Marian Act, denouncing the ministers who: 'make their refuge to the Popes Law, that was made to uphold the Popish Clergy by, when they did uphold the Masse made by Queen Mary'. Farnworth's complaint focused on the fact that the Marian legislation had been repealed at Elizabeth's accession, and that ministers and magistrates were therefore acting unlawfully. Farnworth advised readers to 'see the Statute in the first of Mary 2. Ass. 3. Ch: and againe see if it be not repealed by Elizabeth, in the first yeare of her reigne, 2. chap last clause'.[84] He was similarly explicit in a more prophetic tract, *Moses message to Pharaoh*, which warned that the ministry of England, Satan's officers, were 'cunning, and had trained up their schollers' to uphold the pope's laws. Not only this, but 'he hath the Justices to take his part': Satan was 'every way armed against the Lord . . . and will not suffer the truth to be declared'.[85] Here the reference to the Marian Act and its repeal appeared in the margin of the tract,

---

[80] Richard Farnworth, *A call out of Egypt and Babylon* (London, 1653), F474 (29 June, 1653); [Richard Farnworth], *A discovery of faith* (London, 1653), STC F479 (29 June); Farnworth, *A discovery of truth and falsehood* (London, 1653), STC F479A, (29 June); Farnworth, *An Easter-Reckoning* (London, 1653), STC F480 (29 June); Farnworth, *The generall-good to all people* (London, 1653), STC F483 (29 June); Farnworth, *God's covenanting with his people* (London, 1653) [bound as part of F483] (29 June); James Nayler, *Several petitions answered* (London, 1653), STC N316A (29 June); Richard Farnworth, *Englands warning piece gone forth* (London, 1653), STC F482 (2 July; published for Thomas Wayte).

[81] This was James Nayler's *A discovery of the first wisdom from beneath* (London, 1653), STC N272 dated by Thomason on 25 April, shortly after the forcible dissolution of the Rump Parliament.

[82] Farnworth referred to this Act in *A brief discovery of the kingdom of Antichrist* [n.p., 1653], STC F472A, which Farnworth dated March 1653, *The general good to all people* (London, 1653), STC F483, dated April 1653 by Farnworth, and 29 June by George Thomason; *Gods covenanting with his people* (London, 1653), no STC entry, dated 29 June by Thomason, and *Moses message to Pharaoh* [n.p., 1653], STC F491B, not obtained by Thomason.

[83] Farnworth, *A brief discovery of the kingdom of Antichrist*, p. 2.

[84] *Ibid.*, pp. 7–8. His source for the repeal of the Marian Act was Michael Dalton's instructions for justices of the peace, *The countrey justice*, first published in 1618 and reprinted regularly until at least 1635: Farnworth directed his readers to pp. 103–04 of Dalton's work.

[85] Richard Farnworth, *Moses message to Pharaoh* [n.p., 1653], STC F491B, p. 11.

along with numerous scriptural citations. Thus in both an account of suf-
ferings in Yorkshire, and in a prophetic work, Farnworth emphasised that
the Marian Act was being misused to silence the Quakers. In another tract,
God's covenanting with his people, which was addressed to the Council of
State, the caretaker government established by Cromwell prior to the calling of Barebones, Farnworth transcribed in full the Marian Act under which
Quakers were arrested. He also cited the Elizabethan statutes which repealed
Marian religious legislation, noting darkly that the 'Priests' of Farnworth's
day were running 'to Queen Maries Law, for the upholding of Mass . . . Pass-
ing by Queen Elizabeths . . . who stood up for truth, as it doth appear'.[86]
He then reproached ministers and magistrates for using 'unrighteous Laws
to imprison the righteous':

> Never let it be said to the people in other Nations, that the Ministry of Christ, as it
> is said to be, is upheld by a Popish Law; It will open the mouth of blasphemers, to
> cry out against you, that there should be not other Reformation Yet, but what was
> left upon record by the Papists.[87]

By actually transcribing the statutes in question, Farnworth put into practice
radical arguments that the laws of England should be written in English and
available to all. In this, Farnworth was operating in the context of real and
immediate political debate. In July, his northern colleague William West was
appointed to the Barebones law committee, and in August to the more radical
committee to consider a 'new Body of the Law'.[88] In another tract originally
published as a part of *God's covenanting*, Farnworth urged the 'heads and
Rulers of the people':

> to take away that unrighteous Law, or Statute made by Queen Mary, which the
> Priests . . . make their refuge . . . Let such Laws be established as tend to the punish-
> ment of evil doers, and countenancing those that do well . . . Let truth be declared
> freely by any one where it is made manifest; Who art thou that would limit the holy
> one of Israel by thy carnal mind?[89]

The whole of *God's covenanting with his people* can be read as more explicitly political than Farnworth's other works. Addressed to the Council of
State, and urging 'you that are set up' to establish 'righteous Laws, Statutes,
and Ordinances', Farnworth argued that laws should be God's Law, 'according to the Scripture'.[90] In the time of Moses, laws were not set up for the

---

[86] Farnworth, *God's covenanting with his people*, pp. 47–48.   [87] *Ibid.*, pp. 44–45.
[88] Woolrych, *Commonwealth to Protectorate*, pp. 265, 270.
[89] Richard Farnworth, *The general good to all people* (London, 1653), STC F483, p. 6. *The general good* and *God's covenanting* were probably published as one tract. In the Thomason Collection, *The general good* is catalogued as E703(6) and *God's covenanting* as E703(6*). *The general good* is paginated continuously from pp. 1 to 30, sigs. A–EV. *God's covenanting* is paginated pp. 33–51, sigs. E2r–G4r.
[90] Farnworth, *God's covenanting*, p. 34.

righteous, Farnworth wrote, but 'for the wicked, for the transgressors, for the Lawless, and disobedient'. The magistrate was a minister of God, cutting down 'Pride, Covetousness, Lust, and Revenge, Lying and Ungodliness . . . having the power of Godliness ruling in him, which worketh a Reformation'.[91] The Judges and Officers set up by Moses feared God, and knew his Law: they were to 'judge righteous Judgement', were not to respect persons, 'but hear the cause of the poor as well as the great', and were not to take gifts or rewards.[92] 'Let your Laws and Officers be according to the Scriptures', Farnworth warned the heads of the nation; 'Let every cause be heard in plainness of speech.'[93]

THE INAUGURATION OF THE PROTECTORATE

On 12 December 1653, alarmed by the increasingly fractious and radical atmosphere in the Barebones Parliament, conservative members of Parliament resigned their authority to Oliver Cromwell; on 16 December, Cromwell was sworn in as Protector; two weeks later the *Instrument of Government* was formally published as the new constitution.[94] Alan Cole and other scholars have seen the inauguration of the Protectorate as a watershed for the nascent Quaker movement, marking the moment of their alienation and withdrawal from worldly politics.[95] While it is clearly the case that Quakers were scornful of the 'Protector so called', it would seem rather that it was in response to the fall of Barebones and the advent of the Protectorate that the Quaker movement became fully mobilised as a genuinely national movement, and even emerged as an oppositional force to the government.[96] George Thomason obtained a steady flow of Quaker tracts from October 1653 onwards and it becomes more difficult to describe the circulation of tracts in London in terms of a clearly political chronology. However, the growing volume of print was integrated into a wider political campaign, as Quaker leaders began to appear in London in person from late 1653 onwards, lobbying members of Parliament and Oliver Cromwell, and orchestrated a national preaching mission over the summer of 1654 during the elections to the first Protectorate Parliament.

Personal contact between northern Quaker ministers and members of Parliament was made for the first time in November 1653, as the Barebones

[91] *Ibid.*, pp. 39–40.   [92] *Ibid.*, p. 41.   [93] *Ibid.*, p. 43.
[94] Woolrych, *Commonwealth to Protectorate*, pp. 312–64; Peter Gaunt, 'Drafting the Instrument of Government, 1653–54: a reappraisal,' *Parliamentary History* 8: 1 (1989), 28–42.
[95] Cole, 'The Quakers and politics', p. 26.
[96] Anthony Pearson mentioned 'an ordinance of the protector so called' in a letter to Edward Burrough, 21 February 1654, Sw Mss 3: 35. The letter continued in code and mentioned the interception of two Quaker books.

Parliament became increasingly radical in its proposed legislation to abolish lay tithes.[97] Again, initial contact was made between Quaker ministers in the north and army members: from Yorkshire, Richard Farnworth reported that Captain Stoddard 'is gone up to London againe', and that Benjamin Nicholson was 'in the south'.[98] In November, Judge Thomas Fell was again in London, followed later in the same month by Gervase Benson. Benson reported to Nayler and Fox that Quakers were already well known in the capital, suggesting that their publications had already made an impact there. Many people in London were 'enquireinge after frends in the north and the truth made manifest in you', as well as 'much writeinge for and against the preists'.[99] Benson was unimpressed by the atmosphere in London, complaining, 'I find nothinge here that I can have any fellowshippe with.' Although 'a light' was 'raising up' in many, and causing them to speak out against the 'carnal acteings both of Majestrates and Ministers', when he attended a meeting in the company of like-minded Parliament men and ministers, Benson was appalled, and felt obliged to 'declare against their practises at such meetings and to show them their meetings weare not for the better but for the worse they spendinge their tyme in puttinge questions one to another and janglings about things they could not witnes'.[100] Accordingly, Benson stopped attending 'such meetings', resorting instead to writing 'a few proposalls to some members of parliament, which by the goodnes of the lord weare finished this morneing', and the heads of which he sent back to Nayler and Fox.[101]

Although Benson's proposals are no longer extant, a number of Quaker publications circulated in the capital in the autumn and winter of 1653, most of them addressed to Parliament or the rulers of England. As before, the key concern of the authors was to present details of Quaker prosecutions in the localities. A tract by Anthony Pearson, addressed to the 'The Parliament of the Commonwealth of England' and obtained by Thomason on 3 October 1653, provided a list of Quaker prisoners in the north of England, giving the dates and stated causes of their arrests.[102] '[A]rise, stand up and execute Justice and Judgement, that you may be hid in the day of the Lords fierce wrath, which is at hand', Pearson warned his 'Christian Friends' in Parliament.[103] Whereas Farnworth had emphasised the iniquity of the 'popish' Marian Act,

---

[97] Margaret James, 'The political importance of the tithes controversy in the English revolution, 1640–60', *History* 26 (1941), esp. 12–15. James demonstrates that concern over tithes was shared by groups and writers other than the Quakers at this time.

[98] Richard Farnworth to George Fox [November 1653], Sw Mss 3: 52.

[99] Gervase Benson to George Fox and James Nayler, 29 November 1653, Sw Mss 4: 32.

[100] *Ibid.*   [101] *Ibid.*

[102] Anthony Pearson, *To the parliament of the common-wealth of England* [n.p., 1653], STC P992, pp. 3–5.

[103] *Ibid.*, p. 1.

Pearson opposed any magisterial interference in religion. Many of the prisoners named had been committed 'for disturbing a priest', and others had been fined for not removing their hats, and subsequently imprisoned when they refused to pay the fine.[104] By highlighting the variety and pettiness of the charges against Quakers, Pearson argued that magisterial regulation of religion was both ineffective and inappropriate. Not one of the prisoners named, Pearson insisted, had been 'committed for a vice', but because they would not 'put off their hats, no not to a Magistrate'. Here Pearson turned to the proper role of the godly magistracy: to punish vice and wickedness, to act justly and to protect the innocent from evil-doers. Yet the magistrate's power should not extend to 'the life of all Religion'; and Pearson went on to discuss the problematic nature of magisterial interference in religion, arguing that the right to oppose erroneous preaching was essential:

The Priest many times speaks those things, to which, if a present answer might be made, before the peoples minds and memories were distracted with a multitude of vain Notions, the truth might be made manifest, and things that differ discerned.[105]

The main argument for forbidding the interruption of church services which Pearson had encountered was that Quaker interventions bred 'tumults and distraction among the people'; yet for Pearson it was precisely the popular hostility against Quakers and others which the magistrate should properly curb. 'Let the Magistrate look to his duty to punish him that breaks the Peace, or offers violence to any' argued Pearson; but questioned: 'why doth the the Magistrate interpose his Authority to hold up their false worship, and not suffer the Messengers of the Lord to call people to the truth?'[106]

The importance of the immediacy of experience in Quaker religious belief thus took on a political edge in Pearson's work. The individual experiences of prisoners in gaols across the north of England were presented to Parliament as a compelling argument for political legislation. The very publication of Pearson's evidence should force members of Barebones to act: 'Here you are brought to a strait, look to it', yet he also urged the importance of members acting in accordance with their conscience in order to enjoy political legitimacy: 'For as you deal in this matter, so shall you be established.' 'I have done my duty, the sin lyes at your door; Do what seems good to you; consider scruples of conscience are not obvious to every mans reason, if they were, no liberty need be pleaded for tender consciences.'[107]

Other tracts circulated in London towards the end of 1653 made similar points. In a set of papers published and 'intended to have been delivered to every member of Parliament' in November 1653, George Fox denounced the use of both the Marian and Blasphemy Acts, and accused England's rulers of

[104] *Ibid.*, pp. 3–5.   [105] *Ibid.*, p. 6.   [106] *Ibid.*, p. 6.   [107] *Ibid.*, p. 8.

'makeing Lawes in your wils and mindes contrary to this in the Conscience, and above this in the Conscience', and advised them 'to wait upon the Lord, that you may receive the Law of God'.[108] Shortly after the installation of the Protectorate on 16 December 1653, George Thomason obtained another tract in which Fox argued that the Commonwealth governments had failed because there had been insufficient change: 'the same Teachers are standing that were in the time of the King, and the same that were in the time of the Bishops, and many of these are and have been your Counsellers, and the same that held up the Rails, Crosses and Pictures, are standing still'.[109] Fox also enumerated the reforms necessary for the creation of a truly godly commonwealth, in which all 'Heads, Rulers, Judges, Justices and Constables' should fear the Lord.[110] None should be put to death for theft, for this was contrary to the Law of God. Office-holders should not be 'covetous', for they would work for their own ends, nor should they be proud, as they would seek honour from their offices. Justices should not receive money for judging; this would encourage corruption, and the Law should be 'known in every mans language, so every man shall know when he is a transgressor'. People in every town should be able to work or be maintained. Every constable should 'have the law committed to him' in order that he might tell it to the people. Office-holders should not be drunkards; there should be no gambling, drinking of toasts, cock-fighting, bull-baiting, bear-baiting or holy-days 'for these are times of sporting and wantonnes, and filthy pleasures'. Fox (always bearing in mind the needs of the itinerant preacher) also argued that there should be 'no Ale-houses but such as keep lodging for travellers; for they nourish up young and old people to vanity'.[111] He charged 'rulers' to print no more 'ballads nor jesting books,' 'for they stir up lightness and wantonness, and gather the people together to exercise their minds in that which drawes from God'.[112] Fox thus presented a systematic, familiar programme for the furthering of the reformation, which developed into a specific call to the government: 'And call in all your Acts which you have given forth concerning religion, lest you lay it upon them where the seed of God is raised up: And you be found fighters against God'.[113]

THE PROTECTORATE

Following the installation of Oliver Cromwell as Lord Protector, there is evidence of greater Quaker mobilisation on a national scale, as ministers began in a more systematic way to present their views to the political nation,

---

[108] Nayler, *A lamentation*, pp. 13–14.
[109] George Fox, *Newes coming up out of the north sounding towards the south* London (for Giles Calvert), 1654 (21 December 1653), *STC* F1867, p. 19.
[110] *Ibid.*, p. 22.   [111] *Ibid.*, pp. 22–23.   [112] *Ibid.*, p. 23.   [113] *Ibid.*

through sustained lobbying and a national preaching campaign, supported by an increasing volume of printed tracts. In early February 1654, a meeting of several key Quaker ministers was held at the home of Anthony Pearson; later that month Pearson wrote a letter to Edward Burrough which was highly suggestive of political activity, complaining that he had been busy 'in pursuance of an ordinance of the protector so called and his Councell', and warning Burrough that manuscripts he had been carrying to the press had been intercepted. Pearson completed his letter in code, promising, 'when I see thee again I shall tell thee what is not convenient herein to be written'.[114] In March 1654, two senior Quaker ministers, John Camm and Francis Howgill, travelled to London where they met with Cromwell, as well as with key sectarian leaders in the capital and the publisher Giles Calvert. In their meeting with Cromwell they reiterated much of what was already in print, complaining 'of Maries acte', which Cromwell 'vinicated much': generally, Howgill concluded, there was 'a cuninge and suttel Fox and a Serpent in him that we could git nothing fastened upon his conscience'.[115] Accounts of this meeting were duly published, thus presenting in an immediately political context much of what had already been argued in print and orally.[116] (See Plates 11 and 12.)

It has already been suggested that the large meeting held at Pearson's house in February, and Camm and Howgill's trip to London in the spring, may well have been preparing the ground for a national preaching campaign which coincided with the first parliamentary elections of the Protectorate. As has been seen already, Quaker ministers from Lancashire and Westmorland, well supplied with printed tracts, undertook extensive itinerant preaching from June onwards, and convened in London in August and September, while those from Yorkshire, with George Fox, converged on the Midlands.[117] Fox himself wrote a tract addressed 'To the Parliament of England' which was in circulation as the Parliament first assembled.[118] (See Plate 13.) At the end of August 1654, just days before the meeting of the first Protectorate

---

[114] Anthony Pearson to Edward Burrough, 21 February 1654, Sw Mss 3:35. The intercepted papers included George Fox's *A paper sent forth into the world from them that are scornfully called Quakers* (London, 1654), which was later published by Giles Calvert and dated by Thomason on 16 March 1654, and Edward Burrough's *A warning from the Lord to the inhabitants of Underbarrow* (London, 1654), eventually published by Calvert and dated by Thomason 12 April 1654.

[115] Francis Howgill and John Camm to George Fox, 27 March 1654, A. R. Barclay Mss 2:127, fol. 2.

[116] John Camm, *This was the word of the Lord* (London, 1654), STC C392, copy dated by Thomason 8 April; and Camm, *Some particulars concerning the law, sent to Oliver Cromwell* (London, 1654), STC C391, copy dated by Thomason 9 June.

[117] See above, Chapter 2.

[118] George Fox, *A message from the Lord to the Parliament of England* (London, 1654), STC F1863; Thomason dated his copy 15 September.

22

THIS
Was the word of the Lord which

Iohn Camm, φ
AND

Francis Howgill
Was moved to declare and write
TO
OLIVER CROMWELL,
Who is named *Lord-Protector* :

Shewing the caufe why they came to fpeak to
him : and fhewing that they came not to petition
him for any thing , but for the welfare of *Sion*,
and for the righteous feeds fake; and that thofe Laws
which were given forth by the will of man, may be
taken away ; that the Law may go forth of *Sion*, and the
Word of the Lord from *Jerufalem*; and fo the Kingdoms
of the world may become the Kingdom of *Chrift*.

He that hath an ear, let him hear. Rev. 3. 13.

LONDON,
Printed, *Anno Dom.* 1654.

April . 8 . 1654

Plate 11. John Camm and Francis Howgill, *This was the word of the Lord*
(London, 1654), STC c392.

A

Meſſage from the Lord,

TO THE

Parliament

OF

ENGLAND.

That you may all take warning, and be
ye all forewarned, that you act not in the ſteps
of your forefathers, whom the Lord hath caſt out
as an abominable thing, as he hath done all Rulers in all Ages
and Generations, which have ſought themſelves, and eſtabliſhed Laws in
their own wills, whereby the Juſt have ſuffered, and now do ſuffer : The
people which the Lord hath choſen are trodden upon, and the Powers of
the Earth have ſet themſelves againſt the mighty power of the Lord in them.
But now is the Lord ariſing to plead the cauſe of the Juſt, and woe for ever
to all *Sions* Adverſaries.

By him who is a Lover of your ſouls, and a Lover of Iſraels Common-wealth, whom the Lord is returning out of captivity, to
ſerve him in their own Land in perfect freedom.

G E O. F O X. *ỹ Goofe*

*And the Lord ſhall utterly deſtroy the tongue of the Egyptian Sea, and with his
mighty wind ſhall ſhake his hand over the River, and ſhall ſmite it in the ſeven
ſtreams, and make men go over dryſhod,* Iſa. 11. 15.
*And there ſhall be an High-way for the remnant of his people, which ſhall be left
from* Aſſyria, *like as it was to Iſrael, in the day that he came up out of the Land
of Egypt, ver.* 16.

London, Printed in the Year, 1654.

Plate 12. George Fox, *A message from the Lord to the Parliament of England*
(London, 1654), *STC* F1863 sig. A.

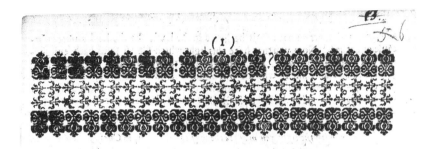

(1)

✤ few Words
To all JUDGES, JUSTICES, and
Ministers of the LAW in
ENGLAND.

From ANTHONY PEARSON.

July 16 1654

TO the Judges of life and death, and Judges of *Nisi prius*, as they call
it, who give oathes to Juftices, Juries and witneffes, and Juftices that give
oathes to Conftables and others. To the light which Chrift Jefus hath enlightned you withal, I fpeake, that with it you may fee you are out of the doctrine
of Chrift, who faith, *Swear not at all, in all your communications let your yea be
yea, and your nay be nay; whatfoever is more, is evil.* So you that fwear are in the
evil, and with the light of Chrift Jefus, you may fee that you be out of the doctrine
of the Apoftle, who faid, my brethren ; fwear not at all, not by heaven, not by
earth, nor any other oath, left you fall into condemnation of the divel; fo you
that fwear are fallen into the condemnation of the divel, and you that caufe o-
thers to fweate, or compel them, or imprifon them, or fine them if they will
not, you are out of the doctrine of Chrift and the Apoftle your felves, and
feek to bring others out of his doctrine, into the fame condemnation of the
divel where you are. Praifed be God, with the light which comes from Chrift,
you are feene to be no brethren of Chrift, who are out of his doctrine, and doth
not doe his will. I am the light of the world, and doth enlighten every one
that comes into the world faith Chrift; now every one loving this light which
Chrift Jefus hath enlightned you withal ; it will bring you to doe his will, and
know his doctrine ; and then in all your communications you will be kept to yea

A   and

Plate 13. Anthony Pearson, *A few words to all judges, justices, and ministers of the
law in England* (London, 1654), STC p988, sig. A.

Parliament, Gervase Benson attended a 'very great meeting of freinds', 'from severall places of the Nation', at Synderhall Green, Derbyshire, reporting the presence of Captain Stoddard from London, Captain William Bradford and 'several other Captaines'. This was obviously a prearranged meeting of some significance: George Fox was reported to have 'sent for some Ranters from severall places to come to him'.[119] At the same time, Thomas Aldam sent a letter to Captain Stoddard, requesting him to deliver two letters in person to Oliver Cromwell relating to the legal prosecution of Quakers.[120] Contact with the army continued as the Quaker movement spread. Thomas Aldam and George Fox had two more meetings with Captain William Bradford in Yorkshire in late October 1654.[121] In Bristol, John Audland and John Camm held meetings at the house of Captain Edward Pyott.[122]

Contact with army officers was significant. The meeting of the first Protectorate Parliament in September 1654 provoked widespread discussion, and political unease, at the constitutional implications of the Instrument of Government, which increased the authority of Cromwell and the Council of State and diminished the standing of Parliament. The Leveller John Wildman drew up a petition with Colonels Okey, Saunders and Alured protesting at the placing of the army under the control of Cromwell and the Council of State at times when Parliament was not meeting.[123] At around the same time, in early September, Wildman and the three Colonels held meetings in London plotting more serious insurrection, involving Major-General Robert Overton, the former governor of Hull who was now in command of the army in the north of Scotland.[124] The potential for contact with Quaker leaders in this plot is striking. The London meetings were attended not only by Anthony Pearson, but also by George Bishop, who had stood as a Bristol candidate in the parliamentary elections; Arthur Haselrig, with whom Pearson was still acquainted, was also associated with the plot.[125] Quakers had known Robert Overton since George Fox stayed in his house in 1652.[126] They were also preaching among army garrisons in Scotland from late 1654 onwards. Wildman's plot is also echoed in the large meeting held at Swannington in Leicestershire in January 1655, attended by Quaker leaders from London, Bristol, Cambridge and York, which was discovered and broken up

---

[119] Gervase Benson to Margaret Fell [1654], Sw Ms 4: 35. Geoffrey Nuttall dates this letter 'after 25 August 1654', and from internal evidence it cannot have been written after the middle of September at the latest.
[120] Thomas Aldam to Oliver Cromwell, 29 August 1654, Portfolio 1: 5.
[121] Thomas Aldam to Margaret Fell, 30 October 1654, Sw Mss 4: 89.
[122] Audland's Journal, 20 September 1654, p. 34.
[123] Gardiner, *Commonwealth and Protectorate*, vol. III, pp. 211–13.   [124] *Ibid.*, p. 228.
[125] *Ibid.*, pp. 228–32.   [126] *Journal of George Fox*, vol. I, p. 32.

by agents of the Protector, and at which Quakers were reported to Cromwell to be armed with pistols.[127]

Thus many of the organisational developments within the movement itself, from the holding of large gatherings of Quaker ministers to the timing of preaching campaigns and the circulation of printed tracts, suggest a politically significant chronology to the movement's growth which forces us to modify the assumption that Quakers were outside mainstream political life and significant only as a marginal group of mystics.[128] Henry Cromwell, acting Lord Deputy of Ireland, warned John Thurloe against precisely this assumption in February 1656, remarking of the Quakers in Ireland: 'Some thinke them to have noe designe, but I am not of that opinion. Their counterfeited simplicitie renders them to me the more dangerous', and went on to report that the republican Sir Henry Vane 'goes up and downe amongst these people and others, endeavouringe to withdrawe them from their submission to the present government'.[129]

The role of print within such a politically engaged movemement was highly important. The authorities were quick to connect Quaker printing with suspected sedition. It was reported to Cromwell that a printer, later identified as Giles Calvert, was present at the Swannington meeting in January 1655, and that six of the Quaker leaders were 'constantly writing' and 'have lett droppe words of ill favour amongst the people frequently'; the following month in February 1655, Calvert's shop was said to have been ransacked by the authorities.[130] In January 1656 Major General Goffe informed John Thurloe that George Fox and 'two more eminent northerne quakers' were in Hampshire, 'doing much worke for the devill', and 'att the same time there are base bookes against the lord protector disperst among the churches'.[131]

Despite the authorities' alarm, however, relatively few of the Quaker publications were concerned explicitly with issues of national political

---

[127] Wildman's plot had also featured meetings to be held in Leicestershire in January 1655. Gardiner, *Commonwealth and Protectorate*, vol. III, p. 30; Thomas Birch (ed.), *A collection of the State Papers of John Thurloe* (7 vols., London, 1742), vol. III, pp. 94, 116.

[128] See Derek Hirst's suggestion that Freud rather than Marx is appropriate for the interpretation of religious radicals in the 1650s, Hirst, *Authority and conflict England 1603–1658* (London, 1986), p. 289; also Barry Reay, 'Popular hostility towards Quakers in mid-seventeenth-century England', *Social History* 5 (1980), *passim*.

[129] Birch (ed.), *State Papers of John Thurloe*, vol. IV, pp. 508–09.

[130] Birch (ed.) *State Papers of John Thurloe*, vol. III, pp. 94, 116; John Hetet, 'A literary underground in restoration England: printers and dissenters in the context of constraint, 1660–89', unpublished Ph.D thesis, University of Cambridge, 1987, p. 130; George Taylor to Margaret Fell, 26 February 1655, Sw. Mss 1: 214. Disruption to Quaker publishing around February 1655 is further indicated by the fact that George Thomason failed to obtain any Quaker tracts during February, and only one in January 1655. This compares with the thirteen he obtained in March 1655.

[131] Birch (ed.), *State Papers of John Thurloe*, vol. IV, p. 408.

significance, and, before 1659, none offered specific constitutional proposals.[132] From as early as 1653, a pattern had been established whereby accounts of local confrontations with magistrates were published, and, at appropriate moments, these appeared as addresses or warnings to national government. The content of these publications was remarkably consistent throughout this period: Quaker authors continued to protest about specific legislation, urged the need to establish a truly godly magistracy, and stressed the importance of recourse to conscience in governing. However, the ways in which these printed tracts were used and presented suggest that Quakers were indeed involved in debates with profound constitutional implications. Local accounts of trials, or pleas to national government, were clearly intended to inform wider audiences of the judicial and legislative context in which Quakers were prosecuted. The fact that Gervase Benson went to court armed with copies of the relevant statutes, and handed them out to bystanders after the trial, indicates that Quaker leaders were keen to foster informed debate with magistrates about their judicial and constitutional legitimacy. The circulation of such information in print would serve to magnify the potential for such debate. In the summer of 1654, at the height of the national preaching campaign, Anthony Pearson addressed a tract to all 'Judges, Justices, and Ministers of the law in England' which outlined his objections to swearing oaths, prosecuting itinerant preachers as vagabonds, and enforcing the payment of tithes (See Plate 13).[133]

It is clear, therefore, that tracts addressed to national government were in fact intended to inform much wider audiences. Very few publications were addressed exclusively to political leaders. More frequently, specific sections only of tracts were addressed to the 'heads' or rulers of England; and such addresses often appeared inside the tracts rather than emblazoned on the frontispiece.[134] Quaker authors specifically resisted petitioning or appealing to political leaders in print and indeed were well able to communicate with

---

[132] Anthony Pearson, *To the parliament of the common-wealth of England* [London] 1653, STC P992; George Fox, *A message from the Lord to the parliament of England* (London, 1654), STC F1863; George Fox, *This for each parliament-man* (London, 1656), STC F1933. Rather more generically, see Fox, *To all the magistrates and governors in the whole world* ([London], 1656), STC F1871, and Henry Clark, *England's lessons, set to be learned by her rulers* (London, 1656), STC C4454.

[133] Anthony Pearson, *A few words to all judges, justices, and ministers of the law in England* (London, 1654), STC P988, pp. 1–8. Thomason obtained his copy on 16 July 1654.

[134] See, for example, William Dewsbery, *A true prophecy of the mighty day of the Lord which is appeared in the north of England* (London, 1654), STC D1279, p. 6; Richard Farnworth, *A discovery of truth and falsehood* (London, 1653), STC F479A, pp. 34–35; Farnworth, *The generall-good to all people* (London, 1653), STC F483, Farnworth, *Moses message to Pharaoh* [London], (1653), STC F491B, p. 1; Margaret Fell, *False Prophets, antichrists, deceivers* (London, 1655), STC F631, Christopher Fell, *A few words to the people of England* ([London], 1655), STC F840, p. 8; George Fox, *Newes coming up out of the north sounding towards the south* (London, 1654), STC F1867, Fox, *A word from the Lord to*

political leaders through private letters or meetings.[135] Personal meetings and letters were not unusual. The Lancashire-born Quaker, Leonard Fell, met Cromwell in March 1655 and gave him a paper, 'soe I cleared my selfe of that which had long laid upon me'.[136] These private letters were mainly concerned with individual cases of wrongful imprisonment: Thomas Aldam's letter to Cromwell in August 1654 was concerned with a legal fine.[137] In December 1654, George Taylor, the manager of the Kendal Fund, advised Margaret Fell to change the wording of a letter to Cromwell, suggesting that one clause of the letter 'which is spoken in the general (as we etc.)' should be changed to the particular, since 'putinge that in the particuler will binde out all Cavills that might be made'.[138] It is remarkable that an ironmonger should advise a gentlewoman on the wording of a letter to the Protector, affirming Kunze's argument that Margaret Fell's gentry status was on occasion subsumed below her gender; but suggesting also that George Taylor, as the chief scribe and co-ordinator of Quaker papers, was well acquainted with the wording of letters to Cromwell.[139] His concern that a letter in the 'particuler' would 'binde out all Cavills' suggests a hesitancy to petition Cromwell in the collective name of Quakers. Taylor was also concerned with the delivery of the letter to Cromwell, suggesting that they should send it by post: 'and write two words in the end of it of excuse in case he have received the same formerly, and date it from Swarthmoor, that wee have friends enough that wold have that care and Couriage to deliver it to him'.[140] Taylor did not want Fell's letter to be devalued by its unwarranted

---

all the world, and all professors in the world, spoken in parables (London, 1654), STC F1991A, p. 8; [Richard Hubberthorne, *A true testimony of obedience to the heavenly call* ([London], 1654), STC H3239, pp. 3–4; James Nayler, *Churches gathered against Christ and his kingdom* ([London], 1654), STC N267, p. 17; Nayler, *A few words occasioned by a paper lately printed*. ([London], 1654), STC N279, pp. 19–20; Nayler, *A lamentacion (by one of Englands Prophets) over the ruines of this oppressed nacion*. (n.p., 1654), STC N292, pp. 1, 12, 20; Nayler, *The power and glory of the Lord shining out of the north* (London, 1653), STC N302, pp. 12–15; Nayler, *Several petitions answered that were put up by the priests of Westmorland* (London, 1653), STC N316A, sig. A3v; Martha Simmonds, *A lamentation for the lost sheep of the House of Israel* (London, 1655), STC S3791, p. 4; Thomas Stubbs, *A call into the way to the kingdom* (London, 1655), STC S6084, p. 9; Christopher Taylor, *The whirlwind of the Lord gone forth as a fiery flying roule* (London, 1655), STC T268, sig. Ar; Francis Ellington, *A true discovery of the ground of the imprisonment of Francis Ellington, Thomas Cocket and Edward Ferman* (London, 1655), STC T2683, p. 8; George Whitehead, *The path of the just cleared* (London, 1655), STC W1944, pp. 17, 18–19.

135 Alan Cole, 'The Quakers and politics', p. 55, n. 1.
136 Leonard Fell to Margaret Fell, 31 March 1655, Sw Mss 1: 120.
137 Thomas Aldam to Oliver Cromwell, 29 August 1654, Portfolio 1: 5.
138 George Taylor to Margaret Fell, 25 December 1654, Sw Mss 1: 211.
139 Bonnelyn Young Kunze, 'Religious authority and social status in seventeenth-century England: the friendship of Margaret Fell, George Fox, and William Penn', *Church History* 57: 2 (1988), 170–86.
140 Taylor to Fell, 25 December 1654, Sw Mss 1: 211.

duplication before Cromwell. Thus Quaker leaders were able to approach political leaders on matters of individual redress in private; and access to Cromwell seems to have been quite straightforward. On another occasion, Margaret Fell charged John Stubbs with forwarding a letter 'to Oliver, which I would have thee git carfully Convaied to him, ther is Sarvants in his house that is freinds, if it can be saftly gotten to any of them . . . its like they will gett it to him'.[141]

Thus personal communication with political leaders about the resolution of individual cases, or even the expression of broader political concerns, was relatively straightforward. Print, by definition, was a public medium, intended to foster widespread political debate and activity. In their tracts, Quaker authors frequently asserted their political credentials by emphasising their loyalty to the parliamentary cause in the 1640s. A published declaration of 1653, addressed to the Parliament and Army of the Commonwealth, stated that its 329 signatories had been 'faithful to the Parliament, and serviceable in their places to this Commonwealth, to the hazard of their Lives, Liberties and Estates'. Their constant prosecution by local magistrates eager to 'deprive them of that Liberty which the Parliament hath afforded' was carried out by 'several got into the Commission of the peace, formerly Malignants, and some that have been actually in Arms against the Parliament, contrary to the Act of Parliament'.[142] The subscribers of the declaration not only asserted their political credentials over those of their local magistrates, but specifically reminded their readers that their 'dear Brother James Nayler', imprisoned in Appleby gaol, 'served the Parliament under the Command of Major General Lambert, betwixt eight and nine years, as we believe some of the Army can witness'.[143]

Other Quaker authors made reference to their military service in the civil wars, most often in accounts of the cross-examining which took place at their trials; and sometimes in accounts of their religious awakening. William Dewsbery explained to Northamptonshire magistrates that he had not finished his apprenticeship because he went 'into the service for the Parliament'; Dewsbery's colleague John Whitehead prefaced an account of his own sufferings in Northamptonshire with a religious testimony which included his army service to Parliament.[144] At the end of John Stubbs's account of his trial at Maidstone in Kent, he emphasised his loyalty to Parliament's cause,

---

[141] Margaret Fell to John Stubbs, 1656, Spence Mss 3: 40.
[142] *Several petitions answered, that were put up by the priests of Westmorland* (London, 1653), STC N316A, pp. 61–63 [mispaginated, sigs. I3r–I4r.]
[143] *Ibid.,* pp. 63–64 [mispaginated; sigs. I4r-I4v].
[144] William Dewsbery, *A discovery of the ground from whence persecution did arise* (London, 1655), STC D1266, p. 11; John Whitehead, *The enmitie between the two seeds* (London, 1655), STC W1975, pp. 3, 7.

presenting his personal sacrifices in mockery of criticisms levied at Quakers who abandoned their families and livelihoods for the sake of their ministry:

> you have been warned by one who have felt and born the Bishops and prelats rigour over the Conscience by them then, suffered the loss of Liberty, Friends, Means, and all outward, dear and near Relation whatsoever, not onely so, but travelled many years in the Parliaments Army, through much Scarcity, Watchfulness, Dangers, Perills, many cold Stormy nights and Dayes; for severall Years past over my head, much pretious time spent, WIFE and small CHILDREN forsaken, and LIFE Engaged many times in the WAR, yet in the midst of the greatest straits and extremities still hoping a DAY of FREEDOME would come, and not to be thus rewarded by this POWER which is now in being, for which I have beene made willing for many YEARS past, to sustaine the loss of all to do him good to my utmost against HIS and the NATIONS ENEMIES, and now to be thus served a poor REQUITALL, what EVIL have I done, let that in the CONSCIENCE speak.[145]

John Stubbs and his co-religionists were thus keen to advertise their past military service as a means of establishing their political credibility and justification in questioning the actions of the government.[146] Other Quaker authors also defined themselves in clearly political terms, albeit in opposition to the Rump Parliament or the Protectorate: a group of Quaker prisoners at Kendal in 1653 identified themselves as the 'free born of England'; Edward Burrough, writing in 1657, styled himself 'a friend to England's Commonwealth'.[147]

In addition to claiming political identities for themselves, Quaker authors also located their audiences within the body politic, addressing not only Parliament, the army or the Council of State, but crucially also the people of England. Indeed the elision between the government and the people of England in Quaker tracts suggests strongly that their authors sought to achieve widespread political participation through the medium of print. In a set of papers published and 'intended to have been delivered to every member of Parliament' in November 1653, James Nayler expressed his disappointment with the Barebones experiment: 'the People to whom Oppression and Unrighteousness hath been a Burden, have long waited for Deliverance, from

---

[145] John Stubbs and William Caton, *A true declaration of the bloody proceedings of the men in Maidstone* (London, 1655), STC s6072, p. 5.

[146] The Quaker leaders' army roots have been recognised for some time, but the denominational significance of the 1661 Peace Testimony, and the subsequent association of Quakers with pacifism, has obscured the widespread everyday association of Quakers and soldiers in the early years of the movement. See M. E. Hirst, *The Quakers in peace and war* (London, 1923); Barry Reay 'Early Quaker activity', pp. 57–62; Hill, *The world turned upside down*, pp. 241–42; Alan Cole, 'The Quakers and politics', pp. 16–36, who discusses how denominational historians have overemphasised the pacifism of the early Quakers.

[147] 'To the Major and Justices of Kendal', in Christopher Atkinson, *The standard of the Lord lifted up* (London, 1653), STC A4128, p. 31; Edward Burrough, *A just and lawful trial.* (London, 1657), STC B6008, sig. A. The naval captain Anthony Mellidge also wrote as the 'Free-born of England': see Reay, 'The Quakers, 1659, 194.

one year to another, but none comes, from one sort of men to another'.[148] Although Nayler's lamentation was intended to be 'deeply layd to heart by Parliament and Army', it was actually addressed to the people of England, whom Nayler held responsible for the failure of Barebones. The oppression of Nayler and his co-religionists was not performed 'by an open Enemy, for then it had not bin so strange', but 'by those who pretend to be against oppression; and for whom under that pretence thou hast adventured all that is dear unto thee, to put power into their hands . . . Are these not the choicest of thy Worthies, who are now in power?'[149]

The responsibility of the people for their government was made even more explicit in a tract by Christopher Fell written in 1655, which warned the 'people of England' that time was running out: 'many precious days of visitation hath the Lord thy God let thee see'. He reminded them that, in the time of the bishops and prelates, they had covenanted to overthrow their oppressors and persecution in England: 'was not this thy ingagement and promise O people of England, when thou wast under, and in distresse?'[150] Christopher Fell placed the responsibility for England with its people:

The Lord hath brought under thy feet the necks of them that did oppresse thee, and the Lord hath brought into thy power their Authority and their Laws, and subdued them all under thee, to the full request of that which then breathed under did desire . . . God will not be mocked with words nor shews, to the light of Christ in thy conscience look, and it will let thee see, that the same Laws which thou in thy adversity and lownesse didst promise to pull downe are standing still; are not oppressive Laws to compell men to pay Tithes to the maintaining of covetous hirelings and tithe mongers, standing as in great force as ever: . . . and this is not done by an enemy of thine, but even by thee who didst professe to be faithfull in performing thy Vowes to the Lord.[151]

Christopher Fell was thus clear that the 'authority' for the laws in England now rested with the people. Although his tract made no attempt to discuss the finer political or constitutional derivations of this position, Quaker pamphleteering was its practical epitome, urging audiences to challenge and debate with magistrates, and providing them with the legal and constitutional information necessary to do so.

In Quaker tracts, addresses to rulers were made through the voice of the inhabitants or the people of England. These tracts were handed out and read aloud at meetings in market squares, churchyards, and in the meeting houses of London and other towns. While explicitly informing audiences about

---

[148] James Nayler and George Fox, *A lamentation (by one of Englands prophets) over the ruines of this oppressed nation* (n.p., 1653), STC N292, p. 3. This was printed for Thomas Wayte in York, probably in December 1653. George Thomason dated his copy 27 January [1654].
[149] *Ibid.*, p. 4.
[150] Christopher Fell, *A few words to the people of England* [n.p., 1655], pp. 1–2.
[151] *Ibid.*, p. 3.

the ways in which religious liberties and social justice were being under-mined, Quaker publications also reinforced implicitly that the government of England was the responsibility of the people. Quaker authors did not intend, as did the petitions of ministers and magistrates, to persuade governments by their printed tracts. They intended instead to establish a programme for godly reformation which rested with the people of England. Individual religious and legal experience was the foundation of this wider programme. Individual experiences of injustice were transmuted, by the fact of publication, into wider, politicised objections at religious prosecution or ungodly magistracy taking place under the auspices of England's Commonwealth. By the same token, generic complaints against governmental injustice could then be applied by readers to their own experiences, and thus served to politicise the readership further. Quakers' tracts located their readers within the body politic, and demanded their participation in the establishment of a truly godly commonwealth.

8

The James Nayler crisis, 1656

In October 1656, James Nayler and a group of his followers were arrested by Bristol magistrates after staging a symbolic re-enactment of Christ's entrance into Jerusalem as a sign of the presence of Christ within everyone, and perhaps also of the imminence of the second coming of Christ.[1] Nayler was accused of having assumed 'the gesture, words, honour, worship and miracles of our blessed Saviour' as well as his 'names and incommunicable attributes and titles', and was ultimately brought before Parliament where, in December 1656, he was accused and convicted of blasphemy.[2] The *Nayler* case is well known, both for the ructions it caused within the Quaker movement, and for the constitutional problems it posed for the Protectorate. In many ways, it also neatly encapsulates many of the themes discussed in this book and provides a fitting conclusion. In the most obvious sense, the parliamentary examination of a leading Quaker for blasphemy afforded the movement its best opportunity yet to participate in a national debate about the achievement of religious liberty, and the Quakers' published response to Nayler's trial is an eloquent demonstration of how print constituted a central plank in their campaign. At the same time, the severe internal upheavals within the Quaker movement over the Nayler crisis provide further evidence of the impressively tight control Quaker leaders exercised over their publications: in the face of considerable internal uncertainty and division, the Quakers' printed output remained entirely cohesive and consistent. The *Nayler* case is a powerful example that the Quakers' use of print was highly focused, and the tool of a well-organised and purposeful movement. The following case-study reviews Nayler's trial from the perspective of the key themes of this book: first it will show how Quaker leaders viewed Nayler's trial as

---

[1] The most recent and comprehensive account of the *Nayler* case is by Leo Damrosch, *The sorrows of the Quaker Jesus: James Nayler and the puritan crackdown on the free spirit* (Cambridge, Mass., 1996); for a discussion of what his symbolic action meant, see esp. pp. 163–76. I would like to thank Professor John Morrill for reading and commenting upon an earlier draft of this chapter.

[2] *A complete collection of state trials* (6 vols., London, 1730), vol. I, p. 796.

the culmination of their campaign to argue for the political achievement of religious settlement, and acted accordingly; secondly it will show how the Quakers' accounts of the case were carefully controlled in order to suggest a coherent and unified response; and finally it will argue that the tight control wielded by a small handful of Quaker leaders over the movement's publications in the face of considerable internal crisis was a crucial feature of its development. Traumatic though the Nayler crisis undoubtedly was, Quaker leaders were able to incorporate it into a well-established pattern of publication: their impressive command of the press was a central feature of the early Quaker movement's political acuity.

The events surrounding the Nayler affair are well known.[3] James Nayler had been preaching in London since the summer of 1655 with great success; in particular he had become extremely adept in public disputations and by 1656 was undoubtedly the most prolific author of published disputes with the Quakers' opponents, an indication of his considerable authority.[4] His predominance in London was all the greater after Edward Burrough and Francis Howgill, the key Quaker ministers in the capital, left for a preaching mission in Ireland in the late summer of 1655, returning to London in the spring of 1656. Among London Quakers there was a substantial number of vociferous and active women preachers, which, as has been seen already, was often a source of anxiety for their male counterparts. In the summer of 1656, the preaching of Martha Simmonds in particular aroused the ire of Hubberthorne, Burrough and Howgill, and they wrote to her, warning that she and her followers were 'out of the power, out of the wisdom, and out of the Life of God'.[5] Martha Simmonds, the wife of the Quaker publisher Thomas Simmonds and sister of Giles Calvert, had already written a handful of tracts and was thus a Quaker minister of some renown and authority: Patricia Crawford has argued convincingly that the initial conflict with Hubberthorne, Burrough and Howgill was actually a leadership struggle between them and Martha Simmonds rather than James Nayler.[6] Following her rebuke, Simmonds turned to Nayler for support; Nayler initially

---

[3] The following account is drawn from Braithwaite, *The beginnings of Quakerism* (2nd edn, Cambridge, 1955), pp. 241–55; Patricia Crawford, *Women and religion in England 1500–1720* (London, 1993), pp. 160–78; Damrosch, *Sorrows of the Quaker Jesus*, pp. 115–76; William Bittle, *James Nayler 1618–1660: the Quaker indicted by Parliament* (York, 1986), 77–112.

[4] During the course of 1656 alone, Nayler wrote, or contributed to, over ten pamphlet disputes while Edward Burrough engaged in three and William Dewsbery in two. Over the course of the period 1652–56, Nayler wrote approximately half of all the printed exchanges between Quakers and their opponents.

[5] Markey Mss, 120–22, as cited in Patricia Crawford, *Women and religion in England 1500–1720* (London, 1993), p. 174.

[6] Martha Simmonds, *A lamentation for the lost sheep of the House of Israel* (London, 1655), STC s3791; Simmonds, *When the Lord Jesus came to Jerusalem* (n.p., 1655), STC s3794;

hesitated and then conceded that she acted with the power of God. There-after, Simmonds and her followers began addressing Nayler in increasingly Messianic language, while Nayler himself seems to have entered a period of deep spiritual anguish and indecision, to the consternation of his colleagues. Over the following weeks and months, deep rifts appeared within the move-ment; in London, different groups of Quakers pronounced their allegiance either to 'James' or to 'Edward and Francis'; and letters between Quaker min-isters demonstrate the acute concern felt over the behaviour of Nayler. When Nayler and his followers travelled to Bristol fair in July 1656, John Audland and Francis Howgill were sufficiently alarmed by his condition to send him for a meeting with George Fox, who had been imprisoned at Launceston gaol in Cornwall since January 1656. Nayler never reached Launceston but was apprehended and imprisoned at Exeter for travelling without a pass, and eventually it was Fox, released from Launceston in September, who visited Nayler in Exeter gaol. The confrontation between them is well known as a deeply symbolic leadership struggle, Nayler requesting reconciliation, Fox asking Nayler to kiss his foot in recognition of Fox's authority, and Nayler refusing to do so.

During the summer and autumn of 1656, Quaker ministers, although deeply concerned by Nayler's spiritual anguish, were primarily alarmed by the influence and authority wielded by Martha Simmonds, who, with her own entourage, accompanied Nayler to Bristol and thence to Exeter, also visiting Fox in gaol in Launceston where she 'exalted her selfe and Judged him'. In September, Richard Hubberthorne reported to Fell that Nayler was 'pretie low and tender' and that 'his hart was opened towards mee', but as soon as Simmonds 'in her filthines' appeared, Nayler became entirely 'sub-jecte to her'.[7] Walter Clements wrote that things were 'not soe well' with Nayler since his imprisonment at Exeter, 'Martha haveinge beene there with him'.[8] Accounts written at the time and subsequently have dismissed Martha Simmonds as mad, a witch, or a whore, and she has traditionally shouldered much of the blame for the temptation of James Nayler. More recent work by Patricia Crawford and Christine Trevett has modified this view, locat-ing Martha Simmonds's behaviour, and the reactions of her co-religionists, within the context of a highly gendered Quaker leadership struggle.[9] As Chapter 5 has shown, there were indeed considerable tensions and ambigui-ties within the movement surrounding the authority of Quaker women minis-ters, and Nayler's own spiritual crisis clearly stemmed from his recognition of

M. Simmonds, H. Stranger, J. Nayler and N. T., *O England thy time is come* [London, n.d.], STC s3793; Crawford, *Women and religion*, pp. 173–80.

[7] Richard Hubberthorne to Margaret Fell, Cornwall, 16 September 1656, Sw Trs 2: 597.
[8] Walter Clement to Margaret Fell, 4 October 1656, Sw Mss 1:180.
[9] Crawford, *Women and religion*, pp. 168–72.

Simmonds's religious authority. Nevertheless, Simmonds and her entourage regarded Nayler, not Simmonds, as the Messianic figure, and it was Nayler, widely regarded as a, if not the, leader of the Quaker movement, who ultimately bore the brunt of the responsibility and punishment for their actions.

On 12 October, Fox wrote to Nayler blaming him for the growing divisions in the Quaker movement and for his failure to condemn Simmonds and her followers. The rift between Fox and Nayler continued. Still in the company of Simmonds and her entourage, Nayler was released from Exeter in mid-October and the group travelled northeast across Somerset towards Bristol. Here, on Friday 24 October, they staged their symbolic re-enactment of Christ's entrance to Jerusalem, with Nayler apparently seated on horseback, and led by his group of followers as they sang 'Holy, holy, holy'. Upon their arrest by Bristol magistrates, Nayler was found to be carrying a number of letters, including one from two of his followers, Hannah and John Stranger, addressing him in Messianic terms as 'thou fairest of ten thousand' and the 'only begotten Son of God', and declaring 'Thy name is no more to be called James but Jesus.'[10] Members of the group were examined before Bristol magistrates, and Nayler's women followers continued to speak of Nayler in Messianic terms, Dorcas Erbury claiming that he had raised her from the dead.[11] The Bristol magistrates, unsure how to proceed, referred the matter to the second Protectorate Parliament, which had convened in September. On 31 October 1656 the House established a committee of fifty-five members to consider the 'great Misdemeanors and Blasphemies of James Nayler, and others, at Bristoll, and elsewhere . . . And likewise to look upon the Laws and Ordinances made against Blasphemy.'[12]

The transfer of the case to Westminster radically altered its significance. The decision to try Nayler before Parliament starkly exposed the paucity of the Protectorate's religious settlement, and highlighted the constitutional weaknesses of the Instrument of Government and inherent tensions between Protector and Parliament. The remit of Parliament was apparently clear: the parliamentary committee was first to investigate and report on the blasphemy and misdemeanours of James Nayler and his followers, and secondly to prepare a bill 'in reference to such Blasphemies and Misdemeanors, as also for taking away such old Laws made against tender Consciences, as are fit to be taken away'.[13] The authority with which Parliament acted, however, was extremely unclear. After having questioned Nayler and other witnesses, the MP Thomas Bampfield presented the committee's report to

[10] Leo Damrosch, *Sorrows of the Quaker Jesus*, p. 152. His source is the account in Ralph Farmer, *Satan inthron'd in his chair of pestilence* (London, 1657), STC F444, pp. 10–11.
[11] Farmer, *Satan inthron'd*, pp. 18–19, cited in Crawford, *Women and religion*, p. 168.
[12] *Journals of the House of Commons 1651–1659*, vol. VII, p. 448.   [13] *Ibid.*

Parliament on 5 December, which charged Nayler with assuming the 'names and incommunicable attributes and titles of our blessed Saviour'.[14] The whole House then spent the next few weeks debating how to proceed. There was no real precedent for Parliament to act in a judicial capacity and hence to accuse and indict Nayler formally of blasphemy; the grounds for doing so were uncertain in this case and MPs could not agree on the proper procedures. Although the Blasphemy Act 1650 remained on the statutes, MPs were reluctant to make use of it. Resorting to the Blasphemy Act begged the question of Parliament's jurisdiction in the case, which should have been referred back to a civil magistrate. Furthermore, as both Quakers and moderate MPs pointed out, it would have been very difficult to convict Nayler: his actions, and the explanations of them he had given to the Committee, did not constitute blasphemy as defined by the 1650 Act. And, finally, the punishments prescribed by the Act appeared far too lenient in Nayler's case for many MPs who were universally dismayed by his actions, and keen to make an example of the Quakers.[15]

Parliament was also unable to act to its satisfaction within the terms of the Instrument of Government. Clause 37 of the Instrument stated that all those professing faith in God through Jesus Christ 'shall not be restrained from, but shall be protected in, the Profession of the Faith, and Exercise of their Religion'.[16] This was a source of some consternation to many MPs, keen to curb what they saw as the excesses of the religious toleration of the Protectorate. Philip Skippon remarked: 'These Quakers, Ranters, Levellers, Socinians, and all sorts, bolster themselves under [clauses] thirty-seven and thirty-eight of government, which at one breath, repeals all the acts and ordinances against them . . . If this be liberty, God deliver me from such liberty.'[17] Not only this, but the ultimate guarantor of the constitution and of religious liberty was Cromwell, not Parliament, raising a far more serious constitutional issue. If the judicial authority of Parliament was unclear, resorting to their legislative powers would also require the ultimate approval of Cromwell, which they knew they would be unlikely to receive. Ultimately, Nayler's trial exposed a deep constitutional malaise about the authority of the Protector over Parliament which was at the heart of the regime's eventual failure.[18]

[14] *State trials*, vol. I, p. 796.
[15] Theodore A. Wilson and Frank J. Merli, 'Nayler's case and the dilemma of the Protectorate', *University of Birmingham Historical Journal* 10 (1965), p. 48; Damrosch, *Sorrows of the Quaker Jesus*, pp. 196–99.
[16] Firth and Rait, *Acts and Ordinances of the Interregnum* (3 vols., London, 1911), vol. II, p. 822.
[17] *Diary of Thomas Burton* ed. J. T. Rutt (4 vols., London, 1828), vol. I, pp. 49–50.
[18] Wilson and Merli, 'Nayler's case', p. 45.

In the end, the matter was fudged: Parliament assumed judicial powers but failed to clarify the grounds for doing so, voted Nayler guilty of 'horrid blasphemy', and, after further debate, narrowly voted against the death sentence. Instead, on 16 December, Parliament ordered Nayler to be whipped and pilloried before crowds in both London and Bristol, to have his tongue bored and the letter 'B' branded on his forehead, and finally to be imprisoned in Bridewell, where, in recognition of his continuing power and influence, he would be 'restrained from the society of all people' (amended from an earlier draft which suggested he be kept merely from the society of all men) and 'debarred of the use of pen, ink, and paper'.[19] Cromwell expressed considerable irritation with Parliament's actions, and on 26 December wrote to the House requiring an explanation of the grounds of their action. MPs debated a response at length, highlighting precisely the constitutional dilemmas which would be addressed in the Humble Petition and Advice of 1657, but never formally replied.[20]

The *Nayler* case has received extensive attention from historians both of the Protectorate and of the Quaker movement, as a moment of crisis for each. For the Quakers, the rift between Fox and Nayler was fundamental in Fox's asserting his authority over the movement, developing a tighter organisational structure and a wariness of individual expressions of religious enthusiasm. The fissures of the dispute between Fox and Nayler stretched forward into Quaker history, and splits in the later seventeenth century were still attributed to the followers of James Nayler.[21] Fox's subsequent annotations of the early correspondence are an eloquent example of the long-term impact of the *Nayler* case. Fox noted 'mad whimeseye' against an account of a woman raising a man from the dead in 1657; another letter, describing Christopher Atkinson's expulsion from the movement in 1655 for fornication carries an annotation made in the 1670s by Fox: 'if you do not give over youer worke and sprashon [expression] the lord god will blast youer spirit and worke and you then will become hardened and as bad as the ould aposers [opposers] as J-N [James Nayler] his company and J Perot and Pennyman'.[22] Nayler cast a long shadow over the movement.

---

[19] *Diary of Thomas Burton*, ed. Rutt, vol. I, p. 158; *State trials*, vol. I, p. 802.
[20] *Diary of Thomas Burton*, vol. I, ed. Rutt, pp. 246–64.
[21] John Perrot was a Quaker of Irish origin whom Edward Burrough initially hailed as a 'good writer', but who became involved in controversy with George Fox in 1661 over the propriety of keeping one's hat on during prayer, which Perrot argued was idolatry. John Pennyman was of similarly mystical bent, arousing the denunciation of Fox and other Quaker leaders in the later 1660s. *DNB*; W. C. Braithwaite, *The second period of Quakerism* (2nd edn, Cambridge, 1961), pp. 215–55.
[22] Thomas Willan to Margaret Fell, Sw. Mss 1: 270; George Taylor to Margaret Fell, 14 July 1655, Sw Mss 1: 239; on the probable dating of Fox's annotations see Norman Penney, 'Our recording clerks: Ellis Hookes (*c.* 1657–1681)', *JFHS* 1: 1 (1903), 15–17.

By focusing on the shock of Nayler's symbolic action, on the political repercussions of his examination and his punishment, and on the long-term impact on the Quaker movement, historians have tended to ignore the continuities in the *Nayler* case with what had gone before. Viewed from the perspective of the Quakers' use of print, Nayler's trial confirms the very tight organisation which lay behind Quaker pamphleteering and the movement as a whole, and emphasises that pamphleteering had a very clear purpose within the movement. Quaker authors were able to integrate the *Nayler* case easily into the established pattern of publications which underpinned their campaign for religious toleration and which presented the movement as a coherent entity.

First of all, the event itself, although dramatic, was not without precedent. Symbolic actions such as going naked, wearing sackcloth and ashes, or fasting, had been publicly performed by Quaker preachers on previous occasions and had already attracted considerable derision from critics of the movement. Martha Simmonds herself had walked barefoot in sackcloth and ashes through Colchester in 1655; James Nayler and Richard Farnworth had already defended, and indeed even encouraged, such symbolic actions in print.[23] Nayler, indeed, had established arguments to be used at his examination by Parliament when discussing the significance of Quaker signs and wonders in 1654: 'any wise man may know these doe it not according to their owne wills, but in obedience unto God'.[24] Symbolic actions were already well discussed in Quaker literature, and constituted a hallmark of the movement.

There were strong continuities, too, in the political arguments and tactics used to defend James Nayler by his colleagues. As has been shown in Chapter 7, Quaker ministers, chief among them Nayler, had already established an uninvited dialogue in print and in person with government, magistrates and ministers over the Protectorate's religious policies. As recently as September 1656, Edward Burrough had written a tract which denounced members of Parliament for calling a national day of fasting and warned, prophetically: 'That they take heed to themselves lest they make the guiltless to suffer upon the account of Blasphemy or Error, &c., while the evil doers go free, and the false Prophets defenced'.[25] Another Quaker minister, Samuel Fisher, had attended the opening session of Parliament on

---

[23] Patricia Crawford, *Women and religion*, pp. 164–65, 173; Kenneth Carroll, 'Quaker attitudes towards signs and wonders', *JFHS* 54:2 (1977), 70–84; James Nayler, *An answer to the booke called The Perfect Pharisee* ([London], 1654), STC N261, pp. 21 and 28; Richard Farnworth, *The pure language of the spirit of the truth* (London, 1655), STC F494, pp. 6–7 and *passim*; see also Leo Damrosch, *Sorrows of the Quaker Jesus*, pp. 163–76 for a useful discussion of symbolic behaviour in the early movement.

[24] Nayler, *An answer to the booke*, STC N261, p. 28.

[25] Edward Burrough, *The crying sinnes reproved* (London, 1656), STC B5988, sig. A.

17 September and attempted to make a speech denouncing the Protectorate's record on religious liberty.[26] Nayler's trial afforded the best opportunity yet to discuss the political achievement of religious settlement, and as such was welcomed by the more politically astute of Nayler's co-religionists. In a letter written from Westminster on 18 November 1656, three days after the parliamentary committee had begun its examination of James Nayler and his followers, Anthony Pearson wrote to 'Friends', in high praise of Nayler's performance before the Committee: 'Ja: Nayler answered all the accusacions wth soe much wisedome, meeknes and clearnes to the understanding of all indeferent persons, that the whole assemblie (except some violent men of the committee) were strangely astonished, and satisfyed, with his answers.'[27] Moreover, Pearson continued, '[t]he testamonye he hath given is the hyest, hath been made since the daies of Christ . . . and all are amased, and wonders what wilbee the end of itt for now the priestes doctrine is struck att'. Pearson was particularly impressed that Nayler had 'testifyed before the highest Cort in the nation, that god himselfe is come down, to dwell with the sons of men', and concluded rather optimistically: 'all things that hee affirmed before them are clearly to bee owned . . . great is the wisdome of the lord, whoe can turne all things to his own praise'.[28]

Despite Pearson's misplaced optimism, it is significant nevertheless that he welcomed Nayler's testimony 'before the highest Cort in the nation', indicating that whatever the Quakers' publicly voiced concerns about the legitimacy of Parliament's actions, and their privately expressed concerns about Nayler's actions, Pearson recognised on a pragmatic level that Nayler had a tremendous platform from which to bear witness.

The same instinct for political polemic is apparent in the Quaker publications which commented on the Nayler affair. There were only two Quaker tracts directly relating to Nayler's examination, both continuing the Quaker practice of publishing accounts of legal proceedings or court hearings, and providing extensive comments upon them.[29] The first publication, *Copies of some few of the papers*, consisted of copies of the petitions and papers submitted to Parliament in Nayler's support, and was dated by George

---

[26] Samuel Fisher, *The scorned Quakers true and honest account* (London, 1656), STC f1057.
[27] Anthony Pearson to 'Friends SF and AA', 18 November 1656, Sw Mss 3: 78. For an account of the Committee, see Damrosch, *Sorrows of the Quaker Jesus*, pp. 186–92, and Bittle, *James Nayler*, pp. 115–17.
[28] Pearson to 'Friends', Sw Mss 3: 78.
[29] Leo Damrosch argues that these publications give 'a sense of how fascinating the proceedings were by their very secrecy', and that most Quakers would be keen for information on the trial yet excluded from it: Damrosch, *Sorrows of the Quaker Jesus*, pp. 178–79. While this is undoubtedly true to some degree, it should not be forgotten that many Quakers were kept informed through the circulation of much franker letters; nor should we ignore the Quaker publishing strategy relating to other trials, which was very similar to the techniques employed for the *Nayler* case.

Thomason on 5 December, the date on which the whole House began debating the committee's report of James Nayler (see Plate 14).[30] The second and far more substantial publication, *A true narrative of the examination, tryall and sufferings of James Nayler*, was a heavily annotated edition of the parliamentary committee's report (see Plate 15). This tract, dated by Thomason on 14 January 1657, after Nayler's punishment had been dispensed, also included details of the subsequent parliamentary debate on the proper procedures, verdict and punishment for Nayler, and reprinted copies of petitions and papers sent by Nayler's supporters to Parliament and Cromwell.[31] It is not clear who in the Quaker movement compiled *A true narrative*. Robert Rich and William Tomlinson were on the scene and wrote many of the petitions published in *Copies of some few of the papers*; they may have helped in the production of *A true narrative*. Other, perhaps more likely, candidates include Anthony Pearson and Gervase Benson, who were present at some of the Committee's hearings, and who may have had access to the report, as well as substantial experience in shaping the Quakers' published objections to the Protectorate's religious policies.[32]

Throughout *A true narrative*, extensive marginal notes on the report questioned how MPs could arrive at a verdict of blasphemy from the evidence presented: 'what Law of God or man is here broken, or doth say that this is blasphemy, to have his horse led, and one to go barehead before him, or to be accompanied with singing?' demanded the authors; and in another instance: '[i]s it blasphemy to raise from the dead?'[33] At the end of the report, its Quaker commentators advised the reader: 'Take good notice of [Nayler's]

---

[30] G. Fox, R. Rich and W. Tomlinson, *Copies of some few of the papers* ([London], 1657), STC C6080A. It is known that the dates Thomason sometimes ascribed to his tracts were a reflection of the events discussed in the tract, rather than the date of acquisition, so it would be wrong to argue that this tract was published specifically to coincide with the debate in the whole House. However it seems likely, given that Thomason clearly associated the tract with the opening of the Nayler debate, that the tract was in circulation in the capital on 5 December. *Copies of some few of the papers* was effectively reprinted in *A true narrative*.

[31] *A true narrative of the examination, tryall, and sufferings of James Nayler* [London, 1657], STC T2789.

[32] Anthony Pearson to 'Friends', Sw Mss 3: 78. Leo Damrosch attributes the whole of *A true narrative* to Rich and Tomlinson, but in doing so may have assumed that the compilers of *Copies of some few of the papers* also compiled *A true narrative*, for which I have found no evidence. Damrosch, *Quaker Jesus*, p. 178. Although one of his papers appears in *A true narrative*, it is highly unlikely that George Fox was behind the publication of it; as his most recent biographer stated in a discussion of Fox's public defence of Nayler: 'Fox's finest hour it was not.' H. Larry Ingle, *First among Friends: George Fox and the creation of Quakerism* (Oxford, 1994), p. 149. *A true narrative* was obviously compiled in some haste. Although the text reads coherently throughout, the pagination and signatures are not in any chronological order. In subsequent references, both page and signature numbers are included to avoid confusion as far as is possible.

[33] *A true narrative*, pp. 5, 8. Part of the evidence involved Dorcas Erbury's claim, not denied by James Nayler, that he had raised her from the dead.

(1)   13

C O P I E S

OF

Some few of the P A P E R S given into the Houfe of P A R L I A M E N T
in the time of *I A M E S   N A Y L E R S* Tryal there, which began the fifth of *December,* 1656.

To the S P E A K E R *of the* P A R L I A M E N T *of* E N G L A N D, *thefe to
be read.*

F R I E N D S,

Ct nothing cōtrary to that which doth cōvinceyou,though
bound with an Oath, although you bring your felves
in never fo muchdifgrace in breaking your Agreement;
for in fuch a cafe you may rejeƈt the Counfel of God
againft your own Knowledge,and fo appearing to pleafe
the world that looks upon you, the unjuft aƈts againft
the Juft; herein you'l do defpite to the Spirit of Grace,
wilfully aƈting that which he knows he should not: So here comes mans
condemnation juft from God; therefore before you do aƈt confider; and before you do give Sentence fear; for Blafphemy proceeds from the root of
Tranfgreffion; and fee that you be firft out of it before you of it do judge:
There is no Blafphemy in the Light which is truth. And to witnefs the light
is not Blafphemy. And to witnefs the Prophets Life, and the Apoftles Life
that had the Life of Jefus made manifeft in his mortal flefh. And to
witneffe the Life of God, and God dwelling in man, is not Blafphemy.
And to witneffe the fecond *Adam,* the Lord from Heaven, and as he is, fo
to be in this world, is not Blafphemy; but not to witneffe this, and to be in
the tranfgreffion, he is in the Root that will blafpheme; and for a man to fay
he witneffes thefe things, and himfelf in the tranfgreffion, he blafphemes,
and is the Synagogue for Satan, who did tranfgreffe, and not abide in the
truth, who is in the tranfgreffion. Now it is not becaufe men can fpeak the
Scriptures of truth, therefore they are able to judge of Blafphemy; for the
Jews could fpeak the Scriptures of truth, but judged the Truth Blafphemy;
Now if you would know what's Blafphemy, this is blafphemy, and thefe
were out of the life of the truth that judged the life blafphemy; and you do
not read that any that was in the life of Chrift, did whip, banish, prifon, put
to death any for blafphemy: Alas! here is blafphemy heard all up and
down the ftreets, men profeffing what they are not: Now the Jews which
had the Scriptures, and out of the fpirit of Chrift, did put to death for
blafphemy: Now with this examine and judge your felves, that you may
not be judged of the Lord: Although *Darius* could not change after feal-
ed, yet 'twas much grief to him: confider what Aƈt that was, and Law that
                                                                      was

A 2

Plate 14. G. Fox, R. Rich and W. Tomlinson, *Copies of some few of the papers
given in to the House of Parliament* ([London], 1657), STC C6080A.

'A True 6

NARRATIVE

O F

The *Examination*, *Tryall*, and
Sufferings of *James Nayler* in the Cities of *London*
and *Weſtminſter*, and his deportment under them.

With the Copies of ſundry Peti-
tions and other Papers, delivered by ſeverall Perſons
to the *Lord Protector*, the *Parliament*, and many
particular Members thereof, in his behalf. With
divers remarkable Paſſages (relating thereto) before
his Journey to *Briſtol*, whither he is now gone towards the filling up the meaſure of his Sufferings.

Eſth. 3. 8.

*And Haman ſaid unto King Ahaſuerus, There is a certain
people ſcattered abroad, and diſperſed among the people in all
the Provinces of thy Kingdom ; And their Lawes are divers
from all people; neither keep they the Kings Laws. Therefore
it is not for the Kings profit to ſuffer them.*

Jan. 14   London   1656.

Printed in the Year, 1657.

Plate 15. *A true narrative of the examination, tryall, and sufferings of James Nayler*
[London, 1657], STC T2789, sig. A.

answers from first to last, and see if in any of them you can finde blasphemy, or any thing that is contrary to the Scriptures, and the Saints practices.'[34] As has already been seen in other printed accounts of trials or disputations with ministers, Quaker tracts made a point of presenting legal documents and other evidence and asking their audiences to assess them. In the same vein, the compilers of *A true narrative* emphasised that the grounds for the prosecution of Nayler were flimsy indeed, and required members of Parliament to defend their actions:

> You have called him a blasphemer, we desire that you would publish what his blas-phemy is, that we may know it and take heed of it. Christ Jesus himself was called a blasphemer, because he said, *I am the Son of God*; and saith *John, 1 Joh.3.2. Now we are the Sons of God.*[35]

Not only did the Quaker publication censure Parliament for accusing Nayler of blasphemy without first defining it; it also highlighted and attacked the illegitimate proceedings at Nayler's trial, just as many earlier tracts had questioned the judicial procedures against Quakers at Quarter Sessions or assize trials. When Parliament 'Resolved that the Speaker be authorized to issue his warrants' to the sheriffs of London, Middlesex and Bristol so that Nayler's punishment could be carried out, the authors of *A true narrative* remarked caustically on the constitutional implications of its actions: 'It is a question whether this be sufficient warrant (unless the Protector concurre with them in the thing) if the instrument of Government be yet in force.'[36] On the parliamentary decision refusing to allow Nayler to speak before sentence was passed, the authors noted in the margin: 'It is a pity too illegal a thing should stand on record against you' and expressed the hope, 'that no Court of Judicature in these Nations will follow the example, if they should, what will become of the good and wholsome Laws, made by our ancestors'.[37]

Much, then, of *A true narrative* recalls the barrage of Quaker tracts which had denounced prosecutions of Quakers up and down the country since the beginnings of the movement; as in earlier tracts, the Quakers' objections were grounded in legal fact and they were keen to discuss the constitutional implications of the prosecution of religious belief. The high profile of Nayler's examination before Parliament, indeed, allowed more direct political criticism than had been made in earlier tracts. Robert Rich, a wealthy London merchant and shipowner who had been part of Nayler's original entourage, and who sat at Nayler's feet during the course of his punishments, attempted in one of his many addresses to Parliament to place James Nayler's fate in the wider context of what he saw as the clear failure of the Protectorate:

---

[34] *A true narrative*, p. 28; sig. D3v.   [35] *Ibid.*, p. 41, sig. Gr.
[36] *Ibid.*, p. 35; sig. E3r.   [37] *Ibid.*, p. 36, sig. E3v.

ever since the yeer 1648 it was hoped that Opression and all Persecution for conscience sake, would utterly have ceased, according to what hath often been declared;
and instead thereof that Truth and Mercy would have taken place. But contrary
thereto within these three yeers last past, have many hundreds (even in this one
Nation of England, in all parts thereof) been cast into Prisons, Dungeons and Holes,
and some have perished therein; and others have endured cruel whippings, stonings,
and other bodily punishments, besides the spoiling of their goods, for no other cause
save for matters concerning the Law of their God, and that for conscience sake they
could not bow to *Hamans* nature; not so much as one known Law of this Nation
proved that they had transgressed.[38]

In addition to criticising the actions of Parliament, *A true narrative* echoed
other Quaker tracts in denouncing the interference of the civil magistracy in
matters of religion. Again, so stark were the events in the *Nayler* case that
A true narrative was able to make this point far more directly than Quaker
pamphleteers had to date.[39] One of the papers printed at the end of the tract
asserted with great clarity 'that the Civil Magistrate is not the proper Judge of
Error or blasphemy', and expressed fears for the 'safety of the Government,
which is in danger of wrath from the Almighty, for . . . invading the spiritual
jurisdiction of our Lord Jesus'. Finally the petitioners – Quaker sympathisers
rather than Quakers – complained of the consequences to themselves, 'who
by this Rule may be pull'd out; and judged without a Law; yea judged and
sentenced in the highest condemnation as blasphemers, for which the present
temper of the civil Magistrate shall censure to be blasphemy'.[40]

A true narrative may thus be incorporated into the body of Quaker tracts
which had already established the Quakers' views on the need for a proper
religious settlement. Other features of the Quaker response suggest similarly
strong continuities with their political tactics which again underline both
the political acuity of the movement's leadership, and the peculiar role ful-
filled by printed tracts. In the *Nayler* case as in other legal cases, Quaker
leaders sustained a private dialogue and political lobbying of key political
figures. In the course of the parliamentary debate, the MP Gilbert Pickering made it clear he had held discussions with 'a very sober man of that
sect' about James Nayler's frame of mind and appropriate punishment.[41]
The letter from Pearson and Benson makes it clear that they were present
during the Committee's hearings, or at least had a very sympathetic contact.
There is also evidence of considerable lobbying of MPs, the Speaker of the

---

[38] *Ibid.*, p. 36, sig. F2v (*sic*).
[39] The petitioners denied their Quaker status, referring to James Nayler as 'one of the very chief
of that people, (though now dis-owned by the generallity of them, whose case therefore is
the more respected by us.) So that we could no longer, as persons unconcern'd keep silence,
but we must appear from him in a Petition to the Parliament'. *A true narrative*, p. 50,
sig. H v.
[40] *Ibid.*, p. 51, sig. H2r.   [41] *Diary of Thomas Burton*, ed. Rutt, vol. I, p. 153.

House and Cromwell himself, carried out by Quakers and their sympathisers. *Copies of some few of the papers* continued the practice of publishing letters and papers which had already been addressed privately to political figures, echoing Thomas Aldam's original dictum in 1652 that whatever Quaker authors wrote to their political enemies should also be addressed to the 'people', for their gainsayers 'conceale the letters, and will not let them be seene', whereas 'declaring and makeing knowne the same to the people causes many to come to us and many own the truth spoken'.[42] Cromwell's letter to Parliament, requiring explanation of their proceedings against Nayler, was prompted by a petition which had requested him, in accordance with the Instrument of Government, to protect the 'poor people of God'; Parliament was also petitioned with a request to delay Nayler's punishment on the grounds of his ill-health.[43] There is much in the Quakers' political activity to suggest they were capable of making pragmatic approaches to politicians where appropriate. The role of print was clearly to publicise their case to a wider audience of 'Christian Readers'.

Another central strand of this study has shown how print was carefully used by Quaker leaders to present the Quakers as a unified and coherent body of saints. The published defences of Nayler confirm this strategy as Quaker authors drew on the *Nayler* case in order to argue for the cohesion, and true suffering, of the movement. Not surprisingly, perhaps, *A true narrative* skirted around the nature and significance of Nayler's behaviour, focusing primarily on the iniquity of the response he had elicited from the authorities. In discussing the actions of Nayler and his followers, any parallels between Christ and Nayler were couched always in terms of the notion that the light of Christ was in everyone, a message which pervaded early Quaker pamphlet literature. The punishment Nayler had endured was interpreted in terms of a millenarian struggle, signifying the 'great enmity' between the seed of the woman and seed of the serpent, which was at its most intense:

when the appearances of Christ are most signal . . . This was the ground of the sufferings of the Prophets, of Christ himself, and many of the Saints since that time; whether this consideration obtaine not in the present case of *James Nayler*, Upon perusall of this ensuing Treatise, no doubt you will receive full satisfaction.[44]

In its explanation of Nayler's actions, the tract did make a very clear distinction between James Nayler and Christ: Nayler was tempted by worldly desires; Christ was not: '[i]t is not denyed, but a Saint may be subject to many Temptations; twas the priviledge of Christ alone not to bee overcome by them'. Nevertheless, Nayler's temptation was not a matter for a secular court: 'when the True Judge appears, he will embrace his own seed;

---

[42] Thomas Aldam to George Fox and others, York [July] 1652, Sw Trs 1: 13.
[43] Braithwaite, *Beginnings*, p. 264; *A true narrative*, p. 55, sig. H4r.   [44] *Ibid.*, sig. A2r.

and passe sentence, not according to occasional diversions, but according to the constant tenour of the integrity and uprightnesse of our spirits in his sight'.[45]

Discussion of Nayler's actions and his trial is strikingly absent from other Quaker tracts of this time, despite a barrage of hostile publications, and indeed the relative restraint in responding to a large volume of extremely pernicious attacks on the Quaker movement is in itself strong evidence of an almost corporate response to the crisis. The only publication which considered Nayler's behaviour in any detail was George Bishop's *The throne of truth exalted over*.[46] Bishop's publication was a reply to the Bristol presbyterian minister Ralph Farmer, already known to George Bishop and an old opponent of the Quakers, who published a lengthy and vitriolic account of James Nayler's arrest and examination in *Sathan inthron'd in his chair of pestilence*.[47] The main thrust of Bishop's tract was to present the Quakers as a cohesive body, united in its sufferings in the face of unjust prosecution. Bishop was careful to defend James Nayler's authority in the Quaker movement before his fall: 'Whilest I.N. walked in the Light, and in it ruled, he was indeed exceeding precious and honorable amongst the Children of the Day.'[48] In view of the particular significance which Quaker leaders placed on the authority of ministerial writing, discussed in Chapter 1, it should be noted that Bishop was at pains to protect the status of Nayler's early writings, arguing that Nayler's success in disputation against puritan ministers was second to none: 'What mouth was there (then) opened against him that he did not condemn? What Pen replied again when he had answered?'[49] George Bishop went on to affirm the enduring authority of Nayler's writing before his fall: 'And what he (then) wrote, and what he then spoke, and ministred of the Eternal Life shall abide for ever, and shall have an Eternal Witness in that of God in every man's conscience.'[50]

Bishop's tract also asserted the unity of the movement by blaming Nayler's temptation squarely on the shoulders of 'That woman', Martha Simmonds, widely portrayed as the eccentric and malignant force in the whole affair, and whose credibility was far less important to the movement than James Nayler's. He also laughed at Ralph Farmer for trying to argue both that the Quakers were at loggerheads over Nayler, and that all Quakers shared Nayler's views, deriding 'the confusion of the sum of thy Book, *viz. They are divided* (the first was *That they were one)*'.[51] Other key Quaker authors also attempted to portray Nayler's fate as indicative of the movement's

---

[45] *Ibid.*, sig. A2v.
[46] George Bishop, *The throne of truth exalted over the powers of darkness* (London, 1657), STC B3008.
[47] Farmer, *Sathan inthron'd in his chair of pestilence*, STC F444.
[48] Bishop, *The throne of truth*, p. 3.   [49] *Ibid.*, p. 3.   [50] *Ibid.*   [51] *Ibid.*, p. 12.

fundamental unity. Edward Burrough, whose preaching in London had been most directly challenged by James Nayler and his followers, picked up a printed dispute with one of Nayler's many former disputants, John Jackson, in the course of which Burrough avoided almost any reference to Nayler, other than to explain that his fall 'was not suffered of the Lord to be as an occasion to destroy his people, but as an occasion to try them, and to prove them, and thereby are they tryed and proved, and the more setled rather then confounded'.[52]

Not only was Burrough keen to stress in print the unifying impact of the Nayler crisis on the movement, but, like Bishop, he also maintained respect for the authority of Nayler's writings within the corpus of Quaker literature. In the midst of the conflict with Nayler over the summer of 1656, Edward Burrough exchanged letters with him which underline the high esteem with which he regarded Nayler's published writings. In a very warm letter from Burrough to Nayler, written from Oxford in July 1656, Burrough saluted Nayler as 'My dearest Beloved, in who my life dwells; and by whom I am refreshed when I thinke upon thee', and went on to express his confidence in Nayler's spiritual powers: 'I know thou art heard and beloved of the father; and hath answer from him, in thy request; and thy dominion, will be enlarged; and thou art Crowned, in the sight of thy enimies.' Burrough informed Nayler that one of his disputants, the General Baptist and erstwhile Leveller, Jeremiah Ives, had published 'his gatched mischeife' against the Quakers, and that Burrough had written a reply to him, enclosed in the letter to Nayler. Burrough presented his work to Nayler in highly equivocal terms and gave Nayler complete freedom to do with it as he wished: 'either to make an epistle of itt to thy answer, or to putt it in the end or what you will doe with it . . . I will nothing to dow with itt, Contrary to thy will; I leave it to thee, if you thinke it fitt, to putt in some parte of the booke'.[53]

Burrough's respect for Nayler's authority as an author, even in the midst of a bitter internal conflict between the two leaders, is a striking reminder of the significance of print in the eyes of the early Quakers. Both Burrough and Bishop recognised the strength of Nayler's published writings even in the thick of the crisis, Bishop defending them in print and Burrough promoting them in practice. At the same time, both men used the medium of print to

[52] Edward Burrough, preface, in Richard Hubberthorne, *The cause of stumbling removed* (London, 1657), *STC* H3222, sig. A3r.

[53] Edward Burrough to James Nayler, Oxford, 12 July 1656, Portfolio 1:43. Jeremiah Ives, *The Quakers quaking and their foundations shaken* (London, 1656), *STC* I1103, was dated by Thomason on 1 July 1656, and Nayler's reply, *Weaknes above wickednes, and truth above subtilty* (London, 1656), *STC* N327, was dated 18 July 1656. Interestingly, Burrough's contribution did not appear in *Weaknes above wickednes*, which appeared in London six days after his letter to Nayler. Nayler's account of the public debate between Ives and Nayler at the Bull and Mouth in London was witnessed, among others, by Robert Rich, who later was a staunch defender of Nayler, and by George Bishop, who was not.

proclaim the unity of the Quakers: print was a crucial tool in the promotion of a cohesive movement.

Such continuity of printed response is impressive, given the very real fissures and doubts which the actions of Nayler and his companions had aroused. This book has argued that the tight control which Quaker leaders exercised over their publications was their salient feature, and that the evident organisation which underpinned Quaker publishing was an important characteristic of the early movement as a whole. The Nayler crisis reinforces the strong desire (and ability) of Quaker leaders to maintain discipline and cohesion in the movement. While Bishop was quite prepared to defend Nayler in print, his attitude in private was more ruthless, and he may have gone out of his way to isolate Nayler and his followers in the eyes of the authorities. Following the bitter encounter between Fox and Nayler in Exeter gaol, George Fox was reported in early October to have taken charge of a bundle of letters intended for Nayler, and was heading off for a meeting with George Bishop in Reading.[54] On 27 October, three days after Nayler's arrest, George Bishop was able to congratulate himself on the letters found on Nayler's person on his arrest in Bristol. Describing the highly enthusiastic letters from Hannah Stranger and her husband which addressed Nayler as the 'only begotten Son of God', George Bishop reassured Margaret Fell that 'with these were other Letters taken, discovering, and Judging that Spirit that was head [*sic*] in them and seeking to Recover him'. These had included the one by George Fox of 12 October denouncing Nayler's weakness, 'which was written with my hand, and sent lately from Reading when wee were their togather', as well as 'Two of Thyne, and one of Elizabeth Smyth's'. The letters had, Bishop noted, 'exceedingly served the Trueth', and had been 'ordered by the wisdom of God', in order to leave 'us all before the world cleare and Innocent of their Defilement'.[55] At the very least, Bishop was relieved that the authorities had found evidence exonerating Fox and other Quaker leaders from Nayler's actions; it is also conceivable that Bishop had purposely ensured that this would be the case and advised Fox accordingly during their meeting at Reading.[56] Bishop was in many respects one of the most politically pragmatic of early Quaker leaders and his former political career,

---

[54] Walter Clement to Margaret Fell, 4 October 1656, Sw Mss 1:180.

[55] Braithwaite, *Beginnings of Quakerism*, p. 248; George Bishop to Margaret Fell, 27 October 1656, Sw Mss 1: 188.

[56] The crucial role of Bishop as Fox's amanuensis was a matter of public knowledge and some ridicule: in the months following the Nayler scandal, the stationer George Thomason annotated Fox's publications with the words 'Alias Bishop' next to George Fox's name. See George Fox, Robert Rich and William Tomlinson, *A true narrative of the examination, tryall and sufferings of James Nayler* [London, 1657], STC T2789, mispaginated p. 42, sig. H2r; George Fox, *The priests and professors catechisme* (London, 1657), STC F1882, sig. A; George Fox, *The priests fruits made manifest. And the fashions of the world.* (London, 1657), STC F1883, sig. A.

as John Thurloe's predecessor on the Committee of Examinations, would have provided him with ample experience of the presentation or suppression of evidence of sedition.[57] The ability to control the flow of correspondence between Quaker leaders described by Bishop's letter is hugely impressive and again reinforces the political acuity at the heart of the movement's organisation.

The production and distribution of print should be seen as an integral element of the discipline and organisation of the movement. The private correspondence between Quaker leaders indicates deep concerns to maintain discipline within the movement in the immediate aftermath of the Nayler crisis. Although Anthony Pearson, in November, was highly optimistic about the impact of Nayler's performance before the parliamentary committee, other letters circulating at the time were far gloomier, and indicate considerable fears for the unity of the movement. Enclosed with Pearson's letter was a note from Gervase Benson, which consoled: 'lett not your soul (my dear friends) be troubled att reports; the lord our god is over all' and expressed his desire 'that when I come amongst you I may hear of your stedfastnes in the truth, and of your unitye one with another'. George Fox was more direct in his instructions:

This is the word of the lord to you all; in all openings and speakings lett not the man bee lifted upp; for that will not bee the servant but the master, [who] which is to bee throwne downe . . . ; therefore that keepe downe, which would bee lifted upp; in the sight of the world; for that doth fale [fall] in the sight of world.[58]

Many other letters circulating in the wake of Nayler's arrest and trial were deeply concerned with discipline in the movement. Arthur Cotton in Cornwall complained that 'J:N: hath drawn out the mynds of many friends in Many placis'; William Caton in London reported that 'some tymes here is much disturbance in our meettinges by those that adheres after J:N: they are grown very impudent many of them'.[59] As has already been suggested in Chapter 5, and in the work of Patricia Crawford, much of the anxiety at this time focused on the perceived insubordination of women, and a number of women were removed from the ministry. The concern of Quaker leaders to control unruly ministers extended to a desire to check unwarranted printing, and in 1657 a leading Quaker woman minister from London, Sarah Blackborow, was roundly rebuked for defending James Nayler in print.

---

[57] J. W. Martin, 'The pre-Quaker writings of George Bishop', *Quaker History* 74:2 (1985), 20–27; *BDBR*; *DNB*.
[58] Anthony Pearson and Gervase Benson, 18 November 1656, Sw Mss 3: 78.
[59] Arthur Cotton to George Fox, 18 November 1656, Sw Trs 1:630; William Caton to Margaret Fell, 17 March 1657, Sw Mss 1: 367; for expressions of anxiety about women, see above, Chapter 5.

Blackborow, a London matron who was later credited with the establishment of the women's Box Meeting to collect money for the Quaker poor, had gained a certain notoriety during the proceedings against Nayler, and was cited in Parliament's report as having been one of the women followers who addressed Nayler in Christ-like terms.[60] In 1657, Sarah Blackborow wrote the preface to a short pamphlet by Nayler, *How sin is strengthened*, written from gaol, in which he discussed his own experience of having succumbed to, and then defeated, sin.[61] In her preface, Blackborow stated that the work came 'from a pure Fountain, eternal life springing forth itself', and wrote that as she had read it in manuscript, 'a necessity was laid upon me to put it in print, that so it might do service, and have unity with its own'.[62] For her role in its publication, Blackborow was summoned to the house of a leading Quaker merchant, Gerrard Roberts, and made to read a paper by Henry Clark which denounced *How sin is strengthened* as having been ministered by the 'Spirit of the Prince of the Aire'. Sarah Blackborow then wrote her own account of this rebuke which, she directed, was to 'goe forth in City and Cuntry whereever that paper of Henry Clarke shalbe heard of', in which she claimed she was innocent of the charges laid against her, and asserted '[a] necessity is laid upon mee to deny [the spirit] in Henry Clarke'.[63]

Sarah Blackborow's actions reinforce on one level that the Quaker movement was profoundly divided by the Nayler crisis, and bolster Crawford's argument that this was in many ways a highly gendered dispute about the authority of women in the movement. On another level, the determination of the Quaker leadership to curb unruly ministers and control their unwarranted publishing, is striking. While heavyweight authors like Edward Burrough, George Fox and George Bishop, were able to put their names to published defences of Nayler which drew on an existing corpus of Quaker literature to explain his actions, and which focused on the political implications of his trial and punishment, the efforts of Sarah Blackborow to collaborate with the now disgraced James Nayler, were sharply rejected. This was a movement in which print was a carefully deployed tool of an organised and highly purposeful leadership seeking to argue for, and achieve, radical religious reform. The response to the Nayler crisis, both in print, and in activities behind the scenes, underlines this in every respect.

---

[60] *A true narrative*, p. 27. See also Crawford, *Women and religion*, p. 168, Damorosch, *Sorrows of the Quaker Jesus*, p. 126. For her role in the establishment of the London Box Meeting, see Braithwaite, *Beginnings of Quakerism*, p. 341; Phyllis Mack, *Visionary women: ecstatic prophecy in seventeenth-century England* (Berkeley 1992), pp. 220, 285, 327.
[61] [James Nayler], *How sin is strengthened, and how it is overcome* (London, n.d.), STC N285.
[62] SB [Sarah Blackborow], preface in [Nayler], *How sin is strengthened*, sig. Ar.
[63] 'Sarah Blackborow's paper' [1657], Sw Mss 4: 61. I have not located the paper by Henry Clark.

Conclusion

This book has argued that the Quakers were active participants in the political society of the 1650s. The movement engaged with aspects of godly reformation which were of primary concern to many of their contemporaries. Although their enemies portrayed them as salivating agents of antichrist who were intent on turning society on its head, the real nature of the Quaker threat was the plausibility of their views. In 1657, the Essex minister Ralph Josselin was afraid that his neighbour Justice Harlakenden had 'the tang of quakerisme on his spirit'.[1] In the course of the Nayler debate, MP William Strickland denounced the Quakers as 'a growing evil', 'the greatest that ever was', but warned also, 'Their way is a plausible way; all levellers against magistracy and propriety.'[2] Oliver Cromwell's numerous meetings with Quakers are often cited as evidence of the broadly tolerant Cromwellian church; but such meetings also suggest that the Quakers had sufficient credibility to be taken seriously.

Pamphleteering was a central plank to the Quakers' active political participation. Through their tracts, Quakers presented their views about how society should be, and how its members should set about achieving change. As one element in an extensive proselytising campaign which also used preaching, silence and symbolic performance, as well as private letters, the tracts were a major form of interaction with the rest of society. In order to be effective, the tracts had to find some cultural resonance with their audiences. Far from presenting constitutional treatises, or formulaic petitions, Quaker authors deployed a wide range of publishing techniques which could appeal to, and be put to practical use by, their audiences. The rapid growth of the movement, and its immediate recognition by contemporaries as a force to be reckoned with, suggests that they were successful.

Quaker pamphleteering was a self-conscious and carefully conducted activity, and an integral part of the Quaker campaign. It was undertaken

---

[1] Josselin, *The diary of Ralph Josselin 1616–1683*, ed. Alan McFarlane (British Academy Records of Social and Economic History, New Series III, 1976), p. 397.
[2] *Diary of Thomas Burton*, ed. Rutt, vol. I, p. 169.

by a select group of the movement's leaders whose status as authors was an integral part of their authority in the establishment of the movement. The anti-Calvinist thrust of the Quakers' outlook demanded the widest possible proselytising. To this end, tracts were disseminated with great care, often closely supervised by the itinerant Quaker leaders themselves, who made them available for public and individual readings, and presented them to hostile and receptive audiences alike.

The ways in which the tracts were used and produced are vital to our understanding of their impact and the significance of their content. The constant presentation of key issues, such as the denunciation of formal religious worship, the resistance to tithes, or the proclamation of God's law, meant that a body of ideas was repeated among audiences up and down the country. The sense of a nationally uniform 'Quaker' movement stemmed in large part from the ubiquity, and the consistency, of their tracts.

The Quakers' pamphleteering activities are important for the development of our understanding of the significance of print in the English revolution. This book vindicates the growing awareness that print culture and oral culture were inextricably intertwined; and that print could be made accessible to more than just the empirically literate. This goes well beyond the potential power of print to disseminate information and ideas. The Quakers' very focused use of the press was designed to impact on society in a far more profound way, requiring an almost corporate response in their readers, first to change the way in which they led their individual spiritual lives, and then to urge their contribution to the establishment of a truly godly commonwealth. Print involved the politicisation of a reader's own experiences. Printed accounts of local religious persecution or of specific religious disputes were, by virtue of publication, located within national political and religious debates; as more people encountered such accounts, so they were themselves drawn into a generic political context. James Nayler's trial before Parliament was a fitting climax to four years of sustained pamphleteering: his predicament was of immediate national political significance, and yet the printed response of the Quakers was perfectly integrated with their earlier publications.

The Quakers' fluency with the use of the press is an impressive reminder of just how significant was the abundance of print in the English revolution. Quakers developed their own sophisticated publishing strategies; but they were also very aware of the tactics behind salacious gutter-press journalism, and went out of their way to counter them. The presentation of arguments defending women preachers was accompanied by conventional declarations of patriarchal values, while at the same time Quaker leaders carefully regulated the actual preaching activities of Quaker women, and, in the case of Sarah Blackborow, even attempted to intervene in their publications. Quaker authors also easily subverted conventional genres, such as formal pamphlet disputations or petitions, in order to emphasise their own message. Yet these were not London hacks, nor, for the main part, university-educated men. The main body of Quaker authors came from remote parishes in Lancashire and Westmorland, and from parts of Yorkshire only slightly better connected with the capital. Their youth must also be emphasised. Richard Farnworth was about twenty-two in 1652; Edward Burrough was eighteen. They had grown up in a society in which print was widely available, and as zealous religious leaders, they turned to it readily as a means of communicating their views.

In many ways, the Quakers provide us with a unique and unrepresentative case-study of print culture in the 1650s. The meticulous record-keeping by which tracts and correspondence have been preserved, and which describes their pamphleteering so richly, is unparalleled, and owes as much to the Quakers' subsequent denominational tradition as it does to their impressive organisation in the 1650s. It is therefore impossible to claim that the Quaker movement, and the Quakers' use of the press, provide us with a framework on which to model our understanding of other radical groups and other forms of publication. But the Quakers were still operating within many of the same cultural paradigms as their contemporaries, and were clearly effective in their communications. During the course of the Nayler debate, Colonel Sydenham remarked of the Quakers: 'I cannot be in the world but I hear some of their opinions, both in print or otherwise.'[3] Their access to the press, their analysis of their audiences' expectations, and the fact that they used print in clear conjunction with manuscript papers, oral preaching and symbolic silences, all derived from an understanding of their own society, and an unshakable expectation that they would be able to establish meaningful dialogues within it.

Although the Quakers were clearly unusual, and generally reviled, it was central to the evident success of their preaching and pamphleteering that they were not remote from the rest of society. The organisation evident behind Quaker pamphleteering vividly describes the existence of a radical 'milieu', without which Quaker leaders could not have built up a national network of contacts with such rapidity. This book posits that only by gaining an under-standing of the mechanics of how Quakers were able to consolidate their movement does it become possible to assess the nature of their interaction with, and participation in, the political culture of the 1650s. From the outset, print was a crucial element in the developing organisation and discipline of the Quaker movement.

---

[3] *Ibid.*, p. 69.

The Quakers' sophisticated and self-conscious use of the press underlines that pamphleteering itself was a political activity which served to broaden political participation. The outpouring from the printing presses in the 1640s and 1650s should be studied with as much attention to the processes involved in production, distribution and readership, as to the content. Only when we understand why and how people made use of the press, and why and how they read printed pamphlets, can we properly assess the likely significance of the actual material in print.

BIBLIOGRAPHY

Friends' House Library, London.

Abraham Manuscripts. 1 vol.
Abram Rawlinson Barclay Manuscripts. Transcribed by Charlotte Fell Smith, 1915.
2 vols. vol. I: letters 1–125. Vol. II: letters 126–250.
Caton Manuscripts. 3 vols.
Markey Manuscripts. 1 vol.
Portfolio Manuscripts Collections. 36 vols.
Spence Manuscripts. 3 vols.
Swarthmoor Manuscripts. 6 vols.
Swarthmoor Transcripts. Transcriptions of the Swarthmoor Mss., by Emily Jermyn.
7 vols.
'The Journal of John Audland, 1654', in 'Letters of John Audland, 1653', Sw Mss
Box P2/15.
'Mary Pennington her Book', Temp. Mss. 752.
Geoffrey Nuttall, 'Early Quaker letters from the Swarthmoor Mss. to 1660', type-
script calendar and index with annotations, London, 1952 (copy also held at
Cambridge University Library).
Dictionary of Quaker Biography. Typescript collection of biographical details.

Bodleian Library, Oxford

Clarendon State Papers 2624, Mss. Clarendon vol. xxx.

Lancashire Record Office, Preston

Quarter Sessions Recognizances, 1652, QSB1.

Besse, Joseph, *A collection of the sufferings of the people called Quakers*. 2 vols.
London, 1753.
Birch, Thomas (ed.), *A collection of the State Papers of John Thurloe*. 7 vols. London,
1742.
Burton, Thomas, *The diary of Thomas Burton*, ed. J. T. Rutt. 4 vols. London, 1828.
Calendar of State Papers, Domestic Series [1652–56]. London, 189?

Calendar of the Clarendon State Papers, ed. O. Ogle and W. H. Bliss. Oxford, 1872.
Calendar of the Correspondence of Richard Baxter, ed. N. H. Keeble and Geoffrey Nuttall. 2 vols. Oxford, 1991.
A complete collection of state trials. 6 vols. London, 1730.
Eyre, G. E. B. (ed.), *A Transcript of the Registers of the Company of Stationers 1640–1708*. 3 vols. London, 1913; repr. Gloucester, Mass. 1967.
Firth, C. H. and R. S. Rait (eds.), *Acts and Ordinances of the Interregnum*. 3 vols. London, 1911.
Fortescue, G. K. (ed.), *Catalogue of the pamphlets, books, newspapers and manuscripts relating to the Civil War, the Commonwealth, and Restoration, collected by George Thomason, 1640–1661*. 2 vols. London, 1908.
Journals of the House of Commons 1651–1659,
Nickalls, John (ed.), *The Journal of George Fox*. London, 1975.
Fox, George, *The Journal of George Fox*, ed. Norman Penney. 2 vols. Cambridge, 1911.
Josselin, Ralph, *The diary of Ralph Josselin 1616–1683*, ed. Alan McFarlane. Records of Social and Economic History New Series III, London, published for the British Academy, Oxford University Press, 1976.
'Minutes of the Manchester Presbyterian Classes', ed. W. Shaw, *Chetham Society* n. s. 20 (1890).
'Minutes of the Committee of Plundered Ministers', ed. W. Shaw, *Lancashire and Cheshire Record Society* 34 (1896).
Smith, Joseph, *A descriptive catalogue of Friends' books*. 2 vols. London, 1867.
Smith, Joseph, *Bibliotheca anti-Quakeriana; or, a catalogue of books adverse to the Society of Friends*. London, 1873.
Statutes of the Realm. 11 vols. London, 1810–1828. Vol. IV. London, 1819.
Whiting, John, *A catalogue of Friends' books written by many of the people called Quakers, from the beginning of first appearance of the said people*. London, 1708.
Wing, Donald, *Short title catalogue of books printed in England, Scotland, Ireland, Wales and British America, 1641–1700*. 3 vols. New York, 1972–1988.

SECONDARY SOURCES

Acheson, R. W., *Radical puritans in England 1550–1660*. London, 1990.
Achinstein, Sharon, 'The politics of Babel in the English revolution', in James Holstun (ed.), *Pamphlet wars: prose in the English Revolution*. London, 1992.
Amussen, Susan and Mark Kishlansky (eds.), *Political culture and cultural politics in early modern England*. Manchester, 1995.
Aylmer, G. E. (ed.), *The Interregnum: the quest for settlement 1646–1660*. London, 1974.
'Did the Ranters exist?', *Past and Present* 117 (1987), 208–19.
'England's spirit unfoulded, or an incouragement to take the engagement', *Past and Present* 40 (1968), 3–15.
Barbour, Hugh, *The Quakers in puritan England*. New Haven, 1964.
and Arthur Roberts (eds.), *Early Quaker writings, 1650–1700*. Michigan, 1973.
Bauman, Richard, *Let your words be few: symbolism of speaking and silence among seventeenth-century Quakers*. Cambridge, 1983.
'Aspects of seventeenth-century Quaker rhetoric', *The Quarterly Journal of Speech* 56 (1970), 67–74.

'Speaking in the light: the role of the Quaker minister', in Richard Bauman and Joel Sherzer (eds.), *Explorations in the ethnography of speaking*. Cambridge, 1974.

Bell, Maureen, 'Elizabeth Calvert and the "Confederates"', *Publishing History* 32 (1992), 5–49.

'"Her usual practices": the later career of Elizabeth Calvert, 1664–75', *Publishing History* 35 (1994), 5–64.

'Mary Westwood, Quaker publisher', *Publishing History* 23 (1988), 5–66.

Bell, Richard and Patricia Crawford, 'Statistical analysis of women's printed writings 1600–1700', in Mary Prior (ed.), *Women in English society 1500–1800*. London 1985.

Bittle, William G., *James Nayler 1618–1660: the Quaker indicted by Parliament*. York, 1986.

Brailsford, Mabel, *Quaker women 1650–1690*. London, 1915.

Braithwaite, William C., *The beginnings of Quakerism*. [1911] 2nd edn. Cambridge, 1955.

The second period of Quakerism. 2nd edn. Cambridge, 1961.

'The Westmorland and Swaledale Seekers in 1651', *JFHS* 5: 1 (1908), 3–10.

Brinton, Howard, *Quaker Journals: varieties of religious experience among Friends*. Wallingford, Penn., 1972.

Brockbank, Elizabeth, *Edward Burrough: a wrestler for truth 1634–1662*. London, 1949.

Burke, P. and R. Porter (eds.), *Language, self and society: a social history of language*. Cambridge, 1991.

Cadbury, H. J., 'Early use of the word "Quaker"', *JFHS* 49:1 (1959), 3–5.

Caldwell, Patricia, *The puritan conversion narrative: the beginnings of American expression*. Cambridge, 1983.

Capp, Bernard, *The Fifth Monarchy Men*. London, 1972.

Fear, myth and furore: reappraising the Ranters. Comment 2', *Past and Present* 140 (August 1993), 164–71.

'Godly rule and English millenarianism', *Past and Present* 52 (August 1971), 106–17.

'The Fifth Monarchists and popular millenarianism', in J. F. McGregor and B. Reay (eds.), *Radical religion in the English revolution*. Oxford, 1986.

Carroll, Kenneth, 'Quaker attitudes towards signs and wonders', *JFHS* 54:2 (1977), 70–84.

'Quakerism and the Cromwellian army in Ireland', *JFHS* 54:3 (1978), 135–54.

'Sackcloth and ashes, and other signs and wonders', *JFHS* 53:4 (1975), 314–25.

Chadd, David (ed.), *Religious dissent in East Anglia III* (Norwich, 1996).

Chartier, Roger, 'Texts, printings, readings', in Lynn Hunt (ed.), *The new cultural history*. London, 1989.

Clyde, William, *The struggle for the freedom of the press from Caxton to Cromwell*. London, 1934.

Cole, Alan, 'The Quakers and the English revolution', *Past and Present* 10 (1956), 39–54.

'The social origins of the early Friends', *JFHS* 48 (1957), 99–118.

Collinson, Patrick, *The birthpangs of Protestant England: religious and cultural change in the sixteenth and seventeenth centuries*. London, 1988.

The Elizabethan Puritan movement. London, 1967, repr. 1982.

The puritan character: polemics and polarities in early seventeenth-century English culture. William Andrews Clark Memorial Library, Los Angeles, 1989.

The religion of protestants: the church in English society 1559–1625. Oxford, 1982.
'A comment: concerning the name Puritan', *Journal of Ecclesiastical History* 31:4 (1980), 483–88.
'Towards a broader understanding of the early dissenting tradition', in R. C. Cole and M. E. Moody (eds.), *The dissenting tradition: essays for Leland H. Carlson*. Columbus, Ohio, 1975.
Cope, Jackson I., 'Seventeenth-century Quaker style', *Publications of the Modern Languages Association*, 71: 2 (1956), 725–54.
Corns, Thomas N., 'The freedom of reader-response: Milton's *Of Reformation* and Lilburne's *The Christian Mans Triall*', in R. C. Richardson and G. M. Ridden (eds.), *Freedom and the English revolution: essays in history and literature*. Manchester, 1986.
D. Loewenstein (eds.), *The emergence of Quaker writing: dissenting literature in seventeenth-century England*. London, 1995, pp. 99–111.
Crawford, Patricia, *Women and religion in England, 1500–1720*. London, 1993.
'Women's published writings, 1600–1700', in Mary Prior (ed.), *Women in English society 1500–1800*. London, 1985.
Creasey, Maurice, '"Inward" and "outward": a study in early Quaker language', *JFHS* supplement 30 (1962).
Cressy, David, *Literacy and the social order: reading and writing in Tudor England*. Cambridge, 1980.
Cross, Claire, 'The church in England 1646–1660', in G. E. Aylmer (ed.), *The Interregnum: the quest for settlement 1646–1660*. London, 1974.
Cust, Richard and Ann Hughes (eds.), *Conflict in early Stuart England*. London, 1989.
Damrosch, Leo, *The sorrows of the Quaker Jesus: James Nayler and the puritan crackdown on the free spirit*. Cambridge, Mass., 1996.
Davies, Adrian, *The Quakers in English society 1655–1725*. Oxford, 2000.
Davis, J. C., *Fear, myth and history: the Ranters and the historians*. Cambridge, 1986.
'Cromwell's religion' in John Morrill (ed.), *Oliver Cromwell and the English revolution*. London, 1990.
'Fear, myth and furore: reappraising the "Ranters"', *Past and Present* 129 (1990), 79–103.
'Fear, myth and furore: reappraising the "Ranters". Reply', *Past and Present* 140 (August 1993), 194–210.
'Gerrard Winstanley and the restoration of true magistracy', *Past and Present* 70 (1976), 76–93.
'Puritanism and revolution: themes, categories, methods and conclusions', *Historical Journal* 33:3 (1990), 693–704.
'Radical lives', *Political Science* 37:2, (1985), 166–72.
'Radicalism in a traditional society: the evaluation of radical thought in the English Commonwealth, 1649–60', *History of Political Thought* 3:2 (1982), 193–213.
'Religion and the struggle for freedom in the English revolution', *Historical Journal* 35:3 (1992), 507–30.
Donagan, Barbara, 'Puritan ministers and laymen: professional claims and social constraints in seventeenth-century England', *Huntington Library Quarterly* 47 (Spring 1984), 81–111.
Duffy, Eamon, 'The Godly and the multitude in Stuart England', *Seventeenth Century Journal* 1: 1 (1986), 31–55.

Durston, C. and J. Eales (eds.), *The culture of English puritanism, 1560–1700*. London, 1996.

Durston, Christopher, 'Puritan rule and the failure of cultural revolution, 1645–1660', in Durston and Eales (eds.), *The culture of English puritanism, 1560–1700*. London, 1996.

Eley, G. and W. Hunt (eds.), *Reviving the English revolution*. London, 1988.

Eyre, G. E. B. (ed.), *A transcript of the registers of the Company of Stationers 1640–1708*. 3 vols. London, 1913; repr. Gloucester, Mass., 1967.

Ezell, Margaret, 'Breaking the seventh seal: writings by early Quaker women', *Writing women's literary history*. Baltimore, 1993.

Ferguson, Moira (ed.), *First Feminists: British women writers 1578–1799*. Bloomington, Ind., 1985.

Firth, Charles and Godfrey Davies, *The regimental history of Cromwell's army*. 2 vols. Oxford, 1940.

Fletcher, Anthony, *Reform in the provinces: the government of Stuart England*. New Haven and London, 1986.

Fletcher, Anthony, 'The godly divided: the end of religious unity in protestant England', *Seventeenth Century* 5: 2 (1990), 185–94.

Fletcher, Anthony, 'Oliver Cromwell and the godly nation', in John Morrill (ed.), *Oliver Cromwell and the English revolution*. London, 1990.

Fox, Adam, 'Ballads, libels and popular ridicule in Jacobean England', *Past and Present* 145 (1994), 47–83.

Frank, Joseph, *The beginnings of the English newspaper, 1620–1660* Cambridge, Mass., 1961.

Freist, Dagmar, *Governed by opinion: politics, religion and the dynamics of communication in Stuart London, 1637–1645*. London, 1997.

Gardiner, S. R., *The history of the Commonwealth and Protectorate, 1649–1656*. 4 vols. London, 1894–1903.

(ed.), *Constitutional documents of the puritan revolution 1625–1660*. Oxford, 1906, repr. 1979.

Gaunt, Peter, 'Drafting the instrument of government, 1653–54: a reappraisal.' *Parliamentary History* 8: 1 (1989), 28–42.

Gentles, Ian, *The New Model Army in England, Ireland and Scotland, 1645–1653*. Oxford, 1992.

Gerth, H. H. and C. Wright Mills (eds.), *From Max Weber: essays in sociology*. London, 1993.

Greaves, Richard, 'The ordination controversy and the spirit of reform in puritan England', *Journal of Ecclesiastical History* 21: 3 (July 1970), 225–41.

and Robert Zaller, *Biographical dictionary of British radicals in the seventeenth century*. 3 vols. Brighton, 1982–84.

Higgins, Patricia, 'The reactions of women, with special reference to women petitioners', in Brian Manning (ed.), *Politics, religion and the English civil war*. London, 1973.

Hill, Christopher, *The Collected Essays of Christopher Hill*. 3 vols. Brighton, 1985–6.

Vol. I: *Writing and revolution in seventeenth-century England*.

Vol. II: *Religion and politics in seventeenth-century England*.

Vol. III: *People and ideas in seventeenth-century England*.

The experience of defeat. Harmondsworth, 1985.

Winstanley: the law of freedom and other writings. Harmondsworth, 1973.

The world turned upside down: radical ideas during the English Revolution. Harmondsworth, 1987.

'The lost Ranters? A critique of J. C. Davis'. *History Workshop Journal* 24 (1987), 134–40.

'Radical prose in seventeenth-century England: from Marprelate to the Levellers', *Essays in Criticism* 32: 2 (April 1982), 95–118.

Hill, C., B. Reay and W. Lamont, *The world of the Muggletonians.* London, 1983.

Hirst, Derek, *Authority and conflict: England 1603–1658.* London, 1986.

'The failure of godly rule in the English republic', *Past and Present* 132 (August 1991), 33–66.

'The fracturing of the Cromwellian alliance: Leeds and Adam Baynes', *English Historical Review* 429 (October, 1993), 868–94.

Hirst, M. E., *The Quakers in peace and war.* London, 1923.

Hobby, Elaine, *Virtue of necessity: English women's writing 1649–1688.* London, 1988.

' "Oh Oxford thou art full of filth": The prophetical writings of Hester Biddle, 1629[?]–1696', in Susan Sellers (ed.), *Feminist criticism: theory and practice.* London, 1991.

Hodgkin, Lucy, *A Quaker saint of Cornwall: Loveday Hambly and her guests.* London, 1927.

Holstun, James (ed.), *Pamphlet Wars: prose in the English revolution.* London, 1992.

Hope Bacon, Margaret, *Mothers of feminism: the story of Quaker women in America.* San Francisco, 1986.

Horle, Craig, *The Quakers and the English legal system, 1660–1688.* Philadelphia, 1988.

'Quakers and Baptists, 1647–1660', *Baptist Quarterly*, 26: 8 (1976), 344–62.

Huber, Elaine, ' "A woman must not speak": Quaker women in the English left wing', in Rosemary Reuther and Eleanor McLaughlin (eds.), *Women of spirit: female leadership in the Jewish and Christian traditions.* New York, 1979.

Hughes, Ann, ' "Popular" presbyterianism in the 1640s and 1650s: the cases of Thomas Edwards and Thomas Hall', in Nicholas Tyacke (ed.), *England's long reformation, 1500–1800.* London, 1998.

'The pulpit guarded: confrontations between orthodox and radicals in revolutionary England', in Anne Laurence, W. Owens and Stuart Sims (eds.), *John Bunyan and his England, 1628–88.* London, 1990.

Hutton, Ronald, *The British republic, 1649–1660.* London, 1990.

Ingle, H. Larry, *First among friends: George Fox and the creation of Quakerism.* Oxford, 1994.

Isichei, Elizabeth, 'From sect to denomination among English Quakers', in B. R. Wilson (ed.), *Patterns of sectarianism.* London, 1967.

James, Margaret, 'The political importance of the tithes controversy in the English revolution, 1640–60', *History* 26 (June, 1941), 1–18.

Johnson, Francis R., 'Notes on English retail book-prices, 1550–1640', *The Library*, 5th ser., 5: 2 (1950), 83–112.

Jones, Rufus M., *Spritual reformers in the sixteenth and seventeenth centuries.* London, 1914.

Keeble, N. H. and Geoffrey Nuttall, *Calendar of the correspondence of Richard Baxter* 2 vols. Oxford, 1991.

Knott, John R., *Discourses of martyrdom in English literature, 1563–1694.* Cambridge, 1993.

Lake, Peter, 'Anti-popery: the structure of a prejudice', in Richard Cust and Ann Hughes (eds.), *Conflict in early Stuart England*. London, 1989.

'Puritanism, Arminianism and a Shropshire axe-murder', *Midland History* 15 (1990), 37–64.

Lambert, Shiela, 'Richard Montagu, Arminianism and censorship', *Past and Present* 124 (1989), 36–68.

Lamont, William, *Godly rule: politics and religion, 1603–1660*. London, 1969.

'The left and its past: revisiting the 1650s', *History Workshop Journal* 23 (1987), 141–53.

'The Muggletonians 1652–1979: a "vertical approach"', *Past and Present* 99 (1983), 22–40.

'Pamphleteering, the Protestant consensus and the English Revolution', in R. C. Richardson and G. M. Ridden (eds.), *Freedom and the English revolution: essays in history and literature*. Manchester, 1986.

Littleboy, Anna, 'Devonshire House Reference Library, with notes on early printers and printing in the Society of Friends', *JFHS* 18 (1921), 1–16; 66–80.

Lloyd, Arnold, *Quaker social history, 1669–1738*. London, 1950.

Ludlow, Dorothy, 'Shaking patriarchy's foundations: sectarian women in England, 1641–1700', in R. L. Greaves (ed.), *Triumph over silence: women in protestant history*. London, 1985.

McGregor, J. F., 'Fear, myth and furore: reappraising the Ranters. Comment 1', *Past and Present* 140 (August 1993), 155–64.

McGregor, J. F., 'Ranterism and the development of early Quakerism', *Journal of Religious History* 9: 4 (1977), 349–63.

and B. Reay (eds.), *Radical religion in the English revolution*. Oxford, 1986.

Mack, Phyllis, *Visionary women: ecstatic prophecy in seventeenth-century England*. Berkeley, 1992.

'The prophet and her audience: gender and knowledge in the world turned upside down', in G. Eley and W. Hunt (eds.), *Reviving the English revolution*. London, 1988.

'Women as prophets during the English civil war', *Feminist Studies* 8: 1 (1982), 19–45.

Manners, Emily, *Elizabeth Hooton: first Quaker woman preacher (1600–1672)*, *JFHS* Supplement 12. London, 1914.

Manning, Brian, *1649: the crisis of the English revolution*. London, 1992.

Martin, J. W., 'The pre-Quaker writings of George Bishop', *Quaker History* 74: 2 (1985), 20–27.

Matthews, A. G. (ed.), *Calamy revised: being a revision of Edmund Calamy's account of the ministers and others ejected and silenced, 1660–62*. Oxford, 1934, repr. 1988.

Walker revised: being a revision of John Walker's Sufferings of the Clergy during the Grand Rebellion, 1642–60. Oxford, 1988.

Morgan, John, *Godly learning: puritan attitudes towards reason, learning and education, 1560–1640*. Cambridge, 1986.

Morrill, John, *The nature of the English revolution*. London, 1993.

(ed.), *Reactions to the English civil war, 1642–1649*. London, 1982.

(ed.), *Revolution and restoration: England in the 1650s* London, 1992.

'Review article: Christopher Hill's Revolution', *History* 27:241 (1989), 243–52.

Mortimer, Russell, 'Biographical notices of printers and publishers of Friends' books to 1750: a supplement to Plomer's Dictionary', *Journal of Documentation* 3: 2 (1947), 107–25.

'Bristol Quaker merchants', *JFHS* 45: 1 (1953), 81–91.

'The first century of Quaker printers', *JFHS* 40 (1948), 37–49.

'Some notes on early dictionary references to Quakers', *JFHS* 43 (1951), 29–34.

Norbrook, David, *Writing the English Republic: poetry, rhetoric and politics, 1627–1660.* Cambridge, 1999.

Nuttall, Geoffrey, *The holy spirit in puritan faith and experience.* Oxford, 1946.

'James Nayler: a fresh approach', *JFHS*, Supplement 26, 1954.

The puritan spirit: essays and addresses. London, 1967.

Studies in Christian enthusiasm. Wallingford, Penn., 1948.

Visible saints: the Congregational way, 1640–1660. Oxford, 1957.

'Notes on Richard Farnworth', *JFHS* 48 (1956), 79–84.

O'Day, Rosemary, 'Immanuel Bourne: a defence of the ministerial order' *Journal of Ecclesiastical History* 27:2 (April 1976), 101–13.

O'Malley, Thomas, '"Defying the powers and tempering the spirit": a review of Quaker control over their publications 1672–1689', *Journal of Ecclesiastical History* 33:1 (January 1982), 72–88.

'The press and Quakerism, 1653–59', *JFHS* 54:4 (1979), 169–84.

Ormsby-Lennon, Hugh, 'From Shibboleth to apocalypse: Quaker speechways during the puritan revolution', in P. Burke and R. Porter (eds.), *Language, self and society: a social history of language.* Cambridge, 1991.

Penney, Norman (ed.), *The First Publishers of Truth*, *JFHS* Supplements 1–5, London, 1907.

'Our recording clerks: Ellis Hookes *c.* 1657–1681', *JFHS* 1:1 (1903), 12–22.

Peters, M. K. 'Quaker pamphleteering and the growth of the Quaker movement in East Anglia, 1652–1656', in David Chadd (ed.), *Proceedings of the Third Symposium on the History of Religious Dissent in East Anglia.* Norwich, 1996, pp. 141–65.

Phillipson, Laurel, 'Quakerism in Cambridge before the Act of Toleration (1653–1689)', *Proceedings of the Cambridge Antiquarian Society* 76, (1987), 1–25.

Plomer, H. R., *Dictionary of booksellers and printers . . . 1641–1667.* Oxford, 1907.

Purkiss, Diane, 'Material girls: the seventeenth-century woman debate', in Clare Brant and Diane Purkiss (eds.), *Women, texts and histories 1575–1760.* London, 1992.

Reay, Barry, *The Quakers and the English revolution.* London, 1985.

'The Muggletonians: a study in seventeenth-century English sectarianism', *Journal of Religious History* 9: 1 (1976), 32–49.

'Popular hostility towards Quakers in mid-seventeenth-century England', *Social History* 5:3 (1980), 387–407.

'Quaker opposition to tithes 1652–1660', *Past and Present* 86 (1980), 98–120.

'Quakerism and society' in J. F. McGregor and B. Reay (eds.), *Radical religion in the English revolution.* Oxford, 1986.

'The Quakers, 1659, and the restoration of the monarchy', *History*, 63 (1978), 193–213.

'The social origins of early Quakerism', *Journal of Interdisciplinary History* 11: 1 (Summer 1980), 55–72.

Roberts, Stephen, 'The Quakers in Evesham, 1655–1660: a study in religion, politics and culture', *Midland History* 16 (1991), 63–85.

Robinson, Howard, *The British post office: a history.* Princeton, 1948.

Ross, Isabel, *Margaret Fell, mother of Quakerism.* 2nd edn, York, 1984.

Russell, Conrad, 'Losers', *London Review of Books* 6: 18 (1984), 20–22.

Sharpe, K. and P. Lake (eds.), *Culture and politics in early Stuart England*. London, 1994.

Shaw, William A., *A history of the English church during the civil wars and under the Commonwealth 1640–1660*. 2 vols. London, 1900.

Siebert, Frederick, *Freedom of the press in England 1476–1776: the rise and decline of government controls*. Urbana, Ill., 1952.

Smith, Nigel, *A collection of Ranter writings in the seventeenth century*. London, 1983.

　Literature and revolution in England, 1640–1660. New Haven and London, 1994.

　Perfection proclaimed: language and literature in English radical religion 1640–1660. Oxford, 1989.

　'Fear, myth and furore: reappraising the Ranters. Comment 3', *Past and Present* 140 (August 1993), 171–78.

　'Richard Overton's Marpriest Tracts: towards a history of Leveller style', *Prose Studies* 9:2 (1986), 39–66.

Spencer, Lois, 'The politics of George Thomason', *The Library* (5th ser.) 14 (1959), 11–27.

　'The professional and literary connexions of George Thomason', *The Library* (5th ser.) 13 (1958), 102–18.

Spufford, Margaret, *Small books and pleasant histories. Popular fiction and its readership in seventeenth-century England*. Athens, G., 1982.

　(ed.), *The world of rural dissenters, 1520–1725*. (Cambridge, 1995).

　'First steps in literacy: the reading and writing experiences of the humblest seventeenth-century autobiographers', *Social History* 4: 3 (1979), 407–35.

Spurr, John, *The restoration Church of England, 1646–1689*. New Haven, 1991.

Swanson, Robert (ed.), *Gender and Christian religion: studies in church history* (vol. IV, Ecclesiastical History Society, Woodbridge, 1998).

Taylor, Ernest E., 'The first Publishers of Truth: a study', *JFHS* 19 (1922), 66–81.

Terry, Altha, 'Giles Calvert's publishing career', *JFHS* 25 (1938), 45–49.

Thomas, Keith. 'The meaning of literacy in early modern England', in G. Bauman (ed.), *The written word: literacy in transition*. Oxford, 1986.

　'Women and the civil war sects', *Past and Present* 13 (1958), 42–62.

Thompson, E. P., 'On the Rant', in G. Eley and W. Hunt (eds.), *Reviving the English revolution*. London, 1988.

Trevett, Christine, *Women and Quakerism in the seventeenth century*. York, 1991.

　'The women around James Nayler, Quaker: a matter of emphasis', *Religion*, 20 (1990), 249–73.

Tyacke, Nicholas, *Anti-Calvinists: the rise of English Arminianism c. 1560–1640*. Oxford, 1987.

　'Puritanism, Arminianism and counter-revolution', in Conrad Russell (ed.), *The origins of the English civil war*. London, 1973.

Underwood, T. L., 'Early Quaker eschatology', in Peter Toon (ed.), *Puritans, the millennium and the future of Israel: puritan eschatology 1600–1660*. London, 1970.

Vann, Richard, *The social development of English Quakerism, 1655–1755*. Cambridge, Mass., 1969.

　and David Eversley, *Friends in life and death: the British and Irish Quakers in the demographic transition*. Cambridge, 1992.

　'Quakerism and the social structure in the interregnum', *Past and Present* 43 (1969), 71–91.

Wabuda Susan and Caroline Litzenberger (ed.), *Belief and practice in Reformation England: a tribute to Patrick Collinson by his students*. Aldershot, 1998.

Wallis, Amy E., 'Anthony Pearson (1626–1666)', *JFHS* 51: 2 (1966), 77–95.

Watkins, Owen C., *The puritan experience*. London, 1972.

Watt, Tessa, *Cheap print and popular piety, 1550–1640*. Cambridge, 1991.

Watts, Michael, *The dissenters*. Vol. 1: *From the reformation to the French Revolution*. Oxford, 1985.

Weber, Max, *The sociology of religion*. Trans. Ephraim Fischoff. Boston, 1963.

White, Peter, 'The rise of Arminianism reconsidered', *Past and Present* 101 (1983).

Williams, J. B., 'Henry Walker, Journalist of the Commonwealth', *The Nineteenth Century and After* 63 (1908), 454–64.

Wilson, Bryan. R., *Religion in sociological perspective*. Oxford, 1982.

(ed.), *Patterns of sectarianism: organisation and ideology in social and religious movements*. London, 1967.

Wilson, T. A. and F. J. Merli, 'Nayler's case and the dilemma of the Protectorate', *University of Birmingham Historical Journal* 10 (1965), 44–59.

Woolrych, Austin, *Commonwealth to Protectorate*. Oxford, 1986.

'The Cromwellian Protectorate: a military dictatorship?', *History* 75 (1990), 207–31.

'The Good Old Cause and the fall of the Protectorate', *Cambridge Historical Journal* 13:2 (1957), 133–61.

Worden, Blair, *The Rump Parliament 1648–1653*. Cambridge, 1974.

'The Bill for a new representative?', *English Historical Review* 86 (1971).

'Providence and politics in Cromwellian England', *Past and Present* 109 (1985), 55–99.

'Toleration and the Cromwellian Protectorate', *Studies in Church History* 21 (1984), 199–233.

Wright, Luella M., *The literary life of early Friends*. New York, 1932.

'Literature and education in early Quakerism', *University of Iowa Humanistic Studies* 5:2 (1933), 5–60.

Young Kunze, Bonnelyn, *Margaret Fell and the rise of Quakerism*. London, 1994.

'Religious authority and social status in seventeenth-century England: the friendship of Margaret Fell, George Fox, and William Penn', *Church History* 57: 2 (1988), 170–86.

Zaret, David, 'Petitions and the "invention" of public opinion in the English Revolution', *American Journal of Sociology* 101: 6 (May 1996), 1497–1555.

Unpublished dissertations

Bell, Maureen, 'Women publishers of puritan literature in the mid-seventeenth century: three case studies', unpublished Ph. D thesis, University of Loughborough, 1987.

Bohn, Ralph, 'The controversy between puritans and Quakers to 1660', unpublished Ph. D thesis, University of Edinburgh, 1955.

Cole, W. Alan, 'The Quakers and politics, 1652–1660', unpublished Ph. D thesis, University of Cambridge, 1955.

Cotton, Anthony, 'The London newsbooks in the civil war: their political attitudes and sources of information', unpublished D Phil. thesis, University of Oxford, 1971.

Davies, T. A., 'The Quakers in Essex 1655–1725', unpublished D Phil. thesis, University of Oxford, 1986.

Freist, Dagmar, 'The formation of opinion and the communication network in London 1637–*c*. 1645', unpublished Ph. D thesis, University of Cambridge, 1992.

Hetet, J. S. T., 'A literary underground in restoration England: printers and dissenters in the context of constraint, 1660–89', unpublished Ph. D thesis, University of Cambridge, 1987.

Ludlow, Dorothy, ' "Arise and be doing:" English "preaching" women, 1640–1660', unpublished Ph. D thesis, University of Indiana, 1978.

More, Ellen, 'The New Arminians: John Goodwin and his Coleman Street Congregation in Cromwellian England', unpublished Ph. D thesis, University of Rochester, New York, 1979.

Reay, Barry, 'Early Quaker activity and reactions to it, 1652–1664', unpublished D Phil. thesis, University of Oxford, 1979.

Seymour, Michael, 'Pro-government propaganda in interregnum England, 1649–1660', unpublished Ph. D thesis, University of Cambridge, 1986.

Stephenson, W., 'The economic and social status of protestant sectarians in Huntingdonshire, Cambridgeshire and Bedfordshire (1650–1725)', unpublished Ph. D thesis, University of Cambridge, 1990.

Young Kunze, Bonnelyn, 'The family, social and religious life of Margaret Fell', unpublished D Phil. dissertation, University of Rochester, New York, 1986.

INDEX

Titles in the series

*Also published as a paperback